Lying, Cheating, and Stealing

A Moral Theory of
White-Collar Crime

STUART P GREEN

OXFORD
UNIVERSITY PRESS

OXFORD
UNIVERSITY PRESS

Great Clarendon Street, Oxford OX2 6DP

Oxford University Press is a department of the University of Oxford.
It furthers the University's objective of excellence in research, scholarship,
and education by publishing worldwide in

Oxford New York

Auckland Cape Town Dar es Salaam Hong Kong Karachi
Kuala Lumpur Madrid Melbourne Mexico City Nairobi
New Delhi Shanghai Taipei Toronto

With offices in

Argentina Austria Brazil Chile Czech Republic France Greece
Guatemala Hungary Italy Japan Poland Portugal Singapore
South Korea Switzerland Thailand Turkey Ukraine Vietnam

Oxford is a registered trade mark of Oxford University Press
in the UK and in certain other countries

Published in the United States
by Oxford University Press Inc., New York

British Library Cataloguing in Publication Data

Data available

The Library of Congress has catalogued the hardback edition as follows:

Green, Stuart P.
  Lying, cheating, and stealing: a moral theory of white-collar crime /
Stuart P. Green.
    p. cm.
  ISBN–13: 978–0–19–926858–0 (alk. paper)   1. White collar crimes—
Philosophy. I. Title.
  K5018. G694 2006
  345′. 0268—dc22

                                                          2005030677

Typeset by Newgen Imaging Systems (P) Ltd., Chennai, India
Printed in Great Britain
on acid-free paper by
Ashford Colour Press Limited, Gosport, Hampshire

ISBN 978–0–19–926858–0 (Hbk.)
ISBN 978–0–19–922580–4 (Pbk.)

3 5 7 9 10 8 6 4 2

LYING, CHEATING, AND STEALING

Acknowledgments

Various pieces of this book, from brief passages to major parts of whole sections, have previously appeared in print. I am grateful to the following publications for their permission to reprint these materials here: 'Why It's a Crime to Tear the Tag Off a Mattress: Overcriminalization and the Moral Content of Regulatory Offenses' (1997) 46 *Emory Law Journal* 1533; 'Lying, Misleading, and Falsely Denying: How Moral Concepts Inform the Law of Perjury, Fraud, and False Statements' (2001) 53 *Hastings Law Journal* 157; 'The Concept of White Collar Crime in Law and Legal Theory' (2004) 8 *Buffalo Criminal Law Review* 1; 'Moral Ambiguity in White Collar Criminal Law' (2004) 18 *Notre Dame Journal of Law, Ethics & Public Policy* 501; 'Cheating' (2004) 23 *Law and Philosophy* 137; 'Uncovering the Cover-Up Crimes' (2005) 42 *American Criminal Law Review* 9 (reprinted with permission of the publisher, American Criminal Law Review © 2005); 'What's Wrong with Bribery,' in RA Duff & Stuart P Green (eds), *Defining Crimes: Essays on the Special Part of the Criminal Law* (Oxford: Oxford University Press, 2005); and 'Theft by Coercion: Extortion, Blackmail, and Hard Bargaining' (2005) 44 *Washburn Law Journal* 553.

To my mother,
and the memory of my father

General Editor's Introduction

This monograph breaks new ground by investigating the moral foundations of those parts of the criminal law that might fairly be described as 'white-collar crime'—notably fraud, perjury, blackmail, tax evasion and related offenses. In order to uncover these foundations, Stuart Green examines various moral wrongs relevant to such offenses, such as lying, cheating and promise-breaking. What he finds is a measure of ambiguity in the definitions and boundaries of these kinds of behaviour; and, having analyzed those uncertainties, he then goes on to give critical scrutiny to the typical elements of the various 'white-collar crimes'. The result of this enquiry is to demonstrate the often fine and socially-situated distinctions that underlie the relevant laws and their practical applications, and to carve out an important new field of development for the theory of the criminal law.

Andrew Ashworth

Preface

I first began to think about what would become the subject of this book when I was practicing law at a Washington, D.C. law firm, in the early 1990s. It was hardly what one would call a criminal defense practice. We represented, so far as I know, not a single drug dealer, murderer, or rapist. Instead, our client list included airlines, investment banks, pharmaceutical companies, consumer products manufacturers, and communications conglomerates. Most of these clients had achieved success through what seemed, at least at first, to be lawful, if aggressive, business practices. Their managers and employees viewed themselves as law-abiding citizens. Their conduct was, I am sure, no more 'deviant' than that of most other large corporations.

Many of these clients came to the firm because they were having a problem with one or another federal agency—the Securities and Exchange Commission, the Food and Drug Administration, the Environmental Protection Agency, and the like. Often, they wanted to know how they could avoid violating some provision of federal law. Other times, there was a concern that some law had already been violated.

What struck me, again and again, was that what seemed at first like merely 'sharp conduct'—or, at worst, a question of civil liability—turned out, on further inspection, to raise the specter of criminal liability. The sanctions that, I had assumed, were meant to be reserved for society's most wrongful or harmful conduct seemed instead like they might be applied to conduct that was much more morally ambiguous.

By the late 1990s, I had left law practice and gone into law teaching. Although I maintained an interest in the subject of corporate and white-collar crime, I became, like most criminal law scholars, preoccupied with basic 'general part' concepts like act and omission, harm and culpability, and justification and excuse, as well as with a few specific core offenses such as murder and rape.

And then came the corporate scandals of 2001 and 2002. Figures like Enron's Kenneth Lay, WorldCom's Bernie Ebbers, HealthSouth's Richard Scrushy, ImClone's Samuel Waksal, Credit Suisse First Boston's Frank Quattrone, Arthur Andersen's Nancy Temple, and Tyco's Dennis Kozlowski became household names. In some cases, their conduct was shown to be clearly and unequivocally criminal. But often it was not: Scrushy, despite the testimony of a half dozen former lieutenants who said he had orchestrated a $2.7 billion accounting fraud, was acquitted on all counts. Home decorating mogul Martha Stewart, despite her conviction for obstruction of justice and false statements in connection with the government's investigation of her sale of ImClone stock, was widely viewed as having done nothing all that wrong. And the obstruction of justice conviction of accounting firm Andersen, based on its shredding of thousands of pages of documents related to the Enron affair, was reversed by the US Supreme Court on the grounds that, as Chief Justice Rehnquist put it, 'It is, of course, not wrongful for a manager to instruct his employees to comply with a valid document retention policy.'[1]

Time and again, it seemed, there was uncertainty as to whether some course of conduct constituted lawful, if hard-hitting, business behavior, or whether instead it constituted serious criminal conduct. Depending on one's perspective, 'creative accounting' could look like fraud, 'tax avoidance' like tax evasion, 'witness preparation' like witness tampering, 'document retention procedures' like obstruction of justice, 'hard bargaining' like extortion, 'wiliness on the witness stand' like perjury, 'zealous advocacy' like criminal contempt, 'savvy investing' like insider trading, 'political contributions' like bribery, and permissible 'field-of-use restrictions' like illegal market allocation. At the end of the day, it was hard to know which conduct should be regarded as merely aggressive business behavior, and which as criminal. The gap between law and norms seemed to be growing wider. The moral foundations on which the criminal law is supposed to rest seemed increasingly shaky.

I wanted to see if it was possible to find some firmer foundation in which to ground this body of law: in a series of articles, I began to examine the moral content of white-collar crime—one offense at a time. At some point, I realized that I had covered quite a lot of ground. I began this book with the idea of pulling all of these disparate pieces together into a unified whole, of filling in some crucial gaps, and correcting some errors.

*   *   *

Much of the substance of this book was written during the 2002–03 academic year while I was a visiting scholar at the University of Glasgow Law School. I would like to express my thanks to my colleagues there and to the US and UK Fulbright Commissions for their backing during that sabbatical year. I am grateful as well to Chancellor John Costonis and my colleagues at the LSU Law School for their abiding support over the years, and to my assistant Ms Carmel Cucinotta for her help in preparing the manuscript. I would also like to thank John Louth, Rebecca Smith, Rowena Lennon, Nick Pepper, and Professor Andrew Ashworth, all of Oxford University Press, for their assistance throughout the publication process.

While working on the papers that make up the core of this book, I was fortunate to have the opportunity to present my ideas at more than a dozen universities in the United States and Europe, and to have the benefit of insightful

---

[1] *Arthur Andersen v United States* 125 S Ct 2129, 2135 (2005).

comments from numerous friends and colleagues, most of whom (I hope)
I thanked in earlier publications. For offering helpful comments on parts of
the book that have not previously been published, I would now like to thank
Bill Corbett, Jeremy Horder, Ron Scalise, Andrew Simester, Ken Simons, and
Stephen Shute. The influence of the late Joel Feinberg's work, I assume, will
be evident throughout this book, and I am grateful to him as well for his
encouragement at a time when I most needed it. Hugo Bedau has been my
mentor since undergraduate days, and he has long since become a dear friend
and reliable reader of my work. Antony Duff is a friend, mentor, and inter-
locutor of more recent vintage, but one who is no less cherished. Both of them
were a great help in my efforts here.

I must of course reserve a final word of thanks for my family. My children,
Samuel, Rose, and Jonathan, are a constant source of wonder, pride, and
diversion: were it not for them, I probably would have finished this book by
the original contractual deadline. My wife, Jennifer Moses, has listened to
more of my jabbering about the morality of white-collar crime than any
spouse should be asked to endure, and she did it always with patience and
good humor. Confirmed agnostic though I am, I know what it means to be
blessed.

Stuart P Green
Baton Rouge, Louisiana
July 2005

Contents

Table of Cases

Table of Legislation

Introduction

According to the traditional view of our criminal justice system, penal sanctions—the most weighty kind of sanction we have in a civil society—should be reserved for conduct that is truly and unambiguously blameworthy. We view criminal penalties as the 'heavy artillery'[1] of our legal system, to be used only as a 'last resort,'[2] when other kinds of legal or non-legal sanctions prove inadequate. Before such sanctions can be imposed, it is thought, we need to be sure that the conduct punished can be clearly distinguished from—indeed, is qualitatively worse than—other kinds of conduct not similarly subject to criminal penalties.

In reality, however, our criminal justice system is far more complicated than this simple sketch would suggest, and nowhere more so than in the context of what I shall refer to as white-collar crime. What is interesting and distinctive about this group of crimes is that, in a surprisingly large number of cases, there is genuine doubt as to whether what the defendant was alleged to have done was in fact morally wrong. In such cases, the issue is not, as it is with necessity, whether the defendant was confronted with some extraordinary choice between either obeying the law, and allowing significant harm to occur, or violating the law, and preventing such harm.[3] Rather, the question is whether the conduct engaged in was more or less acceptable behavior, at least in the realm in which it was performed, and therefore should not have been subject to criminal sanctions in the first place.

Such ambiguity reflects more than just the effectiveness of white-collar defense counsel in promoting their clients' causes, though the influence of counsel in such cases is surely significant. It is, more fundamentally, the manifestation of a widely felt sense—expressed by judges, jurors, scholars, journalists, and the average citizen—that the law in this area involves a kind of moral uncertainty that distinguishes it from that which governs more familiar 'core' cases of crime, an uncertainty that raises important, and often troubling, questions about the law's legitimacy, coherence, and authority.

---

[1] Francis A Allen, 'The Morality of Means: Three Problems in Criminal Sanctions' (1981) 42 *University of Pittsburgh Law Review* 737, 738.

[2] Douglas Husak, 'The Criminal Law as Last Resort' (2004) 24 *Oxford Journal of Legal Studies* 207; Nils Jareborg, 'Criminalization as Last Resort (*Ultima Ratio*)' (2005) 2 *Ohio State Journal of Criminal Law* 521.

[3] Of course, this is not to suggest that questions of necessity do not also occasionally arise in the context of white-collar crime.

TWO EXAMPLES OF MORAL COMPLEXITY IN
WHITE-COLLAR CRIMINAL LAW

As an illustration of the kind of moral complexity and uncertainty I have in mind, let me begin by describing two recent cases of alleged criminality. (It is, I should note, merely a coincidence that both cases involve prominent American political figures: The great mass of white-collar crime, of course, need not have anything explicitly to do with politics.) The point here is merely to raise the kinds of questions that such cases tend to provoke, not to reach any kind of conclusion: we will return to these examples, as well as to a host of others, throughout the course of the book.

The Case of Tom DeLay

In November 2003, in the midst of an intense lobbying effort by the administration of President George W. Bush to pass its Medicare bill, House Majority Leader Tom DeLay and fellow Republican members of the US House of Representatives allegedly told retiring Congressman Nick Smith that, in return for his vote, they would give Smith's son, Brad, substantial financial and political support in his campaign to succeed his father. When Nick declined, DeLay and his fellow leaders allegedly told him that they would ensure that Brad would never win his race for Congress.[4]

The Case of Bill Clinton

In December 1997, some time after she began having an affair with President Bill Clinton, White House intern Monica Lewinsky was subpoenaed to testify in a sexual harassment suit brought against Clinton by former Arkansas state employee Paula Jones. Shortly thereafter, Clinton allegedly told Lewinsky to be 'evasive' in her testimony. He also asked his personal secretary, Betty Currie, to go to Lewinsky's apartment to reclaim various gifts that he had given her. The next month, Clinton himself was deposed in the *Jones* case. When asked whether he had had 'sexual relations with Monica Lewinsky,' as

---

[4] See Charles Babington, 'Ethics Panel Rebukes DeLay,' *Washington Post* (1 Oct. 2004), at A1; Timothy Noah, 'Nick Smith Recants: Did the Pressure Get to Him?' *Slate* published online 5 Dec. 2003 <http://slate.msn.com/id/2092054/>; Robert Novak, 'GOP Pulled No Punches in Struggle for Medicare Bill,' *Chicago Sun-Times* (27 Nov. 2003). Nick Smith ultimately voted against the legislation. In August 2004, Brad Smith was defeated in the Republican congressional primary. Two months later, the Republican-controlled House Ethics Committee issued a report 'admonishing' DeLay for offering to help Smith's son in return for his vote on the Medicare bill, but recommending no further action. US House of Representatives, Committee on Standards of Official Conduct, 'Investigation of Certain Allegations Related to Voting on the Medicare Prescription Drug, Improvement, and Modernization Act of 2003,' 108th Congress, 2d Session (30 Sept. 2004). In late September 2005, as this book was going to press, Representative DeLay was indicted on charges, unrelated to the Medicare lobbying scheme, that he conspired to violate Texas state campaign finance laws.

that term was used in the unusually narrow definition that appeared in 'Deposition Exhibit 1, as modified by the Court,' Clinton responded that he had 'never had sexual relations with Monica Lewinsky.'[5]

The questions I want to ask about the two cases are similar: What exactly did DeLay, the House leaders, and Clinton, respectively, do that was morally wrong? Did DeLay and his House colleagues engage in coercion? Did Clinton engage in deception or wrongful covering up? If Nick Smith had accepted the offer made to him by the House leaders, would he have done something wrong? Who or what was harmed by such conduct? Are these the kinds of wrongs and harms with which the criminal law is properly concerned? If so, which crimes were actually committed? How can such acts be distinguished from other kinds of at least superficially similar conduct that is not regarded as criminal—such as (in the case of DeLay and the other House leaders) 'log rolling,' 'horse trading,' 'back scratching,' and 'hard bargaining,' and (on the part of Clinton) 'witness preparation,' 'zealous advocacy,' and 'wiliness' on the witness stand?

One of the things that is so intriguing about such cases is how dramatically people's moral and legal judgments of them vary. To some extent, of course, the way one feels about the merits of such cases reflects nothing more than one's attitudes towards the polarizing figures who populate them; and one could hardly ask for more polarizing figures than Tom DeLay and Bill Clinton. But such 'personality' explanations only go so far. We believe that we should be able to separate our feelings about a person's overall character—whether empathetic or antipathetic—from judgments about whether such person deserves to be prosecuted, convicted, and sentenced for a specific criminal act.[6] We like to think that we are capable of making rational, impartial, and consistent judgments about matters as important as these. In fact, as I shall argue, the strikingly broad range of moral judgments that surrounds such cases has less to do with the identity of individual defendants than with deeper moral ambiguities, confusions, and uncertainties that pervade our understanding of white-collar crime more generally.

A ROADMAP

The goal of this book is to delve into the moral concepts that underlie the body of white-collar criminal law, and thereby bring some clarity to an area of law that is in many ways confused. Part I lays the groundwork for the

---

[5] 'Referral to the United States House of Representatives Filed in Conformity with the Requirements of Title 28, United States Code §595(c), Submitted by the Office of the Independent Counsel,' H.R. Doc. No. 105–310 (1998). The year-long investigation into Clinton's activities by Independent Counsel Kenneth Starr culminated in the December 1998 impeachment of Clinton by the US House of Representatives. Two months later, following his trial in the Senate, Clinton was acquitted.

[6] Not every criminal law theorist necessarily agrees with this point. For a discussion of the debate over 'character' vs 'choice' theory, see ch. 2 text accompanying nn 3–4 below.

analysis that follows by developing a three-part framework for analysis. I begin by explaining what I mean by 'white-collar' crime—a construct that is closer to the way the term has been used in law and legal culture than by many criminologists and sociologists. Unlike the prevailing sociological approach, the legal approach to defining white-collar crime focuses not on the social class and circumstances of the offender, but rather on the elements of the offense. The concept that emerges from my analysis is one based on 'family resemblances'—a loosely defined collection of criminal offenses, forms of deviance, kinds of offenders, and moral concepts that share a series of similarities and relationships. It is a concept that is essentially defined by the analysis that follows.

I then offer some reflections on why it is so important to develop a coherent understanding of the moral concepts that underlie white-collar criminal law. The focus here is on the ambiguity and ambivalence with which white-collar crime is treated by legislatures, judges, prosecutors, the media, and the academy. I argue that without a clearer understanding of the relationship between morality and white-collar criminal law, the retributive principles on which the criminal law is founded are placed in serious jeopardy.

Part I concludes with a three-part framework for analyzing the moral content of white-collar criminal offenses, consisting of: (1) the mental element with which the criminal act is committed; (2) the harm the act causes, or risks causing; and (3) the moral wrongfulness that such act entails. Although this approach was designed specifically with the white-collar offenses in mind, it is a framework that could potentially be applicable to other kinds of criminal offenses as well.

The aim of Part II is to develop a detailed account of the notion of moral wrongfulness, which is described in terms of a range of everyday, but nevertheless powerful, moral norms that inform and shape the leading white-collar criminal offenses. In particular, I want to analyze what we mean when we say that someone has violated the norms not only against lying, cheating, and stealing, but also against other forms of deception, and against coercing, exploiting, being disloyal, breaking a promise, and being disobedient; to show how such norms are distinct from each other, and where they overlap.

My project here can be understood primarily as an exercise in descriptive moral theory, rather than in saying why, as a normative matter, we *should* refrain from lying or cheating or stealing. Nor am I much concerned with the meta-ethical task of describing the foundations of the moral system within which such norms exist. Instead, my main interest consists in examining a range of important, but often theoretically neglected, moral concepts. There is no claim that the content of criminal law is exhausted by such a list. It is rather that such concepts are useful in considering such white-collar offenses. My hope is that the discussion in this Part will be of interest even to those readers whose primary interest is in ethics and moral philosophy, rather than in law.

In Part III, we turn at last to a detailed discussion of what I regard as some of the most important, interesting, and problematic white-collar offenses: perjury, fraud, false statements, obstruction of justice, bribery, extortion, blackmail, insider trading, tax evasion, and certain kinds of 'failure to comply' regulatory offenses. The goal here is to offer a fairly general assessment of the moral content of such offenses, with attention paid not only to moral wrongfulness but also to harmfulness and *mens rea*.

Although much of the discussion here is dependent on the way in which such white-collar offenses are defined in American federal law, this should be viewed only a starting point. The attempt is to find, to the extent possible, a more universal conception of these key white-collar offenses, or at least to identify where different systems define them differently. To that end, frequent reference is made to the way in which various offenses are defined outside the United States, especially in Great Britain.

What this analysis will reveal is that certain fine-grained distinctions in our criminal law are a reflection of equally fined-grained distinctions in our moral thinking, and vice versa. Thus, white-collar crime doctrine that may at first glance seem puzzling and internally inconsistent can often be explained through reflection on the moral concepts that underlie it. And, by the same token, ostensibly baffling distinctions we make in our everyday moral lives can in some cases be traced to distinctions that first appeared, or are most clearly articulated, in the criminal law.

WHAT THIS BOOK IS NOT

Having said what this book is about, it is also worth mentioning a few things that it is *not* intended to do. First, the book does not attempt to offer a comprehensive analysis of the law of white-collar crime, either statutory or judge-made; and it is concerned even less with the procedural context within which white-collar crime prosecutions tend to be litigated. Instead, it deals with doctrinal issues only on a selective basis, focusing on those points of law that are most illustrative, or problematic, within the theoretical framework that is developed.

Secondly, the book makes little attempt to explain the social, political, economic, and psychological causes and effects of white-collar crime. This is properly the province of social scientists, who defined and first studied the concept of white-collar crime.[7] Nor does the book attempt to offer anything like a thorough study of the recent epidemic of corporate and white-collar crime scandals, though I freely draw on the rich trove of examples that such cases provide.

[7] See ch. 1 below.

Finally, the book does not purport to offer a foundational theory of either moral philosophy or criminal law. Rather, it is a work of applied philosophy, an effort to engage white-collar criminal law in a process of 'normative reconstruction.'[8] Thus, my method is primarily descriptive and analytical rather than prescriptive. Although I pull no punches in saying where I think white-collar crime doctrine has gone astray, I do not propose anything like wholesale reform, even with respect to the controversial issue of overcriminalization. In general, my goal is to explain the underlying moral content of white-collar criminal law as I find it.

---

[8] The phrase appears, among other places, in Nicola Lacey, 'Normative Reconstruction in Socio-Legal Theory' (1996) 5 *Social & Legal Studies* 131.

PART I
GETTING STARTED

1

The Meaning of White-Collar Crime

Use of the term 'white-collar crime' to refer to some category of illegal, or at least deviant, conduct is now a common feature of our linguistic landscape. Sociologists and criminologists have been using it for more than 60 years. The majority of American law schools have a course in the subject. Journalists and politicians refer to it regularly. Law enforcement agencies, prosecutors, and defense attorneys all claim expertise in the area. And the term is increasingly being used outside the United States, both in English and in translation.

Nevertheless, the meaning of 'white-collar crime,' like that of other abstract terms in legal, social science, and philosophical discourse (think, for example, of 'coercion,' 'violence,' and 'victim'), is deeply contested.[1] Definitions vary both within and across disciplines and linguistic practices. White-collar crime scholars have sometimes sought to find an agreed-upon meaning of the term; other times, they have looked for substitutes. But none of these efforts has been successful: whatever definitions have been offered have failed to find general acceptance; whatever alternatives have been suggested have proved inadequate. Despite its fundamental awkwardness, the term 'white-collar crime' is now so deeply embedded within our legal, moral, and social vocabularies that it could hardly be abandoned. The term persists and proliferates not so much in spite of its lack of definitional precision, but because of it. Speakers attribute to it those meanings that correspond to their own particular analytical or ideological concerns. In this section, I want to explore some of these various meanings and explain how I intend to use the term in this book.

1. THREE CRITICAL ISSUES IN DEFINING 'WHITE-COLLAR CRIME'

One difference between 'white-collar crime' and other contested concepts in law, the humanities, and the social sciences is that its origins are so easily known and so widely acknowledged. The term was first used only 65 years

---

[1] Kip Schlegel has compared the controversy over the meaning of 'white-collar crime' to that over the meaning of 'privacy.' 'Recalling Status, Power and Respectibility [sic] in the Study of White-Collar Crime', in Proceedings of the Academic Workshop, *Definitional Dilemma: Can and Should There be a Universal Definition of White-Collar Crime?* (Richmond, Virginia: National White-Collar Crime Center, 1996) 98.

ago by Edwin Sutherland, the most influential American criminologist of his day, in a presidential address to the American Sociological Association.[2] Sutherland was famously vague and inconsistent in saying exactly what the term should mean. But even if he had been precise and consistent in his usage, it seems likely that the term still would have generated uncertainty and misunderstanding among other users of the term. The concept that Sutherland was the first to define is one that is so inherently complex and multi-faceted that it seems unlikely that one single definition could ever prevail.

The story of how the term 'white-collar crime' has been used in the social sciences has been told on many occasions.[3] Rather than repeating that history here, I would like to focus on three critical issues that have arisen in the battle over the meaning of white-collar crime: (1) should the term refer only to activity that is actually criminal, or also to other forms of non-criminal 'deviance'?; (2) should the term refer to behavior (whether criminal or not) engaged in exclusively or primarily by particular kinds of actors, such as those who occupy certain jobs or have a high socio-economic status; or should it refer instead to some particular kinds of acts?; and (3) assuming that the term should refer to a particular category of criminal acts or other deviant behavior (rather than to actors), what factors should determine which such acts will be included?

Crime vs Deviance

To lawyers, the term 'crime' denotes a legal category. It refers to particular kinds of conduct that our legal institutions recognize as 'criminal.' Such conduct must be defined in a particular manner, employing certain characteristic concepts such as *actus reus* and *mens rea*; it must have a certain 'public' character in the sense that it is a wrong that concerns the public as a whole, or is committed against the public's defining values; criminal charges are usually brought in the name of the government or 'the People'; the question whether a crime has been committed must be adjudicated in a particular manner, with various actors playing distinctive roles, employing distinctive procedures and burdens of proof, and recognizing distinctive procedural rights; and it must

[2] Edwin H Sutherland, 'White-Collar Criminality' (1940) 5 *American Sociological Review* 1, reprinted in Gilbert Geis and Robert F Meier (eds.), *White-Collar Crime* (New York: Free Press, 1977); see also Edwin H Sutherland, *White-Collar Crime: The Uncut Version* (New Haven: Yale University Press, 1983).

[3] See, eg Gilbert Geis, 'White-Collar Crime: What Is It?,' in Kip Schlegel and David Weisburd (eds.), *White-Collar Crime Reconsidered* (Boston: Northeastern University Press, 1992) 31–52; David Weisburd et al., *Crimes of the Middle Classes: White-Collar Offenders in the Federal Courts* (New Haven: Yale University Press, 1991) 3–9; Stanton Wheeler and Dan Kahan, 'White-Collar Crime: History of an Idea', in Joshua Dressler (ed.), *Encyclopedia of Crime & Justice* (2nd edn., New York: Macmillan, 2002), vol. 4, at 1672; Proceedings of the Academic Workshop, *Definitional Dilemma: Can and Should There Be a Universal Definition of White-Collar Crime?* (Richmond, Virginia: National White-Collar Crime Center, 1996).

entail certain characteristic forms of punishment.[4] To lawyers, therefore, it seems obvious that when one talks about 'white-collar' crime, one should be talking about some subcategory of conduct that reflects such criminal law-like characteristics.

To social scientists, this point is less clear. Sociologists and criminologists are concerned less with legal labels and categories than with describing patterns of behavior, the causes of such behavior, and society's attitudes towards it. Thus, for Sutherland and many of his fellow sociologists, white-collar crime is not 'crime' in the legal sense of the term.[5] At the time he was writing, much of the activity with which he was concerned—including restraint of trade, violation of patents, unfair labor practices, and adulteration or misbranding of food and drugs—either was not subject to criminal sanctions at all, or, if it was, was rarely prosecuted as such. Indeed, this was precisely Sutherland's point: a good deal of conduct that is at least as, or even more, harmful or wrongful than what has traditionally been viewed as criminal is subject to a range of procedures and penalties that differ from those used for (and is largely excluded from official statistics on) traditional crime.

This is not to say, however, that everyone has agreed with Sutherland's approach to defining white-collar crime. Indeed, there have been two distinct responses to the confusion caused by including in the notion of white-collar 'crime' conduct that is not regarded as criminal by the law. The first is simply to insist, as Paul Tappan and others have done, that only conduct regarded as criminal by the law should be included in the notion of white-collar crime.[6] The second is to set aside the term 'white-collar crime' and instead use terms such as 'elite deviance' to refer not only to actual crimes committed by the elite but also to deviant activities of the elite that do not violate the law.[7]

From a sociological perspective, this second alternative makes some sense. Much of the conduct we will be dealing with in this book could be treated either as: (1) a crime (whether a serious felony or a relatively minor misdemeanor); (2) a non-criminal violation of law (eg a tort, breach of contract, or statutory violation)[8]; or (3) a merely 'deviant,' aggressive, or anti-social act which is violative of some informal norm but is not contrary to either criminal or civil law. In light of such overlaps, one can easily imagine a sociological

---

[4] cf Antony Duff, 'Theories of Criminal Law', in Edward N Zalta (ed.), *Stanford Encyclopedia of Philosophy*, <http://plato.stanford.edu/entries/criminal-law/> accessed 22 August 2005.

[5] Sutherland acknowledged this point in his essay, 'Is "White-Collar Crime" Crime?' (1945) 10 *American Sociological Review* 132.

[6] Paul W Tappan, 'Who is the Criminal?' (1947) 12 *American Sociological Review* 96; see also Robert G Caldwell, 'A Re-Examination of the Concept of White-Collar Crime', in Gilbert Geis (ed.), *White-Collar Criminal: The Offender in Business and the Professions* (New York: Atherton Press, 1968); Herbert Edelhertz, *The Nature, Impact and Prosecution of White-Collar Crime* (Washington, DC: National Institute of Law Enforcement and Criminal Justice, 1970).

[7] See, eg David Simon, *Elite Deviance* (7th edn., Boston: Allyn & Bacon, 2002).

[8] See John E Conklin, *Illegal But Not Criminal: Business Crime in America* (Englewood Cliffs, NJ: Prentice Hall, 1977). This point is discussed further below ch. 2, n 7.

study in which the distinction between deviant activity that is criminal and that which is not would seem arbitrary.

Moreover, to the extent that one is concerned with *reforming* the criminal law—so that currently non-criminalized behavior is made criminal, or currently criminalized behavior is decriminalized—there is much to be said for a general term that refers to both kinds of conduct. Indeed, there is a significant polemical or reformist strain that runs through much of the sociological literature on white-collar crime.[9] Although Sutherland himself claimed that his theory was 'for the purpose of developing the theories of criminal behavior, not for the purpose of muckraking or reforming anything except criminology,'[10] his real motives surely included the reform of the legal system. To be sure, many students of white-collar crime cannot help but be incensed by the fact that such conduct, even when apparently more harmful than traditional street crime, has traditionally been dealt with more leniently by legislatures and courts.

From the perspective of law and legal theory, however, the term 'elite deviance' is highly problematic. The discipline of criminal law is defined by what is criminal. A wide range of critically important procedural questions turn on whether conduct alleged is violative of the criminal law. To replace the concept of white-collar crime with the concept of deviant behavior is thus to blur a distinction that, at least in legal discourse, is foundational.

Moreover, not only is there deviant behavior that is not criminalized, there is also criminal activity that is not generally regarded as deviant. For example, as we shall see below, a good deal of regulatory crime involves so-called *malum prohibitum* conduct, which is not wrongful prior to its legal regulation, but becomes wrongful (and thus, it is argued, legitimately criminalizable) in virtue of its being regulated. And there are other forms of conduct that may well be regarded as deviant in one social setting (eg courtside at Wimbledon), but not in another (say, on the trading floor of the Chicago Board of Trade).

A final problem with substituting the term 'elite deviance' for 'white-collar crime' is that much white-collar crime is not in fact committed by elites. For example, many people would consider insider trading to be a quintessentially white-collar offense. Yet, as one scholar has pointed out, the Supreme Court first addressed the subject in a case in which the defendant was not a high-level corporate executive at all, but rather a blue collar 'markup man' for a printing press.[11] Indeed, it seems obvious that many cases of what I shall provisionally assume to be white-collar crimes—such as perjury, obstruction of justice, fraud, bribery, and tax fraud—frequently involve defendants who are not, in any meaningful sense of the term, elite.

---

[9] Susan P Shapiro, 'The New Moral Entrepeneurs: Corporate Crime Crusaders' (1983) 12 *Contemporary Sociology* 304 (criticizing this tendency).

[10] Sutherland, 'White-Collar Criminality' (n 2 above, at 1).

[11] J Kelly Strader, 'The Judicial Politics of White-Collar Crime' (1999) 50 *Hastings Law Journal* 1199, 1207 (discussing *United States v Chiarella* 455 US 222 (1980)).

Actors vs Acts

To refer to a crime as 'white-collar' is to draw attention to the characteristics of the person (or entity) that committed it. Indeed, it was the qualities of the offender, rather than those of the offense, that was the main focus of Sutherland's critique. Sutherland sought to question the then-prevalent theory that associated crime with the activities of the lower classes and emphasized poverty as its principal cause. He argued that, because there is a significant category of crimes that are committed by persons of wealth, 'respectability,' and social status, poverty cannot be viewed as the sole, or main, cause of crime.[12] And, in fact, recent cases involving the likes of super-wealthy alleged white-collar criminals such as Martha Stewart, Kenneth Lay, Bernard Ebbers, Richard Scrushy, and Dennis Kozlowski seem to demonstrate the truth of such an assertion.

From the perspective of the criminal law, however, such an approach is once again problematic. Deeply rooted equal protection-type norms forbid us from distinguishing among offenders on the basis of wealth, occupation, race, gender, ethnicity, or other personal characteristics. To be sure, there are special immunity rules that apply to certain kinds of actors performing certain kinds of governmental functions (eg prosecutors). But outside of such narrow exceptions, the law is not ordinarily permitted to take account of a defendant's social status in determining criminal liability. Nor, ordinarily, does legal theory.

One alternative is to change the focus of the inquiry from social class to occupation. Thus, Marshall Clinard and Richard Quinney have suggested that the term 'white-collar crime' be replaced by two constitutive terms: 'corporate crime' and 'occupational crime.'[13] The first category is meant to include offenses committed by corporations and their officials for the benefit of the corporation.[14] The second category entails crimes that are committed 'in the course of activity in a legitimate occupation' and is meant to apply to offenses involving persons at all levels of the social structure. As such, occupational crimes can be committed by employees against employers (as in the case of embezzlement), employers against employees (as in the case of workplace safety violations), and by those who provide services and goods to the public (eg consumer fraud, health care fraud, procurement fraud, environmental pollution).[15]

In somewhat more precise terminology, we might say that, under this approach, white-collar crime should be understood as requiring, as an element, that the offender be: (1) a corporate entity or officer of such entity

---

[12] Sutherland (n 2, above).

[13] Marshall B Clinard and Richard Quinney, *Criminal Behavior Systems: A Typology* (New York: Holt, Rinehart & Winston, 1967, 1973); see also Gilbert Geis, 'Toward a Delineation of White-Collar Offenses' (1962) 32 *Sociological Inquiry* 160.

[14] Geis (n 13 above, at 189).   [15] Geis (n 3 above, at 39–40).

acting in her capacity as such; or (2) performing a particular job or serving in a particular position at the time she committed the offense. And, indeed, such an approach is not at all foreign to the criminal law. For example, one cannot commit the offense of receiving a bribe under the principal federal bribery law unless one is performing an act as a member of Congress, a juror, a witness, or 'an officer or employee or person acting on behalf of the United States, or any department, agency or branch of Government thereof.'[16]

Such an approach would likely forestall the anomaly of having to include under the category of white-collar crime cases in which a person of high social status and wealth commits a presumptively non-white-collar crime such as murder, rape, or possession of a controlled substance. But it would at the same time create a host of other problems. Much of what could presumably be included within the category of 'occupational' crime—including theft of office equipment, workplace assaults, police brutality, and serial killings of patients by doctors and nurses—would not ordinarily be regarded as white-collar crime.[17] Even more problematic is the fact that a great many white-collar crimes have nothing at all do with either corporations or a defendant's occupation. Indeed, perjury, obstruction of justice, the offering of bribes, extortion, false statements, and tax evasion are only rarely committed by employees against employers, employers against employees, or by those who provide goods and services to the public; and they only rarely involve corporations.[18] In short, there is a vast range of presumptively white-collar crime that falls outside the categories of both corporate and occupational crime.

2. WHICH OFFENSES SHOULD BE REGARDED AS WHITE-COLLAR CRIMES?

In the remainder of this book, I shall assume that, at least in the limited context of law and legal theory, the term 'white-collar crime' should refer neither to non-criminalized, deviant behavior, nor to crimes committed by offenders holding particular kinds of jobs or enjoying a particular social

---

[16] 18 USC §201(a)(1). See ch. 16 below.

[17] Here, it should be pointed out that there is a range of ways in which the term 'occupational crime' has been used. For example, David O Friedrichs has suggested that the term should be restricted to illegal and unethical activities committed for individual financial gain in the context of a legitimate occupation—thereby excluding crimes such as workplace assault. 'Occupational Crime, Occupational Deviance, and Workplace Crime: Sorting Out the Difference' (2002) 2 *Criminal Justice* 243. Others, such as Gary Green, have used the term more broadly. *Occupational Crime* (Chicago: Nelson-Hall Publishers, 1997). My point is simply that the term is a poor all-purpose substitute for 'white-collar crime.'

[18] Cf Herbert Edelhertz, *The Nature, Impact and Prosecution of White-Collar Crime* (Washington, DC: National Institute of Law Enforcement and Criminal Justice, 1970) (arguing that we ought not to exclude from the definition of white-collar crime offenses such as tax evasion, receiving illegal social security payments, and consumer fraud).

status. Instead, I shall use 'white-collar crime' to refer exclusively to a category of criminal offenses that reflects some particular group of legal and moral characteristics.

Not surprisingly, this is the sort of approach taken by various lawyers and law enforcement officials interested in formulating a standard definition of white-collar crime. For example, in 1970, US Department of Justice official Herbert Edlehertz described white-collar crime as 'an illegal act or series of illegal acts committed by nonphysical means and by concealment or guile, to obtain money or property, or to obtain business advantage.'[19] Nineteen years later, the FBI defined white-collar crime as 'those illegal acts which are characterized by deceit, concealment, or violation of trust and which are not dependent upon the application or threat of physical force or violence. Individuals and organizations commit these acts to obtain money, property, or services; to avoid the payment or loss of money or services; or to secure personal or business advantage.'[20]

From the perspective of legal analysis, an act-focused definitional approach such as these is much preferable to the actor-focused approach discussed above.[21] Nevertheless, each of the definitions offered presents significant problems: first, it is unclear what it means to commit a crime by 'nonphysical' means; many criminal law theorists would argue that every crime commission requires a physical act.[22] Nor is it even clear what it means for a crime to be 'nonviolent.'[23] For example, would the release of toxic chemicals into a public water source in violation of the Clean Water Act, or the sale of adulterated drugs in violation of the Federal Food, Drug, and Cosmetic Act, qualify as such?

---

[19] *Ibid* 3 (emphasis omitted).

[20] US Department of Justice, Federal Bureau of Investigation, *White-Collar Crime: A Report to the Public* (Washington, DC: US Department of Justice, 1989) 3. The influential formulation offered by the US Department of Justice, Bureau of Justice Statistics seem to combine both act- and actor-based elements. See Bureau of Justice Statistics, US Department of Justice, *Dictionary of Criminal Justice Data Terminology* (2nd ed., Washington, DC, 1981) 215 (defining 'white-collar crime' as

'[n]onviolent crime for financial gain committed by means of deception by persons whose occupational status is entrepreneurial, professional or semi-professional and utilizing their special occupational skills and opportunities; also, nonviolent crimes for financial gain utilizing deception and committed by anyone having special technical and professional knowledge of business and government, irrespective of the person's occupation').

[21] Cf Susan P Shapiro, 'Collaring the Crime, Not the Criminal: Reconsidering the Concept of White-Collar Crime' (1990) 55 *American Sociological Review* 346 (arguing for act-based approach).

[22] Although it should be noted that there is a debate on this question. See, eg Douglas Husak, 'Does Criminal Liability Require an Act?,' in RA Duff (ed.) *Philosophy and the Criminal Law: Principle and Critique* (Cambridge: CUP, 1998) 60; R A Duff, *Intention, Agency and Criminal Liability: Philosophy of Action and the Criminal Law* (Oxford: Blackwell, 1990).

[23] 'Violence,' of course, is another famously contested term. See, eg CAJ Coady, 'The Idea of Violence' (1986) 3 *Journal of Applied Philosophy* 3; Robert Paul Wolff, 'On Violence' (1969) 66 *Journal of Philosophy* 601. Cf *Leocal v Ashcroft*, 125 S Ct 377 (2004) (interpreting definition of term 'crime of violence' as used in 18 USC §16(a)).

Secondly, there is virtually no explanation for why the definition of white-collar crime should be limited to those offenses committed for the purpose of obtaining 'money,' 'property,' or 'services,' or to secure 'financial gain' or 'business advantage.' To the extent that such an approach would exclude many cases of presumptively core white-collar offenses such as perjury, bribe giving, and obstruction of justice, and at the same time include presumptively non-white-collar offenses such as larceny, robbery, and embezzlement, it would seem to require some justification. Indeed, this may explain why some scholars now prefer the term 'economic' or 'business' crime to 'white-collar crime.'[24]

Thirdly, and even more problematic, is the unexplained use of the terms 'deceit,' 'concealment,' 'guile,' and 'violation of trust.' Even if the meanings of such terms were not highly contested (as they are), one could not help but wonder whether this limited list of moral wrongs would fully capture the moral content of the range of presumptively white-collar offenses that will be discussed in this book.

Legal Education and Scholarship

Within the last generation, white-collar crime has developed into a standard subject in the curriculum of American law schools. There are now at least five major casebooks, two hornbooks, an anthology, an annual student-edited law review survey, and scores of law school courses expressly devoted to the subject.[25] Indeed, white-collar, federal, business, and environmental crime

[24] See, eg Harry First, *Business Crime: Cases and Materials* (Westbury, NY: Foundation Press, 1990); Frank O Bowman, III, 'Coping With "Loss": A Re-Examination of Sentencing Federal Economic Crimes Under the Guidelines' (1998) 51 *Vanderbilt Law Review* 461; Jayne W Barnard, 'Allocution for Victims of Economic Crimes' (2001) 77 *Notre Dame Law Review* 39. In my view, the problem with the term 'economic' crime is that it fails to capture the crucial moral distinction between presumptively white-collar crimes, such as fraud, and ordinary street crimes, such as larceny. For a discussion of this distinction, see Stuart P Green, 'Deceit and the Classification of Crimes: Federal Rule of Evidence 609(a)(2) and the Origins of *Crimen Falsi*' (2000) 90 *Journal of Criminal Law & Criminology* 1087, 1093–94 & n 21. For a contrary view, see Bowman, above, at 490–97.
[25] See Kathleen Brickey, *Corporate and White-Collar Crime: Cases and Materials* (3rd edn., New York: Aspen Publishers, 2002); Pamela H Bucy, *White-Collar Crime: Cases and Materials* (2nd edn., St. Paul, Minnesota: West Publishing, 1998); Jerold H Israel et al., *White-Collar Crime: Law and Practice* (2nd edn., St. Paul, Minnesota: West Publishing, 2003); Julie R O'Sullivan, *Federal White-Collar Crime: Cases and Materials* (2nd edn., St. Paul, Minnesota: West Publishing, 2003); J Kelly Strader and Sandra Jordan, *White-Collar Crime: Cases, Materials and Problems* (Newark, NJ: LexisNexis, 2005); see also Leonard Orland, *Corporate and White-Collar Crime: An Anthology* (Cincinnati, Ohio: Anderson Publishing, 1995); Ellen S Podgor and Jerold H Israel, *White-Collar Crime in a Nutshell* (2nd edn., St. Paul, Minnesota: West Publishing, 1997); J Kelly Strader, *Understanding White-Collar Crime* (Newark, NJ: LexisNexis, 2002). There are also several casebooks dealing with 'federal criminal law' or 'business crime' that cover many of the same topics, e.g. Norman Abrams and Sara Sun Beale, *Federal Criminal Law and Its Enforcement* (3rd edn., St. Paul, Minnesota: West Publishing, 2000). The annual student-written white-collar crime survey of the *American Criminal Law Review* deals with antitrust, computer crimes, corporate criminal liability, employment-related crimes, false

are among the most rapidly proliferating subjects in the American law school curriculum.[26]

Legal academics are clearly less inclined than their social science counterparts to think of white-collar crime in terms of either offender characteristics or mere deviance. Almost all law school courses and texts in white-collar crime deal with the specific offenses of mail and wire fraud, perjury, obstruction of justice, conspiracy, and the Racketeer Influenced, and Corrupt Organizations Act ('RICO') as well as with the general principles of corporate criminality. But, beyond this, there is little consensus: many courses emphasize white-collar crime as a body of substantive law, while others focus on the procedures associated with its prosecution and defense, particularly in the federal courts. Some, but by no means all, of the courses emphasize constitutional issues raised by the supposedly increasing federalization of criminal law. Others cover grand jury and forfeiture proceedings. Still others deal with specific offenses such as insider trading and other forms of securities fraud, computer crimes, bribery, gratuities, money laundering, environmental and other regulatory crimes, extortion, false claims, bank fraud, and tax crimes.

In any event, given the tortuous definitional history of white-collar crime in the social sciences, it is surprising that legal academics have expended relatively little effort in defining the term or explaining the criteria upon which specific offenses are included in a given curriculum. Most of the textbooks and law review literature deal with the definitional question only briefly,[27] and some not at all.[28] Rather, there seems to be an assumption that the subject matter of white-collar criminal law is somehow self-defining.

3. SALVAGING WHITE-COLLAR CRIME AS A CONCEPT OF LAW AND LEGAL THEORY

If one were starting from scratch, 'white-collar crime' is surely not the term one would choose to describe the concept that is to be considered in this book. The term was vague and imprecise when first conceived, and seems at least as much so today. Frequently, it means exactly the opposite of what it says, as

---

claims, false statements, criminal conflicts of interest, conspiracy, food and drug violations, financial institutions fraud, foreign corrupt practices, health care fraud, intellectual property crimes, mail and wire fraud, money laundering, obstruction of justice perjury, RICO, securities fraud, and tax violations.

[26] Deborah Jones Merritt and Jennifer Cihon, 'New Course Offerings in the Upper-Level Curriculum: Report of an AALS Survey' (1997) 47 *Journal of Legal Education* 524.

[27] See Israel, et al. (n 25 above, at 1–9); O'Sullivan (n 25 above, at 1–7); Strader, *Understanding White-Collar Crime* (n 25 above, at 1–3); Podgor (n 25 above, at 1–3).

[28] See, eg Brickey (n 25 above); Dan M Kahan and Eric A Posner, 'Shaming White-Collar Criminals: A Proposal for Reform of the Federal Sentencing Guidelines' (1999) 42 *Journal of Law & Economics* 365; Kenneth Mann et al., 'Sentencing the White-Collar Offender' (1980) 19 *American Criminal Law Review* 479, 481 & n 8.

when it is used to refer to merely deviant, non-criminalized activity. Sometimes it has been used overinclusively, such as when it refers to RICO, conspiracy, and corporate homicide. Other times it has been used under-inclusively, as when it excludes various regulatory crimes and non-business-related offenses such as perjury and obstruction of justice. It has been used to refer to characteristics of persons rather than of offenses in a manner that is unacceptable within the framework of equal protection norms. Its ideological overtones are significant and, in the pursuit of objective scientific and legal analysis, unforgivable. And although it was coined only 60 years ago, the point at which all parties might agree on a definition has long since passed.

In light of all these problems, is there any justification for the term's continued use? It would be presumptuous of me, an academic lawyer, to offer advice to social scientists, law enforcement officials, practicing attorneys, social activists, or journalists, among others, on whether and, if so, how, the term should be used. From the perspective of moral and legal theory, however, it seems to me that—in the absence of any viable alternative, and in light of its powerful cultural resonances—the term 'white-collar crime' *is* worth preserving, provided that certain features are understood, and various caveats observed.

White-Collar Crime as a Family Resemblance Category

We would do better to think of the term 'white-collar crime' as referring to a set of offenses connected by a series of what philosophers call 'family resem-blances,' rather than as susceptible to definition through a precise set of necessary and sufficient conditions. As linguist George Lakoff has put it, under the traditional, Aristotelian, or classical approach to classification, categories are 'assumed to be abstract containers, with things either inside or outside the category. Things [are] assumed to be in the same category if and only if they ha[ve] certain properties in common. And the properties they ha[ve] in common [are] taken as defining the category.'[29] Under the classical model, then, categories are thought to have clear boundaries and be defined by common properties. Such an approach seems appropriate, at least as an ideal, in the context of defining criminal offenses. We want to know, to the extent possible, precisely which acts will fall within the category of, say, 'murder,' 'rape,' or 'theft,' and which will not.

But many concepts in the social sciences, the humanities, the arts, and in our daily lives are simply not susceptible to such precise in-or-out definition. Such concepts have 'fuzzy' boundaries that do not fit into the classical model. Wittgenstein gives the example of the category 'game'[30]: Some games involve competition and strategizing (like chess and capture-the-flag). Others involve

---

[29] George Lakoff, *Women, Fire, and Dangerous Things* (Chicago: University of Chicago Press, 1987) 6.

[30] Ludwig Wittgenstein, *Philosophical Investigations* (GEM Anscombe trans.) (3rd edn., Oxford: Basil Blackwell, 1968) 66–71.

merely amusement (like ring-around-the-rosy). With categories of this sort, it seems impossible to find any single collection of properties that all members (and only those members) share. Instead, categories like 'game' seem to consist of a collection of members who share what Wittgenstein called 'family resemblances.' Just as family members may resemble each other in a variety of different traits (say, hair or eye color, facial features, or physical stature), what defines the category of games is not some single well-defined collection of common properties, but rather a collection of different resemblances, a whole series of similarities and relationships shared by the class.

It seems obvious that, at least for purposes of legal theory, 'white-collar crime' is better approached as a family resemblance-, rather than classical-, type category. As the discussion above suggests, if we expect to find some fixed and universally-agreed-upon collection of necessary and sufficient conditions that all members of the category (and only those members) share, that thereby define the category of white-collar crime across all disciplines, we are bound to be disappointed.[31] Nevertheless, I believe that it would be a mistake to give up on the term entirely. Provided that we recognize its context-specific, loosely-defined, family-resemblance-like-quality, 'white-collar crime' can remain for the legal theorist a term both powerfully evocative and ultimately indispensable.

How the Term 'White-Collar Crime' will be Used in This Book

The main purpose of this book is to explore the moral content of a specific collection of interesting, but mostly under-theorized, crimes: perjury, fraud, false statements, obstruction of justice, bribery, extortion and blackmail, insider trading, tax evasion, and certain regulatory offenses. I use the term 'white-collar crime' as a kind of shorthand to refer to the crimes contained on this list, but I recognize some potential problems with my doing so. First, I acknowledge that there undoubtedly are other offenses, not on my list, that deserve to be considered white-collar crimes. This does not seem to be a particularly serious problem, however, as I make no claim to exhaustiveness. Secondly, there may be some offenses that are on my list that some readers would not consider to be white-collar crimes. While I will try to make the case for the 'white-collar-ness' of such offenses, the truth is that not much ultimately depends on such a label: my analysis of any given offense should work or not, regardless of whether such labeling is proper.

In any such definitional enterprise, there is, of course, always the potential for circularity: in deciding which offenses fall within the category of

---

[31] Thus, I am in agreement with the sociologist David Friedrichs, who has suggested that any definition of white-collar crime is ultimately meaningful only in relation to its stated purpose. David O Friedrichs, *Trusted Criminals* (2nd edn., Belmont, CA: Wadsworth/Thomson, 2004) at 4–12; David O Friedrichs, 'White-Collar Crime and the Definitional Quagmire: A Provisional Solution' (1992) 3 *Journal of Human Justice* 5.

white-collar crime, we will be forced to assume that certain paradigmatic qualities define the category; and in determining which qualities define the category, we will have no choice but to assume that certain offenses fall within it. In the remainder of this chapter, my goal is to begin to compile a catalogue of family resemblances that characterize the list of offenses that I have just enumerated.

2

Some Generalizations About the Moral Content of White-Collar Crime

In the previous chapter, I suggested that the most sensible way to characterize the concept of white-collar crime is in terms of a loose collection of family resemblances relevant to the task at hand. In this section, I want to begin the task of looking at white-collar crime through the lens of criminal law theory. And what do I mean by criminal law theory? The term is broad enough to encompass inquiry into matters such as the purpose of punishment, the difference between crimes and civil wrongs, the proper scope and limits of the criminal law, the question of criminalization, and the manner in which the criminal law should address the citizenry. Each of these areas of inquiry will, in turn, involve an investigation into the relationship between the criminal law and morality. For the moment, I will offer some broad generalizations on the last of these subjects.

1. THE PLACE OF RETRIBUTION IN CRIMINAL LAW THEORY

What justifies the imposition of formal, legally sanctioned punishment by the state on criminals? While recognizing the enormous complexity of the literature addressing this question, I shall for present purposes simply assume that retribution, in one form or another, is a necessary, if not sufficient, goal of the criminal law.[1]

Although there are many versions of retributivism, the core notion is that punishment is justified when it is deserved, and that criminals deserve punishment

---

[1] Most criminal law scholars subscribe to a theory that mixes retributive and preventative (including both deterrent and incapacitative) goals. See, eg Andrew von Hirsch, *Doing Justice: The Choice of Punishments* (Boston: Northeastern University Press, 1986); HLA Hart, *Punishment and Responsibility* (Oxford: OUP, 1968) at 158–85. Only 'pure' retributivists believe that retribution should be the only goal of punishment. See, eg Michael S Moore, *Placing Blame* (Oxford: Clarendon Press, 1997).

when they are morally at fault.[2] A system of law that imposed punishment on people who were not at fault, or did so in a way that was disproportionate to their fault, would be unjust. Thus, determining whether, and to what extent, the commission of a given crime entails moral fault is crucial to determining whether, and how much, punishment should be imposed. Moreover, without an adequate grounding in widely held moral values, the criminal law loses its legitimacy. If the criminal sanction is overused, or misused, its potency is diluted, its sting is lost, and it is ultimately rendered ineffective. Assessing the moral content of criminal law is thus also an essential step in assessing its likely effectiveness.

Character and Choice, Types and Tokens

In recent years, one of the most important debates in the criminal law theory literature has focused on whether the criminal law should be concerned exclusively with the quality of the acts that criminal offenders perform, or also with the motivation and character that lie behind such acts.[3] The traditional approach has been to focus solely on the nature of the defendant's 'choice' in engaging in such conduct. Under this approach, we assume that people have free will and that, when they make the wrong choice, by engaging in illegal or immoral behavior, rather than doing what is right, they are at fault and deserve to be punished. According to this view, it does not matter, at least at the liability stage of criminal adjudication, *why* the defendant did what he did, or whether he made the right choice at other times in the past.

In response, a number of scholars have argued that a choice-based approach to criminal liability provides an overly restrictive basis on which to assess the merits of a defendant's conduct.[4] According to this view, what really matters is the defendant's character; punishing a person for his bad acts is just a means of punishing him for the bad character that produced such acts and, ultimately, to encourage the development of good character traits in the future.[5] And, these theorists say, the best way to assess a person's character is in terms of traditional notions of virtue and vice, or perhaps motive and emotion.

---

[2] For a helpful summary and analysis, see John Cottingham, 'Varieties of Retribution' (1979) 29 *Philosophical Quarterly* 238. For a discussion of this central component of retributivism, see, eg David Dolinko, 'Three Mistakes of Retributivism' (1992) 39 *UCLA Law Review* 1623 (1992); Jeffrie G Murphy, 'Retributivism, Moral Education, and the Liberal Estate' (Winter/Spring 1985) *Criminal Justice Ethics* 3; Joel Feinberg, 'Justice and Personal Desert,' in *Doing and Deserving: Essays in the Theory of Responsibility* (Princeton: Princeton University Press, 1970) 55, 67–73; Hugo Adam Bedau, 'Retribution and the Theory of Punishment' (1978) 75 *Journal of Philosophy* 601, 608–11.

[3] For a helpful summary, see Claire Finkelstein, 'Excuses and Dispositions in Criminal Law' (2002) 6 *Buffalo Criminal Law Review* 317. See generally Symposium, 'The New Culpability: Motive, Character, and Emotion in Criminal Law' (2002) 6 *Buffalo Criminal Law Review*, 1.

[4] eg Michael D Bayles, 'Character, Purpose, and Criminal Responsibility' (1982) 1 *Law & Philosophy* 5; Peter Arenella, 'Character, Choice and Moral Agency: The Relevance of Character to Our Moral Culpability Judgments' (1990) 7 *Social Philosophy & Policy* 59.

[5] Finkelstein (n 3 above, at 320–21); see also, eg Kyron Huigens, 'Virtue and Inculpation' (1995) 108 *Harvard Law Review* 1423.

So, between these two possibilities (there could of course be others), which approach should apply when assessing the moral content of white-collar crime? At first glance, an analysis based on the choices that an offender makes when he engages in criminal conduct seems more relevant to the task at hand than one based on the offender's character. After all, the focus here is not on the culpability of individual defendants committing specific acts of white-collar crime—crime tokens—but rather on the degree to which particular kinds of conduct—crime types—can be said to entail moral fault.[6] We can think of the latter inquiry as a kind of generalization about criminal conduct, similar to the sort of inquiry that a legislature makes (or ought to make) in determining whether a certain kind of conduct justifies criminal penalties and, if so, what kind and what amount. We ask, in effect, to what extent can the sort of defendant who obstructs justice or lies on the witness be said *on average*, or *typically*, to be at fault. In making such an assessment, we normally assume that no applicable exculpatory conditions, such as mistake or duress, apply; and we are not ordinarily concerned about the motivations or personal histories of particular defendants who commit such acts.

At the same time, it would be a mistake to ignore the virtue/vice/emotion/ motive approach to criminal culpability entirely. Despite its focus on the character of individual offenders, this literature has had the effect of broadening the vocabulary we use to talk about the moral content of criminal acts as well. As I argue below, the moral content of criminal offenses consists not solely in the extent to which a defendant intentionally or knowingly or recklessly causes harm, and does so without excuse or justification, but also includes the extent to which his act was morally wrong. And, as we shall see, it is with respect to the concept of moral wrongfulness that concepts developed in connection with the character-based approach to fault will prove most useful.

2. MORAL AMBIGUITY IN WHITE-COLLAR CRIMINAL LAW

Whatever specific approach to theorizing we take, it seems evident that the relationship between crime and moral fault needs to be attended to closely. Before we can determine which conduct should be criminalized, and what punishment should be applied, we need to have a clear idea of the degree to which such conduct entails moral fault. In Chapter 3, I offer a methodology for assessing moral fault on a detailed, offense-by-offense basis. Before we arrive at that, however, I want to offer some more generalized observations concerning the moral content of white-collar crime.

---

[6] The type-token distinction is discussed, among other places, in Michael Moore, *Act and Crime* (Oxford: OUP, 1993) 295.

Three Kinds of Moral Ambiguity

The body of white-collar criminal law is characterized by at least three kinds of moral or legal ambiguity. First, there are many cases in which precisely the same conduct can be treated as a crime or as a civil violation. In American law, such 'hybrid' criminal/civil character is particularly evident under regulatory-type statutes such as the Securities Exchange Act of 1934, Sherman Act, Clean Water Act, Bankruptcy Code, Tax Code, Truth in Lending Act, False Claims Act, and Federal Food, Drug and Cosmetic Act.[7] Under such statutes, the decision whether to pursue criminal or civil penalties is solely within the discretion of the prosecutor. In such cases, there is little or no qualitative distinction, at least not at the level of statutory definition, between what should be regarded as criminal and what should not.

There is another group of white-collar criminal statutes in which core cases can be treated as unambiguously criminal, but peripheral cases only controversially so. Consider again the case of Tom DeLay that was mentioned in the Introduction. Had DeLay offered Congressman Smith, in return for his vote, a briefcase full of hundred-dollar bills, or had he threatened to break his knees, most people, I assume, would think that DeLay had committed a serious crime and would deserve to be punished. But the more ambiguous, and more interesting, sorts of cases arise, not in such presumptively core cases, but rather at the periphery of criminality, where the defendant merely offers 'support' for a political campaign, or threatens to bring political pressure to bear unless his colleague complies with his demand. In such cases, the line between serious criminality—here, bribery or extortion—and non-criminality—mere 'log rolling,' 'horse trading,' or 'back scratching'—can be blurry indeed.

Finally, there are some white-collar and regulatory offenses that are controversial even at their core. In contrast to offenses such as bribery, extortion, and fraud, these offenses involve conduct that—even in the most central cases—is not universally viewed as worthy of criminalization. In some cases, the problem is one of 'sticky norms'—where there exists a gap between what the law regards as morally wrongful and what a significant segment of society views as such. Here we say that prevailing norms have not yet 'caught up' to legislation.[8] In other cases, conduct is viewed as wrong, but not so wrong as to justify criminal penalties.

---

[7] See Margaret V Sachs, 'Harmonizing Civil and Criminal Enforcement of Federal Regulatory Statutes: The Case of the Securities Exchange Act of 1934' (2001) *University of Illinois Law Review* 1025, 1027. See also Andrew Ashworth, 'Is the Criminal Law a Lost Cause?' (2000) 116 *Law Quarterly Review* 225, 234–35 (on blurring of civil and criminal categories in intellectual property and competition law); Lawrence M Solan, 'Statutory Inflation and Institutional Choice' (2003) 44 *William & Mary Law Review* 2209. See also Keith Hawkins, *Law as a Last Resort: Prosecution Decision-Making in a Regulating Agency* (Oxford: OUP, 2001).

[8] See Dan M Kahan, 'Gentle Nudges Vs. Hard Shoves: Solving the Sticky Norms Problem' (2000) 67 *University of Chicago Law Review* 607.

Let me offer several examples of cases in which such sticky norms exist. The first is the category of so-called *malum prohibitum* or 'trivial' offenses—such as failing to file a required government report or selling liquor without a license. Such (arguably white-collar criminal) conduct is often thought to be insufficiently serious to justify the imposition of criminal sanctions.[9] The view is that imposing criminal penalties on such conducts tends to dilute the sanction, and diminish its meaning in more traditional contexts.

Another example of sticky norms occurs in connection with the criminalization of various intellectual property offenses, such as criminal copyright and trademark infringement, theft of trade secrets, and the manufacture and sale of devices that can be used to circumvent technological protection measures.[10] Recent studies have shown that many such offenses fail to correspond to widespread moral norms: for example, more than 70 per cent of people polled do not believe it is wrong to make unauthorized photocopies of a book or magazine, more than half do not regard the unauthorized downloading of music as immoral, 49 per cent do not think it is wrong to make unauthorized copies of CDs and tapes, 35 per cent do not believe it is wrong to make unauthorized copies of videocassettes, and 25 per cent do not believe it is wrong to make unauthorized copies of computer software.[11]

A final example is insider trading. In the view of certain law and economics scholars, insider trading makes the market more efficient by causing market prices to reflect more complete information about the value of the traded securities than would otherwise be possible.[12] They see nothing wrong with such conduct. Thus, they believe that insider trading, even in core cases, should not be a crime.[13] The point is not that white-collar crime is the only area of the criminal law that suffers from such controverisies. Certainly, there is significant debate about the criminalization of various 'morals offenses,' such as abortion, drug use, and allegedly deviant sexual practices. In such

---

[9] See Herbert Packer, *The Limits of the Criminal Sanction* (Stanford, CA: Stanford University Press, 1968); Paul H Robinson and John M Darley, *Justice, Liability and Blame* (Boulder, CO: Westview Press, 1995) at 201–02; Francis Sayre, 'Public Welfare Offenses' (1933) 33 *Columbia Law Review* 55, 79–80. For a critique of this literature, see Stuart P Green, 'Why It's a Crime to Tear the Tag Off a Mattress: Overcriminalization and the Moral Content of Regulatory Offenses' (1997) 46 *Emory L.J.* 1533. For a recent collection of essays from the libertarian perspective, see Gene Healy (ed.), *Go Directly to Jail: The Criminalization of Almost Everything* (Washington, DC: Cato Institute, 2004).

[10] See generally Stuart P Green, 'Plagiarism, Norms, and the Limits of Theft Law: Some Observations on the Use of Criminal Sanctions in Enforcing Intellectual Property Rights' (2002) 54 *Hastings Law Journal* 167; Geraldine Szott Moohr, 'Defining Overcriminalization Through Cost-Benefit Analysis: The Example of Criminal Copyright Laws' (2005) 54 *American University Law Review* 783.

[11] See Geraldine Szott Moohr, 'The Crime of Copyright Infringement: An Inquiry Based on Morality, Harm, and Criminal Theory' (2003) 83 *Boston University Law Review* 731, 767–68; Green (n 10 above, at 236–37) (both citing studies). There is, of course, an interesting question as to why views of wrongfulness differ so substantially depending on which medium is being copied.

[12] The most influential such work is Henry G Manne, *Insider Trading and the Stock Market* (New York: Free Press, 1966).   [13] *Ibid.*

cases, the argument is not simply that such conduct should be beyond the reach of government control, but that there is nothing morally wrong with such conduct in the first place. My point is simply that such sticky norms are surprisingly common in the area of white-collar crime.

Diffusion of Responsibility

Much white-collar crime is committed by abstract entities such as corporations, partnerships, non-profit associations, and governmental agencies, or by individuals working within the complex institutional structures that characterize such entities; and these facts pose special complications for assessing the moral fault of those who engage in white-collar crime. In such organizations, responsibility for decision-making and implementation is shared among boards of directors, shareholders, top and mid-level managers, and ground-level employees.[14] Such diffusion of responsibility, together with other factors discussed in the next section, make it difficult to determine exactly who (or what, in the case of an entity) should be held responsible for such conduct.

Consider the case of Arthur Andersen.[15] In 2001, as Enron's financial difficulties became public, its auditor, Andersen, instructed its employees to destroy documents pursuant to its so-called document 'retention' policy. At the time, Andersen was one of the 'big five' international accounting firms, with more than 25,000 employees in the United States alone, and thousands more employees working at affiliated offices around the world. According to the indictment charging Andersen with obstruction of justice, documents were destroyed not only in Houston, but also in London, Chicago, and Portland, Oregon. The order to destroy the documents came from within a complex corporate hierarchy and was carried out by hundreds of employees. A low-level secretary or clerk who shredded documents knowing that she would be subject to an SEC subpoena would surely deserve blame for her conduct. But our judgment of such a person would likely be tempered—made more ambivalent, I would say—by the fact that the employee acted within the context of a large organization and shared responsibility with numerous other actors.[16]

---

[14] See generally Michael Tonry and Albert J Reiss, Jr. (eds.), *Beyond the Law: Crime in Complex Organizations* (Crime and Justice: Volume 18) (Chicago: University of Chicago Press, 1993).

[15] *Arthur Andersen v United States*, 125 S Ct 2129 (2005). For a helpful analysis of the facts, see Stephan Landsman, 'Death of An Accountant: The Jury Convicts Arthur Andersen of Obstruction of Justice' (2003) 78 *Chicago-Kent Law Review* 1203 (2003).

[16] Indeed, it was the diffuseness of responsibility that presumably led prosecutors to name Andersen itself, rather than its individual employees, as the defendant in its indictment for obstruction of justice. My point here is not to engage in the surprisingly still persistent debate over whether corporations and other entities should be subject to criminally liability. For a useful summary, see Wayne A Logan, 'Criminal Law Sanctuaries' (2003) 38 *Harvard Civil Rights-Civil Liberties Law Review* 321, 348–64; see also Stuart P Green, 'The Criminal Prosecution of Local Governments' (1994) 72 *North Carolina Law Review* 1197. My point is simply that our judgment of individuals who commit criminal offenses while working in a corporate or

Legislative, Judicial, and Prosecutorial Attitudes

The complex and often ambiguous moral character of white-collar crime is both a cause and an effect of how it has been treated by legislatures, judges, and prosecutors. Three points about the legislative treatment of white-collar crime are particularly worth noting. First, as we have already seen, much of the conduct we will be looking at is enforceable by means of both criminal prosecution and private or governmental civil actions. Indeed, it has been suggested that, in the case of certain forms of white-collar wrongdoing, criminal law may even be the less preferred approach.[17] Under such statutes, precisely the same conduct can give rise to criminal or civil penalties, with the discretion to pursue one or the other (or both) wholly in the hands of prosecuting officials.

Secondly, many of the crimes we shall be considering are dealt with in specialized, regulatory portions of state and federal law rather than in the criminal law proper. For example, securities fraud is dealt with in the part of the US Code dealing with securities law, tax evasion in sections dealing with tax law, criminal price-fixing in the antitrust provisions, and environmental crimes in the titles dealing with environmental law. Because such offenses are codified separately from 'real crimes,' they are perhaps less likely to be thought of as such.

Thirdly, and perhaps most significantly, white-collar offenses seem, in general, to be subject to less severe penalties than street crimes.[18] Admittedly, comparing white-collar and non-white-collar crimes in terms of seriousness is bound to be difficult. Nevertheless, one cannot help but be struck by US Sentencing Commission statistics indicating that, during 2001, the average sentence for white-collar crimes was just over 20 months, while the average sentence for drug and violent crimes was 71.7 and 89.5 months, respectively.[19] Indeed, when Jamie Olis, a former mid-level executive at Dynegy, was sentenced to 24 years in prison after being convicted for his role in the company's $468 million fraud, commentators across the country condemned the sentence as excessive[20]—an exception that would seem to prove the rule.

One can also observe an interesting inversion in attitudes towards white-collar crime held by judges, apparently based on political ideology and class consciousness: while 'conservative' judges tend to be more aggressive than

---

organizational setting are likely to be different from our judgment of people who commit equally serious offenses in a non-organizational setting.

[17] Darryl K Brown, 'Street Crime, Corporate Crime, and the Contingency of Criminal Liability' (2001) 149 *University of Pennsylvania Law Review* 1295, 1298.

[18] See generally Ilene Nagel and John Hagan, 'The Sentencing of White-Collar Criminals in Federal Courts: A Sociological Exploration of Disparity' (1982) 80 *Michigan Law Review* 1427.

[19] US Sentencing Commission, *Sourcebook of Federal Sentencing Statistics* (2001), at 32, Fig. E.

[20] Purva Patel, 'Observers Call Former Dynegy Vice President's Sentence in Loan Case "Overkill",' *Houston Chronicle* (26 March 2004).

their 'liberal' counterparts in their attitudes toward the investigation, prosecution, and punishment of street crime, in the case of white-collar offenses, just the converse seems to be true.[21] The effects of such apparent bias is particularly striking at the sentencing stage. To cite just one example, in the late 1990s, officials of Archer Daniels Midland were caught red-handed on videotape rigging prices of agricultural products with competitors. The trial judge sentenced the two ringleaders to a mere two years in prison each. An outraged appeals court increased the sentence to the statutory maximum of three years. Even so, as Kurt Eichenwald has put it, the result was that 'executives who effectively cheated every grocery store in the country received shorter sentences than if they had robbed just one.'[22]

There is also evidence that white-collar crime is more likely than street crime to be dealt with leniently by prosecutors. A striking example is provided by a recent study of the federal Occupational Safety and Health Administration (OSHA).[23] During the period 1982 to 2002, the agency investigated 1,242 cases in which it concluded that workers had died because of 'willful' safety violations on the part of their employers. All of these cases would seem to have involved a violation of criminal law. Yet in 93 *per cent* of the cases, OSHA declined to prosecute, apparently owing to a 'culture of reluctance [that] rules [the agency] regardless of which party controls Congress or the White House.'[24]

The Criminal Defense Bar, Publicists, the Media, and the Academy

Public attitudes towards white-collar crime are affected not only by how such offenses are treated by government officials, but also by the criminal defense bar, the media, the public relations industry, and the academy. Defendants in white-collar criminal cases are much more likely than those in street crime cases to have the money to hire lawyers, investigators, paralegals, jury consultants, and others to promote their cause. Highly paid white-collar criminal defense lawyers are more successful than their public defender counterparts at almost every stage in the criminal justice process: They do a better job of persuading prosecutors not to indict, preventing the prosecution from obtaining evidence needed to convict, keeping witnesses from talking to prosecutors, presenting their case in the media, obtaining favorable plea bargains, pursuing post-conviction appeals, and arguing mitigation in sentencing.[25] Some white-collar defendants even hire publicists and launch websites intended to help repair

[21] See J Kelly Strader, 'The Judicial Politics of White Collar Crime' (1999) 50 *Hastings Law Journal* 1199, 1202.
[22] Kurt Eichenwald, 'White-Collar Defense Stance: The Criminal-less Crime,' *New York Times* (3 March 2002), at D1.
[23] See David Barstow, 'U.S. Rarely Seeks Charges for Deaths in Workplace' *New York Times* (22 Dec. 2003), at A1.   [24] *Ibid.*
[25] See generally Kenneth Mann, *Defending White-Collar Crime: A Portrait of Attorneys at Work* (New Haven: Yale University Press, 1985).

reputations damaged by allegations of criminal conduct. All of those retained are expert at exploiting the moral ambiguity of white-collar crime, whether at trial or in the larger court of public opinion.

The seriousness of white-collar crime also tends to be minimized by the media. Both newspapers and broadcast media tend to give more attention to conventional, interpersonal, sensational, and violent forms of criminality than to their more subtle white-collar counterparts.[26] The more limited media coverage of such crimes seems to be attributable to the complexity and supposed 'dullness' of the conduct involved, the more indirect nature of the harm experienced by individual victims, and the fact that such criminality tends to produce fewer striking visual images on which television news in particular thrives.[27] In addition, it may be that media organizations are more likely to be intimidated in their coverage of white-collar crime by the possibility that corporate sponsors might withdraw advertising and that deep-pocketed targets of white-collar investigations might institute defamation suits.[28]

Finally, it is worth noting that the academic treatment of white-collar crime may also contribute to its morally ambiguous character. Social scientists going back to Edwin Sutherland have complained that their colleagues neglect white-collar criminality in favor of street crime. A similar phenomenon can be observed in the law schools. White-collar offenses are almost never dealt with in introductory courses in criminal law, and are only rarely mentioned in the general literature on criminal law theory. There are, of course, courses in 'white-collar' and 'federal' crime that deal with offenses such as mail fraud, perjury, and obstruction. But to the extent that law school curricula deal at all with the subject of regulatory crime, it is only in passing, in more general courses on environmental, tax, securities, antitrust, intellectual property, labor, and administrative law. The result is that such offenses (if not white-collar crime more generally) tend to be viewed more as 'violations' than as genuine 'crimes.'

---

[26] For a useful discussion of how the media deal with white-collar crime, see Friedrichs, *Trusted Criminals* (ch. 1, n 31 above at 17–19).   [27] *Ibid* at 18–19.
[28] *Ibid*.

3

A Three-Part Framework for Analysis

Given the ambiguities and uncertainties described in the last section, it seems evident that we need some more precise method for assessing the moral content of white-collar offenses than we currently have. To this end, I propose that we focus on three kinds of moral element that we should expect to find in any criminal offense: (1) *mens rea* (or omission of *mens rea*), (2) harmfulness, and (3) moral wrongfulness. I offer no argument that such elements comprise a set of necessary and sufficient conditions for criminalization (although the lack of any such element should at least put such status into question). Rather, I intend to use this three-part framework as an analytical framework for describing white-collar crime's moral complexity.

1. Mens Rea

Perhaps the most familiar element of moral content in criminal offenses is *mens rea*. I shall use the term here in its narrow 'elemental' sense, to refer to the particular mental state either required in the definition of an offense, or with which a defendant actually commits a crime.[1] The Model Penal Code famously provides a concise list of *mens rea* terms—purposely, knowingly, recklessly, and negligently—though there are of course many other *mens rea* terms that are regularly used in non-MPC jurisdictions as well.

Such elemental usage is in contrast to the broad 'blameworthiness' sense of *mens rea* (perhaps more helpfully referred to as 'culpability'), which refers not only to the mental element of particular offenses but also to the absence of potentially applicable defenses, such as insanity, duress, intoxication, and necessity. My point is not that such defenses and motives are not applicable to white-collar crimes, or not important in assessing the moral status of individual offenders who commit such crimes. Indeed, it may be that, under a broad, family resemblance-type approach to defining the concept of white-collar

---

[1] See generally Stuart P Green, 'Six Senses of Strict Liability: A Plea for Formalism,' in AP Simester (ed.), *Appraising Strict Liability* (Oxford: OUP, 2005)1, from which some of the discussion here is derived.

crime, the motive of greed plays a prominent role. My point is simply that such concepts have little relevance to the assessment of the moral content of white-collar crime offenses in the abstract, at the level of legislative crime definition.

Assessments of *mens rea* are crucial to determining the extent to which an act entails fault and is therefore deserving of punishment. Other things being equal, we say that an offense committed purposefully is more blameworthy (and therefore more deserving of punishment, or perhaps deserving of more punishment) than an offense committed recklessly; and that an offense committed recklessly is more culpable than one committed negligently. And we say this even when the harm that the offense entails is precisely the same in each case.[2]

White-collar offenses are characterized by three distinct patterns of *mens rea*. Two of these patterns are almost direct opposites: Some white-collar crimes, particularly in the regulatory area, require a significantly lower level of *mens rea* than traditionally required by the criminal law, while in other white-collar crimes the requirement of *mens rea* is so important that it is in fact the only thing that distinguishes the conduct criminalized from conduct that is not otherwise considered criminal. In addition, the fact that white-collar crime is often committed by corporate entities creates another distinct pattern of culpability. Let us consider each pattern in turn.

Reduced *Mens Rea* and Strict Liability

At common law, the paradigm of criminality traditionally required a high level of subjective *mens rea*. But, as more criminal offenses began to be enacted in statutory form, the requirement of *mens rea* began to be diluted,[3] a trend that has been particularly common, and frequently criticized,[4] in the context of white-collar and regulatory crime.

There are two ways in which a diminution of *mens rea* has occurred among white-collar and regulatory crimes. The first is through a move from the relatively high-level *mens rea* requirements that existed at common law (viz., purpose, intent, and knowledge) to relatively low-level *mens rea* requirements

---

[2] Of course, there might be cases in which a victim suffers more harm simply by knowing that the offender's act was intentional. So let us assume for present purposes that the victim has no such knowledge.

[3] See Francis Sayre, 'Public Welfare Offenses' (1933) 33 *Columbia Law Review* 55.

[4] Such diminution in culpability, particularly in the form of strict liability, has been viewed as problematic by generations of criminal law scholars, inasmuch as it is said to expose defendants to punishment even when they are not properly 'at fault,' eg Norman Abrams, 'Criminal Liability of Corporate Officers for Strict Liability Offenses—A Comment on *Dotterweich* and *Park*' (1981) 28 *UCLA Law Review* 463; Kathleen F Brickey, 'Criminal Liability of Corporate Officers for Strict Liability Offenses—Another View' (1982) 35 *Vanderbilt Law Review* 1337; Rollin M Perkins, 'Criminal Liability Without Fault: A Disquieting Trend' (1983) 68 *Iowa Law Review* 1067; Henry Hart, 'The Aims of the Criminal Law' (1958) *Law & Contemporary Problems* 402, 422. For some recent reassessments of strict liability, see the essays in AP Simester (ed.), *Appraising Strict Liability* (Oxford: OUP, 2005).

such as recklessness and negligence. A good example is Clean Water Act section 1319(c)(1)(B), which provides that 'any person who negligently introduces into a sewer system . . . any pollutant or hazardous substance which such person knew or reasonably could have known could cause personal injury or property damage . . . shall be punished.'[5] A second way in which the requirement of *mens rea* has been diminished is through the enactment of strict liability crimes, which do away with *mens rea* as to one or more elements of *actus reus*. A good example here is the Federal Food, Drug & Cosmetic Act, which makes it a crime to introduce into interstate commerce any food, drug, device, or cosmetic that is adulterated or misbranded, regardless of whether the defendant had knowledge of such adulteration or misbranding.[6]

My claim, of course, is not that all white-collar or regulatory offenses reflect reduced culpability of these sorts. As we shall see below, there are a number of key white-collar offenses, such as bribery, false statements, and obstruction of justice, that do in fact require as high a level of *mens rea* as any conventional crime. Nor, of course, am I denying that there are *non*-white-collar offenses that also reflect a reduced level of culpability: one need only think of strict liability offenses such as statutory rape and felony murder to see that this is so.[7] What I am suggesting is simply that, as a family of offenses, white-collar crime—and particularly the subset of regulatory crimes—has gone quite far in reducing the kind of culpability required for liability.[8]

Mens Rea as What Distinguishes Criminal from Non-Criminal Conduct

There is also another distinctive pattern of *mens rea* that figures in white-collar criminal law, which is in some sense the converse of the pattern of reduced culpability just described. Under this second pattern, proof of *mens rea* is so crucial to the definition of the white-collar offense that conduct performed without it either fails to expose the actor to criminal (as opposed to civil) liability, or is not even regarded as unlawful in the first place.

Consider, for example, the crime of obstruction of justice, which, as defined in 18 U.S.C. § 1512(b)(2)(B), requires that one 'destroy . . . an object' that

---

[5] 33 USC § 1319(c)(1)(B).   [6] 21 USC § 331(a).

[7] In the case of statutory rape, although the defendant must be shown to have engaged intentionally in sexual intercourse with an under-age person, the offense does not require that the defendant know that the victim was under age. In the case of felony murder, although the prosecution must typically prove the defendant's intent to commit the underlying felony, the more serious offense does not require that the defendant intend that his conduct will cause death.

[8] Indeed, strict liability is so common in the area of regulatory crime that some commentators have mistakenly viewed the terms 'strict liability crime' and 'regulatory crime' as synonymous, eg Laurie L Levenson, 'Good Faith Defenses: Reshaping Strict Liability Crimes' (1993) 78 *Cornell Law Review* 401, 413–15 & n 77. Of course, the terms are not equivalent: as I will explain below, in ch. 20, whether a crime is 'regulatory' has at least as much to do with types of harmfulness and wrongfulness as *mens rea*.

would be used 'in an official proceeding.'[9] Almost every modern business concern has a euphemistically-named 'document retention procedure' pursuant to which it destroys documents it no longer needs to maintain. So how should we distinguish between lawful and unlawful destruction of documents? Well, as the Supreme Court's recent decision in *Arthur Andersen v United States*[10] makes clear, a crime is committed only if the defendant destroyed documents 'corruptly'—ie only if in doing so it intends to impede some pending investigation or court proceeding.[11] Absent such *mens rea*, the defendant has done nothing wrong; it has merely carried out its own lawful policies.

A similar analysis applies in the case of bribery. Imagine that *X*, a private citizen, gives Congressman *Y* a check for $10,000. Assuming that *X* acts with the 'intent to influence' an official act, he has committed a bribe.[12] Alternatively, if he has acted with the intent to 'thank' *Y* for his services, then he has committed the offense of gratuities.[13] But if *X* acts neither with the intent to influence nor to thank *Y* for his services, he has committed no offense; he has merely made a legal gift or campaign contribution. Thus, in such cases, the presence or absence of *mens rea* would provide an unusually decisive (though, in terms of proof, a frequently elusive) factor in determining whether *X* has committed a crime.

Corporate *Mens Rea*

As noted earlier, the concept of white-collar crime is distinct from that of corporate crime. Yet the fact remains that a significant amount of white-collar crime *is* committed by abstract entities such as corporations, partnerships, non-profit associations, and governmental agencies. Exactly how *mens rea* should properly be ascribed to such entities (or, indeed, *whether* such entities should even be viewed as capable of forming *mens rea*) raises a host of complex and interesting questions that lie beyond the scope of this work.[14] For the moment, it is enough to note simply that such difficulties constitute yet another way in which white-collar crime differs from conventional crime.

---

[9] § 1512 is actually titled 'Tampering with a Witness, Victim, or an Informant,' but is known generically, along with several other provisions, as Obstruction of Justice.

[10] 125 S Ct 2129 (2005).

[11] As an example of conduct that would not be considered corrupt, the Court offers the case of a mother who suggests to her son that he invoke his right against compelled self-incrimination or a wife who persuades her husband not to disclose marital confidences. *Ibid* at p. 2135.

[12] 18 USC § 201(b)(1)(A).   [13] 18 USC § 201(c)(1)(A).

[14] For an excellent treatment of such issues, see Celia Wells, *Corporations and Criminal Responsibility* (2nd edn., Oxford: OUP, 2001); Brent Fisse and John Braithwaite, *Corporations Crime and Accountability* (Cambridge: CUP, 1993). I have previously dealt with some of these questions in Stuart P Green, 'The Criminal Prosecution of Local Governments' (1994) 72 *North Carolina Law Review* 1197, 1222–28.

2. HARMFULNESS

I shall refer to the second basic element of moral content as 'harmfulness'—ie the degree to which a criminal act causes (or risks causing[15]) harm. And what is harm? For present purposes, I shall rely on Joel Feinberg's definition of harm as some relatively lasting or significant setback to a person's interests.[16] An interest, in turn, is something in which a person has a stake.[17] The concept of harm was also helpfully characterized by Jean Hampton, who referred to it as 'a disruption of or interference in a person's well-being, including damage to that person's body, psychological state, capacities to function, life plans, or resources over which we take this person to have an entitlement.'[18] For present purposes, we can also assume that the harm caused by criminal acts is 'public' in a way that the criminal law considers relevant—ie that it is the sort of harm that somehow properly concerns the community as a whole, rather than just individual citizens within such community.[19]

The concept of harmfulness is clearly distinguishable from that of *mens rea* or culpability. It is quite possible to cause harm without intending to do so or even being aware that such harm is likely to occur. For example, a person who, though driving in a cautious and lawful manner, hits a child who darts out from behind a parked car, thereby causing the child serious injury, has obviously caused harm, but she has not done so culpably or with *mens rea*. A driver would not be criminally liable in such a case unless causing harm to a person while driving a car was a strict liability offense.

Harmfulness plays a distinctive role in white-collar crime in at least four significant ways: (1) the kinds of harm white-collar crime causes are different from the kinds of harms caused by conventional crime; (2) the manner in which white-collar crime harms its victims is different from that in which conventional crime harms its victims; (3) white-collar crime often conflates choate and inchoate liability in a manner that is foreign to conventional criminal law; and (4) the harm white-collar crime causes is often mitigated by the value of surrounding legitimate conduct. Let us consider each of these factors in turn.

[15] For an argument that the risk of harm is itself a kind of harm, see Claire Finkelstein, 'Is Risk a Harm?' (2003) 151 *University of Pennsylvania Law Review* 963.

[16] Joel Feinberg, *Harm to Others* (New York: OUP, 1984) 31–36. *Harm to Others* is the first of Feinberg's four-volume opus, *The Moral Limits of the Criminal Law*. For reference to a refinement of the concept of harm that Feinberg makes in a later volume, see n 36 below.   [17] *Ibid.*

[18] Jean Hampton, 'Correcting Harms Versus Righting Wrongs: The Goal of Retribution' (1992) 39 UCLA Law Review 1659, 1662; see also Hyman Gross, *A Theory of Criminal Justice* (New York: OUP, 1979) 115 ('Harm is an untoward occurrence consisting in a violation of some interest of a person.').

[19] For a helpful discussion, see RA Duff, *Punishment, Communication and Community* (Oxford: OUP, 2001); Jonathan Schonsheck, *On Criminalization: An Essay in the Philosophy of Criminal Law* (Dordrecht: Kluwer Academic Publishers 1994).

Kinds and Quality of Harm

The kinds of harm that occur as a result of white-collar criminality tend to differ from those associated with traditional street crime. Many conventional street crimes involve identifiable physical injury to the victim, such as death, serious injury, or physical violation; are committed through sudden violent force; and occur in an identifiable physical location in a brief, relatively discrete period of time. White-collar crime, by contrast, often is committed through non-violent means; causes harm that is incorporeal, such as financial loss or injury to an institution; and occurs at a nonspecific physical location over a difficult-to-define period of time.

White-collar offenses also tend to involve harms that are more difficult to identify than in the case of conventional street crimes. For example, there is not likely to be much controversy about the proposition that the principal harm caused by homicide is the death of a human being. In the case of white-collar crimes such as tax evasion, bribery, and insider trading, however, the identification of harm presents real difficulties. Some direct harms seem relatively straightforward: presumably, tax evasion leads to reduced revenues for the public treasury, bribery to biased governmental decision making, and insider trading to unfair transactions in the securities markets. But there are also significant indirect, diffuse, and aggregative harms caused by such conduct—eg loss of investor and consumer confidence, distrust of government, and bad decisions made by public officials—that are harder to quantify.

The complexity of harms caused by white-collar crime is in part a function of the complexity of the underlying activity that white-collar crime statutes are meant to regulate. Such activities can occur over an extended period of time and in disparate locations. They frequently involve elaborate forms of behavior such as those associated with manufacturing and industrial processes, marketing, corporate finance, the stock market, document retention procedures, government contracts, financial auditing, trial and litigation procedures, and political fundraising. Such activity often occurs within large and complex organizations, involving numerous individuals occupying a wide range of different positions, and many series of complicated transactions. Understanding how such processes work can require a fairly sophisticated understanding of disciplines such as finance, economics, engineering, medicine, political science, organizational theory, management, accounting, environmental science, and information technology. It is often hard enough for the lay public to understand how these processes are supposed to work when they are conducted in a legal manner; it is all the more difficult to understand how they function when they involve criminal activity. Because the context in which white-collar crime occurs is often so complex, it can be difficult to understand exactly how a defendant has violated a given criminal provision.

The Nature of Victimization

Given the diffuseness and complexity of harms associated with white-collar offenses, it is not surprising that the identification of victims is also more difficult than in the case of conventional offenses.[20] In core, violent street crimes, such as murder, rape, and arson, the harm is focused and obvious: a human being is killed, a person's body is violated, a building is burned. We have no problem in saying that the principal victim of a homicide is the decedent.[21] Even in the case of non-violent crimes such as larceny and forgery, a victim or discrete group of victims are easily identified.

But white-collar crime presents much greater difficulties: how can we say exactly which citizens are victimized by environmental violations and government corruption; which taxpayers are the victims of false claims and tax evasion; which employees are wronged by labor law violations and accounting fraud; and which consumers are harmed by price fixing, violations of the food and drug and product safety laws, and fraudulent marketing practices? Many white-collar crimes involve small harms to a large number of victims, and are significant only in the aggregate.[22] And, of course, some victims of white-collar crime are never even aware that they have been victimized. Indeed, the identity of the victims harmed may be unknown even to the white-collar offender herself.

Inchoate Liability

Another way in which the harms associated with white-collar crime differ from those associated with traditional, non-white collar offenses is in terms of their inchoateness. The criminal law has traditionally distinguished between inchoate and completed forms of criminality. Inchoate offenses, such as attempt, conspiracy, and solicitation, are generally not punished as severely as completed offenses (although there is a lively scholarly debate about whether this should be so[23]). White-collar crime, by contrast, tends to merge complete and incomplete conduct into a single offense, punishable by

---

[20] This argument borrows from Stuart P Green, 'Victims' Rights and the Limits of Criminal Law' (2003) 14 *Criminal Law Forum* 335.

[21] This is not to say that there are not difficult and interesting questions about the extent to which, say, the family and friends of the principal victim should also be regarded, and perhaps eligible for compensation, as 'victims.' See generally Markus Dirk Dubber, *Victims in the War on Crime: The Use and Abuse of Victims' Rights* (New York: NYU Press, 2002) 245–333. My point is simply that the task of determining who is the principal victim of violent crime is generally easier than that of determining who is a victim of white-collar crime. For more on this point, see Green (n 20 above).

[22] Cf Feinberg, (n 16 above, at 187–217) (assessing and comparing harms).

[23] See generally RA Duff, *Criminal Attempts* (Oxford: OUP, 1996) 116–27. Most scholars have maintained that inchoate crimes should be punished as severely as completed ones. See, eg Model Penal Code § 5.05(1) (Proposed Official Draft, 1962); Stephen J Schulhofer, 'Harm and Punishment: A Critique of Emphasis on the Results of Conduct in the Criminal Law' (1974) 122 *University of Pennsylvania Law Review* 1497; Gross (n 18 above, at

a single penalty. And, often, it criminalizes conduct that involves nothing more than the creation of a *risk* of harm.[24]

Extortion, for example, is defined as the 'obtaining of property from another, with his consent, induced by wrongful use of actual or threatened force, violence, or fear, or under color of official right.'[25] In order to be convicted under the federal Hobbs Act, however, one need not actually obtain any property from another. It is enough that one affect commerce by *attempting* to obtain property in this manner.[26] Similarly, the principal federal obstruction of justice statute requires that a defendant 'obstruct' or '*endeavor* to obstruct' the due administration of justice.[27] In other words, federal law tends to merge completed and inchoate extortion into a single, undifferentiated offense; and imposes the same penalty on each.

Sometimes the same effect is reached by defining an offense in terms of prohibited *conduct* rather than, or in addition to, a prohibited *result*. For example, the federal bribery statute speaks in terms of 'giving' *or* 'offering' (or 'receiving' *or* 'seeking') a bribe.[28] In other words, the offense of bribery can be committed either by achieving a result (namely, a completed bribe) or by engaging in conduct that falls short of that end result (namely, offering or seeking a bribe). An analogous statute in the area of homicide law would speak in terms of causing the death of a human being *or* 'engaging in murderous conduct' (even if no death actually occurs). By merging results and conduct in this manner, such statutes achieve the same blurring effect as those statutes that merge choate and inchoate forms of liability.

Countervailing Value of Surrounding Legitimate Conduct

A final way in which white-collar crime differs from traditional street crime is in terms of the surrounding legitimate conduct that often mitigates the harmfulness of such conduct. Many of the offenses we will be considering are committed in the course of conduct that is otherwise legal, and even socially productive. For example, government officials who accept bribes are frequently also involved in legitimate governmental functions; investors who trade on the basis of inside information tend to be engaged in legal investment as well; and people who commit regulatory crimes are also typically engaged in the business of providing socially valuable products and services.

423–36); Larry Alexander, 'Crime and Culpability' (1994) 5 *Journal of Contemporary Legal Issues* 1. A few others have taken a contrary position. See, eg Michael S Moore, 'The Independent Moral Significance of Wrongdoing' (1994) 5 *Journal of Contemporary Legal Issues* 237.

[24] See generally RA Duff, 'Criminalizing Endangerment,' in RA Duff and Stuart P Green (eds), *Defining Crimes: Essays on the Special Part of the Criminal Law* (Oxford: OUP, 2005) 43.

[25] 18 USC § 1951(b)(2).　　[26] 18 USC § 1951(a).

[27] 18 USC § 1503(a) (emphasis added).　　[28] 18 USC § 201(b).

Consider the case of Mikhail Khodorkovsky, the former chief executive and principal owner of Russia's largest oil company, Yukos, who in 2005 was convicted of fraud and tax evasion and sentenced to nine years in prison.[29] Khodorkovsky was once considered not only Russia's richest man, but also an important symbol of Russia's transition to a capitalist economy, and a hero to many. By most accounts he did a lot of good for his country, even if he greatly enriched himself, partly through illicit means, in the process.[30] The same surely cannot be said of most drug dealers, burglars, and serial killers.

The perceived harmfulness of at least some white-collar criminality is also arguably mitigated by the philanthropic purposes to which some alleged white-collar criminals put their ill-gotten gains. Enron's Kenneth Lay (to be tried in early 2006) donated over $2.5 million to more than 250 organizations through his family's foundation.[31] WorldCom's 'Bernie Ebbers (convicted of fraud and other charges in March 2005) raised record sums of money for Mississippi College, arranged scholarships for local children, aided local businesses, gave to churches, [and] helped neighbors become millionaires through WorldCom stock.'[32] HealthSouth's Richard Scrushy (acquitted of all charges in June 2005) served on the boards of trustees of Troy State University, Birmingham-Southern University, and the University of Alabama; and actively supported United Cerebral Palsy, the Arthritis Foundation, the March of Dimes, and many other worthwhile charities.[33] And in the most ironic of cases, Alberto Vilar, a wealthy stock investor and prominent patron of the Metropolitan Opera and other prominent cultural institutions, allegedly defrauded a client of $5 million in order to make good on charitable pledges he could not meet with funds earned legally.[34] The fact

[29] 'Russian Tycoon Jailed for Nine Years', *The Guardian* (31 May 2005), <http://www.guardian.co.uk/print/0,3858,5205164-103610,00.html>.

[30] The Kremlin portrayed Khodorkovsky as a self-interested tax cheat with little respect for the law or the state. But Khodorkovsky's supporters had a very different take: for example, Leon Aron, director of Russian studies at the American Enterprise Institute, published an op-ed piece in the *New York Times* arguing that, while Khodorkovsky may have 'broke[n] some laws . . . in the chaotic Russian economy of the [1990s], when the state was privatizing its assets on a grand scale, no large business was 'clean'—and the larger the company, the greater the chance it committed violations.' According to Aron, given the tax scheme then in force in Russia, '[t]ax evasion was the only strategy that allowed an entrepreneur to pay salaries and invest in his business.' Leon Aron, 'Crime and Punishment for Capitalists,' *New York Times* (30 Oct. 2003), at A29. Other defenders pointed that any number of Russia's business leaders could have been charged with the same crimes and that the case against Khodorkovsky was driven largely by political motives. Even after Khodorkovsky was convicted and sentenced to nine years in prison in June 2005, the debate seemed likely to continue. CJ Chivers & Erin E Arvedlund, 'Russia Tycoon Given 9 Years On Tax Charge' *New York Times* (1 June 2005), at A1.

[31] See Heather Bourbeau, 'The Redemption of Swine: Can Ken Lay Make a Comeback?', *Slate* (19 Sept 2002), <http://slate.msn.com/id/2071203>.   [32] *Ibid.*

[33] See Biographical Sketch of Richard Scrushy, <http://www.richardmscrushy.com/bio.aspx?id = 1> accessed 22 August 2005. By most accounts, Scrushy's popularity in his home town of Birmingham, fueled by his philanthropy, was a major factor in his acquittal. See Reed Abelson and Jonathan Glater, 'A Style That Connects with Hometown Jurors,' *New York Times* (29 June 2005), at C1.

[34] Kurt Eichenwald and Daniel J Wakin, 'The Double Ups and Downs of a Philanthropist,' *New York Times* (30 May 2005) A1.

that defendants such as these have engaged in socially beneficial conduct of this sort is relevant not only at the sentencing stage of their trials, but also to the way we perceive the harmfulness of their underlying acts.

3. MORAL WRONGFULNESS

The third element of moral content in criminal offenses—moral wrongfulness—refers to the violation of a moral norm that occurs when a criminal act is committed. The approach to wrongfulness that I shall take is primarily non-consequentialist, or deontological, in its orientation.[35] Under this approach, what makes an act wrongful is some intrinsic violation of a freestanding moral rule or duty, rather than the act's consequences. Such wrongfulness is typically directed towards a particular person or group of persons who are 'wronged'—as opposed to being, in Feinberg's term, a 'free-floating' evil.[36] Thus, familiar vices such as hypocrisy, vanity, gluttony, sloth, lust, and envy would not qualify as wrongs unless they have, or are intended to have, some negative impact on another. It is moral wrongfulness in this sense that will be the major analytical focus of this book.

Distinguishing Wrongfulness from Harmfulness and *Mens Rea*

Although moral wrongfulness, harmfulness, and *mens rea* frequently overlap, the concepts are analytically distinct. People who do wrongful acts such as exploiting or telling lies can undoubtedly cause harm to those whom they exploit or lie to. Indeed, it may well be that norms prohibiting exploitation and lying originally developed because of the social harms such acts are likely to cause. Nevertheless, harms and wrongs are distinct moral concepts. Natural disasters, like tsunamis and earthquakes, and diseases like cancer and diabetes all cause vast harms. But none of these harms involves moral wrongfulness, since none of them involves a violation of moral norms. Even human acts can be harmful without being wrongful, and the presence or absence of wrongfulness is frequently what distinguishes an act that is criminal from one that is not. For example, if *X* and *Y* are boxing, there is

[35] For a helpful introduction to such concepts, see Samuel Scheffler, *The Rejection of Consequentialism: A Philosophical Investigation of the Considerations Underlying Rival Moral Conceptions* (Oxford: OUP, rev. edn. 1994); Nancy (Ann) Davis, 'Contemporary Deontology' in Peter Singer (ed) *A Companion to Ethics* (Oxford: Blackwell, 1991) 205; Philip Pettit, 'Consequentialism' in *ibid*, at 230.
[36] See Joel Feinberg, *Harmless Wrongdoing* (New York: OUP, 1988) 18–20. It is worth mentioning here the distinction Feinberg draws between harms₁ and harms₂. Harms₁ are harms in the neutral sense of causing a setback to interests. Harms₂ cause a setback to interests and in so doing constitute a wrong or violation of another's rights. *Ibid* at xxvii–xxix. Because I believe that the concepts of harming and wronging are better understood if they are kept separate, I have resisted Feinberg's move towards merger into a single integrated notion of wrongful harm.

a reasonable chance that X will cause Y serious harm. But, assuming that Y has 'consented' to such conduct (and that X is playing by the rules), we would say that X had not *wronged* Y, and therefore that he should not be subject to prosecution for battery. Similarly, if X kills Y in justified defense of himself or others, we would once again say that Y has been harmed without being wronged, since one cannot be wronged by a justified act; and because X's act was not wrongful, he would not be liable for criminal homicide.

As we shall see below, whether a harmful act is also wrongful has particular significance in the realm of white-collar crime, where harms caused by conduct that is unlawful are often indistinguishable from harms caused by conduct that is lawful. For example, the harms caused by unlawful price fixing, insider trading, and fraud, on the one hand, and lawful (if ruinous) competition, on the other, are virtually the same: loss of money, a business, a job, market share. But, assuming that the relevant players 'played by the rules,' and violated no one's rights, we would not consider the kinds of harms that result from lawful 'fair' competition wrongful (unless, perhaps, we are looking at the situation from a Marxist perspective). And because such acts are not wrongful, they should not be subject to criminal sanctions.[37]

Conversely, acts can be wrongful without being harmful. For example, a witness who lies on the stand about a matter that is not 'material' to the proceeding has done an act that is wrongful, but not harmful in the way that the law of perjury considers relevant.

Moreover, even when a single act entails both harmfulness and wrongfulness, the two concepts will often be viewed as distinct. For example, if X steals a car owned by Y, the *wrong* X has committed is principally done to Y, although X might also cause indirect harm to Y's family (who are deprived of transportation) and to Y's neighbors (who might suffer a feeling of insecurity). Similarly, as we shall see in Chapter 18, if X trades securities on the basis of inside information that is not available to Y, then it appears that X has wronged Y. But the *harm* X causes (at least in the aggregate) is more general: in theory, insider trading is detrimental to investor confidence and ultimately harmful to the market as a whole.

The concept of wrongfulness is also distinguishable from that of *mens rea* or culpability, though less clearly than from that of harmfulness. Whether an act is wrongful often depends on whether it is intentional. As we shall see in Chapter 4, it makes little sense to speak of X's cheating Y unless X has broken a rule intentionally. And the same can be said of deception: X must intend for Y to believe something that is untrue in order for us to say that X has deceived Y. If X has been reckless or negligent in his attitude toward the truth, or

---

[37] As Dan Kahan has put it, in explaining the difference between theft and legal, but nevertheless harmful, competition, only theft involves 'disrespect for the injured party's moral worth.' Dan M. Kahan, 'The Secret Ambition of Deterrence' (1999) 113 *Harvard Law Review* 413, 420. See also AP Simester and Andrew von Hirsch, 'Rethinking the Offense Principle' (2002) 8 *Legal Theory* 269, 270–72 (distinguishing between harms and wrongs).

toward following rules, we might still say that X had done a wrongful act, but we would probably not say that he had been deceitful or cheated. On the other hand, one can certainly break a promise even if one does not intend to do so. Imagine a case in which I have promised to arrive in time to see the beginning of my son's track meet, and then turn up 20 minutes late because I was caught in traffic along the way. Assuming that I was at least negligent in failing to anticipate the traffic jam that caused me to be late, we would probably say that I had broken my promise.

What Makes Acts Wrongful?

So what exactly is it that makes an act wrongful? From the non-consequentialist or deontological perspective, the most familiar way of speaking of wrongfulness is in terms of a violation of a victim's rights, of disrespect to a victim, as 'an affront to the victim's value or dignity,' in the words of Jean Hampton.[38] In Feinberg's definition, '[o]ne person *wrongs* another when his indefensible (unjustifiable and inexcusable) conduct violates the other's right.'[39]

In recent years, criminal law scholars have become increasingly sensitive to the important role that wrongs play in defining crimes. Much of this recognition has occurred in connection with the turn towards 'character' or 'virtue' theory, referred to earlier.[40] Such examination has occurred, in the context of a variety of particular criminal offenses, on a more or less ad hoc basis. John Gardner, for example, has argued, in connection with the English Offences Against the Person Act, that the concept of harm fails to 'capture all that is interesting, or rationally significant, about' the seriousness of various offenses; that we need to focus as well on the *way* in which harm is brought about; on how various criminal acts are 'wrongful.'[41] More recently, Gardner and Stephen Shute have focused on a hypothetical case of 'harmless rape' as a vehicle for analyzing the 'wrongness' of rape, which, they find, involves a violation of the victim's autonomy and proprietary rights.[42] Similarly, Shute and Jeremy Horder have looked at two offenses that involve essentially the same harm—theft and obtaining property by deception—and found that the latter offense involves a form of moral wrongfulness not present in theft—namely, an abuse of the victim's

---

[38] Hampton (n 18 above), at 1666.

[39] Feinberg, n 16 above, at 34. Cf Alan Brudner, 'Agency and Welfare in the Penal Law,' in Stephen Shute, et al (eds) *Action and Value in Criminal Law* (Oxford: Clarendon Press, 1993) 21, 31 ('A [criminal] wrong is an exercise of freedom wherein the self claims a right of action *vis-à-vis* another that the other cannot, consistently with his equal end-status, recognize as valid; or wherein the will makes claims for its worth in excess of those objectively validated through the framework of mutual recognition.').

[40] See text accompanying nn 3–4, ch. 2 above.

[41] John Gardner, 'Rationality and the Rule of Law in Offences Against the Person' (1994) 53 Cambridge Law Journal 502, 511.

[42] John Gardner and Stephen Shute, 'The Wrongness of Rape' in Jeremy Horder (ed.) *Oxford Essays in Jurisprudence* (Oxford: OUP, 2000) 195–200.

autonomy.[43] And Andrew Simester and Bob Sullivan have examined a hypothetical case of harmless—indeed, socially beneficial—theft as a means for examining the 'wrongdoing' inherent in theft, which they say consists in a violation of the victim's proprietary rights.[44]

Part of what is at stake here is the principle of fair labeling, the concern of which is, in Andrew Ashworth's words, to 'see that widely felt distinctions between kinds of offences and degrees of wrongdoing are respected and signalled by the law, and that offences should be divided and labeled so as to represent fairly the nature and magnitude of the law-breaking.'[45] One frequent context in which concern with the principle of fair labeling arises is the law of theft: if people regard stealing and swindling as distinct forms of wrongdoing, it is said, the criminal law should reflect such a distinction by resisting the conflation of larceny and fraud into the single offense of theft.[46] Accordingly, in the discussion below, we will see the relevance of fair labeling repeatedly in the context of offenses such as fraud (stealing by deception) and extortion (stealing by coercion).

But the principle of fair labeling also applies more broadly. We need to refer to the idea of wrongdoing not only in distinguishing among various offenses but also in deciding which conduct to criminalize in the first place, how offense elements should be defined, and what defenses should be available. For example, as we shall see, the divergent ways in which the offenses of perjury and fraud treat the requirement of deception (perjury requires a literal falsehood, while fraud does not) reflect deep-seated and fine-grained distinctions concerning the concept of deception that we make in our everyday moral lives. When legal rules fail to square with people's common understanding of what is wrong, the result is unfair labeling.

Wrongfulness, Legal Moralism, and the Harm Principle

Another context in which criminal law theorists have been concerned with the concept of moral wrongfulness is the debate over legal moralism. While there is near unanimous support for the notion that the state should have the power to prohibit, and, indeed, impose sanctions for, intentionally wrongful conduct that causes serious harm or injury to others (such as murder and rape),[47] there is considerable controversy among scholars (and policy

---

[43] Stephen Shute and Jeremy Horder, 'Thieving and Deceiving: What is the Difference?' (1993) 56 *Modern Law Review* 548, 553.

[44] AP Simester and GR Sullivan, 'On the Nature and Rationale of Property Offences,' in RA Duff and Stuart P Green (eds.), *Defining Crimes: Essays on the Special Part of the Criminal Law* (Oxford: OUP, 2005) 168, 174–75.

[45] Andrew Ashworth, *Principles of Criminal Law* (4th edn., Oxford: OUP, 2003) 89–90.

[46] *Ibid* at 72. See also Shute and Horder (n 43, above).

[47] A dissenting handful of radical scholars have argued that the criminal justice system as we now know it—based on notions of individual culpability for disobedience to supposedly shared moral norms—should be abolished entirely. See Antony Duff and David Garland (eds.), *A Reader*

makers) as to whether the state should have the power to criminalize morally wrongful conduct that is not obviously harmful to self or others.

Theorists who subscribe to legal moralism, at least as that term has traditionally been used,[48] believe that it is acceptable for the state to impose criminal sanctions to enforce prohibitions on conduct that is supposedly immoral but not directly harmful (or even offensive) to others or self. They thus embrace the anti-liberal view that the state may legitimately criminalize so-called 'victimless' conduct, such as incest, prostitution, and obscenity, even when carried out in private among consenting adults.[49]

The 'liberal' view—that criminal sanctions are justified only in cases in which conduct causes harm (or, possibly, offense) to others, and not for mere harmless immoralities or harms to self—is most famously associated with John Stuart Mill,[50] and is explored most comprehensively by Feinberg in his *Moral Limits of the Criminal Law*. According to Feinberg's harm principle:

It is legitimate for the state to prohibit conduct that causes serious private harm, or the unreasonable risk of such harm, or harm to important public institutions and practices. In short, state interference with a citizen's behavior tends to be morally justified when it is reasonably necessary (that is, when there are reasonable grounds

on Punishment (Oxford: OUP, 1994) 331–35; Herman Bianchi, 'Abolition: Assensus and Sanctuary,' in *Ibid* at 336–51.

[48] I offer this qualification because the term 'legal moralism' is also sometimes used to refer to the view that, as Dan Kahan has put it, 'law is suffused with morality and, as a result, can't ultimately be identified of applied . . . without the making of moral judgments.' Dan M Kahan, 'Ignorance of the Law is an Excuse—But Only for the Virtuous' (1997) 96 *Michigan Law Review* 127, 128. Scholars who subscribe to legal moralism of this sort need not take any particular position on the criminalization of non-harmful or non-offensive acts.

Michael Moore uses 'legal moralism' in what is arguably yet another sense of the term. According to Moore, a legislator who subscribes to legal moralism 'would believe that in some sense there are right answers to moral questions . . . and that such right answers do not depend on what most people in his society happen to think about these matters. Further, a theorist of this type would believe that every legislator has the right and the duty to legislate his view of what the correct moral order is, into law.' Michael Moore, *Placing Blame: A General Theory of the Criminal Law* (Oxford: Clarendon Press, 1998) 645. Ultimately, the *content* of the 'liberal' legal moralism that Moore endorses looks very different from the content of the 'conservative' legal moralism embraced by writers such as Patrick Devlin, *The Enforcement of Morals* (Oxford: OUP, 1965). (For example, because Moore believes that 'morality is indifferent to sexual practices, and that avoidance of much else in the way of conventionally regarded "vice" is only supererogatory but not obligatory,' he would decriminalize 'much of what passes as 'morals offences' in our current criminal code.' *Ibid* at 662.) Nevertheless, from a methodological standpoint, Moore's version of legal moralism seems less like the primarily descriptive version used by Kahan than like the primarily prescriptive version referred to by Devlin and other conservative legal moralists.

[49] For examples of the legal moralistic approach, see Robert P George, *Making Men Moral: Civil Liberties and Public Morality* (Oxford: Clarendon Press, 1993); Devlin (n 48 above); James Fitzjames Stephen, *Liberty, Equality, Fraternity* (University of Chicago Press edn. 1991) (orig. publ. 1874).

[50] John Stuart Mill, *On Liberty* (London, 1859), ch. 1, para. 9 ('the only purpose of which power can be rightfully exercised over any member of a civilized community, against his will, is to prevent harm to others').

for taking it to be necessary as well as effective) to prevent harm or the unreasonable risk of harm to parties other than the person interfered with.[51]

At first glance, my interest in moral wrongfulness might be understood as suggesting that I am sympathetic to the traditional legal moralist view, since the legal moralists are also concerned with the ways in which the criminal law might be used to 'enforce morality.'[52] I should make clear at the outset, however, that any such understanding of my position would be mistaken. Although I am concerned with the ways in which the criminal law reflects moral values, my position is well within the liberal tradition of Mill and Feinberg, in the sense that I would oppose the use of the criminal law to punish acts that do not satisfy some form of the harm principle. Under the approach taken here, the only proper use of criminal sanctions is to prevent not simply harm, but a certain subset of harms—namely, wrongful harms. Indeed, Feinberg himself maintains that acts are properly criminalized only if they are both harmful and wrongful.[53] To put it another way, I am interested in the requirement of moral wrongfulness not because I think it should be viewed as sufficient to justify criminalization, but because I think it should be viewed (*along with* harmfulness and culpability) as necessary.[54]

Requiring that acts be both wrongful *and* harmful also has the effect of ensuring that mere *private* wrongs not become criminalized. For example, if

---

[51] Feinberg (n 16 above, at 11). See also Ronald Dworkin, 'Do We Have a Right to Pornography?', in R Dworkin, *A Matter of Principle* (Oxford: OUP, 1985); HLA Hart, *Law, Liberty, and Morality* (Oxford: OUP, 1963); Packer, (ch 2 n 9 above, at 296–354); Sanford Kadish, 'The Crisis of Overcriminalization' (1957) 374 *Annals of American Academy Political & Social Science* 157, 169; Edwin M Schur and Hugo Adam Bedau, *Victimless Crimes: Two Sides of a Controversy* (Englewood Cliffs, NJ: Prentice Hall, 1974) 76–84. Bernard Harcourt has argued that the terms of the liberal/legal moralist debate have shifted in recent years. According to Harcourt, those who want to prohibit prostitution, pornography, drug use, and other kinds of conduct that once were viewed as 'harmless wrongdoing,' now argue that such acts are in fact harmful to others or self. See Bernard E Harcourt, 'The Collapse of the Harm Principle' (1999) 90 *Journal of Criminal Law & Criminology* 109.

[52] Although the idea of using law to 'enforce morality' has negative connotations for most liberals, it does not seem to me inherently objectionable. Indeed, every retributivist is in some sense committed to the view that law can properly be used to sanction immoral behavior, though not as such. The real question is, what kind of immoral behavior is to be prohibited and punished? If we use the term 'enforce morality' to refer to the criminalization of harmless wrongdoing, then the liberal concern is warranted. But if we use the term to refer to the punishment of wrongful harmdoing, it is hard to see any valid objection. cf Joel Feinberg, 'Some Unswept Debris from the Hart-Devlin Debate' (1987) 72 *Syntheses* 260 (quoted in Jean Hampton, 'How You Can Be Both a Liberal and a Retributivist: Comments on *Legal Moralism and Liberalism* by Jeffrie Murphy' (1995) 37 *Arizona Law Review* 105, 106).

[53] Feinberg (n 16 above, at 31–36). See also RA Duff, 'Harms and Wrongs' (2001) 5 *Buffalo Criminal Law Review* 13, 16–26; Hamish Stewart, 'Harms, Wrongs, and Set-Backs in Feinberg's Moral Limits of the Criminal Law' (2001) 5 *Buffalo Criminal Law Review* 47.

[54] Cf RA Duff and Stuart P Green, 'Introduction: The Special Part and its Problems,' in RA Duff and S Green (eds.), *Defining Crimes* (Oxford: OUP, 2005) 7 (principle of legal moralism as understood by Feinberg (and Moore) 'is not that the prevention of wrongdoing constitutes a good reason to criminalize conduct; it is rather the wrongfulness of the conduct itself that gives us reason to criminalize it').

I breach an important promise to a friend, I have violated a moral norm—namely, to keep one's promises. I have clearly done a wrong to my friend and, assuming that he relied on my promise in some significant way, may even have caused him significant harm. But unless the harm I did to my friend is 'public' in the way that the criminal law considers relevant,[55] my action should remain a private matter between the two of us, well beyond the reach of the criminal law.[56]

Wrongfulness as a Violation of Everyday Norms

The approach to moral wrongfulness that I shall take in this book consists of examining a collection of everyday, but nevertheless powerful, moral norms—specifically, the norms against cheating, deception, coercion, exploitation, disloyalty, promise-breaking, and disobedience. My goal is to show how such familiar concepts, properly understood and clearly articulated, inform and help shape a collection of key white-collar crimes. Indeed, it is the very 'everyday-ness' of such norms that helps explain the difficulties we encounter in distinguishing between white collar crime and lawful, if aggressive, kinds of behavior.

Such an approach has several advantages over the generalized rights-based approach mentioned earlier. Unlike rights, which can be maddeningly abstract ('nonsense upon stilts,' in Bentham's memorable phrase), the norms that I will be describing are fairly concrete. Although there will be significant disagreement over the precise content and application of such norms, almost every civilized person will have some rudimentary understanding that it is morally wrong, at least in certain core cases, to lie, cheat, steal, coerce, exploit, break promises, and the like. Moreover, such an approach is more suggestive of the richly nuanced way people actually think about the content of their moral lives. Even people who have never had occasion to read a single page of moral philosophy are capable of making remarkably fine-grained distinctions about, say, what properly constitutes cheating or stealing.

At the same time, it should be clear that the norms- and rights-based approaches are not mutually inconsistent. I have no quarrel at all with the proposition that subjecting a fellow human being to coercion or deceit constitutes a violation of such person's (moral or legal) rights. My point is simply that saying that V's rights were violated is often less informative than saying that V was deceived or coerced or cheated.

Finally, although my everyday norm-based approach to moral wrongfulness in criminal law does have advantages over the rights-based approach, it is hardly without its own problems. For one thing, the list itself is limited: I have not attempted to find an everyday norm or set of norms that underlies every

[55] See discussion above, text accompanying n 19.
[56] A somewhat similar point is made in Duff and Green (n 54 above, at 8) although cast there (I now think incorrectly) in terms of public 'wrongs' rather than public 'harms.'

criminal offense, and indeed there may well be offenses for which no readily identifiable, independent moral norm can be found. In such cases, we might be able to say nothing more informative than that X wronged V by intentionally (or knowingly, recklessly, or negligently) causing V some particular kind of harm.

Social Consensus and the Law's Educative Function

Another aspect of the principle of fair labeling, referred to above, is that of 'assisting the law's educative or declaratory function by sustaining and reinforcing social standards.'[57] That is, by labeling and punishing certain conduct as 'criminal,' our legal system sends a message that such conduct is worthy of censure.[58] Thus, just as the decision to make certain conduct criminal reflects publicly held moral norms, so too are public perceptions of morality affected by what has been made criminal.[59] When such labeling is consistent with what society as a whole regards as morally wrongful, law and norms are mutually reinforcing, or reciprocal. But when there is a gap between what the law regards as morally wrongful and what a significant segment of society views as such, moral conflict and ambiguity are likely to be the result.

Indeed, the idea of consensus is important to all three elements of the criminal law's moral content—culpability, harmfulness, and wrongfulness. When we say that a person is culpable or that an act is wrongful or harmful, we mean, at least in part, that a consensus of society would, or should, view the person or act in that way. Indeed, it is the supposed gap in what John Coffee has called the 'close linkage between the criminal law and behavior deemed morally culpable by the general community'[60] that is at the core of the overcriminalization critique.[61]

Several points about the significance of social consensus should be clear, however. First, to acknowledge the place of consensus in moral judgments is

---

[57] Ashworth (n 45 above, at 72).

[58] The *locus classicus* for this kind of argument is Joel Feinberg, 'The Expressive Function of Criminal Punishment,' in Joel Feinberg, *Doing & Deserving: Essays in the Theory of Responsibility* (Princeton: Princeton University Press, 1970) 95.

[59] Harry V Ball and Lawrence M Friedman, 'The Use of Criminal Sanctions in the Enforcement of Economic Legislation: A Sociological View' (1965) 17 *Stanford Law Review* 197, 206–07; see also Paul H Robinson & John M Darley, 'The Utility of Desert' (1997) 91 *Northwestern University Law Review* 453 (describing the process by which the law plays a role in the creation of societal norms); John C Coffee, Jr., 'Does "Unlawful" Mean "Criminal"?: Reflections on the Disappearing Tort/Crime Distinction in American Law' (1991) 71 *Boston University Law Review* 193, 198; Packer (n 9, ch. 2 above, at 43); Philip Soper, 'The Moral Value of Law' (1985) 84 *Michigan Law Review* 63, 85 ('a basic institution like law may be one of the ways that we learn about morality in the first place'). For a review of the empirical evidence on this point, see Tom R Tyler and John M Darley, 'Building a Law-Abiding Society: Taking Public Views About Morality and the Legitimacy of Legal Authorities into Account When Formulating Substantive Law' (2000) 28 *Hofstra Law Review* 707, 712–13.

[60] Coffee (n 59 above, at 198).

[61] See Green (n 9, ch. 2 above); see also Henry M Hart, Jr., 'The Aims of the Criminal Law' (1958) 23 *Law & Contemporary Problems* 401, 404–05, 422 (arguing that criminal sanctions cannot be 'justifie[d]' unless 'accompanie[d]' by 'the judgment of community condemnation.').

not meant to suggest that we can derive an 'ought' from an 'is'[62] or that we should decide what is morally right by taking a vote. Nor is it to deny that there is a significant difference between 'critical' and 'conventional' (or 'intuitive') morality.[63] Secondly, it is important to recognize that society's views of morality change over time, and that what one generation views as morally wrongful or socially harmful frequently deviates from the views of earlier and succeeding generations.[64]

Recognizing the existence of the relationship between social consensus and the criminal law does not require one to believe that it will always be possible to find such a consensus, or that criminal penalties should never be authorized or imposed unless we are able to do so. For present purposes, I shall take as a given that society is capable of reaching, and frequently does reach, a consensus about the moral status of many acts. Determining precisely how and when this phenomenon occurs, however, is beyond the scope of this study.[65]

[62] See WD Hudson (ed.), *The Is-Ought Question: A Collection of Papers on the Central Problems of Moral Philosophy* (New York: St Martins Press, 1969).

[63] See Joel Feinberg, *Harm to Self* (New York: OUP, 1986) 124–25; RM Hare, *Moral Thinking: Its Level, Method, and Point* (Oxford: OUP, 1981) 25 (contrasting 'intuitive' and 'critical' morality). Conventional or intuitive morality consists of the moral rules and principles regarding our dealings with each other and the valuation of social goods that are widely accepted in a particular society. Critical morality, by contrast, consists of moral rules and principles best supported by reasoned argument. In a corrupt society, the conventional morality is viewed as abhorrent from the perspective of critical morality.

[64] The process by which public morality changes over time has been referred to by Ball and Friedman as 'intergenerational drift.' See Ball & Friedman (n 59 above, at 221).

[65] For a discussion of the difficulties in finding social consensus regarding issues of values, see generally Neil Cooper, *The Diversity of Moral Thinking* (Oxford: Clarendon Press, 1981).

PART II
DEFINING MORAL
WRONGFULNESS

This Part offers an analysis of eight kinds of moral wrongfulness: cheating, deception, stealing, coercion, exploitation, disloyalty, promise-breaking, and disobedience—dealt with here in roughly decreasing order of their importance in the context of white-collar criminal law. The subject, of course, is a vast one: one could write an entire volume on each kind of moral wrongfulness individually, and, as the notes to this Part indicate, many such books have in fact been written. My own 'ramble through a moral minefield'[1] is intended primarily to give the reader a 'feel' for each kind of moral wrongfulness and to pick out those defining features that seem most relevant to the task of criminal law theorizing that follows.

---

[1] This is the phrase that Judith Shklar used to refer to her own discussion of what she called the 'ordinary vices'—cruelty, hypocrisy, snobbery, betrayal, and misanthropy. Judith Shklar, *Ordinary Vices* (Cambridge, Mass.: Harvard/Belknap, 1984).

4

Cheating

Cheating is a subject we hear, and talk, about all the time: top officials of Enron have been facing charges that they cheated shareholders and employees by, among other things, redistributing assets and liabilities among shell companies to mask the firm's true financial condition. One-hundred-and-twenty-two students at the University of Virginia were charged with cheating after it was discovered that they had submitted plagiarized answers to a homework assignment in an introductory physics class. In Britain, Army Major Charles Ingram, his wife, and a college lecturer were found guilty of cheating by using 'coded coughs' to win the top prize in the television game show, 'Who Wants to Be a Millionaire?' At the 2002 Winter Olympics, Russian cross-country skiers were stripped of their medals for cheating after it was discovered that they had used performance-enhancing drugs. Former Tyco head Dennis Kozlowski, who allegedly bought six paintings to decorate his Fifth Avenue apartment and then shipped empty boxes to his home in New Hampshire, has been indicted for cheating on New York State sales tax. A one-vote majority of the Supreme Court is said to have cheated by halting the Florida vote recount and effectively awarding the 2000 presidential election to George W Bush. And Bill Clinton, it is said, cheated on his wife, Hillary, by having an affair with White House intern Monica Lewinsky.[2]

Although use of the term is common, however, we seldom stop to think about what exactly we mean when we say that someone has cheated. Presumably, we intend to convey the normative judgment that she has committed a morally wrongful act. But is cheating anything more than a generalized, unreflective

---

[2] See Kurt Eichenwald, 'Enron Paid Huge Bonuses in '01; Experts See a Motive for Cheating' *New York Times* (1 Mar. 2002), at A1; Lew Freedman, '3 Expelled for Doping Violations' *Chicago Tribune* (25 Feb. 2002), at 5 ('[H]ours before the violations were officially announced, skiers were abuzz, speaking of how drug cheaters had tarnished their sport.'); Beth Piskora, 'The Art of the Steal; Dumped Tyco Chief Kozlowski Indicted' *New York Post* (5 June 2002), at 35 ('Former Tyco CEO Dennis Kozlowski was indicted yesterday for cheating New York out of $1.87 million in taxes he should have paid on $13.2 million worth of art purchases.'); Jeevan Vasagar, 'Guilty: Trio Who Cheated Their Way to a Million,' *The Guardian* (8 April 2003), at 11; Diana Jean Schemo, 'University of Virginia Hit by Scandal Over Cheating' *New York Times* (10 May 2001); Alan M Dershowitz, *Supreme Injustice: How the High Court Hijacked Election 2000* (New York: OUP, 2001), 174 ('[T]he decision in the Florida election case may be ranked as the single most corrupt decision in Supreme Court history, because it is the only one that I know of where the majority justices decided as they did because of the personal identity and political affiliation of the litigants. This was cheating, and a violation of the judicial oath').

term of moral disapprobation? Is there some common group of qualities that link all of these various instances of cheating? If so, how does cheating differ from other kinds of morally wrongful acts, such as deceit, exploitation, coercion, promise-breaking, and disloyalty? Given its ubiquity and seeming importance to our moral discourse, it is surprising that the concept of cheating has engendered so little in the way of philosophical analysis. It is as if theorists have simply assumed that the concept is too vague in its meaning or too general in its application to be of much interest.

This section offers a 'normative reconstruction' of the concept of cheating. My aim is not to conduct a linguistic study of all the various ways in which the term is used. Rather, I want to develop a framework for thinking critically about a paradigmatic concept of cheating; and, if not to reach consensus on every point, then at least to identify those aspects of cheating about which there is likely to be agreement (or disagreement). What I hope to demonstrate is that there is, in fact, a widely recognized concept of cheating that it is distinguishable—both analytically and expressively—from other forms of moral wrongfulness.

1. THE CONCEPT OF CHEATING IN THE SCHOLARLY LITERATURE

What is most striking about the scholarly treatment of cheating is how little there is of it. Although the concept of 'fairness' is dealt with extensively in the literature on political and social philosophy, the concept of cheating—despite its apparent importance in our everyday lives—has been mostly ignored in the literature of moral philosophy.[3]

Cheating as Non-Cooperation

One place in which talk of cheating does occur regularly is the economics literature, particularly that involving game theory, in which the idea of a game is used as a tool or metaphor for analyzing how groups of people interact.[4] In this context, cheating is often used a synonym for various forms of non-cooperative behavior. As such, it is typically used in a non-moral sense. And,

---

[3] On justice as fairness, see, most famously, John Rawls, *A Theory of Justice* (Cambridge, Mass.: Belknap Press of Harvard University Press, 1971). The only works of analytic philosophy I am aware of that deal explicitly with the concept of cheating are Bernard Gert, *Morality: A New Justification of the Moral Rules* (New York: OUP, 1988) 129–33; and Michael Sean Quinn, 'Practice-Defining Rules' 86 *Ethics* 76 (1975). For a popular treatment of the subject, see David Callahan, *The Cheating Culture: Why More Americans Are Doing Wrong to Get Ahead* (New York: Harcourt, 2004).

[4] The classic work is John von Neumann and Oskar Morgenstern, *The Theory of Games and Economic Behavior* (2nd edn., Princeton: Princeton University Press, 1947). See also Douglas G Baird, et al., *Game Theory and the Law* (Cambridge, Mass.: Harvard University Press, 1994).

even when a moral sense is implied, it is left unanalyzed. For example, the word 'cheater' has been used to refer to parties who: in the Prisoner's Dilemma, elect to 'rat' on each other even though they would both be better off if they jointly remained silent; succumb to the 'tragedy of the commons' by overusing collective goods; defect from cartel pricing arrangements; fail to cooperate with other franchisees in the same geographic market; and engage in various other forms of non-cooperative behavior.[5]

What is significant about the use of the term 'cheating' in each of these contexts is its primarily descriptive, non-normative quality. For example, the party in the Prisoner's Dilemma who engages in non-cooperative behavior cannot necessarily be said to have done something morally wrongful. She has not broken any rules or promises or failed to perform any duties. She has merely made a strategic decision, on the basis of limited information, about how best to optimize her outcome. While there surely are games in which a participant's non-cooperation could be characterized as morally wrongful, the literature fails to explain which of these various forms of conduct would qualify, and why.

Cheating in Punishment Theory and Developmental Psychology

Two other views of cheating—each problematic in its own way—can be found in the literature of punishment theory and in the literature of developmental psychology. An influential article by Herbert Morris, entitled 'Persons and Punishment,' is representative of the former. In it, Morris argues that:

[I]t is just to punish those who have violated the rules and caused the unfair distribution of benefits and burdens. A person who violates the rules has something others have—the benefits of the system—but by renouncing what others have assumed, the burdens of self-restraint, he has acquired an unfair advantage. Matters are not even until this advantage is in some way erased. Another way of putting it is that he owes something to others, for he has something that does not rightfully belong to him. Justice—that is punishing such individuals—restores the equilibrium of benefits and burdens by taking from the individual what he owes, that is, exacting the debt.[6]

Although he does not use the term itself, Morris does a good job of explaining the basic dynamic of what is, in essence, cheating: in violating a rule that others follow, and thereby breaching an obligation to restrict his liberty in a manner agreed, the cheater gains an unfair advantage.

The problem with Morris's theory, however, is that it puts far more weight on the concept of cheating than it is capable of supporting. Morris is wrong

---

[5] See, eg Björn Brembs, 'Chaos, Cheating, and Cooperation: Potential Solutions to the Prisoner's Dilemma' (1996) 76 *Oikos* 14; Garrett Hardin, 'The Tragedy of the Commons' (1968) 162 *Science* 1243; Andrew R Dick, 'When Are Cartels Stable Contracts?' (1996) 39 *Journal of Law & Economics* 241, 242; Natalie Angier, 'The Urge to Punish Cheats: Not Just Human, but Selfless,' *New York Times* (22 Jan. 2002) (reporting on Ernst Fehr & Simon Gächter, 'Altruistic Punishment in Humans' (2002) 415 *Nature* 137).

[6] Herbert Morris, 'Persons and Punishment' (1968) 52 *The Monist* 475.

to suggest that the idea of cheating underlies *all* crimes. As Jean Hampton explained, Morris's approach 'makes sense only if we believe that constraining ourselves so that we do not rape or murder or steal imposes a cost upon us. Yet that idea makes sense only if [we accept the absurd notion that] raping, murdering, and stealing are viewed by us as desirable and attractive.'[7] On the other hand, while the idea that certain kinds of acts create an 'unfair distribution of benefits and burdens' is insufficient to provide a general theory of criminalization, it does, as we shall see in Part III, play a significant role in defining certain key white-collar offenses, such as tax evasion, insider trading, and various 'failure to comply' regulatory violations.

The concept of cheating also appears in the vast literature on developmental psychology. Here again, the term is used to convey a sense of moral wrongfulness, but it is never defined with any precision. Since the focus of such literature is often the moral development of children, there have been many studies of conduct, in school or on the playground, generically characterized as 'cheating.' Typical are studies showing that: children with high IQs are less likely to cheat than children with low IQs; as children age, the incidence of cheating on school assignments tends to increase, while the incidence of cheating in games tends to decrease; students who believe they are likely to be caught are less inclined to cheat in school than students who believe they are unlikely to be caught; and participation in a moral education program makes children less likely to engage in cheating behavior.[8] By and large, this literature is concerned with common, and uncontroversial, forms of cheating, and fails to shed light on its deeper meaning or outer limits.

2. A Paradigmatic Account of Cheating

Like the concept of cheating that occurs in the literature of developmental psychology and punishment theory, and unlike that which appears in the literature of game theory, the concept of cheating that is the focus of the analysis here is a distinctly moral one. In this section, I seek to develop a positive theory of cheating, beginning with a description of its paradigmatic formal elements. Then, we consider the extent to which cheating is analytically distinguishable from other morally wrongful acts, such as promise-breaking and deceiving.

---

[7] Jean Hampton, 'Correcting Harms Versus Righting Wrongs: The Goal of Retribution' (1992) 39 *UCLA Law Review* 1659, 1660.

[8] See, eg Robert M Liebert, 'What Develops in Moral Development?,' in William M Kurtines and Jacob L Gewirtz (eds.), *Morality, Moral Behavior, and Moral Development* (New York: Wiley, 1984) 187–88 (citing studies); Moshe M Blatt and Lawrence Kohlberg, 'The Effects of Classroom Moral Discussion Upon Children's Level of Moral Judgment' (1975) 4 *Journal of Moral Education* 129, reprinted in Bill Puka (ed.) *Fundamental Research in Moral Development* (New York: Garland, 1994).

Formal Elements of Cheating

Under my account, in order for us to say that X has cheated, X must (1) violate a fair and fairly enforced rule, (2) with the intent to obtain an advantage over a party with whom she is in a cooperative, rule-bound relationship.

Before we proceed to a discussion of these two elements, however, it is worth noting another possible two elements that will not be included in my account of cheating—namely, deception and covertness. The two concepts are distinct. Rule-breaking can be covert without being deceptive and decept-ive without being covert. Deception entails an intent to cause someone to believe something that is untrue. Covertness requires no such intent. It merely requires an intent to conceal or make secret. Deception, moreover, constitutes a prima facie moral wrong; covertness, by contrast, appears to be morally neutral.[9] From a lexicographic standpoint, there is some reason to think that both are part of the concept of cheating. For example, the *Oxford English Dictionary* defines the verb 'to cheat' as 'to defraud; to deprive of by deceit,' 'to deceive, impose upon, trick,' or 'to deal fraudulently, practice deceit.'[10] And Michael Sean Quinn, in one of the very few philosophical works to deal with the concept of cheating, defines a cheater as 'someone who knows the rules of the game, purports to follow them, but *covertly* and deliberately breaks them (usually for his own advantage).'[11]

Although I agree with Quinn (and the *OED*) that cheating often does involve deception or covertness, I am doubtful that either element is required. Consider, for example, a case in which a driver drives on the soft shoulder of the freeway in order to avoid sitting in a line of traffic waiting to get around an accident or other obstruction. The driver is breaking a rule ('wait your turn in line') and doing so to obtain a competitive advantage, but he is not doing so covertly or deceptively since all of the other drivers can observe him. Nevertheless, it seems likely that he is cheating. In light of cases like this, I intend to exclude the elements of covertness and deception from my discus-sion and focus exclusively on rule-breaking and advantage-seeking.

---

[9] See generally Sissela Bok, *Secrets: On the Ethics of Concealment and Revelation* (New York: Pantheon Books, 1982) 26–27 ('Given both the legitimacy of some control over secrecy and openness, and the dangers this control carries for all involved, there can be no presumption either for or against secrecy in general. Secrecy differs in this respect from lying, promise-breaking, violence, and other practices for which the burden of proof rests on those who would defend them. Conversely, secrecy differs from truthfulness, friendship, and other practices carrying a favorable presumption.')

[10] *Oxford English Dictionary* (2nd edn. 1989) (entry on *cheating*).

[11] See Quinn n 3, at 78 above (emphasis added). Quinn offers his discussion of cheating in the context of a critique of John Rawls's argument that engaging in a practice requires rule-following. See John Rawls, 'Two Concepts of Rules' (1955) 64 *Philosophical Review* 3. According to Quinn, the implication of Rawls's argument is that if one is ostensibly engaged in a game, but cheating at it, then one is not actually playing the game. Quinn says this is self-contradictory because one cannot both be playing a game and not playing it. As an alternative, Quinn argues, we should simply say that the cheater is not playing fairly rather than not playing at all. 86 *Ethics* 76, at 80. For more on Quinn's analysis, see n 43 below.

Rule-Breaking

Cheating requires that X violate some rule. Merely playing things close to the line may earn X a reputation as dodgy or wily or unsportsmanlike, but, unless X actually crosses the line, she has not cheated. The question is: what kind of line must X cross? Moral and legal theorists have developed a large and complex body of learning about rules, their structure, and the way we use them.[12] My purpose here is not to review all of this learning, but rather to identify those features of rules that are specifically relevant in the context of cheating.

Rules have been defined as 'hypothetical propositions, stipulating that if certain circumstances ... obtain, then certain consequences are to (or "must" or "ought to") follow or be implemented.'[13] One of the crucial things to note about rules is their general or universalizable character. A rule is general in that is concerned with *types* of actions or events in *types* of circumstances, rather than with a particular set of actions in a particular set of circumstances.[14] In this sense, rules are distinguishable from *commands*, which typically apply only in a given instance.

Descriptive and Prescriptive Rules

To start, we can think of the general category of *rules* as a genus that contains two species: *descriptive rules* and *prescriptive rules*. Descriptive rules state an empirical regularity or habit.[15] They are used to make sense of the world, to describe it, rather than to alter it. Some descriptive rules apply to the physical world: 'As a rule, it rains a lot in Scotland.' 'As a rule, fast food is high in salt and fat.' 'Energy is conserved; it is neither created nor destroyed.' Other descriptive rules apply to human conduct: 'As a rule, Smith parts his hair on the right.' 'As a rule, Jones leaves her house before 8 a.m.'

Prescriptive rules, by contrast, are used to guide or control behavior.[16] They typically include an explicit or implicit 'must,' 'may,' or 'may not': 'Patrons must wear shoes and a shirt.' 'No smoking allowed.' 'Fasten your seatbelt.' 'Brush your teeth after every meal.' 'Honor your mother and father.' 'Act only on that maxim by which you can at the same time will that it should become a universal law.' 'Just say no.' 'Do the right thing.'

By and large, cheating involves the violation of prescriptive rules—a fact that is not surprising, since, as we shall see, the goal of obtaining an unfair advantage is more likely to occur in the context of what one should or should not do. There are, however, some interesting cases in which we might speak of cheating even in the context of descriptive rules. For example, imagine that

---

[12] See, eg Neil MacCormick, *Legal Reasoning and Legal Theory* (Oxford: OUP, rev. edn. 1995); William Twining and David Miers, *How to Do Things With Rules* (London: Weidenfeld & Nicholson, 1991); Frederick Schauer, *Playing by the Rules* (Oxford: OUP, 1991).

[13] MacCormick, (n 12 above, at x).

[14] Twining & Miers (n 12 above, at 123).   [15] Schauer (n 12 above, at 2).

[16] *Ibid.*

a person is involved in a terrible car accident that 'ought to have killed him,' but nevertheless emerges unscathed. In such cases, we might well say that the person has 'cheated death' in the sense that he's broken the (descriptive) rule that 'people who are in accidents of this type usually die or suffer serious injury.' Analogously, we might say that someone has cheated 'sleep' or 'time'. Notwithstanding such usage, however, the kind of cheating with which we shall be concerned here is that which typically concerns the violation of a rule that is prescriptive.[17]

Optional vs Mandatory Rules

Among the species of rules that are prescriptive, we can, in turn, distinguish between two subspecies of rules, which I shall refer to as optional (or prudential) and mandatory (or normative) rules.[18] Optional rules are sometimes referred to as 'rules of thumb.' They provide instructions about how best to perform some task: 'Always keeps your eye on the ball' (in baseball). 'Never drive against the spin' (in cricket). 'Prepositions are a bad thing to end a sentence with.'[19] 'For a healthy diet, eat five servings of fruit or vegetables every day.' 'Wash bright colors separately.' As Frederick Schauer explains, such rules contain[] an explicit or implicit 'if' clause limiting the application of the rule to those seeking success in some enterprise.'[20] Thus, their force is 'congruent with our assessment of the likelihood that they will produce the desired result.'[21] If one believes that, in a given case, following a given rule will fail to lead to the desired result, then one is free to ignore the rule, since the rule itself exerts no normative force.

Optional rules can be distinguished from mandatory rules. To those who accept the authority of one or another mandatory rule, such rules (again, in Schauer's words) 'furnish reasons for actions simply by virtue of their existence *qua* rules, and thus generate normative pressure even in those cases in which the justifications (rationales) underlying the rules indicate the contrary result.'[22] Examples of mandatory rules are: 'Remember the Sabbath Day,

[17] Also problematic are those cases in which it is difficult to distinguish between prescriptive and descriptive rules. For example, imagine that X and Y regularly play tennis together and that X's game is in many ways predictable: As a rule, X can be counted on to play with no great effort or skill. Over the summer, however, X takes tennis lessons, lifts weights and runs, and greatly improves his physical condition. In the Fall, when X and Y play again, X's game is much stronger. Presumably, X has broken the descriptive rule that 'X plays without any great skill or effort.' But it seems odd to call this cheating, since he is obviously still playing by the rules. Perhaps X has also broken some other, less obvious, prescriptive rule, such as that 'one shouldn't defy the expectations of a long-time sporting partner by secretly taking lessons and getting in shape,' or something to that effect. Thus, what may at first seem like the violation of a descriptive rule can plausibly be re-characterized as the violation of a prescriptive rule.

[18] Here again, I follow Schauer, (n 12 above, at 3–4). Twining and Miers make an analogous distinction between prudential and normative rules. Twining & Miers, (n 12 above, at 124–25).

[19] About this rule, Churchill famously remarked: 'This is the sort of pedantry up with which I will not put.'   [20] Schauer (n 12 above, at 3).

[21] *Ibid.*   [22] *Ibid.*

to Keep it Holy.' 'Curb your dog.' 'Pay your taxes.' 'No state shall ... deny to any person within its jurisdiction the equal protection of the laws.'[23] Of course, to claim that a rule is mandatory is not to claim that compliance with it is always the morally right thing to do. Rather, it is merely to suggest that at least part of its moral or normative force is derived from its being a rule.

Once again, it is not always easy to distinguish between optional and mandatory rules. Some rules, such as 'don't drive drunk' and 'fasten your seatbelt' function as both. Other rules, such as that posted outside my law school office door—'Office Hours: Monday and Wednesday, 2–4 p.m'—are intended to be mandatory, but are often understood (at least by my students!) to be merely rules of thumb.

In some unusual cases, we might say that a person who violates an optional rule has cheated. This is what we might say, for example, if X baked a delicious cake using a store-bought mix rather than making it from scratch. But, again, this is not to use 'cheating' in its moral sense. The kind of cheating with which we shall be concerned here involves the violation of mandatory, as opposed to optional, rules. As we shall see below, it is precisely the fact that others will feel morally bound by the mandatory nature of such rules that gives the cheater an opportunity to seek an unfair advantage.

Practice-Defining vs Regulative Rules

A further distinction, associated most famously with John Rawls's early essay, 'Two Concepts of Rules,' is often made between those mandatory rules that define a practice and those that merely regulate actions that fall within such practice.[24] Practice-defining (or 'constitutive') rules are logically prior to regulative rules.[25] For example, the rule that says that a batter in baseball gets three strikes is a practice-defining rule because it helps define the practice of baseball itself. The same is true of the rule that 'a sonnet must consist of 14 lines in iambic pentameter with a fixed rhyme scheme, usually divided into three quatrains and a couplet.'[26] A piece of verse that does not follow those rules may be very fine, but it is not a sonnet. Such rules, though conditional, are mandatory in the sense that, *if* one wants to play baseball or write a sonnet, then one must follow them.

Practice-defining rules are distinguished from regulative rules.[27] Consider the rule in baseball that is intended to prevent the throwing of spitballs: 'The pitcher

---

[23] US Const. Amendment XIV.

[24] Rawls (n 11 above). A similar distinction is discussed in John Searle, *Speech Acts* (Cambridge: CUP, 1969) 33–42.

[25] Rawls (n 11 above, at 8).

[26] TWH Crosland, *The English Sonnet* (London: M. Secker, 1917).

[27] Rawls uses the distinction between constitutive and regulative rules to demonstrate the difference between justifying a practice as a system of rules to be applied and enforced, and justifying a particular action that falls under such rules. According to Rawls, utilitarian arguments are appropriate with regard to questions about practices, while retributive arguments fit the application of particular rules to particular cases. Rawls (n 11 above, at 5).

shall not expectorate on the ball, either hand, or his glove.'[28] This rule is regulative rather than practice-defining, because it is logically dependent on the existence of the game of baseball, as established by its constitutive rules. Similarly, the rule that says that one should stop at a red light is regulative, because the practice to which the rule applies (driving a car on public streets) exists prior to, and does not define, the practice of driving itself.

Cheating can involve the violation of both constitutive and regulative rules, although it seems more likely to involve the latter. For example, using a spitball (in violation of a regulative rule) and taking an extra strike when the umpire loses the count (a violation of what is presumably a constitutive rule) would both constitute cheating. On the other hand, a person who plays a game that regularly allows four strikes rather than three might more accurately be said to be playing some game other than, rather than cheating at, baseball.[29]

Decision vs Conduct Rules

Legal theory offers yet another distinction between two sorts of rules (or, more precisely, between two sorts of functions that legal rules play, since the same rule frequently serves both functions): 'conduct rules' (sometimes referred to as 'primary rules'), which are addressed to the general public and are designed to guide its behavior; and decision rules (sometimes called 'secondary rules'), which are directed to the officials who adjudicate cases involving the violation of conduct rules.[30] A good example of a conduct rule is the first half of the rule in baseball concerning spitballs, previously quoted. The rule serves as a conduct rule in the sense that it tells players that certain conduct is prohibited. An example of a decision rule is the second half of the same rule: 'For violation of this part of the rule the umpires shall immediately call a ball.'[31] The rule serves as a conduct rule because it tells officials what decision to make in the event that the conduct rule is violated.

Cheating usually involves the violation of a conduct, rather than a decision, rule. As I shall explain at greater length below, *X* cheats by violating a rule by which *Y* is also bound. Although there are cases in which a judge can be said to have cheated,[32] the rule violated is usually not a decision rule, but rather a special kind conduct rule that happens to apply to judges—namely, the rule that they shall be impartial and fair in their decision-making.

---

[28] Official Baseball Rule 8.02(a)(3). The rule is discussed further in text accompanying n 61 below.   [29] On this point, compare Quinn (n 3 above).

[30] The distinction is made by, among others, Jeremy Bentham, *A Fragment on Government and an Introduction to the Principles of Morals and Legislation* (Oxford: Blackwell, 1960); HLA Hart, *The Concept of Law* (Oxford: OUP, 1994); Meir Dan-Cohen, 'Decision Rules and Conduct Rules: On Acoustic Separation in Criminal Law' (1984) 97 *Harvard Law Review* 625; Paul Robinson, 'Rules of Conduct and Principles of Adjudication' (1990) 57 University of Chicago Law Review 729; see also Gerald J Postema, *Bentham and the Common Law Tradition* (Oxford: OUP, 1986) 403–13 (concerning Bentham's views on this distinction).

[31] Official Baseball Rule 8.02(a).

[32] See discussion below nn 47–50 and accompanying text.

Rules vs Principles, Policies, and other Generalized Standards

Yet another distinction among kinds of rules, found in Dworkin's famous assault on Hart's version of legal positivism, is between standards that function as rules, and standards that function as principles or policies.[33] As used by Dworkin, the term 'rules' refers to narrow standards that are 'applicable in an all-or-nothing fashion'; if the rule is valid, then it dictates the result in a given case.[34] Principles, by contrast, help guide behavior, but do not necessarily determine it. They have a 'dimension that rules do not—the dimension of weight or importance.'[35] Principles do not specify a particular outcome or mode of behavior. Rather, they are merely a factor among others that a decision-maker needs to take into account in making a decision.[36] According to Dworkin, the law is primarily made up of principles rather than rules.

Dworkin's distinction between rules and principles—whatever its shortcomings in the context of his argument against legal positivism[37]—is useful to us in our discussion of cheating. The fact is that standards do differ dramatically in their level of specificity. Some rules are very precise: 'The speed limit on the freeway is 65.' 'A sonnet must consist of fourteen lines.' 'Three strikes and you're out' (in baseball). Others are quite general: 'Drivers shall not drive at an excessive speed.' 'No one shall be permitted to profit by his own fraud.'[38] 'The right of the people to be secure in their persons, houses, papers, and effects, against unreasonable searches and seizures, shall not be violated.'[39]

In the case of cheating, the standard violated is typically a rule, in Dworkin's sense, rather than a principle or policy. For example, it would be odd to say that violating the principle that 'one should love one's neighbor as oneself'[40] constitutes cheating. A person who violates such a principle might be said to be evil or wicked or immoral in any number of ways, but we would not ordinarily say that he was ipso facto a cheater. The rule violated is simply too general in its application. With cheating, we would expect to see the violation of a rule that is more specific.

---

[33] Ronald Dworkin, 'The Model of Rules,' in Ronald Dworkin, *Takings Rights Seriously* (Cambridge, Mass.: Harvard University Press, 1977) 22–28.   [34] *Ibid* at 24.
[35] *Ibid* at 26.
[36] *Ibid*. In some cases, Dworkin also distinguishes between principles and policies. A policy is 'that kind of standard that sets out a goal to be reached, generally an improvement in some economic, political, or social feature of the community.' A principle is a standard that is to be observed, not because it will advance or secure an economic, political, or social situation deemed desirable, but because it is a requirement of justice or fairness or some other dimension of morality.' *Ibid* at 22. The distinction is of no real relevance in the context of cheating.
[37] See, eg MacCormick (n 12 above, at 229 et seq.); John Gardner, 'Legal Positivism: 5½ Myths' (2001) 46 *American Journal of Jurisprudence* 199, 214; Larry Alexander and Ken Kress, 'Against Legal Principles,' in *Law and Interpretation* 279 Andrei Marmor (ed.) (Oxford; OUP, 1995), reprinted in (1997) 82 *Iowa Law Review* (all discussing problems with Dworkin's distinction).
[38] *Riggs v Palmer*, 115 NY 506, 22 NE 188 (1889), discussed in Dworkin, (n 33 above, at 23–24).   [39] US Const. Amendment IV.
[40] *Leviticus* 19:18.

Unfair Advantage-Seeking

Having examined the kinds of rules involved in cheating, we can now turn our attention to its other elements. Although all instances of cheating involve rule-breaking, there are many cases of rule-breaking that do not involve cheating. In this subsection, we consider what additional conditions are necessary to turn a mere rule-breaking into cheating. I offer four: first, the rule broken must be fair and enforced in an even-handed manner and not subject to a justified exception. Secondly, the rule-breaking must be intentional. Thirdly, the rule-breaker must be part of a cooperative rule-governed activity that involves another party. Fourthly, the rule-breaker must intend to gain an advantage through her rule-breaking. This discussion will also provide the opportunity for thinking more generally about why cheating is morally wrongful.

Fair Rules

The rule that the cheater violates must be fair, issued by a legitimate authority, enforced in an even-handed manner, and not subject to a justified exception. For example, it would not have been cheating for a girl in Afghanistan under the Taliban to violate the law that made it a crime for her to attend school, since the law itself was surely unjust and issued by an illegitimate authority. Of course, what exactly it means for a rule to be just and issued by a legitimate authority is an enormously difficult question—one that lies at the very core of political and legal philosophy.[41] For present purposes, I shall simply assume that the rules violated are just.

Moreover, even what would otherwise be a violation of a rule that is just and legitimate is not cheating if the violation falls within a justified exception to the rule. For example, there is an exception to the baseball rule intended to prevent the use of spitballs: in cold weather, provided that the managers of both teams agree, pitchers are permitted to put their hands to their mouths (though not of course to apply lubricant to the ball).[42] Obviously, a player who puts his hand to his mouth under these circumstances has not cheated. Similarly, a driver is permitted to exceed the speed limit if she is rushing to the hospital to deliver a woman in labor. Such acts do not constitute cheating because, under the applicable exception, no rule is actually violated.[43]

---

[41] See, eg Rawls (above n 11); Michael J Sandel, *Liberalism and the Limits of Justice* (2nd edn., Cambridge: CUP, 1999); Joseph Raz, *The Morality of Freedom* (Oxford: OUP, 1988).

[42] Official Baseball Rule 8.02(a)(1) (exception).

[43] There is also a question about the status of so-called 'professional fouls': imagine that in a game of basketball or football (whether American or non-American), a player is about to score a goal. An opposing player then intentionally incurs a foul (and, typically, a penalty) so as to stop play and prevent the goal from being scored. The rule-breaking is clearly intentional and for the purpose of obtaining a competitive advantage, but does it constitute cheating? Opinions vary. One argument, offered by Michael Sean Quinn, is that such cases actually involve two sets of rules—the rules of the game and a separate set of strategic rules. According to Quinn, there is no cheating

Rule-Breaking is Intentional

Imagine two baseball players, each of whom fails to touch first base before heading to second base on a double. Player *A* knows that he is required to touch first base but 'cuts corners,' so as to save time on his way around the bases. Player *B* is unaware that he is required to touch the base and violates the rule out of ignorance. Because cheating requires intent, only player *A* would be regarded as cheating.

This is not to say that unintentional or unknowing rule-breaking may not be every bit as harmful as intentional rule-breaking. For example, it hardly matters whether one who violates the rules promulgated by the Food and Drug Administration governing the production and distribution of adulterated food and medicines has done so intentionally. Even a person who unknowingly violates a rule of etiquette can cause great offense in the proper circumstances. Indeed, intentional and unintentional rule-breaking are often punished in precisely the same way. The important point, though, is that, from a moral perspective, only intentional rule-breaking counts as cheating.

The Rule-Breaker Must be Engaged in a Cooperative, Rule-Governed Activity

The basic social dynamic of cheating is as follows: the cheater and his victim are engaged in a mutually beneficial cooperative enterprise, such as a game, a market, or a political contest. In order to make the scheme work, the parties have implicitly agreed to restrain their liberty by adhering to a series of rules. In restricting their liberty in this way, those who share in the scheme's benefits have both an obligation to follow the rules and a right that others follow them. In violating a rule that others follow, and thereby breaching an obligation to restrain his liberty in the manner agreed, the cheater is able to gain an (unfair) advantage over those who do abide by the rules.[44] The next two subsections examine the nature of the relationship in which *X* is involved. The subsequent subsection looks at the nature of the advantage sought.

Relationship Between at Least Two Parties

Cheating generally involves a relationship between at least two parties: the cheater and her intended victim or victims. Both cheater and victim must be moral agents, but neither need be a human being: Corporations, institutions,

when 'deliberate rule breakage is condoned by the accepted strategic rules of that particular game.' Quinn (n 3 above, at 81).

[44] This aspect of my account of cheating is derived in part from the account contained in A John Simmons, 'Fairness' in Lawrence C Becker and Charlotte B Becker (eds.) *Encyclopedia of Ethics* (New York: Routledge, 1992) vol. 1, at 355, 356. Herbert Morris, quoted in text accompanying n 6 above, also characterizes what amounts to cheating in a similar way.

governments, and perhaps even society at large can serve as both cheater and victim of cheating. Nor is it necessary that X know the actual identity of her victim. As long as X believes that she will obtain an unfair advantage over some other party, that is sufficient.

What, then, are we to make of the notion of 'cheating oneself?' Is it really cheating, say, to sneak a candy bar when one is supposed to be on a diet? Whether such behavior constitutes cheating is a difficult question that raises broader issues about the extent to which moral duties to self are comparable to moral duties to others.[45] Such questions also arise in connection with other moral concepts that we will be dealing with here: for example, can one truly be said to deceive, break a promise to, or be disloyal to, oneself? [46]

For the moment, we can simply note that cheating requires that the rule-breaker be motivated by a desire to obtain an advantage of some sort. Thus, in order to conclude that one can cheat oneself, we would have to find that one can seek an advantage over oneself. What we refer to as 'cheating oneself' typically occurs when X seeks some short-term pleasure (such as can be gained by eating a candy bar) at the expense of some longer-term interest (eg losing weight). Whether such behavior really can be said to constitute 'seeking an advantage over oneself' seems to me doubtful (although it may in some instances be a sign of *akrasia*, or moral weakness).

Cooperative Rule-Governed Relationship

Ordinarily, we would not say that X had cheated unless he was seeking to gain an advantage over another party, Y, with whom he was engaged in what can loosely be characterized as a mutually beneficial, or cooperative, rule-governed relationship. To say this is not to say that X and Y's interests must be aligned or that they must be consciously working toward a common goal. Rather, it means simply that they have given up some form of liberty so as to make possible a group activity that benefits, or has the potential to benefit, the two of them.

Cooperative relationships can, of course, be quite competitive. For example, although in a given game of baseball only one team can win, players on both teams have the potential for achieving fun, good exercise, camaraderie, admiration from spectators, and perhaps even financial rewards. Similar dynamics apply in a wide range of different areas of human activity: students in school, firms competing in a market for goods or services, buyers and sellers, employers and employees, and political adversaries all compete with each other, but

---

[45] See WD Falk, 'Morality, Self and Others' in Judith Jarvis Thomson and Gerald Dworkin (eds.), *Ethics* (New York: Harper & Row, 1968).

[46] For a useful discussion of the morality of self-deception, see Mike W Martin, *Self-Deception and Morality* (Lawrence, Kansas: University Press of Kansas, 1986); Stephen L Darnell, 'Self-Deception, Autonomy, and Moral Constitution,' in Brian P McLaughlin and Amélie Oksenberg Rorty (eds.), *Perspectives on Self-Deception* (Berkeley: University of California Press, 1988) 407; Marcia Baron, 'What is Wrong with Self-Deception?' in *ibid* at 431.

do so in a context of shared rules. All agree, explicitly or implicitly, to abide by certain rules and thereby limit their liberty, in return for the prospect of achieving some good. Even in war, there are rules that, when broken, can be said to involve cheating.

Rule-Breaking for Purpose of Gaining Advantage

Not only must X and Y be in a cooperative relationship with each other, X must also intend to gain some advantage over Y. Thus, if X breaks a rule merely out of spite, on a whim, or for her personal convenience or pleasure, she has not cheated. For example, violating the traffic laws by speeding is not cheating if there are no other drivers on the road. But driving on the soft shoulder while everyone else waits in traffic to get around an accident is cheating because X is violating a rule in order to gain an advantage vis-à-vis other drivers.

When X cheats, she seeks an advantage by violating a rule that Y is believed to be obeying. Typically, X and Y will be competing over a limited resource, and X's gain will be Y's loss. For example, if X cuts ahead of Y in line, X has broken the rule that says that one should wait one's turn, and has done so to Y's disadvantage: X spends less time waiting in line, while Y spends more. (We'll talk below about cases in which X violates a rule in order to neutralize a perceived advantage that another party has gained through cheating.) Of course, X need not be successful in obtaining an advantage in order for us to conclude that she has cheated. Her rule violation may turn out to be ineffective or counterproductive in ways that she has not anticipated. Nor is there any requirement that she view her rule-breaking as necessary to win: even if X would have won the race without the benefit of steroids, it is still cheating for her to use them.

3. Some Problematic Cases of Cheating

In this subsection, I want to examine a number of cases that might pose a problem for the account of cheating just offered: rule-breaking involving judges, rule-breaking to benefit others (altruistic cheating), rule-breaking intended to negate an unfair advantage ('everyone else is doing it' cheating), and cheating by changing the rules in the middle of the game.

Rule-Breaking Involving Judges

An interesting problem arises when cheating is alleged to be committed by judges. Consider two recent cases in the news: that of Marie-Reine Le Gougne, the French figure skating judge who, allegedly, unfairly favored a Russian couple in the finals of the pairs figure skating competition at the 2002 Winter Olympics; and the decision by five justices of the US Supreme Court in *Bush v Gore* to halt the recount of votes in Florida and effectively award the

2000 presidential election to George W Bush.[47] In order to determine if Judge Le Gougne and Justices Rehnquist, Scalia, O'Connor, Kennedy, and Thomas cheated, we need to ask at least two questions: First, what rules, if any, did they violate? Secondly, was their rule-breaking intended to obtain an advantage over a party with whom they were in a cooperative relationship?[48]

Let us assume, if only for purposes of discussion, and recognizing the provocative nature of the claim, that: Le Gougne violated the rule that points should not be assigned to skaters on the basis of their nationality; the five Supreme Court justices violated the rule that cases should not be decided on the basis of the personal identity or political affiliation of the parties. Next we must ask whether such rules were broken with the purpose of obtaining an advantage over a party with whom they were in a cooperative relationship.

Judge Le Gougne and the five Supreme Court justices were in a cooperative relationship with both their fellow judges and the parties whom they were judging. But was their rule-breaking intended to 'gain an advantage' over such parties? The French skating judge allegedly agreed to favor the Russian team in return for a Russian judge's agreement to favor the French team in a separate competition. A number of commentators have suggested that some of the Supreme Court justices were motivated by an ambition to be appointed chief justice or to be succeeded by like-minded jurists.[49] If these allegations are true, then it seems reasonable to say that—at least with respect to their peers—such judges were seeking a competitive advantage, and that they therefore cheated.

A harder question is whether the judges cheated the litigants and participants whom they were judging. For the most part, we have been speaking of cheating in the context of what we might think of as horizontal, rather than vertical, relationships. In the paradigm case of cheating, the rule-breaking contestant, student, litigant, or other party seeks to gain an advantage over some party with whom she is in a competitive contest—eg other contestants, fellow students, or rival litigants. For example, a lawyer who breaks a rule of ethics by, say, concealing evidence can certainly be said to have cheated with respect to the opposing litigants over whom she has sought an advantage.

---

[47] *Bush v Gore*, 531 US 98 (2000). The term 'cheating' has also been used by Barry Smith to refer to cases in which judges disregard well settled precedent in order to achieve what they regard as the 'right result' (particularly in the appeal of state criminal convictions). MBE Smith, 'Do Appellate Courts Regularly Cheat?' (1997) 16 *Criminal Justice Ethics* 11; MBE Smith, 'May Judges Ever Nullify the Law?' (1999) 74 *Notre Dame Law Review* 1657. However, unless such judges violate the rules in order to obtain unfair advantage, this would not constitute cheating on my account.

[48] There is also, perhaps, a third question concerning the type of rule violated. Earlier, it was suggested that cheating typically involves the violation of a conduct, rather than decision, rule. Unfortunately, it is unclear which kind of rules were involved here. Being impartial is a decision rule in the sense that it tells judges how to decide an issue, but it is also a conduct rule in the sense that it regulates judges' conduct *qua* judges. Deciding skating competitions and lawsuits on the basis of merit both appear to be decision rules.

[49] See, eg, Jack M Balkin, '*Bush v. Gore* and the Boundary Between Law and Politics' (2001) 110 *Yale Law Journal* 1407, 1440 (Scalia and Kennedy motivated by desire to be Chief Justice); Louise Weinberg, 'When Courts Decide Elections: The Constitutionality of Bush v. Gore' (2002) 82 *Boston University Law Review* 609, 615 (Rehnquist and O'Connor anxious to resign and be replaced by conservative justices).

But can cheating also occur between a judge and the party she is judging? Does it make sense to say that Judge Le Gougne cheated the Canadian figure skaters whom she was judging, or that a lawyer who conceals evidence cheats not only his rival litigants but also the court? And is it cheating when rules are broken by the sole student in a given class or a child with no siblings or other rivals?

While recognizing that the word 'cheating' often is used in such a manner, I would recommend a different approach. It seems to me that our moral discourse would be more precise if we reserved the term *cheating* for rule-breaking between rivals. For rule-breaking between a judge and the judged, I propose that we use two alternative terms: litigants who fail to comply with rules set down by the court would be referred to as *disobedient* vis-à-vis the court. Judges who fail to judge their cases impartiality would be understood as having *breached a duty of loyalty* (to their office).[50]

Rule-Breaking to Benefit Others

Another perplexing issue arises in cases in which the rule-breaker intends to gain an advantage for someone other than himself, or for himself as well as for others. Consider, first, those cases in which teachers supply their students with the answers to a standardized test, such as the New York State Regents exam.[51] Although it is the students who benefit from such rule-breaking in the first instance, it seems that their teachers also benefit, though indirectly, because they and their schools receive rewards when their students do well. Such conduct clearly deserves to be called cheating.

Such rule-breaking to obtain benefits indirectly should be contrasted to what might be referred to as 'altruistic' rule-breaking.[52] Consider the recent case of a frustrated golfer at the Tillicoultry Golf Club, in Scotland, who cut down several conifers that had blocked a clear tee shot at the ninth hole. To the extent that everyone who plays that hole has been equally advantaged by having the trees removed, it seems that *X* has not cheated, since *X* has gained no advantage vis-à-vis his competing golfers. On the other hand, if *X* cut down the trees in order to negate an advantage enjoyed by *Y*, a competing

[50] For more on the difference between cheating, breach of fiduciary duty, promise-breaking, deceiving, and other kinds of morally wrongful acts, see subsection 4 below.

[51] See, eg Brian A Jacob and Steven D Levitt, 'Catching Cheating Teachers: The Results of an Unusual Experiment in Implementing Theory,' in William G Gale and Janet Rothenberg Pack (eds.), *Brookings-Wharton Papers on Urban Affairs 2003* (New York: Brookings Institution Press, 2003).

[52] What exactly it means to be altruistic is an enormously difficult question, which cannot be resolved easily here. Suffice it to say that the headmaster who cheats on behalf of his students or the father who cheats on behalf of his son's Little League team typically do so, at least in part, out of selfish motives. On the meaning of altruism, see generally Thomas Nagel, *The Possibility of Altruism* (Princeton: Princeton University Press, 1979); see also Christine Korsgaard, *Creating the Kingdom of Ends* (New York: CUP, 1996) (critiquing Nagel); James R Ozinga, *Altruism* (Westport, CT: Prager Publishers, 1999).

golfer who is particularly adept at aiming his shots between trees, then we should say that X has cheated.

We can also consider a case in which E is playing golf with his boss. E believes that, if his boss wins, she will enjoy the game more and look more favorably on E when it is time to consider raises and promotions. E has an ulterior motive. So while his boss's back is turned, E moves her ball closer to the hole, thereby allowing her to win. Has E cheated? It is certainly true that E is seeking a competitive advantage. But note that the advantage sought is not vis-à-vis the party with whom E is playing golf (namely, his boss), but rather against fellow employees and others who might otherwise receive the raise or promotion that E covets. With respect to the larger game of 'organizational life' (as opposed to playing golf), however, it seems unlikely that E has broken any rules, since 'impressing the boss' is an important and widely practiced element of that game.[53] Thus, in the language of the criminal law, the two elements— rule-breaking and advantage-seeking—do not concur, and I would therefore conclude that E has not cheated.

Rule-Breaking Intended to Negate Unfair Advantage

Is it cheating to break a rule when 'everyone else is doing it too'? To put things more precisely, is it cheating to break a rule solely for the purpose of negating the advantage that a competitor or group of competitors have themselves gained through cheating? Imagine that X and Y are the only competitors in a boxing match and that X knows that Y is using steroids. Under these circumstances, would it be cheating for X to use steroids as well?

We can distinguish between two different scenarios. In the first, Y is cheating, but the referee is looking the other way. Here, we might say that X was not cheating, since cheating requires that the rules be fair and that they be administered in an even-handed manner. In the second case, Y is cheating but the rules are being administered in an even-handed manner. Here, the question is closer. A reasonable argument could be made, however, that, even here X is not cheating, since X has not sought an 'advantage'; rather, he has merely sought to negate the 'unfair disadvantage' that Y has caused him.[54]

---

[53] Cf Lynda Cardwell, 'Sure You Shot a 79, Mr. President. Of Course You Did,' *New York Times* (9 May 2003) (reviewing Don Van Natta, Jr., *First Off the Tee: Presidential Hackers, Duffers and Cheaters from Taft to Bush* (New York: Public Affairs, 2003)).

[54] In connection with the possibility of widespread violations of a given rule, it is worth considering Hume's distinction between natural and artificial virtues. See David Hume (L A Selby-Bigge, ed.), *A Treatise of Human Nature* (Oxford: OUP, 1978), bk. III, part III, section I. For Hume, virtues are the motives that lead to an agent's actions. Virtues such as compassion and friendship he refers to as 'natural' virtues because they arise naturally out of human nature. Other virtues, such as justice, promise-keeping, and allegiance, he says, are 'artificial,' because they arise out of social conventions as a means of ordering society. While it is not possible to consider Hume's distinction between the natural and artificial virtues here in any detail, it is nevertheless worth noting the possibility that, unlike natural virtues, presumably artificial virtues such as 'playing fair' and 'not cheating' might be regarded as having comparatively less force in a society in which such virtues were widely and regularly disregarded.

Changing the Rules in the Middle of the Game

During the Spring of 2005, Republican members of the US Senate sought to change the rules of the chamber, under which a minority of two-fifths plus one, or 41 of the current 100 senators, has traditionally been entitled to block the Senate's vote on almost any debatable proposition (such as a bill or nomination) through a process of extended debate known as a filibuster. The proposed rule change was popularly known as the 'nuclear option.' Although the filibuster had been used on many occasions, by both parties, since at least the 1850s, the Republicans argued that judicial nominees should be entitled to an 'up or down vote,' and they proposed doing away with the filibuster procedure by means of a simple majority vote. In response, the minority leader, Democratic Senator Harry Reid, and others contended that the Republicans were attempting to 'change the rules in the middle of the game,' and that doing so thereby constituted a kind of 'cheating.'[55]

For our purposes, the obvious question is: does 'changing the rules in the middle of the game' really constitute cheating? In this case, the Republicans clearly sought to obtain an advantage over a party with which they are in a cooperative, rule-bound relationship. So the second element of the paradigm was clearly satisfied. The more difficult question, though, is whether, by attempting to change the rule regarding filibusters, the Republicans were violating some *other* rule. The answer seems to be that they were: they were violating the rules regarding *changing* the rules. The Senate's rules provide that when any change to the Senate Rules (including the rules governing debate) is proposed, one-third of the members present and voting plus one (or 34 of the current 100) can prevent the Senate from resolving a filibuster and taking a vote.[56] By trying to force a vote on a procedural rule on the basis of a simple majority, without complying with the second-order rule regarding rule-changes, it appears that the majority was in fact attempting to cheat.[57]

4. Relationship Between Cheating and Other Forms of Moral Wrongfulness

Although there are cases in which the same act might constitute both cheating and one or more other form of moral wrongfulness, cheating is not reducible to any other form of moral wrongfulness, and reflects a distinctive moral

---

[55] 'House Ethics Battle Rages On,' National Public Radio, *Morning Edition* (13 April 2005) <http://www.npr.org/templates/story/story.php?storyId = 4598160>.

[56] Senate Rule XXII, Standing Rules of the Senate, S Doc No 106-15, 106th Cong, 2d Sess 15-17, available at <http://rules.senate.gov/senaterules/menu.htm>.

[57] As it turned out, the rule change never came to pass. A bipartisan group of senators ultimately reached a compromise under which the Democrats agreed to use the filibuster only in 'extraordinary' cases. Carl Hulse, 'Compromise in the Senate: Bipartisan Group in Senate Averts Judge Showdown,' *New York Times* (24 May 2005), at A1.

character. That is, to express the view that 'X cheated' is to express something quite different from the view that X 'lied' or 'broke a promise' or was 'disloyal.'

In some cases, the underlying rule that the cheater violates is a morally neutral rule, such as that a baseball batter gets three strikes. (For lack of a better term, we can call this type of cheating *malum prohibitum* cheating.[58]) In such cases, moral content derives solely from the fact of rule-breaking. Rule-breaking, in turn, is an important element not only in cheating but also in disobedience. But although they overlap, disobedience and cheating are morally and analytically distinct. Cheating—unlike disobedience—requires that the rule-breaker seek an unfair advantage. The wrong in such cases occurs horizontally: the party wronged is a second party, also bound by the rule, against whom an unfair advantage is sought. In the case of disobedience, by contrast, the wrong occurs vertically: the party wronged is the authority that has issued, or is charged with enforcing, the rule.

In other cases of cheating, the rule violated has independent moral content. For example, consider a case in which the rule against deceiving or promise-breaking is violated by the stereotypical dishonest realtor or used car sales-man. Assuming that such rules are violated with the intent to seek an unfair advantage, we could say that such acts constitute not only lying or promise-breaking but also cheating. (We can call this kind of cheating *malum in se* cheating.)

There are also plenty of cases of deceiving, promise-breaking, stealing, disloyalty, and exploitation that do not involve cheating. For example, if X lies about his age or the fact that he uses Botox, he may do so out of pure vanity, rather than with any intent to gain an unfair advantage. Similarly, if X promises to meet Y for lunch and then breaks that promise solely for her own convenience rather than out of any desire to gain an advantage over Y, it would be incorrect to say that X, selfish and inconsiderate though she may be, has cheated.

In some cases, the rule that the cheater breaks is so morally weighty that the fact of her cheating will seem trivial in comparison. To take a somewhat out-rageous example, imagine that two competing mobsters, in an effort to reduce police scrutiny of their activities, agree not to engage in any acts of murder during a given 6-month time period. If one of the mobsters reneges on the promise and commits a murder for the purpose of gaining a competitive advantage against her rival, then, technically, we could say that she had engaged in at least three distinct forms of moral wrongfulness: cheating, promise-breaking, and, of course, unjustified killing. In the real world of moral discourse, however, we would be likely to focus on that form of moral wrongfulness that is by far the most serious—namely, the killing—rather than the lesser wrongs of cheating and promise-breaking.[59]

---

[58] For a discussion of the concepts of *malum prohibitum* and *malum in se*, see below ch. 10.

[59] As Alan Wertheimer has suggested, 'when we offer a moral description of an act, we typically invoke the strongest applicable moral description' of that act. Alan Wertheimer, *Exploitation*

Even stealing—which generally does involve an intent to gain an unfair advantage—need not entail cheating. As we shall see in Chapter 6, the moral focus of stealing is quite different from the moral focus of cheating. Stealing involves the violation of Y's property rights. If X, out of spite, takes Y's property and immediately disposes of it, X has stolen from Y, but it is hard to see how X has necessarily gained any unfair advantage over Y, as cheating would require.

5. Non-criminalized Forms of Cheating

Cheating, like most of the other forms of moral wrongfulness being considered in this book, is a part of life. People cheat, break promises, deceive, disobey, exploit, and are disloyal all the time; yet we rarely think that their conduct should be subject to legal, let alone criminal, sanctions. Under the liberal tradition, as noted above, only those acts that are criminally harmful are eligible for criminalization. But how exactly are we to know which acts of cheating are sufficiently harmful to justify criminalization? To answer this question adequately would entail a vast undertaking: a catalogue of all of the various instances of cheating and the harms they cause. I shall not attempt such a project here. When we arrive at Part III, we shall consider several contexts in which cheating is criminalized. In this subsection, I want to consider several contexts in which it is not.

Sports and Games

It seems likely that we first learn about the concept of cheating as small children, while playing games. Starting at the age of four or five, children learn to play competitive games with other children, follow rules, and develop a concept of winning and losing.[60] Beginning at about age six, a child who fails to win a contest will accuse other children of cheating. Long before we develop an awareness of moral notions such as duties and rights, we begin refining our sense of fair play. As we develop and continue to play games and sports, we continue to be aware of cheating, as when Little League baseball teams use overage pitchers, bicycle racers use performance enhancing drugs, and college football teams use players who have failed to meet the required academic qualifications.

In all but the rarest of cases, cheating in games and sport is dealt with either informally through social stigma or more formally through sub-legal

(Princeton: Princeton University Press, 1996) 15. An analogous tendency occurs in the criminal law. Technically, a defendant who commits a murder has also committed an assault or a battery. But in charging the defendant, battery 'drops out' as a charge and we focus exclusively on the murder. *Ibid.*

[60] See generally Lawrence Kohlberg (Thomas Likona, ed.), *Moral Development and Behavior; Moral Stages and Moralization* (New York: Holt, Rinehart and Winston, 1976); Jean Piaget, *The Moral Judgment of the Child* (New York: Free Press, 1965).

procedures. A victory gained through cheating is viewed as illegitimate. Even one who loses (but plays by the rules) is viewed as more worthy of respect than one who wins through cheating. A player who has a reputation for cheating will be ostracized, passed over when invitations go out for the next tournament, or left without a partner.

Many games also have more formal sanctions for cheating. Frequently, the sanctions seek to equalize the potential advantage gained by the cheater by imposing some form of disability. Thus, when a pitcher in baseball violates the rule regarding spitballs, the opposing batter is given a kind of restitution—a ball.[61] Clipping in American football (blocking an opposing player from behind or below the waist) results in a 15-yard penalty. In more extreme cases, the cheater is disqualified, fined, or suspended; medals and titles are rescinded. Only in unusual cases, such as where money is at stake and cheating amounts to a kind of fraud, is it treated as a crime.

Schools and Academia

Like sports and games, schools and universities provide a fertile ground for cheating. Each involves highly rule-bound activities with many parties competing over limited resources, such as, in the case of schools, academic honors. Students cheat in an almost endless variety of ways: they hand in homework and project assignments copied from others, or written by their parents, or even purchased; they plagiarize from books and the Internet, copy from others in examinations, and try to discover advance information about examinations; they take more time than is permitted, use cheat sheets on exams, and confer with classmates when that is prohibited.[62]

Most educational institutions have an explicit list of rules by which students are bound,[63] but rules need not be explicit in order for there to be cheating. Cheating in the academic setting can be a serious offense, but one that is generally dealt with through internal disciplinary mechanisms. Punishment can consist of students receiving a failing grade, a suspension, or expulsion. Only in the rarest cases, such as when a student cheats in order to obtain scholarship funding, will cheating in school invite the possibility of more serious legal remedies.[64]

Love and Marriage

A married or ostensibly committed person who is sexually unfaithful to his or her regular partner is often said, particularly in American usage, to have

[61] See n 28 above.

[62] Donald McCabe, 'Cheating: Why Students Do It and How We Can Help Them Stop' (2001) *American Educator*, Winter, 38.

[63] For a useful database of university honor code provisions, see <http://academicintegrity.org> (website of Duke University's Center for Academic Integrity).

[64] See, eg *United States v Frost*, 125 F 3d 346 (6th Cir 1997), *cert. denied*, 525 US 810 (1998).

cheated. (What exactly it means to be sexually unfaithful—whether, for example, mere kissing or fondling would count—is, fortunately, an issue that need not be resolved here.) Although adultery was once a crime in many American jurisdictions, and remains on the books in some, it is almost never prosecuted as such today.[65] The question I want to ask is whether being unfaithful in love satisfies the paradigm described above.

Recall that cheating requires rule-breaking intended to obtain an advantage in a cooperative relationship. Being unfaithful in marriage clearly does involve both (1) a violation of the rule that one be faithful to one's spouse, and (2) a cooperative relationship. The harder question is whether it involves an intent to gain an unfair advantage over one's spouse. The cheating partner may be seeking sexual pleasure, emotional intimacy or gratification, or the excitement of engaging in a forbidden act.[66] The problem is that such benefits are not necessarily gained *at the expense of* the cheated-upon spouse. Accordingly, I would conclude that being unfaithful in marriage is not really cheating. Rather, a better way to characterize such behavior is as a breach of loyalty, or betrayal.

6. CHEATING AND CRIMINAL OFFENSES

At first glance, the idea of speaking of cheating in the context of crimes seems odd. We are accustomed to thinking about cheating in terms of everyday, non-legalized, morality, enforced through an informal system of norms or, perhaps, in more serious cases, by a baseball umpire or school principal. It is somewhat surprising, then, that the term 'cheating' and the criminal law bear a strong etymological connection. The word 'cheat' (or, more accurately, 'chete') first appeared in English in the 14th century as a shortened form of 'escheat,' a term that referred to real property that fell to a Lord or to the Crown by forfeiture, fine, or lapse, and which was often obtained by means of fraud or trick.[67] A century later, the word appears again, in the form of 'common law cheat,' a criminal offense consisting of a fraud perpetrated by means of a false token, such as false weights or measures.[68]

---

[65] Although it is almost unimaginable that adultery could be found to satisfy the requirements of the liberal harm principle, it remains on the books as a crime, amazingly, in some 28 US states. Naturally, prosecutions are extremely rare. See Richard A Posner and Katharine B Silbaugh, *A Guide to America's Sex Laws* (Chicago: University of Chicago Press 1996) 104–10 (listing state adultery laws). In some fundamentalist Islamic countries governed by *Shar'iah* law, adultery is still regarded as a capital crime. See Purva Desphande, 'The Role of Women in Two Islamic Fundamentalist Countries: Afghanistan and Saudi Arabia' (2001) 22 *Women's Rights Law Reporter* 193.

[66] See generally David M Buss, *The Evolution of Desire: Strategies of Human Mating* (New York: Basic Books, 1994); David P Barash and Judith Eve Lipton, *Myth of Monogamy: Fidelity and Infidelity in Animals and People* (New York: W. H. Freeman, 2001).

[67] *Oxford English Dictionary* (2nd edn., Oxford: OUP, 1989) (entry on *cheating*); see also Edward Coke, *The First Part of the Institutes of the Lawes of England, or, A Commentarie Upon Littleton* (1628, Garland Publ. Repr. 1979), at 140a.

[68] On the crime of common law cheat, see below ch. 13.

In modern usage, the term 'cheating' has become disassociated from the law. For example, the direct statutory descendant of common law cheat, Model Penal Code §224.71(1),[69] no longer makes any explicit reference to cheating. We now tend to think of cheating as a purely moral concept. Nevertheless, as we shall see in Part III, the concept of cheating continues— *sub silentio*—to play a significant role in a wide range of important white-collar crimes, including tax evasion, insider trading, certain forms of fraud, and various regulatory offenses. In some cases, the law criminalizes the breaking of a rule contained in the criminal law itself (eg the rule against committing theft). In other cases, the law criminalizes the breaking of a rule contained in a separate provision of civil law (eg the rule that a trader who possesses material non-public information about a given securities transaction must either 'disclose' such information or 'abstain' from trading). In yet other cases, the law criminalizes the breaking of a rule that is arguably independent of the law (eg the rule against using steroids in professional sports).

---

[69] Model Penal Code § 224.71(1) (making it a crime, in the course of business, to use or possess for use a 'false weight or measure, or any other device for falsely determining or recording any quality or quantity').

5
Deception

Unlike cheating, the concept of deception has been the subject of extensive scholarly attention. My interest here is primarily in describing the formal structure of deception, rather than in explaining why it is morally wrong.[1] In particular, I want to describe the difference between four analytically distinct kinds of deception which I shall refer to, respectively, as 'lying,' 'merely misleading,' 'falsely exculpating,' and 'falsely inculpating.'

1. The General Concept of Deception

As I shall use it here, the term deception refers to the communication of a message with which the communicator, in communicating, intends to mislead—that is, the communication of a message that is intended to cause a person to believe something that is untrue. A few points about this definition are worth making: The first is that there is no deception unless the communicator intends to deceive. Untrue statements made by mistake are not deceptive, although they might cause a listener to be misled. For example, if Bill mistakenly tells Hillary that he was at home in Chappaqua on the night of 3 February, when in fact he was in New York City, Bill might cause Hillary to be misled, but he has not deceived her. Secondly, there is no requirement that the message itself be untrue, since 'literally true' statements (a concept that is discussed below) can obviously be deceptive. For example, if Bill is asked where he was on the night of 3 February and says he was either in Chappaqua or in the City, while knowing for certain that he was in the City, he has deceived his questioner into believing that he is unsure about his whereabouts on that night, even though his statement is in fact true. Thirdly, deception requires some affirmative act or at least an omission to do an affirmative act that one has an obligation to perform. Thus, merely failing to correct a false belief held by another is not deception unless one is positively obligated to do so. Fourthly, deception can come in a variety of different forms. One can deceive by

---

[1] On why deception is morally wrong, see generally Sissela Bok, *Lying: Moral Choice in Public and Private Life* (New York: Vintage Books, 1979); Charles Fried, *Right and Wrong* (Cambridge, MA: Harvard University Press, 1978) 54–78; Joseph Kupfer, 'The Moral Presumption Against Lying' (1982) 36 *Review of Metaphysics* 103; Neil MacCormick, 'What is Wrong with Deceit?' (1982) *Sydney Law Review* 5.

making a statement, asking a question, issuing a command, stating an opinion, displaying a picture, making a facial expression or gesture, or engaging in various other forms of verbal and non-verbal behavior. Kant gives a famous example: *A* deceives *B* into believing that he is headed on a journey by conspicuously packing a suitcase, and hoping that *B* will draw the intended conclusion.[2]

2. LYING VS MERELY MISLEADING

In this subsection, I describe some distinctions, both formal and substantive, between lying and merely misleading.

Formal Distinctions

Lying constitutes a subset of deception, involving a much narrower range of behavior than deception generally. As generally used, the term *lying* refers to (intentional) deception that (1) comes in the form of a verifiable assertion, and (2) is literally false. By verifiable assertion, I refer to a statement that has a determinable truth value (ie is either true or false, although its truth value may not be known at the time the assertion is made).[3] Because they have no truth value, questions, commands, statements of opinion, greetings, apologies, christenings, and so forth are not capable of being lies, although they can certainly be misleading.[4] The same is true of deceptive nonverbal acts like Kant's bag packer packing his luggage.[5]

What does it mean for a statement to be 'literally false'? Assuming that a sentence is unambiguous, literal meaning is derived by determining the meaning of the individual words in a sentence and applying the grammatical rules of the language to those words.[6] The 'literal meaning' of the sentence is to be distinguished from what the speaker intends by the sentence when she utters it. A statement that is literally false is thus one that is false on its face, without reference to the speaker's meaning. For example, the statement, 'in the final days of his term, President Clinton pardoned convicted financier Michael Milken,' is a literally false statement, even if the speaker has confused

---

[2] Immanuel Kant, *Lectures on Ethics* (Louis Infield, trans.) (Indianapolis: Hackett, 1963) 226.

[3] This definition is adapted from Jill Humphries, 'The Logic of Assertion and Pragmatic Inconsistency' (1973) 3 *Canadian Journal of Philosophy* 177, 179.

[4] The classic analysis of the way in which such utterances function in our communication is JL Austin, *How to Do Things With Words* (2nd edn., Oxford: Clarendon Press, 1975) 5–6.

[5] On the other hand, it should be noted that a lie need not involve an utterance. One can lie, for example, by nodding or shaking one's head in response to a question, using sign language, sending smoke signals, or making other gestures. See Roderick M Chisolm and Thomas D Feehan, 'The Intent to Deceive' (1977) 74 *Journal of Philosophy* 143, 149. One can even lie by remaining silent in the face of certain kinds of questions.

[6] See Peter Meijes Tiersma, 'The Language of Perjury: "Literal Truth," Ambiguity, and the False Statement Requirement' (1990) 63 *California Law Review* 373, 379–80 & n 18.

Marc Rich (a man who *was* pardoned by Clinton) with Michael Milken (who was not) and has intended to refer to the former.

The difference between lying and non-lying verbal deception (which I shall henceforth refer to simply as 'misleading') is, therefore, essentially the difference between (1) asserting what one believes is literally false, and (2) leading the listener to believe something false by saying something that is either true or has no truth value.[7] For example, if Bill knows that he was in New York City on the night of February 3, but tells Hillary that he was 'either in the City or Chappaqua,' Bill has deceived Hillary by leading her to believe that he either doesn't know or is uncertain about where he was on that night. He has, in Evelin Sullivan's phrase, led Hillary 'down the garden path'[8]; he has been deceptive, but he has not lied, because his statement is literally true; he has 'asserted too much.'[9] Similarly, a person might deceive by 'asserting too little.' Imagine that Bill is asked by Hillary whether he was in New York City last week. If Bill was in fact in the City every day last week, but answers, 'well, I *was* in the City on Thursday of last week,' he has misled Hillary into believing that he was in the City only one day last week, but he has not lied, since he was, in fact, in the City on Thursday.

Caveat Auditor: the Moral Distinction Between Lying and Merely Misleading

Assuming a formal distinction between lying and merely misleading, we need next to ask whether there exists any *moral* difference between the two concepts. Imagine that Bill, who was in Chappaqua from 1–5 February, is asked about his whereabouts on 3 February. Is there really any moral difference between his responding, 'no, I was not in Chappaqua on February 3' (a lie), and the statement, 'well, I *was* in Chappaqua on 4 February' (a literally true statement that nevertheless creates the misleading impression that he was not in Chappaqua on 3 February)? The fact is, people sometimes go to great lengths to avoid not only telling the truth, but also to avoid lying. If lying and merely misleading were morally equivalent, such behavior would be irrational. How can it be explained?

My claim is that, other things being equal,[10] merely misleading is less wrongful than lying because what I call the principle of *caveat auditor*, or 'listener beware,' applies to cases of merely misleading but does not apply to lying. Like the principle of *caveat emptor*, which says that a buyer is responsible

---

[7] Cf Jonathan E Adler, 'Lying, Deceiving, or Falsely Implicating,' (1997) 94 *Journal of Philosophy* 435, 437.

[8] Evelin Sullivan, *The Concise Book of Lying* (New York: Farrar, Straus & Giroux, 2001) 81.

[9] See DS Mannison, 'Lying and Lies' (1969) 47 *Australasian Journal of Philosophy* 132.

[10] By restricting the claim in this manner, my intention is to anticipate the obvious objection that some lies, about relatively trivial subjects, are less morally wrongful than non-lying deception concerning more serious matters. In addition, I defer until later, see below nn 23–36 and accompanying text, discussion of cases in which deception might be justified or excused.

for assessing the quality of a purchase before buying,[11] the principle of *caveat auditor* says that, in certain circumstances, a listener is responsible, or partly responsible, for ascertaining that a statement is true before believing it.[12]

When *A* lies to *B*, *A* tells *B* that she herself believes what she is saying. As a result, *B* is justified in putting her faith in *A*; *B* need not be on her guard or question *A*'s veracity. If *A* is mistaken about her assertion, then she is wholly responsible for *B*'s false belief. And if *A*'s untrue statement has been intentional, it is *A* who is wholly to blame.

Merely misleading involves a very different dynamic. When *A* misleads *B* without making an assertion, she has not told *B* that she believes what she is saying is true (since what she is saying is neither true nor false). There is thus no warranty of truth that *B* could rely on.[13] Again, Kant's bag packer provides a good example. If the bag packer lies and asserts that he is going on vacation, then he will be wholly responsible for the spectator's false belief. But if the bag packer merely acts *as if* he is going on vacation, and his spectator draws the wrong conclusion from those actions, then the spectator will be partly responsible for his mistaken belief. The underlying idea, as explained by Jonathan Adler, is 'that each individual is a rational, autonomous being and so fully responsible for the inferences he draws, just as he is for his acts. It is deception, but not lies, that requires mistaken inferences and so the hearer's responsibility.'[14]

---

[11] The doctrine of *caveat emptor* is discussed in ch. 13 below, in connection with the development of English theft law.

[12] The principle of *caveat auditor* also bears analogy to the tort law doctrine of comparative negligence, under which damages are apportioned between injurer and victim according to the parties' relative fault in bringing about harm. See, eg Fleming James, Jr, Foreword: 'Comparative Negligence at Last—By Judicial Fiat' (1976) 64 *California Law Review* 239; William L Prosser, 'Comparative Negligence' (1953) 51 *Michigan Law Review* 465; Gary T Schwartz, 'Contributory and Comparative Negligence: A Reappraisal' (1978) 86 *Yale Law Journal* 697.

[13] Several philosophers have attempted to explain the moral difference between lying and non-lying deception in terms of rights and duties. Although I would prefer to avoid talk of rights and duties in this context, such talk may ultimately be unavoidable in attempting to construct a full analytical account. See Alasdair MacIntyre, 'Truthfulness, Lies, and Moral Philosophers: What We Can Learn from Mill and Kant?', in GB Petersen (ed.) *The Tanner Lectures* (Salt Lake City, UT: University of Utah Press, 1995) vol 16, at 309, 337 ('my duty is to assert only what is true and the mistaken inferences which others draw from what I say or what I do are, in some cases at least, not my responsibility, but theirs'); Chisolm and Feehan, (n 5 above, at 153) (in telling a lie, 'the liar "gives an indication that he is expressing his own opinion." And he does this in a special way—by getting his victim to place his faith in him'; '[I]f a person L *asserts* a proposition *p* to another person *D*, then *D* has the *right to expect* that L himself believes *p*. And it is assumed that L knows, or at least that he ought to know, that, if he asserts *p* to *D*, while believing himself that *p* is not true, then he violates this right of *D*'s. But analogous assumptions are not made with respect to all other types of intended deception.').

[14] Adler (n 7 above, at 444). Traditional Jewish and Christian ethics both seem to recognize the moral distinction between lying and merely misleading. On the former, see Nachum Amsel, 'Truth and Lying,' in *The Jewish Encyclopedia of Moral and Ethical Issues* (Northvale, NJ: Jason Aronson, Inc., 1994) 295 (in certain situations, ambiguous statements that can be construed as partial truths are permitted). See also Joseph Telushkin, *Jewish Wisdom: Ethical, Spiritual, and Historical Lessons from the Great Works and Thinkers* (New York: William Morrow & Co., 1994) 58–64 (surveying Jewish approach to question of justified lying and deception). The Jesuits, moreover, seem to have espoused an even more aggressive doctrine of permissible non-lying

Lying and merely misleading can also be distinguished on the grounds that each tends to elicit a different set of 'reactive emotions,' and cause a different set of harms, in its victims.[15] A victim who is deceived by a non-lie feels foolish and embarrassed, presumably because he believes he has contributed to his own harm by drawing unwarranted inferences from misleading premises. By contrast, a victim of lies is much more likely to feel 'brutalized' (in Adler's word) by some external force.[16] Even Bernard Williams, who in his study of truth and truthfulness is generally dismissive of the moral distinction between lying and non-lying deception, at least concedes that 'in some circumstances, and among people who in general have reason to trust one another, there is something particularly odious or insulting about the "lie direct," that it is a special kind of affront.'[17]

Lying and merely misleading not only feel different to the victim, they also evoke different reactions in the perpetrator. One who lies is likely to feel a different degree, or at least different kind, of guilt than one who merely misleads. The non-lying deceiver will be much more able to rationalize his conduct than the liar—a fact that may explain why people go to such considerable lengths to avoid actually lying. Finally, there may be a kind of consequentialist rationale for distinguishing between lies and non-lying deception. As Larry Alexander and Emily Sherwin have put it:

> If we cannot eliminate all deceptions from human interaction, we should at least try to preserve core conventions of dialogue. One such convention is that positive assertions of fact are true in the ordinary sense of the words used. If this convention is generally respected, speakers can signal their seriousness by choosing to make assertions, and listeners will have a safe haven of confidence.[18]

deception, or equivocation. See Leo Katz, *Ill-Gotten Gains: Evasion, Blackmail, Fraud, and Kindred Puzzles of the Law* (Chicago: University of Chicago Press, 1996) 29 (quoting Blaise Pascal, *The Provincial Letters* (A.J. Krailsheimer, trans.) (Baltimore: Penguin Books, 1967) ('One of the most embarrassing problems is how to avoid lying, especially when one would like people to believe something untrue. This is where our doctrine of equivocation is marvelously helpful, for it allows one to use ambiguous terms, conveying a different meaning to the hearer from that in which one understands them himself.'). For a contrary view—ie that the form of deception is irrelevant to its moral content, see TM Scanlon, *What We Owe Each Other* (Cambridge, Mass.: Harvard University Press, 1998) 317–22. See also sources cited in nn 17 and 18 below.

It should be emphasized that simply because a distinction between lying and non-lying deception can be found in Jewish and Catholic sources does not mean that the distinction is universally recognized or that non-lying deception is generally condoned. Indeed, the traditional Yiddish proverb that a 'half truth is a full lie' would seem to indicate a rejection of precisely the distinction that I have been seeking to draw. More importantly, it should be stressed that both Jewish and Catholic authorities place a very high value on truth-telling, and that they would permit deception only in the narrowest of circumstances. On the Jewish approach to deception more generally, see Amsel (above, at 291–96). On the Catholic approach, see Sullivan, (n 8 above, at 77–80) (Jesuit doctrine of equivocation applies only when such deception is otherwise justified—for example, in order to avoid religious persecution). See also n 30.

[15] The concept of reactive emotions is discussed in ch. 10 below.

[16] Adler (n 7 above, at 432).

[17] Bernard Williams, *Truth and Truthfulness* (Princeton: Princeton University Press, 2002) 108–09.

[18] Larry Alexander and Emily Sherwin, 'Deception in Morality and Law' (2003) 22 *Law and Philosophy* 393, 403–04. It should be noted, however, that Alexander and Sherwin ultimately

In arguing that lying is distinguishable from other forms of deception, I do not of course mean to suggest that lying is always wrong or that it is always worse than other forms of deception. A lie told to avoid some greater harm is not likely to be viewed as wrongful. And non-lying deception about a matter of real importance will be viewed as more wrongful than an outright lie about some trivial concern. Moreover, in some unusual cases, a 'bald-faced' lie may actually seem less objectionable than other forms of deception—with all of their subterfuges, dissembling, and pretense. At this point, my claim is simply that there are real and articulable differences in moral content between lying and other forms of deception, and that, *ceteris paribus*, lying tends to be more wrongful than merely misleading.

3. False Exculpation and False Inculpation

Having distinguished in the foregoing subsection between lies and non-lying deception, I now want to introduce two additional moral categories, which I shall refer to as 'false exculpation' and 'false inculpation.' These categories cut across those discussed above: that is, false exculpation and inculpation can occur by means of both lies and merely misleading. My contention is that we accord: (1) a distinct moral status to lies and other forms of deception that occur when a person falsely *denies* an accusation of wrongdoing (whether by himself or others); and (2) yet another moral status to deception that occurs when a person falsely *accuses* another (or, more unusually, himself) of wrongdoing.

False Exculpation

The pattern of false exculpation occurs when a person who is suspected of having engaged in, or having information about another's involvement in, some alleged course of wrongful conduct, falsely denies such involvement (eg by falsely denying guilt during a criminal investigation or on the witness stand) or makes it harder for another to obtain truthful information about such information (eg by intimidating a witness or destroying incriminating evidence). The distinctive moral character of false exculpation reflects two conflicting norms: the norm that says that one should accept responsibility for one's wrongdoing, and the norm that says that one should be able to 'preserve' oneself from harm that others might try to inflict against one.

Most people would agree that it is a virtue to accept responsibility for one's wrongdoing. We teach our children that it is better to admit to a wrongful act than to cover it up by lying; indeed, one of the great American national myths is that of George Washington and the cherry tree (according to an apocryphal

reject the moral distinction between lies and non-lying deception, because, they say, it results in a prohibition that is too easy to evade and relies on a distinction between direct and indirect assertion that is too difficult to maintain.

story first recorded by Mason Weems, the young Washington tried out a new axe by chopping down his father's cherry tree. When questioned by his father he responded famously, 'I cannot tell a lie. It was I who chopped down the cherry tree.')[19] Most religious thought, as well, regards repentance as a centrally important concept.[20] Even in our criminal justice system, we put considerable value on the role of contrition and remorse, recognizing that they serve important moral, social, and psychological ends.[21] Covering up one's own wrongdoing thus cuts directly against such positive norms.

On the other hand, we recognize that there is something potentially unfair about enforcing the norm against deception in such contexts. That is, we are more forgiving of someone who lies in order to protect himself because, other things being equal, we regard such deception as less wrongful than other kinds of deception.

In order to understand the special moral status of false exculpations of self, we need to consider the familiar distinction between justification and excuse. Conduct that is justified is conduct that is right and good, or at least not wrong. Conduct that is excused, though itself morally wrong, is conduct for which the perpetrator should not be punished or blamed.[22] Thus, to say that a lie or other act of deception is justified is to say that it was the right thing to do in a given instance. To say that an act of deception is excused is to say that, though the act was bad, the deceiver should not be blamed for it.

Under what circumstances might a lie or other deception be justified? Much of the literature on lying and deception deals with just this issue.[23] While almost everyone (save a Kantian[24] would agree that it is permissible to

---

[19] Mason L Weems, *The Life of Washington* (Cambridge, MA: Harvard University Press, 1962) (orig. publ. 1800) 11–12. See also Henry J Friendly, 'The Fifth Amendment Tomorrow: The Case for Constitutional Change' (1968) 37 *University of Cincinnati Law Review* 671, 687. ('No parent would teach [a doctrine of self-incrimination] to his children; the lesson parents teach is that while a misdeed ... will generally be forgiven, a failure to make a clean breast of it will not be.').

[20] Of course, different religions understand the role of repentance in different ways. Cf *Luke* 15 (Christian parable of Prodigal Son) with Abraham Isaac Kook, *Philosophy of Repentance* (New York: Yeshiva University Press, 1968, Alter B Metzger, trans.) (expounding a Jewish philosophy of *t'shuvah*).

[21] See, eg Stephanos Bibas and Richard A Bierschbach, 'Integrating Remorse and Apology into Criminal Procedure' (2004) 114 *Yale Law Journal* 85, 104; Stephen P Garvey, 'Symposium: Punishment as Atonement' 46 *UCLA Law Review* 1801 (1999); Michael M O'Hear, 'Remorse, Cooperation, and "Acceptance of Responsibility": The Structure, Implementation, and Reform of Section 3E1.1. of the Federal Sentencing Guidelines' (1997) 91 *Northwestern University Law Review* 1507.

[22] The classic discussion of excuse is JL Austin, 'A Plea for Excuses' in JO Urmson and GJ Warnock (eds.) *Philosophical Papers* (Oxford: OUP, 1961) 123.

[23] Bok (n 1 above); Robert N Van Wyk, 'When is Lying Morally Permissible? Casuistical Reflections on the Game Analogy, Self-Defense, Social Contract Ethics, and Ideals' (1990) 24 *Journal of Value Inquiry* 155.

[24] Kant took the famously categorical view that lying is never justified, even to save an innocent life. Immanuel Kant, 'On the Supposed Right to Lie from Altruistic Motives,' in Peter Singer (ed.), *Ethics* (New York: OUP, 1994) 280. Perhaps Kant's unusually hard line on lying may help explain his desire to distinguish lies from merely misleading. For more on

lie to protect an innocent human life, there is a wide range of opinion on questions such as whether and when it is justifiable for doctors to lie to their patients, political leaders to lie to their constituents, and parents to lie to their children.[25] Among legal scholars, there has been particular concern with the circumstances, if any, under which it is permissible for lawyers and police officers to lie in the exercise of their duties.[26] In addition, many people would agree that it is permissible to engage in certain kinds of trivial or white lies when such deception will serve, say, to avoid giving offense to others or to maintain good social relations.[27]

The generally accepted consequentialist principle seems to be that it is permissible to lie or deceive in order to prevent some greater harm from occurring. At the same time, however, we recognize the strong deontological pull of the rule against lying. The problem of justified lies stems from the clash between these two inconsistent modes of moral thinking. In any event, the claim in these cases is typically that the person who lies or deceives has done the right thing—ie that he is justified in his action. Many writers have argued that, despite the prima facie rule against it, an individual is morally permitted—even required—to use deception when doing so could prevent some greater harm.[28]

The contention that a lie is *excused* (rather than justified) takes a quite different form. Imagine that *A*, while having a gun held to his head by *B*, is forced to lie to *C*, who is on the other end of the telephone. *A* has done something wrongful; he has misled *C*, and he has done so intentionally; he has acted unjustifiably. But *A* has acted under duress. Although *A*'s act itself was

Kant's theory of lying, see Christine M Korsgaard, 'The Right to Lie: Kant on Dealing with Evil' (1986) 15 *Philosophy & Public Affairs* 325; Fried (n 2 above, at 69–78).

[25] Bok (n 1 above); MacIntyre (n 13 above, at 318–23) (discussing the wide range of commonly held attitudes about when lying is permissible).

[26] On lying by lawyers, see, eg David Luban, *Lawyers and Justice: An Ethical Study* (Princeton: Princeton University Press, 1988); Geoffrey M Peters, 'The Use of Lies in Negotiation' (1987) 48 *Ohio State Law Journal*; William H Simon, 'Virtuous Lying: A Critique of Quasi-Categorical Moralism' (1999) 12 *Georgetown Journal of Legal Ethics* 433; Alan Strudler, 'Incommenurable Goods, Rightful Lies, and the Wrongness of Fraud' (1998) 146 *University of Pennsylvania Law Review* 1529, 1537–42; Gerald B Wetlaufer, 'The Ethics of Lying in Negotiations' (1990) 76 *Iowa Law Review* 1219, 1223; James J White, 'Machiavelli and the Bar: Ethical Limitations on Lying in Negotiation,' (1980) *American Bar Foundation Research Journal* 926. On lying by the police, see, eg Christopher Slobogin, 'Deceit, Pretext, and Trickery: Investigative Lies by the Police' (1997) 76 *Oregon Law Review* 775.

[27] Your son wants to know what you thought of his violin solo, your mother-in-law asks your opinion of her new meatloaf recipe, your spouse asks what you think of his or her new outfit. Sometimes, in situations like these, the right thing to do is to lie. Such lies can serve as an element of tact or politeness that helps people to maintain good social relations with family, friends, and colleagues. For the Talmudic view of white lies, see *Babylonian Talmud* 'Ketuvot' 16b (Brooklyn, NY: Soncino Press, 1989). Bok, however, is quite critical of society's tolerance for white lies. See n 1 above, at 60–76.

[28] See sources cited in notes 23–26 above. On the distinction between prima facie duties and absolute duties, which cannot be overcome by competing moral obligations, see WD Ross, *The Right and the Good* (Oxford: OUP, 1930) 18–36.

wrongful, most of us would agree that he should not be blamed for it—that *A*'s conduct, in other words, should be excused.[29]

So what does all this have to do with the morality of false exculpation? The fact is that people often fail to accept responsibility for their wrongful acts. Sometimes they do so by remaining silent. Other times they do so by falsely denying the accusations that are made against them or by engaging in acts of deception to avoid detection. Imagine that *B* asks *A* about some wrongdoing in which *A* has engaged, and *A* responds with a false denial. How should we judge *A*'s conduct? The answer is not likely to be simple: it will depend on a wide range of complex factors, including the circumstances of *A*'s wrong-doing, the nature of the relationship between *A* and *B*, the form of *A*'s denial, the consequences of his denial, and, perhaps, the basis for *B*'s suspicion.[30]

We can envision a small number of cases in which *A*'s false denial might actually be justified.[31] More often, though, *A*'s denial is likely to be unjustified, particularly if: (1) *A*'s prior wrongdoing was harmful, (2) *B* has a relationship of trust with *A*, (3) *A* could easily and without adverse consequences remain silent, or (4) exposure of *A*'s wrongful conduct might help alleviate some additional harm to a victim or facilitate some good, such as restitution.

Nevertheless, the fact that *A*'s conduct is unjustified does not necessarily mean that it should not be excused. Although we admire people who take responsibility for their wrongful acts, we are nevertheless sympathetic to those who not only fail to do the virtuous thing but actually compound their wrongdoing by attempting to conceal it. The basis for this moral sentiment, I believe, is an implicit recognition of the right to self-preservation—a right

[29] As a matter of substantive criminal law, duress can serve as a defense only if the defendant reasonably feared *immediate* death or serious bodily injury which could be avoided only by committing the criminal act charged. In perjury cases, where the crime is generally committed in the relative safety of a courtroom, it is difficult to satisfy the requirement that the danger to the defendant be present, imminent, impending, or unavoidable. As a result, the defense of duress or coercion is usually ineffective in cases of perjury. See, eg *Hall v State*, 187 So 392, 407 (Fla 1939) (jury charge requiring that, for coercion, danger must be real, present, imminent, and unavoidable); *Bain v State*, 70 So 408 (Miss 1890); *Hardin v State*, 211 SW 233, 237 (Tex Ct Crim App 1919); *People v Ricker*, 262 NE 2d 456, 460 (Ill 1970) (threat to perjurer was not sufficiently imminent); *United States v Nickels*, 502 F 2d 1173 (7th Cir 1974); *Edwards v State*, 577 P 2d 1380, 1283 (Wyo 1978). But see *People v Richter*, 221 NW 2d 429 (Ct App Mich 1974) (allowing duress defense); *State v Rosillo*, 282 NW 2d 872, 874 (Minn 1979) (defendant could establish coercion defense to charges of perjury where he 'fear[ed] a shot through a courthouse window').

[30] There is support for such an ad hoc approach, interestingly, in the Roman Catholic Catechism. See *Catechism of the Catholic Church* (Libreria Editrice Vatican trans.) (San Francisco, CA: Ignatius Press, 1995) 596 (catechism on commandment not to bear false witness against one's neighbor: 'The good and safety of others, respect for privacy, and the common good are sufficient reasons for being silent about what ought not to be known *or for making use of a discreet language*.') (emphasis modified).

[31] For example, imagine that: (1) *A* has engaged in some form of harmless or minor wrongdoing, (2) *A* is asked about his conduct by *B*, a busybody neighbor with whom *A* has only a fleeting acquaintance, (3) if *A* were to respond to *B*'s questions about his conduct by refusing to answer or by telling *B* that it is none of his business, *A*'s response would be construed as an admission of guilt and would be broadcast in *A*'s community, and (4) exposure of *A*'s wrongful conduct would cause harm to *A* or to *A*'s family or community.

not to cooperate with those who would seek to bring adverse consequences against oneself. Kent Greenawalt has referred to it as 'a right to avoid destructive consequences to [oneself] even if submission would serve the welfare of others.'[32] Although often associated with a narrow constitutional right 'of silence,' the right of self-preservation is better understood as linked to a broader right against self-incrimination.[33] That the right to self-preservation might include a right to falsely deny seems particularly plausible in cases in which remaining silent in the face of accusatory questioning would be tantamount to admitting guilt.[34] Indeed, to limit the right against self-incrimination to the right to remain silent *simpliciter* would be akin to saying that the right to life is a wholly passive right and does not entail the right to use force, actively, in its defense.[35] Thus, in Continental criminal practice, parties to a lawsuit were exempt from prosecution for perjury on precisely these grounds.[36]

Lest I be misunderstood, however, let me reiterate that I am not contending that it is good that people fail to accept responsibility for their wrongdoing, or that contrition and remorse do not serve important ends. I would regard either contention as perverse. Nor, of course, am I suggesting that the self-incrimination clause of the Fifth Amendment gives one the legal right to lie in one's defense. My purpose has been merely to suggest that we tend to view the false denial of accusations against self as morally distinct from other kinds of unjustified deception, and to offer an account of why that might be.

False Exculpation of Others

We also tend to be more forgiving in our attitude toward deception used to exculpate others. Not only do people have a right not to inform against

[32] Kent Greenawalt, 'Silence as Moral and Constitutional Right' (1981) 23 *William and Mary Law Review* 15, 29. The *locus classicus* concerning the right of self-preservation is Thomas Hobbes, *Leviathan*, (New York: Collier, 1955) ch 14 (Michael Oakeshott, ed.).

[33] On the moral right to self-preservation as it relates to the constitutional right against self-incrimination, see David Dolinko, 'Is There a Rationale for the Privilege Against Self-Incrimination?' (1986) 33 *UCLA Law Review* 1063; Michael S Green, 'The Privilege's Last Stand: The Privilege Against Self-Incrimination and the Right to Rebel Against the State' (1999) 65 *Brooklyn Law Review* 627; Irene Merker Rosenberg & Yale L Rosenberg,' In the Beginning: The Talmudic Rule Against Self-Incrimination' (1988) 63 *New York University Law Review* 955; William J Stuntz, 'Self-Incrimination and Excuse' (1988) 88 *Columbia Law Review* 1227, 1254.

[34] Although in the formal context of court proceedings jurors are instructed not to make adverse inferences from a defendant's exercise of the right to remain silent, see *James v Kentucky*, 466 US 341 (1984), the fact is that, in our normal social dealings, one who remains silent in the face of an accusation often *is* presumed to be guilty.

[35] I have previously dealt with the moral basis for the right of self-defense in Stuart P Green, 'Castles and Carjackers: Proportionality and the Use of Deadly Force in Defense of Dwellings and Vehicles' (1999) 1999 *University of Illinois Law Review* 1, 18–24.

[36] See Mirjan R Damaška, *The Faces of Justice and State Authority: A Comparative Approach to the Legal Process* (New Haven: Yale University Press, 1986) 130 (noting that 'civil parties were actually exempt from liability for perjury in a great number of European jurisdictions. To impose on them the duty to tell the truth and thereby to harm their own interests was proclaimed to be inhumane, akin to a form of a moral torture, even though civil parties had also acquired the right to refuse to testify.') (footnote omitted).

themselves, they may also have a duty not to reveal secrets about others, at least where there exists a relationship of trust between them.[37] In Part III, I describe the antipathy we feel towards the act of taking bribes as being informed by the aversion we feel towards the act of disloyalty that such bribe-taking frequently entails.[38] Here, my suggestion is that the antipathy we feel towards people who take steps to avoid inculpating others is *mitigated* by our sense that such avoidance is, at least in some cases, based on a legitimate sense of loyalty.[39] More generally, a society in which neighbors rat on neighbors, colleagues on colleagues, and family members on other family members is not the sort of society in which most people would want to live.[40]

False Inculpation

The final pattern of deception, false inculpation, occurs less frequently, or at least is less commonly subject to criminal prosecution, than false exculpation. Here, a person who purports to have information about another's conduct either makes a false accusation against another or prevents another from obtaining true information about a third party's wrongdoing. (Of course, a person who makes a false accusation against another so as to throw some third party off the trail of the true suspect would have satisfied both patterns.)

A good example of alleged wrongful inculpation is provided by the 1987 case of Tawana Brawley. The case involved a 15-year-old girl who went missing and was found four days later covered in dog feces and with racial slurs written on her body.[41] With her advisor, the Reverend, and, later, presidential candidate, Al Sharpton, by her side, Brawley claimed that she had been 'kidnapped, abused and raped' by an upstate New York prosecutor named Steven Pagones.[42] A grand jury investigation concluded in late 1988 that Brawley 'was not the victim of forcible sexual assault' and that the whole thing was a hoax.[43]

[37] For a discussion, see generally Sissela Bok, *Secrets: On the Ethics of Concealment and Revelation* (New York: Random House, 1989) 210–29; see also Michael A Simons, 'Retribution for Rats: Cooperation, Punishment, and Atonement' (2003) 56 *Vanderbilt Law Review* 1 (2003); George C Harris, 'Testimony for Sale: The Law and Ethics of Snitches and Experts' (2001) 28 *Pepperdine Law Review* 1.   [38] See ch. 16 below.

[39] For a discussion of the conflict between interpersonal loyalties and duties to society at large as it exists in the context of lawyer informants, see Gerard E Lynch, 'The Lawyer as Informer' (1986) *Duke Law Journal* 491, 527–32.

[40] For a vivid account of life under the eyes of the East German Secret Police, see Timothy Garton Ash, *The File: A Personal History* (New York: Vintage, 1998). See also Alexandra Natapoff, 'Snitching: The Institutional and Communal Consequences' (2004) 73 *University of Cincinnati Law Review* 645.

[41] See William Saletan, et al., 'The Worst of Al Sharpton: A Troubling Tale From His Past. Is it True?,' in *Slate* (8 Sept. 2003), <http://slate.msn.com/id/2087557/>; see also 'Report of the Grand Jury Concerning the Tawana Brawley Investigation,' in court TV.com <www.courttv.com/legaldocs/newsmakers/tawana/part1.html> accessed 22 August 2005; Robert D McFadden, *Outrage: The Story Behind the Tawana Brawley Hoax* (New York: Bantam Books, 1990).

[42] Saletan (n 41 above).

[43] *Ibid*. The grand jury's report specifically exonerated Pagones, and in 1998 Pagones won a defamation lawsuit against Sharpton, Brawley, and Brawley's lawyers. Because Brawley had

It is the wrongfulness of false inculpation that seems be to the primary focus of the biblical commandment that one shall not bear false witness against one's neighbor. This provision is often interpreted as a general prohibition on lying, or more specifically as a prohibition on lying under oath.[44] But a narrower understanding would focus specifically on what it means to bear false witness 'against' another.[45] To the extent that our system of justice views wrongful conviction as worse than wrongful acquittal (at least ten times so, by some accounts[46]), it seems to follow that, *ceteris paribus*, wrongful inculpation should be viewed as morally even worse than wrongful exculpation.

4. DECEPTION AND WHITE-COLLAR CRIME

As we shall see in Part III, the concept of deception plays a central role in defining such key white-collar crimes as perjury, fraud, false statements, and obstruction of justice. Perhaps more surprising is that quite fine-grained moral distinctions, of the sort discussed in this section—between lying and merely misleading, and wrongful exculpation and wrongful inculpation—are directly reflected in legal doctrine. Thus, perjury, like lying, requires a literal falsehood; fraud is satisfied by merely misleading; obstruction of justice frequently involves a form of false exculpation or inculpation; and the offense of false statements involves a complex hybrid of all four concepts. Indeed, as we shall see below, such fine-grained distinctions in the law are so significant that they may well have the effect of reinforcing such distinctions in the moral sphere.

---

never told her story under oath before a grand jury, she was not prosecuted for perjury. Nor, despite their allegedly having given false evidence to the police, were Brawley or any of her advisors ever prosecuted for making false statements.

[44] See, eg Nachum Amsel, 'Truth and Lying' in *The Jewish Encyclopedia of Moral and Ethical Issues* (Northvale, NJ: Aronson, 1994); Catholic *Catechism* (n 30 above).

[45] In fact, the Bible does distinguish between false exculpation and false inculpation. A witness who falsely inculpates is to receive the same punishment as that which would have been given to the falsely accused. *Deuteronomy* 19:18–9. The punishment for false exculpation, on the other hand, does not appear to be stated.

[46] See Alexander Volokh, ''n Guilty Men' (1997) 146 *University of Pennsylvania Law Review* 173.

6

Stealing

At first glance, it might seem as if stealing is less a concept of morality than law. Notwithstanding its inclusion in the Decalogue, we so closely associate the norm against stealing with its legal prohibition and penal consequences that we tend to treat it and the legal concept of theft as if they were one. We may even teach our children that it is wrong to steal because they might 'go to jail.' And, indeed, the concept of stealing is bound up with the law in a way that few other moral norms are. Nevertheless, as I shall argue in this section, the norm against stealing does have an independent moral significance, which is neither wholly derivative of law nor wholly reducible to other moral norms.

1. The Independent Moral Significance of Stealing

In order to determine if stealing constitutes an independent moral norm, we need to ask if it is reducible to some other moral norm. Let us first consider cheating, which was defined earlier as the breaking of a rule with an intent to gain an unfair advantage over another with whom one is in a cooperative, rule-bound relationship. Is it possible to recharacterize the concept of stealing so that it will always fit within this definition? The answer, I think, is no. While it is true that stealing always involves the breaking of some rule, it need not involve either a cooperative, rule-bound relationship or an intent to gain an unfair advantage. Imagine a case in which X takes a worthless piece of personal property from Y without his permission. Suppose that Y never knew that he owned such property (it was contained in an old trunk in the attic of a house that Y inherited) and that, upon taking the property, X immediately destroys it. Let us further assume that X took the property for his own perverse pleasure rather than to gain any advantage over Y. Such a taking would certainly constitute stealing, but it does not appear that it would constitute cheating; thus, stealing is not invariably reducible to cheating.

   Another possibility worth considering is that stealing is reducible to disobedience to the law. In his book, *Morality*, Bernard Gert examines a collection of what he purports to be irreducibly basic moral norms, including 'don't deceive,' 'keep promises,' and 'obey the law.'[1] Among the norms he considers adding to the list, but which he ultimately excludes, is that against stealing. According to Gert:

The point of including a rule in the list of basic moral rules is that it prohibits some action impartial rational persons want prohibited but is not already prohibited by some other rule. To show that an independent rule against stealing is needed, one must show that it prohibits some actions not prohibited by any of the other rules....

Stealing involves taking that which is owned by another; the concept of ownership depends upon the concept of law. Whether you own something, and under what conditions, is determined by the law. Stealing is not merely taking that which is owned by another, it is taking it unlawfully. Thus every case of stealing will be a case of breaking the law. Including as a basic moral rule the rule "Obey the law" guarantees that stealing is immoral, without having an independent rule against it.'[2]

Unfortunately, Gert's approach, at least for our purposes, turns out to be inadequate. Thinking of stealing as lawbreaking may well 'guarantee' that stealing is immoral, but only in the most trivial sense. There are many, many forms of lawbreaking that do not entail stealing. To view stealing as nothing more than lawbreaking is to lose the essence of stealing, to miss what it is that makes it morally distinctive.

So what is it that makes stealing distinctively wrong? Perhaps we should say that stealing is reducible to disobedience not just to any law, but to some particular set of laws—namely, those concerning property. But such an approach would also be flawed. It would seem to imply that stealing is wrong solely because it is prohibited—ie that stealing is a kind of *malum prohibitum*.[3] But this can't be right either: stealing offenses such as theft are paradigmatically *mala in se*; we would surely view stealing as wrong even if it were not unlawful.

A better formulation is as follows: to steal something is to violate, in some fundamental way, another's rights of ownership. Note that this is different from saying that stealing is merely a violation of some particular set of laws concerning property. To be sure, in modern, liberal societies, we tend to think of rights of ownership in legalistic terms, and the law of property certainly plays a significant role in shaping and informing our understanding of what it means to own things, and to have them stolen. But the concept of stealing itself seems to be in some fundamental way pre-legal. Small children and primitive man both have a sense of what it means to own things.[4] And they

---

[1] Bernard Gert, *Morality: A New Justification of the Moral Rules* (New York: OUP, 1988).
[2] *Ibid* at 135–6.
[3] See ch. 10 for a discussion of the concept of *malum prohibitum*.
[4] See, respectively, Estelle Peisach and Mildred Hardeman, 'Moral Reasoning in Early Childhood: Lying and Stealing' (1983) 142 *Journal of Genetic Psychology* 107; and Bruce L Benson, 'Enforcement of Private Property Rights in Primitive Societies: Law Without Government' (1989) 9 *Journal of Libertarian Studies* 1.

undoubtedly have a sense that having such things involuntarily taken from them in some way constitutes a 'wrong.'

This, I believe, is a useful way to begin thinking about the concept of stealing, but it hardly tells the whole story. There remain a number of important issues that need to be attended to. First, it should be clear that stealing, like cheating and deceiving, always entails intent. Taking another's property without intending to do so—eg, if I walk away with your umbrella believing incorrectly that it is mine—is not stealing, although if my belief is unreasonable, I may still have done a morally wrongful, and perhaps even criminally liable, act. Moreover, I need to intend to deprive you of your property permanently, not merely to borrow it.

Secondly, it is necessary to determine what is meant by saying that X violates another's rights of ownership in some 'fundamental' way. It is a commonplace that property rights are really bundles of rights, organized around the idea of securing, for the right of the holder, exclusive use of or access to, a thing.[5] Tony Honoré divides what he calls the liberal concept of full ownership into a list of components: rights to possess, use, and manage a thing; the right to the income from its use by others; the right to sell, give away, consume, modify, or destroy; the power to transmit it to the beneficiaries of one's will; and the right to security from expropriation.[6] But even if it is possible to say which rights constitute 'ownership,' it is difficult to say exactly which incidents of ownership must be violated in order for something to be stolen. If D violates my proprietary rights by *using* my property without permission, we would ordinarily say that he has committed joyriding or trespass, rather than that he has stolen. Similarly, if D *damages* my property without permission, we might say that he has engaged in vandalism, but, once again, not that he has stolen. To 'steal' something, it seems, is to interfere with an owner's fundamental right to *possess* it. This suggests a possible refinement of our definition: in order to steal, it appears that one must subject another to a substantial deprivation of rights in some particular piece of property, including, at a minimum, the right of possession.

Thirdly, we need to consider what kinds of thing must be taken in order to say that X has stolen. For example, taking sex without consent is not stealing: it constitutes a different, and even more serious, kind of violation of the victim's autonomy, which we call rape.[7] Nor, similarly, is it stealing to chop off another's

---

[5] Lawrence C Becker, 'Property' in Lawrence C Becker and Charlotte B Becker, *Encyclopedia of Ethics* (New York: Routledge, 2001), vol. 3, at 1389, 1390.

[6] AM Honoré, 'Ownership,' in Anthony G Guest (ed.), *Oxford Essays in Jurisprudence* (Oxford: Clarendon Press, 1961) 107.

[7] Cf John Gardner and Stephen Shute, 'The Wrongness of Rape,' in Jeremy Horder (ed.) *Oxford Essays in Jurisprudence* (Oxford: OUP, 2000) 193, 199–203. One could imagine a case in which D had consensual sex with a prostitute and then refused to pay. We might say in such a case that D had 'stolen' sex. See generally Patricia J Falk, 'Rape by Fraud and Rape by Coercion' (1998) 64 *Brooklyn Law Review* 39, 76–79. But there is something admittedly troubling about this approach. Perhaps a better solution is to say that D stole the *money* he had falsely agreed to pay for the prostitute's services.

limb without consent; this is mayhem. So what kinds of thing *can* be stolen? To be sure, we sometimes speak of X's 'stealing' Y's 'affection' or Z's 'thunder.' But such usages are metaphorical or derivative (the second, doubly so). In order to be stolen, a thing must be commodifiable—ie, it must be capable of being bought and sold.[8] This does not mean that a good or service must be subject to *legal* purchase or sale in order to be stolen: contraband drugs and human organs can certainly be subject to theft.[9] It merely means that, for something to be stolen, it must be the sort of thing that, in theory, *is capable of* being bought or sold.

Fourthly, we need to make a distinction (an analogue of which will appear again when we discuss coercion, disloyalty, and promise-breaking) between stealing in the 'descriptive' or 'factual' sense and stealing in the 'moral' or 'normative' sense. Imagine a society in which all of the real and personal property, even that which is generated through the work of the citizens, is deemed by law to be owned by a despotic dictator, with the citizens making use of only the most meager resources for their own subsistence. The economic system of such a society would be profoundly unjust. If a citizen of such a society were to take some reasonable share of property from the dictator without his permission, we might say that the citizen had 'stolen' in some descriptive sense of the term—ie he did in fact deprive another of the possession of his property, and had the intent to do so. But we would presumably not say that he had 'stolen' in the moral sense of the term—ie that he had committed a morally wrongful act. Because the dictator had no moral rights to such property in the first place, there was no violation of such rights. Analogously, if A, an abolitionist, helped a slave escape, the slave's owner and his peers would presumably regard A's act as stealing, though, from our more enlightened perspective, A obviously would not have done anything morally wrong; indeed, he would have done what was morally correct.[10] Once again, we would say that A had stolen in the descriptive sense of the term, but not in its moral or normative senses. In order to steal in the moral sense of the term, the rights in property that are violated by the stealer need to be morally legitimate rights. As in the case of cheating, which involves the violation of *fair* and *fairly enforced* rules, we need to be able to exclude those violations that occur against the background of a fundamentally unfair or illegitimate system of property.

---

[8] The concept of commodifiability is discussed in Stuart P Green, 'Plagiarism, Norms, and the Limits of Theft Law: Some Observations on the Use of Criminal Sanctions in Enforcing Intellectual Property Rights' (2002) 54 *Hastings Law Journal* 167, 216–18. For consideration of the argument that bribery should be a crime because it involves the 'commodification of government,' see ch. 16, n 13 below.

[9] *State v Pocinwong*, 1997 WL 435708 (Wash App Div I, 4 Aug 1997) (stealing of illegal drugs constitutes theft); *State v Donovan*, 183 P 127, 129 (Wash 1919) (illegal liquor subject to larceny); but see Jerome Hall, *Theft, Law and Society* (2nd edn, Indianapolis, Ind. Bobbs Merrill, 1952) 84–85 (during Prohibition, some cases held that bootleg liquor was not subject to theft).

[10] Cf AP Simester and GR Sullivan, 'On the Nature and Rationale of Property Offences' in RA Duff and Stuart P Green (eds.), *Defining Crimes: Essays on the Special Part of the Criminal Law* (Oxford: OUP, 2005) 168, 172.

Finally, like many of the norms discussed in this Part, the wrong of stealing is obviously prima facie in character. Even in a society with a 'by and large' just distribution of wealth, there are bound to be cases in which unauthorized appropriations of property will not be viewed as morally wrongful, as where *D* must choose between having his children starve and taking food from a millionaire's well-stocked pantry without his permission. Once again, while we might well say that *D* had 'stolen' in such a case (and the court might well convict him of theft), our intuitions tell us that *D* has done nothing wrong.

2. Stealing and the Criminal Law

The norm against stealing is clearly an essential ingredient in a wide range of criminal law offenses, often combined with some other moral norm to create a distinctive crime: thus, stealing plus deception constitutes fraud or false pretenses; stealing plus disloyalty constitutes embezzlement; stealing plus coercion equals extortion; stealing plus the use of unjustified force equals robbery; and so forth.[11]

It should be emphasized, however, that the fit between stealing and the law of theft is far from perfect. Until recently, the criminal law of theft was quite narrow, applying only to the misappropriation of tangible property, and excluding such intangibles as a ride on a train, a deed to land, and stocks and securities.[12] Thus, there were many instances in which *X* could be said to have 'stolen' something in the moral sense of the term, without being subject to criminal sanctions for theft. Conversely, there are cases in which *X* is subject to what is referred to by the law as 'theft' even though many people would say that he has not stolen anything. Consider leading intellectual property offenses such as the National Stolen Property Act and the No Electronic Theft Act, both of which speak in terms of various forms of (intangible) property being 'stolen.'[13] Indeed, it is likely that such terminology was chosen precisely for the purpose of invoking the moral condemnation traditionally associated with violations of this norm. Yet, as we saw in Part I, a significant percentage of the population believes that there is nothing morally wrong with the underlying conduct that such laws prohibit. Given this, we might infer that such people believe that such acts do not constitute 'stealing.' If this is so, it suggests an even greater divergence between the norm against stealing and the legal prohibition of theft than might previously have been recognized.

---

[11] Cf Stephen Shute and Jeremy Horder, 'Thieving and Deceiving: What is the Difference?' (1993) 56 Modern Law Review 548; CMV Clarkson, 'Theft and Fair Labelling' (1993) 56 *Modern Law Review* 554.   [12] Green, (n 8 above, at 210).
[13] See 18 USC §§ 2314 and 1028, respectively.

7
Coercion and Exploitation

There are at least two ways, speaking broadly, in which the concept of coercion figures in the criminal law. One is as an excusing condition: a defendant who, under the effects of coercion or duress, commits what would otherwise be a criminal act is regarded as blameless for his act, or at least as less blameworthy than he otherwise would have been.[1] The second is as an 'element' of an offense: one who unjustifiably uses coercion on another does a blameworthy act, which will, if other conditions are also met, constitute a criminal offense.[2] Coercion in both contexts has generated a large and sophisticated literature.[3] My concern in this section will be with the second sense of coercion: I offer a brief account of what coercion means in the sense that it occurs in crimes such as extortion and blackmail, and I say something about how the concept of coercion differs from that of exploitation, and why the latter form of moral wrongfulness is less comfortably subject to criminalization than the former. I will reserve my discussion of the relationship between coercion and consent until Chapter 17, when I talk in detail about the crime of extortion.

1. COERCION AS THREAT

There are various techniques that people use to get others to act as they want. Some are perfectly acceptable: a lawyer wants a client to pay him money; he offers him competent service for a reasonable fee and sends a bill at the end of the month. Others we view as morally suspect: for example, X lies to Y about the quality or quantity of some good or service in order to induce him to pay him more money than is deserved. 'Coercion,' in Joel Feinberg's words, is yet

---

[1] See Michael D Bayles, 'A Concept of Coercion' in J Roland Pennock and John W Chapman (eds.), *Nomos XIV: Coercion* (Chicago: Aldine/Atherton, 1972) 74.   [2] *Ibid.*
[3] For some leading works, see Joel Feinberg, *Harm to Self* (Oxford: OUP, 1986) 189–268; Alan Wertheimer, *Coercion* (Princeton: Princeton University Press, 1987); Mitchell N Berman, 'The Normative Functions of Coercion Claims' (2002) 8 *Legal Theory* 45; Harry Frankfurt, 'Coercion and Moral Responsibility,' in Ted Honderich (ed.), *Essays on Freedom of Action* (London: Routledge and Kegan Paul, corrected reprint ed. 1978); Kent Greenawalt, 'Criminal Coercion and Freedom of Speech' (1983) 78 *Northwestern University Law Review* 1081; Robert Nozick, 'Coercion,' in *Socratic Puzzles* (Cambridge, Mass.: Harvard University Press, 1997).

another 'technique for forcing people to act as the coercer wants them to act, and presumably contrary to their own preferences.'[4]

Coercion is usually carried out by means of a threat. When X 'threatens' V, X is promising V (or, perhaps more accurately, stating to V her intention[5]) to bring about some unwanted state of affairs for V. Often, but not always, threats are conditional: in such cases, V is given a choice between doing what is demanded or opting instead for the threatened consequences. When X threatens V, she is stating her intention to make V *worse off* in relation to some relevant baseline position than if V does not accept her proposal. This is in contrast to X's making an 'offer' to V, in which V is given an inducement to action: if V accepts X's proposal, V will be made *better off* in relation to some relevant baseline position.

Assuming that this distinction between threats and offers is valid, the key to determining whether V is subject to a threat is determining V's baseline or benchmark, so as to know whether V will be made better or worse off. Baselines are usually defined with respect to what Robert Nozick referred to as the 'normal or natural or expected course of events.'[6] Thus, if X proposes to kill V if V does not hand over all his money, X is making a threat, because if V does not accept the proposal he will be worse off than in his baseline situation, in which he keeps his money and remains alive. But contrast a case in which X is drowning and V offers to save him in return for a million dollars. Here, X has made an offer, since if V does not accept the proposal he will be no worse off than in the baseline situation (for which, I am assuming, X bears no responsibility).

As Nozick and others have recognized, however, the term 'normal or natural or expected course of events' is ambiguous.[7] It can refer either to the outcome that, as an empirical matter, would likely occur absent the acceptance of the proposal; or it can refer to the action that is morally required. To give one of Nozick's examples, imagine that O, a slave owner, beats S, his slave, each morning, for no reason connected to S's behavior. One day, O says to S, 'Tomorrow I will not beat you if and only if you do γ.'[8] Under the empirical approach, O's proposal is an offer, since S expects to be beaten each morning, and relative to that expectation, his acceptance of O's proposal would make him better off. Under the moral approach, however, O's proposal should be viewed as a threat, for O is morally prohibited from beating S every morning (indeed, he is morally prohibited from having a slave in the first place), and relative to that baseline, O is proposing to make S worse off than he has a right to be.[9]

---

[4] Joel Feinberg, 'Coercion' in *Routledge Encyclopedia of Philosophy* Edward Craig (ed.), (London: Routledge, 1998), vol. 2, at 387.

[5] As I suggest in ch. 9 below, we should perhaps reserve the term 'promising' for cases in which X states an intention to do something that V regards (or at least that X believes V regards) as desirable.   [6] Nozick (n 3 above, at 243).

[7] *Ibid*; Feinberg, (n 3 above, at 219); see also Wertheimer (n3 above, at 208–09).

[8] Nozick (n 3 above, at 27).

[9] *Ibid*; Nozick's slave case is also discussed in David Zimmerman, 'Coercive Wage Offers' (1981) 10 *Philosophy & Public Affairs* 121 (offering alternative theory of baselines that allows some offers to be viewed as coercive).

Such ambiguity in defining the baseline, in turn, reflects a broader debate that runs through the scholarly literature on coercion. Some scholars maintain that coercion is an essentially empirical concept—that the question whether *X* has coerced *V* can be answered based on facts alone, without reference to moral concepts.[10] Others say that the question whether *X* has coerced *V* cannot be answered without reference to moral judgments, such as whether *X* had a right to treat *V* in such manner.[11] For the moment, we need not resolve this debate, although we will revisit it when we consider the offense of extortion in Chapter 17.

2. EXPLOITATION

Another morally suspect way for *X* to get *V* to do what he wants is through exploitation.[12] Exploitation does not involve outright lies or threats. Instead, exploitation involves *X*'s 'using' or 'manipulating' or 'taking advantage of' *V*, usually for his own benefit and often at *V*'s expense.[13] In some ways, exploitation is harder to distinguish from morally acceptable forms of getting another to do what one wants than are deception and coercion.

In Joel Feinberg's formulation, exploitation consists of three elements: First, *X* must 'use' *V* in the sense of 'playing on' him in some way. He can, in Feinberg's words, 'offer inducements, employ flattery, beg or beseech; he can try alluring portrayals or seductive suggestions; he can appeal to duty, sympathy, friendship, or greed, probing constantly for the character trait whose cultivation will yield the desired response.'[14] Secondly, what *X* is exploiting in *V* is either a trait of *V*'s or a circumstance in which *V* is found. Exploitable traits include both virtues (eg, generosity, loyalty, courage, or conscientiousness) and vices (eg, greed, recklessness, lust, or envy). Sometimes these traits may be more or less permanent aspects of *V*'s character; other times they may be short-lived deviations, particularly when brought on by particular circumstances, either unfortunate, such as illness or hunger; or fortunate, such as new-found wealth or freedom. Thirdly, *X* must intend to benefit from the exploitation, typically, though not always, at *V*'s expense, as where a funeral home operator exploits the sorrow of a grieving widow by getting her to buy a more expensive casket than she can properly afford.

---

[10]   eg, Frankfurt (n 3 above); Dennis G Arnold, 'Coercion and Moral Responsibility' (2001) 38 *American Philosophical Quarterly* 53.

[11]   Wertheimer (n 3 above); Nozick (n 3 above).

[12]   The literature on exploitation includes Alan Wertheimer, *Exploitation* (Princeton: Princeton University Press, 1996); Joel Feinberg, *Harmless Wrongdoing* (New York: OUP, 1988), chs. 31–32; and Patricia Greenspan, 'The Problem with Manipulation' (2003) 40 *American Philosophical Quarterly* 155.

[13]   This is exploitation in the moral, pejorative sense of the term, as contrasted to exploitation in the non-pejorative sense of the term, in which one exploits an opportunity or resource. Cf Feinberg (n 12 above, at 177).   [14]   *Ibid* at 181.

3. DISTINGUISHING COERCION AND EXPLOITATION

Despite the differences between coercion and exploitation, it should be clear that the two concepts are not mutually exclusive. As both Feinberg and Alan Wertheimer have emphasized, the two concepts have fundamentally different foci.[15] In considering whether X subjected V to coercion, we look to the effects of X's acts on V's options. The focus of exploitation is quite different: In determining whether X has acted exploitatively, we look to the effects of such conduct on X's interests.[16]

Because these two conditions—effect on Y's options, and effect on X's interests—are independent, a given proposal might reflect one of four possibilities: (1) A proposal can be coercive without being exploitative, as when a doctor tells her patient that she will no longer treat him unless he gives up smoking; (2) A proposal can be exploitative without being coercive, as when a tugboat encounters a ship in distress and offers to tow it for a fee that greatly exceeds the normal market price for such services; (3) A proposal can be both coercive and exploitative, as when an extortionist threatens to break a victim's kneecaps unless the victim pays the extortionist $1,000; and (4) A proposal can be neither coercive nor exploitative, as when a seller offers to sell a buyer some property at a reasonable, market-based price.

4. CRIMINALIZING COERCION AND EXPLOITATION

Although coercion and exploitation are both viewed as morally wrongful acts, the former is more likely to be subject to criminal sanctions than the latter. Indeed, statutes that subject such non-coercively exploitative behavior to criminal or quasi-criminal sanctions are unusual and generally disfavored in the law.

Consider the offense of price gouging, which consists of failing to comply with a requirement that the price of necessities in the aftermath of a major storm or other emergency remain at the average price that existed for some specified period prior to the emergency.[17] A grocery store or lumber yard that prices milk or lumber far above the price at which they were sold before the hurricane is arguably 'playing on' storm victims' unfortunate circumstances for its own benefit. But it is doing so through exploitation rather than coercion, since its proposal involves an offer, not a threat: if the consumer in need of

---

[15] Wertheimer (n 3 above, at 226); Joel Feinberg, 'Noncoercive Exploitation' in Rolf Sartorius (ed.), *Paternalism* (Minneapolis: University of Minnesota Press, 1983) 208.

[16] See generally Wertheimer (n 12 above); Feinberg (n 12 above, chs. 31–32).

[17] Gary E Lehman, '*Force Majeure* Price Gouging: Application of Florida's Deceptive and Unfair Trade Practices in the Aftermath of Hurricane Andrew' (1993) 17 *Nova Law Review* 1029.

such commodities does not accept the seller's proposal, he will be no worse off than in his baseline situation (ie, lacking the needed commodity).

Other quasi-criminal offenses such as ticket scalping and usury reflect a similar dynamic: the ticket scalper prices concert ticket far above their normal face value[18]; the usurer offers 'pay day' loans at an interest rate far above the generally available market rate.[19] In both cases, the exploitee is placed in no worse a position than he would have been absent the offer. The same might be said about the sale of bodily organs, prostitution, and perhaps drug dealing. In each case, the offender engages in what the moralist would regard as a form of exploitation. Yet criminalizing any of these kinds of behaviors is highly controversial.[20]

Now contrast such 'exploitation offenses' to the crime of extortion, which consists of obtaining money or property from another by threatening to commit a wrongful act unless one is paid to forgo it.[21] Extortion clearly involves coercion in the sense that the extortionist states his intention to make his victim worse off than the victim has a right to be unless he pays the price demanded. The question is why the law seems more comfortable in criminalizing coercion offenses such as extortion than it does in criminalizing exploitation offenses such as price gouging and usury.

One possible answer could be that the harms typically associated with coercive behavior are greater than the harms typically associated with exploitation. And this certainly seems plausible: *ceteris paribus*, it may well be that the victim of extortion really does suffer more than the victim of price gouging. Another possible explanation is that the character of the two wrongs is different—that coercion is inherently a more serious wrong than exploitation. Finally, it may be that exploitation is harder to distinguish from merely aggressive but lawful business behavior than is coercion. As a result, exploitation crimes might prove even more morally ambiguous and unstable than other kinds of white-collar offenses.

---

[18] Feinberg (n 12 above, at 231–38).

[19] Creola Johnson, 'Payday Loans: Shrewd Business or Predatory Lending' (2002) 87 *Minnesota Law Review* 1.

[20] Many free-market-oriented scholars have argued that 'price gouging' (a term they deem unnecessarily pejorative) is economically efficient and that laws prohibiting such practices are unneccssary and even counterproductive. See, eg Anita Ramasastry, 'Assessing Anti-Price-Gouging Statutes in the Wake of Hurricane Katrina: Why They're Necessary in Emergencies, But Need to be Rewritten,' *FindLaw.com*, <http://writ.news.findlaw.com/ramasastry/20050916.html> (16 Sept. 2005) (reviewing such arguments).   [21] See ch. 17 below.

8

Disloyalty

The significance of the norm against disloyalty (and the closely related concept of breach of trust) to our understanding of white-collar crime has been both over- and underestimated in the scholarly literature. On the one hand, there are those writers, such as Susan Shapiro, who have argued that violation of trust is *the* defining characteristic of white-collar crime—what distinguishes it from all other kinds of crime.[1] On the other hand, there are scholars such as John Coffee who have expressed considerable skepticism about the role that the concept of breach of trust should play in the criminal law.[2] A more accurate assessment would arrive at a conclusion somewhere between these extremes. While the concept of disloyalty does play a significant role in defining certain key criminal offenses, such as bribery, treason, some acts of insider trading, and some frauds, it has relatively little to do with a whole host of other core white collar offenses.[3] In this section, I offer an explanation of what I mean by disloyalty, and foreshadow some of the ways in which it plays a role in defining white-collar crime.

1. THE DUTY OF LOYALTY

Before we can consider what it means to *violate* a duty of loyalty, we need first to consider what it means to *have* a duty of loyalty. To be loyal involves being true or faithful to someone or something—having a 'persevering commitment to some associational object', as John Kleinig has put it.[4] But what kind of

---

[1] Susan P Shapiro, 'Collaring the Crime, Not the Criminal: Reconsidering the Concept of White-Collar Crime' (1990) 55 *American Sociological Review* 346, 350 ('The violation and manipulation of the norms of trust—of disclosure, disinterestedness, and role competence—represent the modus operandi of white collar crime.'). See also David O Friedrichs, *Trusted Criminals: White Collar Crime in Contemporary Society* (Belmont, CA: Wadsworth/Thomson Learning) 9 (giving a qualified endorsement to the violation-of-trust approach to white-collar crime).

[2] John C Coffee, Jr., 'Does "Unlawful" Mean "Criminal"?: Reflections on the Disappearing Tort/Crime Distinction in American Law' (1991) 71 *Boston University Law Review* 193, 208; John C Coffee, Jr., 'From Tort to Crime: Some Reflections on the Criminalization of Fiduciary Breaches and the Problematic Line Between Law and Ethics' (1981) 19 *American Criminal Law Review* 117.

[3] The FBI is thus probably closest to this in-between position when it says that white-collar crime involves 'deceit, concealment, *or* violation of trust.' US Department of Justice, Federal Bureau of Investigation, *White Collar Crime: A Report to the Public* (Washington, DC., 1989) 3.

[4] This phrase appears in an in-progress draft of a book of Kleinig's entitled *Loyalty and Loyalties*, of which I am grateful to have had the opportunity to read a chapter.

object? Some commentators, such as Marcia Baron and John Ladd, have argued that loyalty must be interpersonal—that one can be loyal only to an individual, or group, or institution.[5] Under this view, loyalty is founded on a specific kind of relationship or tie defined by membership in a group and differentiation within that group.[6] It is typically defined by social roles, rather than any particular characteristics of individuals: thus, I am loyal to *my* family, *my* friends, and *my* colleagues because of their relationship to me, rather than because of any particular qualities they might possess.

Other commentators, including, most prominently, Josiah Royce, have suggested that the proper objects of loyalty are ideals, causes, and practices, rather than individual people or institutions. Thus, for Royce, loyalty consists in the 'devotion of a patriot to his country,' 'the devotion of a martyr to his religion,' and 'the devotion of a ship's captain to the requirements of his office.'[7]

The best view, it seems to me, is that one can be loyal to both people *and* causes or ideals (or, to put it homophonically, to both princip*als* and princip*les*).[8] Loyalty creates in one a prima facie obligation to act *in the best interests* of a particular person or cause, even when doing so would be against one's own self-interest. It helps define many of our most important human relationships, and indeed our very identities as persons. To be loyal is to be guided by such concerns for the relevant others in our dealings with family, friends, colleagues, communities, and nations, and in the pursuit of our most important projects. As Andrew Oldenquist has suggested, 'it is likely that loyalties ground more of the principled, self-sacrificing, and other kinds of nonselfish behavior in which people engage than do [other kinds of] moral principles and ideals.'[9] Take away loyalty and our lives would be empty indeed.

In some cases, we choose our own loyalties: when I decide to marry a particular person, work for a particular employer, or join a particular club, I knowingly and voluntarily assume the moral obligations that go with such relationships. In other cases, loyalties arise involuntarily: we are all born into a web of familial, social, national, ethnic, cultural, religious, ideological, and political relationships. As adults, we may be theoretically free to reject those ties and choose others in their place, but such early bonds are usually strong ones.

Loyalty and Moral Conflict

Sometimes, a person ostensibly subject to a duty of loyalty is forced to choose between acting in a way that is consistent with such duty and complying with

[5] Marcia Baron, *The Moral Status of Loyalty* (Dubuque, IA: Kendall/Hunt, 1984), at 5; John Ladd, 'Loyalty,' in Paul Edwards (ed.) *Encyclopedia of Philosophy* (London: Routledge & Kegan Paul, 1967, reprint edn. 1972) 97.   [6] Ladd, *Ibid* at 97.

[7] Josiah Royce, *The Philosophy of Loyalty* (New York: Hafner Publishing Co., 1908) 17.

[8] Whether one can also properly be said to be loyal to a product or brand, and whether dogs and other animals can truly be said to be loyal, are questions which, for present purposes, need not be answered. See generally Kleinig (n 4 above).

[9] See Andrew Oldenquist, 'Loyalties' (1982) 79 *Journal of Philosophy* 173, 173.

some competing moral obligation. In sorting out such conflicts, it will be helpful to distinguish once again between what we can refer to as (1) loyalty in the factual (or descriptive or empirical) sense, and (2) loyalty in the normative (or moral) sense.[10] Loyalty in the factual sense consists in a certain mental attitude that X has towards the object of his loyalty: it requires that X view himself as obligated to act, and in fact be inclined to act, in the best interests of his principal; and that he be willing to persevere in such an attachment despite the difficulties that might be involved. Loyalty in this sense does not require that the object of one's loyalty be a good person or right cause.

By contrast, to think of loyalty in the normative or moral sense is to think of it as a virtue; it requires not only that X work in the best interests of his principal, but also that such principal in fact be a good person or right cause, or at least not a thoroughly bad person or wrong cause. Thus, whereas one could be loyal in the empirical sense to a Hitler or to the ideology of Nazism, one could not be loyal to such objects in the normative sense.[11] In such cases, we say that one's loyalties are misplaced.

Loyalties, in either form, are not absolute. Loyalty is only one of a series of competing factors, a prima facie consideration, which people take into account in making moral decisions.[12] Sometimes our loyalty to one person or cause conflicts with our loyalty to another person or cause.[13] The obligations of loyalty can also come into conflict with other kinds of moral obligations. For example, if one were questioned by the police about what one knew of criminal wrongdoing by one's spouse or child, the demands of loyalty might well require that one violate one's competing moral (and legal) obligation to tell the truth.

Inasmuch as it is potentially at odds with liberalism, loyalty can seem a disfavored or outmoded virtue. Liberalism in its various forms assumes that all people should be regarded as equal, that they should be treated with like concern and respect, and that moral judgments should be impartial. The ethic of loyalty, by contrast, involves a preference for people in my family or my group over those who are outside it.[14] In some cases, the conflict between the two approaches can be acute. Adherence to the ethic of loyalty has the potential to negate our critical edge, cause complacency, lead us to accept what our

---

[10] Cf Peter Westen, *The Logic of Consent* (Aldershot: Ashgate Publishing, 2004) 4–7 (distinguishing between 'factual' and 'legal' senses of 'consent'); Nozick (n 3 above) (distinguishing between coercion in the 'empirical' sense and coercion in the 'moral sense').

[11] Cf Robert E Ewin, 'Loyalty and Virtues' (1992) 42 *Philosophical Quarterly* 403.

[12] Cf Marcia W Baron, 'Loyalty,' in Lawrence C Becker & Charlotte B Becker (eds) *Encyclopedia of Ethics* 751, 752 (2nd edn., New York: Routledge, 1992).

[13] Compare Forster's famous remark that, 'If I had to choose between betraying my country and betraying my friend, I hope I should have the guts to betray my country.' EM Forster, 'What I Believe,' in *Two Cheers for Democracy* (London: Edward Arnold, 1951).

[14] This point is emphasized in George P Fletcher, *Loyalty: An Essay on the Morality of Relationships* (New York: OUP, 1993), at 11–16.

political leaders do unquestioningly, and to be intolerant of those who are not part of our group. In its most perverse forms, loyalty can lead to bigotry and xenophobia.

Indeed, there are cases in which individuals are encouraged, or even required, to place adherence to some supposedly higher principle (one might even say 'loyalty' to some higher principle) over loyalty to a friend or employer. For example, rules against nepotism require hiring decisions to be made on the basis of what is in the best interest of an institution, rather than according to personal loyalties.[15] Similarly, the Code of Ethics for federal government employees states that such employees should 'expose corruption wherever uncovered,' 'pay loyalty to the highest moral principles,' and 'put country above loyalty to persons, party, or Government department.'[16] And the *qui tam* provisions of the US Federal Civil False Claims Act create significant financial incentives that encourage 'whistle-blowing' employees to betray the interests of their employees, when such betrayal would serve the larger interests of the public.[17]

2. DISLOYALTY

Disloyalty consists of more than merely the absence of loyalty. Just as promise-breaking requires that X be bound by a promise, disloyalty presupposes that X be bound by some duty of loyalty. George Fletcher has described loyalty as a rejection of alternatives that undermine the principal bond: 'A loyal lover is someone who will not be seduced by another. A loyal citizen is someone who will not go over to the enemy in a time of conflict. A loyal political adherent will not "sell out" to the opposition.'[18] Disloyalty, then, can be defined as the pursuit of alternatives that undermine the principal bond.

Disloyalty comes in various gradations. Imagine that third parties are speaking negatively about someone to whom one has an obligation of loyalty. Failing to say anything in the face of such criticism may be seen as disloyal. Adding one's own negative comments seems even more so. And if others are working actively to harm the object of one's loyalty, then it may be disloyal to fail to work against their doing so, and even more disloyal to assist them. In its most virulent form, disloyalty becomes betrayal.[19]

The extent to which one can be said to be disloyal turns on context-specific determinations. Some conservatives seem to think that it is disloyal to criticize

---

[15] See, eg 5 USC § 3110(b) (barring public officials from appointing relatives to positions in agencies over which such officials exercise jurisdiction or control).

[16] Code of Ethics for Government Service, passed by the US House of Representatives in the 85th Congress, 1958, quoted in Sissela Bok, *Secrets: On the Ethics of Concealment and Revelation* (New York: Vintage Books, 1984) 211–12.

[17] False Claims Act, 31 USC § 3730; see also Public Interest Disclosure Act 1998 (UK) (protecting employees from retaliation for whistle blowing).   [18] Fletcher n 14 above, at (8).

[19] See generally Judith Shklar, *Ordinary Vices* (Cambridge, Mass.: Harvard/Belknap, 1984) at 138–91.

one's government, its leaders, or its policies, especially in times of war. In contrast, liberals believe that one can be highly critical of one's country without being disloyal. Indeed, the liberal view is that true loyalty *obligates* one to criticize one's country when it is in the wrong.

Context may also determine the difference between disloyalty and a mere shift in loyalties. For example, while I am working for company X, it would be disloyal of me also to work for its chief rival, Y. But I am free (and, indeed, morally and legally required) to shift my loyalties after I leave my job at X and go to work for Y. On the other hand, even after I have left working for company X, I am still ethically (and legally) constrained from sharing its trade secrets. Similarly, I may decide that I no longer want to be friends or lovers with F without such a decision entailing disloyalty, but it might nevertheless be disloyal to write a tell-all book about F even after our relationship has ended.[20]

The question of shifting loyalties is particularly important in the context of legal ethics. It is sometimes said that a lawyer's duty of loyalty to her client does not extend beyond the life of the attorney-client relationship, and that the only duty that persists beyond the termination of the relationship is the duty of confidentiality.[21] But this seems questionable. Some scholars have suggested that a lawyer is more like a 'special purpose friend'[22] than an employee of the client's. If this is so, then the relevant question is whether a remnant of the duty of loyalty extends beyond the duration of a friendship. Although the matter is certainly debatable, it seems to me plausible that it does. Except perhaps in cases in which X has been betrayed by his former friend, Y, it seems plausible that X should continue to have some residual duty of loyalty to Y even after they are no longer friends. While X surely has no ongoing duty to work affirmatively on Y's behalf, he may nevertheless have a continuing duty not to work affirmatively *against* Y's interests. If this chain of assumptions is correct, then it suggests that a lawyer continues to have some remnant of the duty of his loyalty to his clients even after the attorney-client relationship has been severed.

---

[20] See, eg Claire Bloom, *Leaving the Doll's House* (New York: Little, Brown, 1996) (about her marriage to Philip Roth); Joyce Maynard, *At Home in the World* (New York: Picador, 1998) (about her relationship with JD Salinger); and Paul Theroux, *Sir Vidia's Shadow* (Boston: Houghton Mifflin, 1998) (about his friendship with VS Naipaul). What is unseemly about such books, in my view, is that they reflect a betrayal of trust that once existed between writer and subject, and which ought to continue to have some residual force even after the relationship has ended.

[21] See, eg Ronald D Rotunda, 'Conflicts Problems When Representing Members of Corporate Families' (1997) 72 *Notre Dame Law Review* 655, 662 ('The duty to refrain from taking a case adverse to Corporation A only applies while Corporation A is a client of the law firm. There is no general rule prohibiting a client from suing a former client. Otherwise any corporation, particularly a large one such as General Electric or General Motors, would be able to preclude many lawyers from ever taking positions adverse to them just because, years before, someone in the law firm had represented them. There is, in short, no duty of loyalty to a former client.').

[22] See Charles Fried, 'The Lawyer as Friend: The Moral Foundations of the Lawyer-Client Relation' (1976) 85 *Yale Law Journal* 1060.

3. Distinguishing Disloyalty from Other Forms of Moral Wrongfulness

In what respects is the concept of disloyalty I have described distinguishable from other forms of moral wrongfulness or illegality, such as promise-breaking and breach of fiduciary duty? Disloyalty is both broader and narrower than promise-breaking. If I enter into a contract in which I promise to sell my butterfly collection to a stranger over eBay, and then renege on that promise, I have not been disloyal. Loyalty involves a complex web of obligations and duties arising out of certain kinds of identifiable social relations: friend-to-friend, sibling-to-sibling, employee-to-employer, and so forth. Such relations are not easily reducible to an identifiable promise or set of promises. Moreover, although one who is disloyal will often have made a promise to be loyal, this is not always the case. For example, people are generally thought to have a duty of loyalty to their families even though they will not normally have made any specific promise as such.

The concept of disloyalty is also both broader and narrower than that of breach of fiduciary duty. Unlike loyalty, which is primarily a concept of morality, fiduciary duty is primarily a concept of law; it refers to a set of obligations that the law imposes on parties who stand in a position of trust in relation to other parties, such as agents to principals, lawyers to clients, and doctors to patients. There are obviously cases in which one can have a duty of loyalty without a corresponding duty to a fiduciary. For example, while I certainly have a duty of loyalty to friends and relatives outside my immediate family, I generally owe them no legally enforceable fiduciary duty.

The harder question is whether fiduciary duties are always reducible to duties of loyalty. There is a great deal of debate in the literature about exactly what lies at the core of fiduciary duty. Courts and scholars have variously described the fiduciary duty as: (1) involving a 'duty of care'; (2) fundamentally contractual in nature; and (3) nothing more than a collection of specific, narrower duties, such as avoidance of conflicts, and the obligation to treat beneficiaries of the same class equally and beneficiaries of different classes fairly.[23] There is also an interesting strand of thought that does in fact view loyalty as the foundation of fiduciary duty.[24] While it is beyond the scope of this study to resolve this issue in the law of agency, for the moment it is enough simply to raise the possibility of a connection between a loyalty-based theory of fiduciary duty and a (dis)loyalty-based theory of bribery.[25]

[23] For a sampling of the vast literature on fiduciary relationships, see Robert Flannigan, 'The Fiduciary Obligation' (1989) 9 *Oxford Journal of Legal Studies* 285; Tamar Frankel, 'Fiduciary Law' (1983) 71 *California Law Review* 795; Deborah A DeMott, 'Beyond Metaphor: An Analysis of Fiduciary Obligation,' 1988 *Duke Law Journal* 879.

[24] Gordon Smith, 'The Critical Resource Theory of Fiduciary Duty' (2002) 55 *Vanderbilt Law Review* 1399, at 1406–11.

[25] The connection between fiduciary duty theory and the law of corruption is made explicit in Kathleen Clark, 'Do We Have Enough Ethics in Government Yet?: An Answer from Fiduciary Theory,' 1996 *University of Illinois Law Review* 57.

4. Disloyalty and the Criminal Law

Given the predominantly private and interpersonal nature of the wrong of disloyalty described above, it is somewhat surprising that the concept should play as large a role in the criminal law as it does. Historically, we can observe a particularly striking connection between the concept of disloyalty (or betrayal) and the criminal law of Renaissance Florence. According to Paul Chevigny, Dante's *Inferno* reflects a rough kind of grading of crimes in 14th century Italy.[26] As he descends through the nine circles of Hell, Dante encounters a sequence of increasingly serious sins, most of which are also crimes. Those crimes that are viewed as most damaging of the social fabric, and therefore most deserving of punishment, are those that involve a betrayal of trust. Thus, Dante views crimes of violence such as assault and robbery as less serious than crimes (he views as) involving betrayals of trust, such as fraud and theft. In Dante's view, according to Chevigny, 'crimes of betrayal were the most serious not only because they required the most deliberate exercise of free will, but also because they did the most damage to the ethical net of obligations in society.'[27]

In modern times, the most significant disloyalty crimes are probably bribery and treason; and, indeed, it may be no coincidence that these are the only two offenses specifically identified in the U.S. Constitution as grounds for impeachment.[28] Both acts are viewed as striking at the foundations of the legal order. As Daniel Lowenstein has put it:

Bribery is 'worse' than other crimes. It is a 'crime akin to treason,' a 'despicable act.' Those who, having voluntarily assumed public office, set aside the public trust for private advantage (and those who tempt public officials to do so) engage in morally reprehensible conduct striking at the roots of fairness and democracy. We want a special crime, with a special stigma, for such conduct.[29]

The offense of bribery will be discussed extensively in Chapter 16, as will that aspect of fraud that involves breach of trust. Although the crime of treason[30] is mostly beyond the reach of this study, it is worth mentioning two related, lesser offenses that also seem to criminalize the wrong of disloyalty and that can arguably be classified as white-collar offenses: the Intelligence Identities Protection Act of 1982,[31] and the Espionage Act of 1917.[32] Both statutes received a good deal of attention during the Summer and Fall of 2005 when it

---

[26] Paul G Chevigny, 'From Betrayal to Violence: Dante's *Inferno* and the Social Construction of Crime' (2001) 26 *Law & Social Inquiry* 787.   [27] *Ibid* at 790.

[28] See US Constitution, Art I, § 4.

[29] Daniel H Lowenstein, 'Political Bribery and the Intermediate Theory of Politics' (1985) 32 *UCLA Law Review* 784, at 806 (footnotes omitted).

[30] 18 USC §§ 2381 *et seq*. For a classic discussion of treason, see Rebecca West, *The New Meaning of Treason* (New York: Viking Press, revised and expanded ed. 1964).

[31] 50 USC §§ 421–26.   [32] 18 USC § 793. Similar is Britain's Official Secrets Act 1989.

was revealed that Karl Rove, President George W Bush's chief political strategist, and I Lewis 'Scooter' Libby, Vice President Dick Cheney's chief of staff, during the run-up to the American invasion of Iraq, played what was, at the time of this writing, a still-unclear role in leaking the identity of covert CIA operative Valerie Plame Wilson to *Time* magazine reporter Matthew Cooper and possibly others. Rove and Libby were allegedly motivated by a desire to retaliate against Plame's husband, Joseph Wilson, a former State Department official who had criticized the Bush administration for exaggerating the threat posed by Iraq under Saddam Hussein. The exposure of Plame's identity potentially endangered the safety of both her and her contacts.

In order to violate the Intelligence Identities Protection Act, four conditions must be met: (1) one who has authorized access to classified information that identifies a covert agent, (2) must intentionally disclose information identifying such agent, (3) to an individual not authorized to receive classified information, (4) knowing that the information disclosed so identifies such agent and that the United States is taking affirmative measures to conceal such covert relationship. Violation can result in a maximum penalty of 10 years in prison. At the time of this writing, there remained many unanswered factual questions as to whether: Plame would be considered a 'covert agent' within the meaning of the Act,[33] the government was taking affirmative measures to conceal her identity (and Rove or Libby knew about such measures), and Rove or Libby intentionally disclosed information identifying Plame.

A more straightforward case, perhaps, could be made under the Espionage Act, which requires, inter alia, that the defendant: (1) possess information relating to national defense, (2) have reason to believe that such information could damage the United States or aid a foreign nation, and (3) willfully communicate that information to a person not entitled to receive it.[34] (The penalty here is also a maximum of 10 years.) Under this statute, the person doing the communicating need not actually believe that the revelation of such information would damage the United States; he need only have 'reason to believe' that it would. That fact that such information was classified and that Rove and Libby, both of whom have security clearance, would be obligated to know that fact, would seem to establish a 'reason to believe' that such information could damage the United States or aid a foreign nation. Moreover, there is no requirement under this provision that the defendant had any 'purpose' to damage national security; it is only the act of communication itself that must be willful.[35]

---

[33] The statute defines 'covert agent' to require, among other things, that the agent is serving or has served outside the United States within the last five years. 50 USC §426(4)(A). It is unclear whether Plame would satisfy this requirement.   [34] 18 USC §793(c).

[35] See *United States v Morrison*, 844 F 2d 1057 (4th Cir) (upholding conviction under Espionage Act for leaking classified surveillance photos of a Soviet aircraft carrier to *Jane's Defence Weekly* despite defendant's claim that he had tried to help the media avoid incorrect reporting on an alleged Soviet military buildup), *cert. denied*, 488 US 908 (1988).

Shortly before this book went to press, Special Prosecutor Fitzgerald announced the indictment of Scooter Libby—for perjury, obstruction of justice, and false statements, but not for the underlying leak of Valerie Plame's identity. Nor was Rove charged at all. At the news conference announcing the indictment, Fitzgerald seemed to imply that the reason he was unable to bring charges for the underlying leak was precisely because the cover-up had been so successful. (This aspect of the case is discussed at the end of Chapter 15.) For present purposes, it is enough to note that statutes such as the Intelligence Identities Protection Act and the Espionage Act are clearly intended to criminalize the disloyal act of exposing the identity of a covert agent of the United States government. While it is not now publicly known, and may never be known, exactly who leaked Valerie Plame's identity, it seems reasonable to surmise that senior members of the Bush Administration played some significant role in that process. The irony is that such disloyalty to the country at large seems to have been motivated by, what seems to me, a narrow and misguided notion of loyalty to a president and vice-president determined to justify the invasion of Iraq.

9

Promise-Breaking

Legal theorists have made significant contributions to our understanding of the concept of promising.[1] But their focus has almost invariably been on the law of contract. In light of the minimal degree of opprobrium that usually attaches to promise-breaking in that context, the idea that such moral wrongfulness might play a role in defining the moral content of crimes seems at first thought improbable. Nevertheless, a brief examination of the norm against promise-breaking is appropriate here, if for no reason other than to explain how it differs from the other norms we have been considering. Moreover, it turns out that the moral content of a small but interesting collection of white-collar and regulatory offenses does in fact owe something to the concept of promise-breaking.

1. The Nature of Promising

Before we consider what it means to break a promise, let us first consider what it means to make, and be bound by, a promise.

Formal Elements

Promising can be understood as a social practice the rules of which, including the rule that promises must in general be kept, we are bound to obey.[2] When *A* (the promiser) promises *B* (the promisee) that he will ϕ, *A* communicates to *B* that he (1) undertakes an obligation to do ϕ, and (2) in so communicating, intends for *B* to believe that he has undertaken an obligation to do ϕ.[3] Promises must be addressed and communicated by a promiser to a promisee,

---

[1] Among the leading works are Patrick Atiyah, *Promises, Morals, and the Law* (Oxford: Clarendon Press, 1981); Charles Fried, *Contract as Promise: A Theory of Contractual Obligation* (Cambridge, Mass.: Harvard University Press, 1981); Joseph Raz, 'Promises and Obligations' in PMS Hacker and Joseph Raz (eds.) *Law, Morality, and Society* (Oxford: Clarendon Press, 1977) 210; Neil MacCormick, 'Voluntary Obligations and Normative Powers' (1972) 46 *Proceedings of the Aristotelian Society* 59.

[2] For a work emphasizing the 'social practice' aspects of promising, see William Vitek, *Promising* (Philadelphia: Temple University Press, 1993).

[3] Cf Richard Bronaugh, 'Promises,' in Lawrence C Becker and Charlotte B Becker (eds.), *Encyclopedia of Ethics* (New York: Routledge, 2001), vol. 3, at 1386.

unlike vows, intentions, and resolutions, which may be kept private and addressed solely to one's self.[4] In promising, *A* is making a statement about some future action rather than a current or past state of affairs.[5] What is promised must be within the promiser's control, as opposed to a prediction, which is not. Our society has developed various verbal formulas for distinguishing promises from other statements of intention. Although the formula 'I promise' is common, it is not a necessity. Statements such as 'I will do ϕ if you do γ' also provide an effective means of making a (conditional) promise.[6]

When *A* promises *B* that he will do (or not do) ϕ, *A* states his true intention to do ϕ. If *A* is lying about his intention to do ϕ, he has not made a promise; rather, he has deceived, or attempted to deceive, *B*. What is somewhat less clear is whether *B*, the promisee, must also believe that the promiser intends to do ϕ. We can imagine cases in which *B* is highly skeptical of the likelihood that *A* will do what he says he will do. Some commentators have thought that such skepticism would preclude the existence of a binding promise,[7] but this seems to me mistaken. Even when the promisee does not believe the promiser's (true) statement of intention, we should say that a promise has been made, and that the promiser is bound by such promise.

As a result of *A*'s promise, *B* acquires both the right to see ϕ performed and the power to release *A* from his obligation if he should choose to do so.[8] In general, the act (or omission) promised is something that *B* regards (or at least that *A* believes *B* regards) as desirable. By contrast, when *A* states his intention to do something bad to *B*, we call this a threat.[9]

The Moral Force of Promises

Just as promise-making consists of more than simply stating one's intention to carry out some course of action, promise-keeping involves more than simply following through with that intention. Making a promise to do ϕ involves assuming a moral obligation to do ϕ, and keeping such a promise involves performing one's obligation to do ϕ.

---

[4] We do sometimes speak of making (or breaking) a 'promise to oneself,' but this seems to me a non-core usage, like 'cheating' or 'deceiving' oneself. See discussion in chs. 4 and 5 above, respectively.

[5] Of course, people do sometimes use the language of promising in the context of current or past states of affairs. For example, Bartholomew might say, 'I promise you that I saw Beatrice at the disco yesterday' or 'I promise you that I am fluent in Uzbek.' But such statements seem to me quite different from the kind of promise we are considering in the text. Both are merely a way of emphasizing that the speaker is telling the truth. Functionally, they are no different from saying, 'believe me when I tell you that I saw Beatrice at the disco yesterday' or 'believe me that I speak Uzbek.' Such statements do not entail the normative force that attaches to genuine promises: the listener obtains no rights from the speaker's statement beyond the right he already had to rely on the speaker's statement as true.

[6] Bernard Gert, *Morality: A New Justification of the Moral Rules* (New York: OUP, 1988) at 128.   [7] *Ibid* at 128.

[8] Bronaugh (n 3 above, at 1387).

[9] On the distinction between threats and offers, see text accompanying ch. 7 n 5.

The most interesting questions about promises are: exactly how does uttering some convention of speech result in the promiser's being under a moral obligation? And to what extent is the moral obligation created by promising dependent on the moral content of the conduct promised? In particular, what are we to make of promises to engage in morally wrongful conduct? Is there any way to avoid the paradoxical conclusion that a promise to do something evil (eg, 'I promise to murder your boss') should create a moral obligation to perform such an evil act?

There is a considerable literature on such questions which, for present purposes, we need not delve into too deeply. One possibility is simply that promises create a right of reliance in the promisee. By promising B that he will do ϕ, A raises B's expectations that ϕ will take place; and by failing to perform the act, A disappoints such expectations.[10] To put it another way, A, having promised to do ϕ, is now obligated to perform ϕ because B may well have relied on his belief in A's doing ϕ in planning his own activities, possibly to his detriment. Of course, such a view may imply that, other things being equal, promises actually relied upon by a promisee should be accorded more moral weight than promises not relied upon.

As for promises to do clearly immoral acts, one possible approach to the problem is analogous to the approach I recommended in the discussion of disloyalty, stealing, and coercion—that is, to distinguish between the descriptive and normative senses of such concepts. In the current context, we might similarly distinguish between promising in the descriptive sense and promising in the normative sense. Promises in the former sense require nothing more than that A undertake an obligation to do some act, and, in communicating that fact to B, intend for B to believe that he has undertaken an obligation to do such an act. By contrast, promising in the moral sense requires, additionally, that the conduct promised be morally permissible. Thus, if A states his intention to do that which is morally impermissible (eg kill B's boss), he would not have made a promise in the moral sense, and would not thereby be morally bound.

2. PROMISE-BREAKING

The reason why it is morally wrongful to break a promise follows naturally from the moral obligation to keep promises. If promises create a moral obligation in promisers, then promise-breaking entails a violation of such an obligation. In order to break a promise, however, one must be capable of keeping it. This is consistent with the Kantian principle that 'ought implies can.' Thus, if A promises to give a million dollars to his favorite charity, and is subsequently unable to fulfill his obligation because, say, he has been

---

[10] See Richard Craswell, 'Contract Law, Default Rules, and the Philosophy of Promising,' (1989) 88 *Michigan Law Review* 489, 494.

bankrupted through no fault of his own, it seems that A should be relieved (though regrettably) of the obligation he otherwise would have had.

And how should we assess the seriousness of promise-breaking? At first glance, it may seem that promise-breaking is a less serious form of moral wrongfulness than most of the other forms of moral wrongfulness we have been discussing. There are two factors that may contribute to this perception. First, most of the other kinds of moral wrongfulness we have been considering require an affirmative act.[11] By contrast, promise-breaking very often involves an omission, as when A promises B that he will do some action, and then fails to perform. Secondly, unlike the other kinds of moral wrongfulness we have been surveying, promise-breaking is frequently unintentional, as when A promises B that he will do some action and then simply forgets (perhaps negligently) to do it.

Another significant factor in assessing the wrongfulness of promise-breaking is, of course, the content of the promise made. If A promises to do something that B regards as important, and especially if B relies on A's promise to his detriment, then A's promise-breaking will be seen as more wrongful than if the content of his promise had been trivial. In this, promise-breaking tracks a pattern that can be observed in contexts such as deception (the more serious the matter that A lies about, the more serious is his lie), disloyalty (the more significant the relationship between A and B, the more serious is A's disloyalty to B), and stealing (the more valuable the property stolen, the more serious is the theft).

3. DISTINGUISHING PROMISE-BREAKING FROM OTHER FORMS OF MORAL WRONGFULNESS

Although promise-breaking frequently overlaps with other forms of moral wrongfulness, it is important to recognize its distinctive character. For example, while X might use deceit in breaking a promise (eg by telling Y that he must break his promise to have lunch with him because he's snowed under with work, when in fact he's headed to the dog track with Z), promise-breaking and deceiving are nevertheless distinct acts. It is quite possible to break a promise without deception (eg X might simply say, honestly, that he would prefer going to the track with Z than having lunch with Y).

Promise-breaking can also be distinguished from the morally wrongful acts of cheating, disobeying, and being disloyal. As we have seen, cheating requires both rule-breaking and advantage-seeking. In some cases, the cheater's rule breaking will involve the violation of an explicit promise, as when X and Y overtly agree that neither will use steroids in preparation for, or during, their

---

[11] Admittedly, one can deceive through a properly-situated omission, but this is not the most common way of doing so.

bicycle race next month, and X does so anyway. X has both broken a promise and cheated. More commonly, the cheater's rule breaking will involve the violation of what we might recognize as an implicit promise to follow the rules of the game, the sort of promise that arises almost any time one participates in a competitive sport or game. But there are also cases in which a cheater might violate a rule to which he has never promised, either explicitly or implicitly, to adhere. For example, as I shall argue in Chapter 19, it is cheating for X to fail to pay the taxes he is required by law to pay, even if X (like most of us) has never made any specific promise to pay such taxes. Likewise, although an enlisted soldier or Catholic priest both breaks a promise and is disobedient when he disregards an order from (as the case may be) his commanding officer or the Pope, one can be disobedient—to one's parents, to one's parole officer, or to the judge presiding at one's murder trial—without ever violating a promise to obey. Similarly, while one who betrays her friends or law partners engages in both promise-breaking and disloyalty, one who betrays her sister or her country may be disloyal without ever having made a promise to break.

4. Promise-Breaking and the Criminal Law

The vast majority of broken promises (of the 'I-promise-to-cut-the-grass-this-weekend' variety) are beyond the reach of legal sanctions of any kind. Those broken promises that do have legal consequences—mainly, in the context of breach of contract—are almost never dealt with by *criminal* sanctions. And this is as it should be: As a general rule, breaches of contractual duty are viewed as violations of private obligations arising from the assent of the parties, rather than as violations of duties owed to the public.[12]

There are, however, several interesting, and instructive, exceptions to the rule that promise-breaking not be criminalized. First, at English Common Law, criminal sanctions were recognized as an appropriate response to breach of promise in cases in which, as Benno Schmidt has explained, the breach 'violated duties owed to the public or the state, as where a breach endangered human life or caused serious injury, exposed property to destruction, interrupted vital governmental services, or violated a contractual relationship thought to require special security (ie those involving military personnel or seamen).'[13] This approach makes sense: Promise-breaking is no

---

[12] The currently fashionable view among law and economics-oriented scholars, of course, is that promise-keeping is basically irrelevant to the law of contract and that breach of contract remedies are not a 'sanction' for immoral behavior. See Coffee, 'Does "Unlawful" Mean "Criminal"?', (1991) 71 *Boston University Law Review* 193, 208 (quoting Oliver Wendell Holmes, Jr, 'The Path of the Law' (1897) 10 *Harvard Law Review* 457, 462 ('The duty to keep a contract at common law means a prediction that you must pay damages if you do not keep it—and nothing else.')). Indeed, breaches of contract are considered desirable where such breaches would create 'value.' See, eg Richard Posner, *The Economic Analysis of Law* (6th edn., New York: Aspen, 2002).

[13] Benno C Schmidt, Jr, 'Principle and Prejudice: The Supreme Court and Race in the Progressive Era. Part 2: The Peonage Cases' (1982) 82 *Columbia Law Review* 646, 703–04.

less inherently a matter of criminal law than cheating, deception, coercion or disloyalty. When the harm caused by a broken promise is the sort of harm that concerns the public as a whole, criminal sanctions are appropriate.

Secondly, there are cases in which criminal sanctions have been applied to violations of promises that were never valid in the first place, because they were not made truthfully. Consider a case in which *A*, in return for a thousand dollars, promises to supply *B* with a ton of widgets. *A* then fails to supply the widgets despite his having been paid the thousand dollars. If *A* truthfully intended to supply the widgets at the time he entered into the agreement, and only changed his mind subsequently, then we would say that *A* had broken his promise and is liable only for civil breach of contract. But if *A* never intended to supply *B* with the widgets from the start (if, as Schmidt puts it, *A* received the money 'with an aim to swindle')[14], then we would say that *A* had deceived *B* and stolen from him. Conceptually, the distinction is clear, but in terms of proof, it can be quite elusive.

Finally, criminal or quasi-criminal sanctions are frequently used in response to the violation of certain kinds of promises to uphold the law. For example, witnesses promise to tell the truth on the witness stand, public officials promise to uphold the constitution and laws of their jurisdiction, and members of the military promise to uphold the Code of Military Justice. If such witnesses, officials, or members of the military fail to live up to their promises, they can be prosecuted for perjury, subjected to impeachment, or court-martialed, as the case may be.

A similar dynamic occurs in the realm of regulatory law. As we shall see in Chapter 20, persons engaged in regulated industries—such as mining, operating a warehouse, and selling real estate—frequently promise to be bound by the statutes and regulations applicable to that industry, often as a condition for obtaining a permit or license or other government benefit. Even members of the general public, when they apply for permits to fish or hunt, are sometimes required to make an explicit promise to abide by certain applicable rules and regulations. In such contexts, it seems, the moral wrongfulness of the offender's conduct derives not only from the wrongfulness of the underlying substantive violation or the official's disobedience to the applicable law, but also from the offender's breach of the obligation to keep a promise.

There is, however, an important point to be made about such schemes. In assessing the wrongfulness of such promise-breaking, we need to consider whether and to what extent the promiser was obligated or compelled to make the promise in the first place. For example, a witness who is subpoenaed to testify in a court proceeding will not be permitted to testify unless she first

Another, tragic, instance in which criminal penalties were used for breach of employment contracts was during the Jim Crow Era in the South, when certain states enacted racially-motivated statutes that imposed criminal penalties for breach of employment contract, and then applied these statutes almost exclusively to freedmen. *Ibid* at 647.

[14] *Ibid* at 703–04.

promises to tell the truth. Similarly, many regulatory schemes *require* an applicant to make a promise to uphold the law before he may be granted a license or permit to engage in some regulated activity.[15] Assuming, as it seems reasonable to do, that the moral obligation to keep a promise obtained in such a manner is weaker than the moral obligation to keep a promise obtained without such compulsion, it follows that the moral wrongfulness associated with *breaking* a promise made in such circumstances should also be regarded as less serious.

[15] Douglas Husak, in critiquing an earlier work of mine, has emphasized the 'adhesive' or 'take-it-or-leave-it' nature of such promises. Douglas Husak, '*Malum Prohibitum* and Retributivism' in RA Duff and Stuart P Green, *Defining Crimes: Essays on the Special Part of the Criminal Law* (Oxford: OUP, 2005) 65, 84. See discussion below in ch. 20.

10

Disobedience

Having considered the concepts of cheating, deception, stealing, coercion, exploitation, disloyalty, and promise-breaking, we come now to the discussion of our final moral norm, that against disobedience. This is undoubtedly the most controversial of the moral norms that we are considering. Many readers will be skeptical that disobedience to the law is a form of moral wrongfulness in the first place, let alone the kind that should justify penal sanctions. My goal in this section is to dispel some of this skepticism, and to make the case that disobedience to the law is a potentially relevant consideration in assessing the moral content of certain white-collar and regulatory crimes.

1. THE PRIMA FACIE MORAL OBLIGATION TO OBEY THE LAW

In thinking about the supposed moral wrongfulness of disobedience, one obvious question is: disobedience to what or whom? We can speak about disobedience to persons and institutions—eg to parents, judges, or Senate committees—as well as of disobedience to laws, principles, norms, and to the state generally. (We saw a similar dichotomy in the context of disloyalty, which, I argued, can be directed to both persons and principles.) For simplicity's sake, I will focus here primarily on the putative wrongfulness of disobeying laws, although we will at times speak as well of the putative wrongfulness of disobeying courts, administrative agencies, government officials, and the like.

In order for disobedience to the law to be morally wrong, there must be some moral obligation to obey the law that is breached. But to say this is merely to restate the real issue: namely, is there a moral obligation to obey the law and, if so, what accounts for that obligation? Given its centrality to our system of law, it is not surprising that this question has generated a voluminous and complex body of philosophical theory. While Plato and Hobbes both seem to have argued for an absolute duty to obey the law,[1] the modern

---

[1] Thomas Hobbes (Edwin Curley, ed.), *Leviathan: With Selected Variants from the Latin Edition of 1668* (Indianapolis, IN: Hachett Publishing (1994); Plato, 'Crito', in Edith Hamilton and Huntington Cairns (eds.) & Hugh Tredennick (trans.) *The Collected Dialogues* (Princeton: Princeton University Press, 1961) 27.

view is that, if there is a moral obligation to obey the law at all, it is a limited, prima facie, obligation, one that applies only when laws are 'just' and when such obligation is not overridden by competing moral claims.[2]

For example, it could not seriously be contended that there was a moral obligation to obey the fugitive slave laws (which made it a crime to harbor escaped slaves) or the Nuremberg Laws of 1935 (which, among other things, forbade marriage and extramarital relations between Germans and Jews). Indeed, there is a compelling argument that, where it would be unjust to follow a particular law or legal regime, there is a moral obligation to *disobey*.[3] Moreover, there are obviously cases of justification or 'necessity' or 'choice of evils' in which—because of extraordinary circumstances—one has no moral obligation to obey (and may even have an obligation to disobey) a law that would otherwise be considered just.[4]

Our concern here, however, is neither with the question of obedience to unjust laws nor with cases of necessity, but rather with the question of obedience to presumably just white-collar and regulatory laws in non-exceptional circumstances. This is not to deny that there are penal statutes that are unjust, or that there are any readily identifiable conclusive means for distinguishing between just and unjust laws. Rather, I shall simply assume that some regulatory and white-collar crime laws are just, and ask whether they entail any moral obligation to obey.

Social Contract Theory

Since Locke,[5] the most commonly offered theory of why citizens are obligated to obey the law has been the social contract theory—the idea that 'a citizen is obligated to obey the law because he has consented to the government in a manner that includes a promise to abide by its decisions.'[6] As Kent Greenawalt has described:

The government derives its authority to coerce from consent, and citizens are bound to comply so long as the government acts within the authority they have conferred.

---

[2] See MBE Smith, 'Is There a Prima Facie Obligation to Obey the Law?' (1973) 82 *Yale Law Journal* 950, 951. For a helpful overview of the subject and a revision of his earlier views, see MBE Smith, 'The Duty to Obey,' in Dennis Patterson (ed.), *A Companion to Philosophy of Law and Legal Theory* (Oxford: Blackwell, 1999), at 465.

[3] See, eg Martin Luther King, Jr, *Why We Can't Wait* (New York: Harper & Row, 1963) 77, 84; Michael Walzer, 'The Duty to Disobey', in *Obligations: Essays on Disobedience, War, and Citizenship* (Cambridge, Mass.: Harvard University Press, 1970); J Roland Pennock and John W Chapman, (eds.), *Political and Legal Obligation: Nomos XII* (New York: Atherton Press, 1970).

[4] See, eg Kent Greenawalt, *Conflicts of Law and Morality* (New York: OUP, 1987) 286–310; George Fletcher, *Rethinking Criminal Law* (Boston: Little, Brown, 1978), at § 10.2.

[5] John Locke (Thomas P Peardon ed.) *The Second Treatise on Government* (Indianapolis, IN: Bobbs Merrill, 1952; orig. publ. 1690), 54–70.

[6] Kent Greenawalt, 'Promise, Benefit, and Need: Ties that Bind Us to the Law' (1984) 18 *Georgia Law Review* 727, 733; Greenawalt (n 4 above, at 62).

On this account, a person's obligation to obey is based on his autonomous commitment to act in accord with the law: obligation derives from promise.[7]

Despite its longevity, however, the social contract theory is viewed by many commentators as fundamentally flawed. Its basic factual predicate—that citizens consent to the authority of their government—is, at least with respect to most ordinary persons, simply unsound.[8] As Greenawalt has said, 'many persons do apparently have promissory obligations to obey laws and other rules but . . . on no plausible account have all or nearly all citizens or residents of liberal democracies promised to obey.'[9]

There have been various attempts to salvage the theory. It has been suggested, for example, that simply remaining in one's country, receiving government benefits, or voting might constitute a form of consent to be governed.[10] But, on reflection, none of these proposals is adequate to support a generalizable obligation to obey the law. Remaining in one's country is not sufficient to create consent because, it is claimed, emigration is not for most people a serious option, and those who could leave their homeland tend to stay more out of convenience and personal ties than any particular endorsement of their government.[11] Likewise, receiving government benefits does not necessarily entail consent because many government benefits (such as police and military protection, and various forms of infrastructure) cannot be refused, and even when benefits can be refused, they continue to be received 'even when their preferred government is overturned by domestic revolution or foreign invasion.'[12] Finally, the obligation to obey the law would not be very widely shared if government participation were a necessary prerequisite, since many citizens do not vote, and those who do are limited in their choices.[13]

Duty of Fair Play

Partly in response to such problems has come a second influential theory—originally suggested by HLA Hart,[14] and developed by John Rawls in his early writing[15] and others[16]—which concerns the so-called duty of fair play. Unlike

---

[7] Greenawalt (n 6 above, at 733).

[8] See A John Simmons, *Moral Principles and Political Obligations* (New Jersey: Princeton University Press, 1979), 75–100.

[9] Greenawalt (n 4 above, at 62–63); see also Joseph Raz, *The Authority of Law: Essays on Law and Morality* (Oxford: OUP, 1979) 239 (making similar point).

[10] David Hume, 'Of the Original Contract,' in *Essays: Moral Political and Literary* (Indianapolis, IN: Liberty Classics, 1985) 465.   [11] *Ibid*; Greenawalt (n 6 above, at 737).

[12] *Ibid* at 738.

[13] See, eg A John Simmons, 'Consent, Free Choice, and Democratic Government' (1984) 18 *Georgia Law Review* 791, 800; Greenawalt (n 6 above, at 738). An argument might also be made that it is perverse to require citizens to choose, in effect, between exercising their right to vote and assuming an obligation to obey the law. *Ibid*.

[14] HLA Hart, 'Are There Any Natural Rights?' (1955) 64 *Philosophical Review* 175.

[15] John Rawls, 'Obligation and the Duty of Fair Play,' in Sidney Hook (ed.), *Law and Philosophy* (New York: NYU Press, 1964) 3.

[16] See, eg ADM Walker, 'Political Obligation and the Argument from Gratitude' (1988) 17 *Philosophy & Public Affairs* 191, 196; see also Ronald Dworkin, *Law's Empire* (Cambridge,

the social contract or promissory obligation theory, the fair play theory does not rest on the questionable premise that citizens have promised to obey the law. Instead, it suggests that the benefits citizens choose to receive from their government create in them a duty of fair play to their fellow citizens, a duty that includes the obligation to obey the laws that govern their lives together.[17] Citizens who break the law violate this duty by unfairly exploiting the law-abidingness of their fellow citizens.

Notice the difference between the duty of fair play argument referred to here and the related concept of cheating discussed above. The claim that I made previously was that, in certain specific cases, the criminal law punishes people who break rules for the purpose of gaining an unfair advantage over others with whom they are in a cooperative relationship.[18] The very different claim being assessed here is that *all* law-breaking involves a violation of the duty of fair play.

As support for a generalized obligation to obey the law, the duty of fair play is inadequate. There are two basic problems. First, the duty of fair play theory, like the promissory obligation theory itself, rests on the questionable premise that citizens always voluntarily accept the benefits that governments confer.[19] Secondly, as Feinberg and others have argued, there are many cases—such as 'running a red light on empty streets late at night under perfect conditions of visibility'—in which violating the law fails to take advantage of anyone.[20]

2. An Inductive Approach to Assessing the Moral Wrongfulness of Disobedience

So far, we have been approaching the moral obligation to obey the law by seeking a more basic moral obligation upon which the obligation to obey might rest. That is, we have been proceeding deductively, from first principles.

MA: Harvard University Press, 1986) 167–216 (suggesting that the obligations of citizens arise from their having received benefits of their community).

[17] Greenawalt (n 6 above, at 756).   [18] See Chapter 4 above.

[19] See, eg Joseph Raz, 'The Obligation to Obey: Revision and Tradition' (1984) 1 *Journal of Law, Ethics & Public Policy* 139, 152. Other criticisms can be found in Greenawalt (n 6 above, at 756) ('[I]n even the most free political communities, neither participation nor the acceptance of many benefits is voluntary. Many important legal duties do not depend on the voluntary acceptance of benefits, and many benefits cannot be refused.').

[20] Joel Feinberg, 'The Right to Disobey' (1989) 87 *Michigan Law Review* 1690, 1694. As indicated by Feinberg's example, the argument against the moral obligation to obey the law frequently turns on the apparent absence of harm. In addition to Feinberg, critics such as Joseph Raz, MBE Smith, and Donald Regan all have sought to show that there is no independent general moral obligation to obey the law by pointing to acts of disobedience that do not appear to cause any harm. See Raz (n 9 above, at 237–42) (conceding that some people have moral reasons to obey the law, as in cases where a person's disobedience would set a bad example for others, but insisting that, unless an act of disobedience is detected, there is no independent moral reason to obey the law); Smith (n 2 above, at 956–60; 969–73); Donald Regan, 'Law's Halo' (Autumn 1986) *Social Philosophy & Policy* 15, 16, 24. But such arguments are ultimately unpersuasive. As discussed in ch. 3 above, an act need not cause harm for it to be viewed as morally wrongful.

But this approach has proved troublesome: we have been unable to settle on any more fundamental principles to which the moral obligation to obey can be reduced.

Rather than proceeding deductively, I now want to try a different approach: I want to show through what is essentially a process of induction that we often do in fact regard disobedience to the law as a morally wrongful act. I focus on four kinds of empirical 'data': (1) the traditional distinction in the criminal law between *malum in se* and *malum prohibitum*; (2) empirical studies of why people obey the law; (3) the moral psychology of law-breaking; and (4) the way the criminal law deals with recidivism.

Malum in Se and *Malum Prohibitum*

As a first piece of evidence that law-breaking is regarded as a morally wrongful act, I want to examine the traditional common law distinction between *mala in se* and *mala prohibita* crimes. This distinction will also provide a useful analytic tool for the discussion that follows.

In its earliest usage, the term *mala in se* referred to criminal acts that derived their wrongfulness from a source higher than civil authority—from God, or natural law. The term *mala prohibita*, by contrast, referred to crimes that derived their wrongfulness from their being prohibited by civil authorities, such as the king, or more generally, by the positive law.[21]

The modern meaning is somewhat changed. The term *mala in se* now generally refers to criminalized acts that would be viewed by society as morally wrongful regardless of whether they were prohibited by law.[22] (Typical examples are murder, rape, and theft.) The term *mala prohibita*, by contrast, refers to acts or omissions that are wrong only (or primarily) because they have been proscribed by law.[23] (Examples typically given are storing hazardous waste materials with an incorrect permit, possessing a gun without a license, and selling unregistered securities.[24]) The distinction, which is close to Feinberg's distinction between 'primary' and 'derivative' crimes,[25] remains potentially significant in a number of practical contexts.[26]

---

[21] On the history of the distinction generally, see Nancy Travis Wolfe, '*Mala In Se*: A Disappearing Doctrine?' (1981) 19 *Criminology* 131, 132; H Wechsler, 'The Distinction Between *Mala Prohibita* and *Mala In Se* in Criminal Law' (1930) 30 *Columbia Law Review* 74, 74–76; Richard L Gray, Note, 'Eliminating the (Absurd) Distinction Between *Malum In Se* and *Malum Prohibitum* Crimes' (1955) 73 *Washington University Law Quarterly* 1370; Michael L Travers, Note, 'Mistake of Law in *Mala Prohibita* Crimes' (1995) 62 *University of Chicago Law Review* 1301.

[22] *Black's Law Dictionary* (St. Paul, MN: West Publishing Co., 2001) (defining *mala in se* offenses as 'wrongs in themselves, acts morally wrong; offenses against conscience').

[23] *Ibid* (defining *mala prohibita* offenses as 'wrong only as forbidden by law').

[24] See Travers (n 21 above, at 1301 n 3, 1323); Wayne LaFave, *Criminal Law* (4th edn., St. Paul, Minn.: West, 2003), at § 1.6(b).

[25] See Joel Feinberg, *Harm to Others* (New York: OUP, 1987) 19–20.

[26] See Stuart P Green, 'Why It's a Crime to Tear the Tag Off a Mattress: Overcriminalization and the Moral Content of Regulatory Offenses' (1997) 46 *Emory Law Journal* 1533, 1572 n 124.

The term *mala prohibita* has sometimes been used to refer to a collection of crimes that are supposedly devoid of moral content. Blackstone, as much as anyone, is responsible for this usage. He speaks in the *Commentaries* of *mala prohibita* offenses as involving no 'moral offence, or sin'; such offenses, he says, involve no 'moral guilt'; with such crimes, he says, our 'conscience' is not 'concerned.'[27]

As in so many areas of our jurisprudence (whether for better or worse), Blackstone's understanding has had a great influence. Following Blackstone, various commentators have viewed *mala prohibita* offenses as (in Leo Martinez' phrase) 'carr[ying] no moral baggage.'[28] They have suggested that *mala prohibita* offenses involve no 'sin' and therefore should not even be referred to as 'crimes'[29]; that in the case of *mala prohibita*, 'the moral standards of the community' are simply not relevant.[30] This is also the way in which various social scientists have used the term.[31]

There are several problems with such usage, however. First, it defies the literal meaning of the term *mala prohibita*—ie, '*wrongs* that are prohibited.' Secondly, it is at odds with the original historical meaning of the term, as discussed above. Thirdly, such usage seems to beg the important question whether such offenses—and the disobedience to the law that they involve—really are morally neutral.

Indeed, Ronald Dworkin (though avoiding the *mala in se/mala prohibita* terminology itself) has criticized HLA Hart on just this point. Responding to Hart's argument that the existence of certain apparently *mala prohibita*-type offenses such as failing to comply with the English rail transport regulations shows that the criminal law need not apply exclusively to morally wrongful acts, Dworkin says that Hart has failed to distinguish between

two grounds on which a violation of law might be morally wrong. It might be wrong to break a law because the act the law condemns (killing, for example) is wrong in itself. Or it might be wrong, even though the act condemned is not wrong in itself, just because the law forbids it. Perhaps it is doubtful whether it is wise or fair for England

[27] See William Blackstone, *Commentaries* (Philadelphia: University of Pennsylvania Press, 1996) at 57.
[28] See Leo Martinez 'Taxes, Morals, and Legitimacy' (1994) *Baylor Law Review* 521, 524 (explicitly following Blackstone on this point).
[29] See Rollin M Perkins & Ronald N Boyce, *Criminal Law* (3rd edn., Mineola, NY: Foundation, 1982) 886.
[30] See Henry M Hart, 'The Aims of the Criminal Law' (1958) 23 *Law & Contemporary Problems* 401, 420 ('When a criminal enactment proscribes conduct which is *malum in se*, such as murder or manslaughter . . . the moral standards of the community are available always as a guide in the resolution of the indeterminacies, and there is a minimum of unfairness when doubt is resolved against a particular defendant. This guidance is missing when the proscribed conduct is merely *malum prohibitum*.').
[31] See, eg Johannes Andenaes, 'The General Preventive Effects of Punishment' (1996) 114 *University of Pennsylvania Law Review* 949, 957; Jack P Gibbs, 'The Sociology of Law and Normative Phenomena' (1966) 31 *American Sociological Review* 315, 325; Gordon P Waldo and Theodore G Chiricos, 'Perceived Penal Sanction and Self-Reported Criminality: A Neglected Approach to Deterrence Research' (1972) 19 *Social Problems* 522, 524.

to nationalize the railroads; it might still be true that once the law is passed everyone has a moral obligation to obey it.[32]

Thus, the better usage of the term *mala prohibita* is to refer to acts that are, as Jerome Hall said, 'immoral . . . because the actor knows they are legally forbidden.'[33]

---

[32] Ronald Dworkin, *Taking Rights Seriously* (Cambridge, MA: Harvard University Press, 1977). See also AP Simester and ATH Smith, 'Criminalization and the Role of Theory,' in AP Simester & ATH Smith (eds), *Harm and Culpability* (Oxford: OUP, 1996) 4–5 ('Certain crimes *mala prohibita* co-ordinate society by settling which one of alternative possible ways may be adopted in order to satisfy some valuable but more general goal. Such crimes thereby acquire moral force as a conduit to the achievement of that indeterminate goal.').

[33] Jerome Hall, *General Principles of Criminal Law* (2nd edn., Indianapolis: Bobbs-Merrill, 1960) 374 (emphasis removed). This view appears consistent with Aquinas' understanding, as described in Philip Soper, 'Legal Theory and the Problem of Definition' (1983) 50 *University of Chicago Law Review* 1170, 1182 (Under Aquinas' view, 'the merely *malum prohibitum* becomes *malum in se* by virtue of the lawmaker's decision.').

Even so, there remain some serious conceptual problems with the *malum in se/malum prohibitum* distinction. First, it is difficult to find an example of a pure *malum in se* crime—one that is wrong 'without *any* regard to the fact of its being noticed or punished by' law. If there were no legal culture at all, certain acts—such as murder and rape—would still be viewed as morally wrongful. But, given that we do have a legal culture, our view of such acts inevitably reflects that fact. As discussed above, the criminal law serves an important 'educational' or 'socializing' function. In our culture, children often learn that conduct is wrong at the same time they learn that it is illegal. Indeed, the earliest explanation many parents give their questioning child regarding the wrongfulness of certain conduct is 'because you could go to jail for it.' We can hardly think of murder or rape or theft without reference to our legal culture. The acts that constitute these crimes thus seem to derive some part of their moral character from the fact that they have been criminalized.

Secondly, there are also difficulties in finding pure *malum prohibitum* offenses—those that are wrong *only* because they are proscribed by law. Consider a law that requires doctors to have a license to practice medicine. The primary purpose of such laws is presumably to protect patients from being treated by persons who are not qualified to practice medicine. Obviously, an unqualified person who practices medicine without a license has done something wrongful independent of the licensing requirement—namely, he has endangered the health of his patients. But what about an otherwise fully qualified doctor who simply fails to obtain, or renew, his license and thereby violates the law? Has he committed an act that is wrongful for any reason other than that it is proscribed by law? One possibility is that a violation of this sort would make it more difficult for the government to regulate the medical profession. One can surmise that medical licensing agencies typically maintain a database of all the doctors practicing medicine in a particular locale. If a public health emergency were to arise, all of the doctors in the database would be notified. But a doctor who is not licensed would not appear in the database and would therefore not be notified of the emergency. As a consequence, the health of his patients might be endangered. In such a case, one might say that even the qualified doctor's failure to obtain a license was wrongful for a reason other than simply that it was in violation of the law.

The important point is that most crimes seem to have both *mala in se* and *mala prohibita* qualities. Indeed, the most persistent criticism of the *malum in se/malum prohibitum* distinction has been that it is notoriously difficult to determine the category into which many crimes fit. Insider trading, selling cigarettes to minors, drug possession, gambling, and prostitution are all examples of crimes that may or may not be *mala in se*, depending on how society views the moral status of the underlying acts. Given such difficulties, there is thus a good argument that the distinction should be—at least for practical purposes—abandoned entirely. Despite these difficulties, however, the concepts retain analytic power as a means of distinguishing between two kinds of moral content. But the distinction needs some refinement. As I shall use the term here, *mala prohibita* will refer to a cluster of related kinds or qualities of moral content that are derived from, or

Empirical Studies of Why People Obey the Law

In the preceding section, the concept of *malum prohibitum* was offered as one piece of evidence that the criminal law has traditionally viewed law-breaking as a morally wrongful act. In what follows, I want to examine the social science evidence concerning the way in which people view the morality of law-breaking.

Social scientists have conducted numerous studies designed to discover the factors that motivate people to obey or disobey the law and legal authorities. Although early studies focused primarily on the deterrent effects of the threat of sanctions,[34] more recent studies have sought to determine the extent to which people obey the law 'voluntarily'—as a result of factors such as their own personal moral beliefs or the opinion of peers.[35] To the extent that these studies have involved *mala prohibita*-type crimes, they provide further support for the view that the violation of the law itself is viewed as having significant moral content.[36]

---

defined by, acts being made illegal or criminal: (1) An act can be morally wrongful because it has been defined as such by the law. For example, possessing a dangerous thing without a license can be wrong at the possessing/inchoate stage because it violates a prophylactic norm that defines the action as wrong at that stage; (2) Our legal culture also helps to define what we regard as a social harm. We need a legal definition of death, for example, in order to state exhaustively what we will regard as a wrongful killing; (3) Acts can also be harmful *to* our legal culture as a protected interest. Our political and legal institutions are harmed when they are subject to widespread or flagrant or repetitive acts of disobedience.

[34] See, eg Franklin E Zimring and Gordon Hawkins, *Deterrence: The Legal Threat in Crime Control* (Chicago: University of Chicago Press, 1973); Alfred Blumstein, et al, *Deterrence and Incapacitation: Estimating the Effects of Criminal Sanctions on Crime Rates* (Washington, DC: National Academy of Sciences, 1978); Jack P Gibbs, 'On Crime, Punishment, and Deterrence' (1968) 49 *Social Science Quarterly* 515; Charles R Tittle, 'Crime Rates and Legal Sanctions' (1969) 16 *Social Problems* 409. In general, these studies indicate that, the greater the threat of legal punishment, the lower the incidence of crime.

[35] See, eg Robert F Meier and Weldon T Johnson, 'Deterrence as Social Control: The Legal and Extralegal Production of Conformity' (1977) 42 *American Sociological Review* 292; J Richard Eiser, 'Evaluation of Choice-Dilemma Alternatives' (1976) 15 *Journal of Social Clinical Psychology* 51; Raymond Paternoster, et al, 'Perceived Risk and Social Control: Do Sanctions Really Deter?' (1984) 17 *Law and Society Review* 457; Harold G Grasmick and Donald E Green, 'Legal Punishment, Social Disapproval and Internalization as Inhibitors of Illegal Behavior' (1980) 71 *Journal of Criminal Law & Criminology* 325; Paul Robinson and John Darley, *Justice, Liability and Blame: Community Views and the Criminal Law* (Boulder, Col.: Westview, 1995) 201, 217–18.

[36] Early on, some scholars had assumed that, whereas people are deterred from committing *mala in se* crimes by their personal sense of morality, the only thing that keeps them from committing *mala prohibita* crimes is the external threat of sanctions. See, eg Johannes Andenaes, 'The General Preventive Effects of Punishment' (1966) 114 *University of Pennsylvania Law Review* 949; Franklin Zimring, *Perspectives on Deterrence* (Washington, DC: Nat'l Inst. of Mental Health, Center for Studies of Crime and Delinquency, 1971). In light of subsequent studies discussed herein, however, this assumption appears to be unwarranted. In fact, it now appears that, at least for 'strongly socialized' individuals, the threat of sanctions is essentially irrelevant, even in the case of *mala prohibita*-type violations. For such individuals, moral values and peer pressure are such powerful inhibitors that they preclude the possibility that the motivation to break the law will even be felt.

Perhaps the most comprehensive such study was conducted by Tom R Tyler.[37] This study, involving 1,575 randomly selected residents of Chicago, tested the views of participants regarding six offenses: illegal parking, speeding (driving over 55 mph on the highway), making enough noise to disturb neighbors, littering, drunk driving, and stealing inexpensive items from a store.[38] Participants were asked, among other things, whether breaking each of these laws was morally 'very wrong,' 'somewhat wrong,' 'not very wrong,' or 'not wrong at all.'[39] In each case, breaking the law was considered morally very wrong or somewhat wrong by a large proportion of the respondents: 96 per cent in the case of disturbing neighbors (very wrong by 61 per cent); 96 per cent for littering (very wrong by 63 per cent); 100 per cent for drunk driving (very wrong by 95 per cent); 84 per cent for speeding (very wrong by 39 per cent); 99 per cent for shoplifting (very wrong by 92 per cent); and 86 per cent for parking illegally (very wrong by 37 per cent). As Tyler summarizes his findings: 'Citizens seem to view breaking laws as a violation of their personal morality. Almost all the respondents felt it wrong to break any of the six laws studied.' And this is true regardless of whether the offenses were presumptively *mala in se* (like shoplifting) or *mala prohibita* (like parking illegally).

Assuming that these studies accurately gauge people's views,[40] their findings are, for our purposes, quite striking. What they seem to indicate is that many people view both *mala in se* and *mala prohibita*-type violations as morally wrongful.[41] These studies thus provide empirical evidence that seems to undermine the suggestion that *mala prohibita*-type offenses are—at least in the mind of the public—devoid of moral content.

---

[37] Tom R Tyler, *Why People Obey the Law* (New Haven: Yale University Press, 1990).

[38] These laws were 'chosen to represent the range of laws people deal with in their everyday lives,' *Ibid* at 40. The survey consisted of two stages. In the first stage, telephone interviews lasting approximately 25 minutes each were held with 1,575 respondents. A randomly selected subset of 804 respondents was then reinterviewed a year later. *Ibid* at 8.

[39] *Ibid* at 44. The questionnaire that Tyler used indicates that participants were asked whether particular acts of lawbreaking were 'wrong', *Ibid* at 190 (Appendix A). Tyler, however, in characterizing his own study, says that participants were asked whether particular acts of lawbreaking were 'morally wrong.' *Ibid* at 44. It is unclear whether in fact participants understood the term 'wrong' to mean 'morally wrong' or whether any significance should be attached to this difference in terminology.

[40] For a skeptical view of 'what, if anything, one can learn by asking people questions like why they obey laws,' see Alan Hyde, 'The Concept of Legitimation in the Sociology of Law' (1983) 1983 *Wisconsin Law Review* 379, 393–95 & n 28 (discussing RE Nisbett and TD Wilson, 'Telling More Than We Can Know: Verbal Reports on Mental Processes' (1977) 84 *Psychological Review* 23).

[41] Tyler's findings are, at least with respect to 'strongly socialized' individuals, consistent with studies conducted by Grasmick and Green, above n 35, at 328 (moral values and peer pressure are such powerful inhibitors that they preclude the possibility of most actors ever feeling the motivation to break the law), and Matthew Silberman, 'Toward a Theory of Criminal Deterrence' (1976) 41 *American Sociological Review* 442 (maintaining that 'strongly socialized individuals (ie those who measure high on the morality index) are less likely to [commit both *mala in se* and *mala prohibita* offenses] than individuals who are less morally committed').

Disobedience and the 'Reactive Emotions'

Moral philosophers and developmental psychologists have long viewed human emotions such as regret, guilt, and resentment as significant indicators of moral content.[42] Psychologist William Damon, for example, has said that:

Positive feelings like empathy, sympathy, admiration, and self-esteem, and negative feelings like anger, outrage, shame, and guilt are all essential parts of our moral reactions to situations . . . Often it is the perception of a uniquely moral sentiment like guilt or responsibility that makes us first aware of the moral demands of certain life situations.[43]

Legal scholars, particularly retributivists, have seized on the idea of the reactive emotions as a rich source of insight into the theory of punishment, a theory in which criminal sanctions are viewed as a form of moral communication between and among the state, the criminal, and the community. Samuel Pillsbury, for example, has suggested that 'the determination of deserved punishment should be reconceived as a moral-emotive dynamic involving outrage at the offender's acts of disrespect . . . and caring for the offender's positive moral qualities.'[44] Michael Moore, in a narrower context, has argued that the fact that completed crimes are accompanied by a greater amount of guilt and resentment than attempts tends to suggest that completed crimes involve a greater degree of moral culpability, and thus should be punished more severely, than unsuccessful attempts.[45]

My purpose here is not to construct or defend a theory of punishment based on the reactive emotions. I make no claims as to whether guilt or resentment are necessary or sufficient conditions for moral blame. I recognize that there are obviously cases in which persons either fail to have (or express) the appropriate reactive attitudes (a person suffers from an asocial pathology, for

---

[42] The classic discussion is Joseph Butler's 'Upon Resentment, and Forgiveness of Injuries', in *The Works of Joseph Butler* (Bristol: Thoemmes Press, 1997) vol. 2, at 112 (originally published in 1897). The most important modern treatment is P F Strawson's British Academy lecture, 'Freedom and Resentment,' in P F Strawson, *Freedom and Resentment and Other Essays* (New York: Harper & Row, 1974) 1–25 (arguing that responsibility needs to be understood in the context of a central range of sentiments, or 'reactive attitudes,' that we are subject to in our dealings with each other, including, in the specifically moral case, indignation and disapprobation). For a detailed study of the reactive emotions, see R Jay Wallace, *Responsibility and the Moral Sentiments* (Cambridge: Harvard University Press, 1994).

[43] William Damon, *The Moral Child: Nurturing Children's Natural Moral Growth* (New York: Atlantic Monthly Press, 1988), 13.

[44] Samuel H Pillsbury, 'Emotional Justice: Moralizing the Passions of Criminal Punishment' (1989) 74 *Cornell Law Review* 655, 657.

[45] Michael S Moore, 'The Independent Moral Significance of Wrongdoing' (1994) 5 *Journal of Contemporary Legal Issues* 237, 267–71. For other discussions of the reactive emotions in the context of criminal law, see Peter Arenella, 'Convicting the Morally Blameless: Reassessing the Relationship Between Legal and Moral Accountability' (1992) 39 *UCLA Law Review* 1511, 1530, 1537–39; Jeffrie G Murphy and Jean Hampton, *Forgiveness and Mercy* (New York: CUP, 1988); Jean Hampton, 'Correcting Harms Versus Righting Wrongs: The Goal of Retribution' (1992) 39 *UCLA Law Review* 1659; Michael S Moore, 'Causation and the Excuses' (1985) 73 *California Law Review* 1091, 1144.

example), or have inappropriate reactive attitudes (such as where a person suffers from feelings of guilt and resentment brought on by neurosis).[46]

Instead, I merely mean to suggest that, in considering the claim that disobedience is a form of moral wrongfulness, it is appropriate to ask whether such acts tend to be accompanied by feelings of regret and guilt on the part of the lawbreaker, or resentment on the part of others. If the answer is no, then one might well infer that moral content is slight, or even absent. But if the answer is yes, then one might be justifiably skeptical about the claim of moral neutrality.

Unfortunately, there do not appear to be any empirical studies concerning the extent to which the reactive emotions attach themselves to instances of rule-breaking. The best we can do is rely on our intuitions, which, I suspect, will vary widely from reader to reader. Consider the case of a driver who violates a city ordinance by slowing but not stopping at a stop sign at an otherwise deserted intersection at 3 a.m. Would the driver feel guilt about such conduct? And would an observer (say, one flying overhead in an airplane) feel resentment toward the driver? The reader may find it at least plausible that, even in such situations, some psychologically healthy people would feel guilt or resentment, as the case may be.

Perhaps a more persuasive argument can be made in the closely analogous context of religious proscriptions. Some religious laws (eg the commandments prohibiting stealing and murdering) have a strong ethical component and might be analogized to *mala in se*. That is, commission of such acts is regarded as morally wrongful regardless of their being prohibited by religious law. Other religious laws (eg the Jewish dietary laws of *kashruth* and the Mormon rule prohibiting the consumption of alcohol and coffee) might be analogized to *mala prohibita*. These acts seem to derive most of their moral content from the fact that they are prohibited, rather than from the wrongfulness of the underlying act. Commission of such acts is regarded as morally wrongful primarily because such acts are prohibited.

What is important to recognize, however, is that (within the relevant communities) the violation of such *mala prohibita*-type religious laws is regarded as morally wrongful. Religious sources repeatedly speak of both *mala prohibita* and *mala in se* violations in the same language of moral condemnation. And violation of such non-ethically based ritual or religious laws (say, an observant Jew's eating pork or shellfish) is likely to cause guilt on the part of the (otherwise observant) actor and resentment on the part of third parties within the relevant community—just as surely (although perhaps not to the same degree) as the violation of ethically-based rules regarding murder and theft.[47]

---

[46] On the distinction between 'moral' (or appropriate) and 'amoral' (or inappropriate) reactive emotions, see Pillsbury (n 44 above, at 673); Fletcher (n 4 above, at 483); Yoram Shachar, 'The Fortuitous Gap in Law and Morality' (Summer/Fall 1987) *Criminal Justice Ethics* 16–17.

[47] To focus on their *malum prohibitum*-type character is not to deny that these rules might have *malum in se*-type justifications as well. For example, many commentators have attempted

The Treatment of Recidivism

So far we have been looking for evidence that our society views lawbreaking as morally wrongful by considering those cases in which conduct that would not otherwise be regarded as wrongful becomes wrongful as a result of its being prohibited. But there is also another context in which society views law-breaking as morally wrongful, and that is when the lawbreaker is a recidivist.

Imagine that a certain amount of moral disapprobation is associated with a given offender's first violation of crime C. Now assume that the same offender commits C for a second time, and that crimes C_1 and C_2 are otherwise identical in terms of *mens rea*, motive, and harms caused. If we were to find that the moral disapprobation associated with the second occurrence of C was greater than that associated with the first, we should be able to infer that the later violation involved greater moral wrongfulness, and that the source of such moral wrongfulness was the offender's defiance of the law.

Unfortunately, there do not appear to be any empirical studies that measure public attitudes toward recidivism in this manner. In the absence of such studies, the best we can do is observe how recidivism has been treated by the criminal justice system. Frequently (and, controversially, in the case of draconian 'Three Strikes' statutes), habitual offenders do receive greater punishment than first offenders. One supposed justification for this is deterrence: the general view is that because the recidivist was not adequately deterred from engaging in criminal conduct the first time, punishment for subsequent offenses must be greater.[48] But there is also a sense, widely expressed by the courts, that, other things being equal, habitual offenders are more blameworthy, and hence deserving of more punishment, than first time offenders.[49] As the Supreme Court has said, we tend to think of 'the repetition of criminal conduct,' as 'aggravat[ing] [the offender's] guilt and justif[ying] heavier penalties'[50]—a view that has been echoed in dozens of subsequent state and lower federal court opinions.[51]

to justify the laws of *kashruth* by emphasizing the moral content of the requirement that food be 'clean' and that animals be treated in a 'humane' manner. Certainly these are significant aims. At the end of the day, however, it seems obvious that the moral content of violating the laws of *kashruth* has, for the observant Jew, a very different character from the moral content of simply eating food that is unhygienic or comes from an animal that has not been killed in a humane manner.

[48] See, eg *Ewing v California*, 538 US 11 (2003) (upholding California's Three Strikes law on such grounds).

[49] See Andrew von Hirsch, *Doing Justice: The Choice of Punishments* (New York: Hill and Wang, 1976) 85 (arguing that defendant who repeats an offense following conviction is 'more culpable, since he persisted in the behavior after having been forcefully censured for it through his prior punishment'). But note that von Hirsch has subsequently modified his views on this issue. See Andrew von Hirsch, 'Desert and Previous Convictions in Sentencing' (1981) 65 *Minnesota Law Review* 591, 600.

[50] *Graham v West Virginia*, 224 US 616, 623 (1912) (Hughes, J.) (upholding life sentence for an 'apparently incorrigible horsethief').

[51] See Green, (n 26 above, at 1595 n 207) (citing authorities); see also *Spencer v Texas*, 385 US 554, 571 (1967) (Warren, C.J., concurring and dissenting) (considering various rationales for enhanced penalties for recidivists, noting, among others, that: 'A man's prior crimes are thought to aggravate his guilt for subsequent crimes, and thus greater than usual retribution is warranted.').

I do not mean to suggest that this point is uncontroversial. There is certainly a reasonable argument that enhanced penalties for recidivists are redundant, and hence unfair, insofar as they punish repeat offenders for crimes for which they have already paid their debt to society.[52] For now I simply want to suggest the plausibility of the view that what distinguishes the first time and habitual offenders' acts is the amount of disobedience involved. The recidivist has been apprehended and convicted, and yet she persists in her lawbreaking. She refuses to comply with our laws regardless of the fact that she has been punished for doing so. The resentment (or guilt) that we (or the psychologically healthy recidivist) feel toward such acts is based in part on the resentment (or guilt) that we (or he) feel towards acts of disobedience.

3. CRIMINALIZING DISOBEDIENCE

To what extent does, or should, the putative wrongfulness of disobedience play a role in informing the criminal law? In a sense, every violation of law involves disobedience to the government or other lawful authority. But in the case of core *mala in se* offenses (at least for the non-recidivist), the moral content of such disobedience is trivial. For example, we punish murderers not because they violate the law (although the law certainly helps define what should count as murder), but because they violate the norm against unjustified killing. By contrast, the cases I am interested in here are those in which we punish conduct primarily because it involves disobedience to the law or lawful authority.

There are at two main categories of offense that come to mind in this connection. One category consists of parole and probation violations and criminal contempt, in which the defendant is punished primarily because his conduct constituted a violation of a court order, rather than for its underlying wrongfulness. In such cases, the harm is done to the court and the justice system. The second, and more controversial, category is that of regulatory violations. Here, offenders who engage in trivially harmful conduct, such as driving with an expired license, can be subject to criminal sanctions. Once again, the defendant's act would unlikely be regarded as wrongful absent the violation of law. It is this second kind of offense that will be considered in Chapter 20.

---

[52] See Markus Dubber, 'Recidivist Statutes as Arational Punishment' (1995) 43 *Buffalo Law Review* 689, 705 ('Repeat offender laws have long been challenged by retributivists on the grounds that they penalize an offender's insufficient obsequiousness and that they have nothing to do with the offender's moral desert as they punish her not for the present act, but for another act already committed.'); Fletcher, (n 4 above, at 465) ('If the family were an appropriate model for civil society, [Andrew von Hirsch] might be right. But (thank God) the family is not the model for liberal society . . . In a liberal society, based upon the rule of law, authority is not charismatic, but formal. Legislators, judges and law enforcement personnel occupy legally defined offices: they are not entitled to react to the 'persistent' criminal as though their personal authority were challenged.'); see also George P Fletcher, 'The Recidivist Premium' (Summer/Fall 1982) *Criminal Justice Ethics* 54, 57.

11

A Final Thought on Moral Wrongfulness

Our focus in Part II has been on the various distinct ways in which people commit wrongful acts. The attempt has been to think about each kind of wrong in isolation—separated both from harms and one another. But it is important to recognize that such concepts are not wholly separable, and that there is in fact a potential for overlap among them. In this concluding section, I want to say something about the nature of such overlap.

One of the problems we face in attempting to 'reconstruct' a list of basic moral norms is their malleability. Each of the concepts we have been dealing with is so rich in meaning that we may be tempted to try to express one norm in terms of others. Consider the following passage from Khaled Hosseini's bestselling novel of life in modern Afghanistan, *The Kite Runner*, in which the narrator's father, Baba, tells his son:

"[N]o matter what the mullah teaches, there is only one sin, only one. And that is theft. Every other sin is a variation of theft. . . .
"When you kill a man, you steal a life . . . . You steal his wife's right to a husband, rob his children of a father. When you tell a lie, you steal someone's right to the truth. When you cheat, you steal the right to fairness."[1]

In other words, Baba is saying that we do not need a differentiated set of moral norms to know what is the right way to behave; a single concept of 'theft,' or 'stealing,' is broad enough to encompass all of the other moral norms.

Now, whatever the literary merits of Hosseini's novel, and whatever the virtues of Baba's approach to the moral education of his son, such a method strikes me as rather poor philosophizing. It is certainly at odds with the approach I have been taking here, since it blurs precisely the kind of moral distinctions I have been trying to draw. To reduce so fertile and nuanced a set of norms to a single undifferentiated norm against stealing is to obscure the meaning of stealing, as well as that of killing, lying, and cheating.

Even a sophisticated legal theorist such as Charles Fried is not immune from such confusion. Consider his account of lying, which, he says, is wrong

---

[1] Khaled Hosseini, *The Kite Runner* (New York: Riverhead Books, 2003) 17–18.

because when I lie I set up a relation which is essentially exploitative. . . . Lying violates respect and is wrong, as is any breach of trust. Every lie is a broken promise [which] is made and broken at the same moment. Every lie necessarily implies—as does every assertion—an assurance, a warranty of its truth.[2]

Note that Fried describes one moral concept—lying—in terms of three others—exploitation, breach of trust, and promise-breaking. In a sense, Fried's method is the converse of Hosseini's: rather than reducing multiple distinct moral concepts to one, he takes one moral concept and expands it to several. From the perspective of moral theory, however, we would do better to try to preserve those distinctions that track the everyday way we think about our moral lives.

One of the best ways to determine whether a given moral norm deserves the kind of discrete analysis that I have recommended here is to consider the reactive emotions that its violation is likely to evoke.[3] Each violation certainly has the potential to bring about shame, guilt, or regret in the one who has deceived, cheated, stolen, coerced, exploited, been disloyal, or broken a promise; and to cause resentment, outrage, or anger in the one who has been deceived, cheated, coerced, exploited, or betrayed, had something stolen, or had a promise to him broken. But the quality of such reactive emotions will differ depending on which wrong has been committed. That is, such wrongs generally *feel* different from each other—a significant psychological phenomenon since differences in reactive emotions, though not conclusive, are usually a reliable indicator of differences in moral content.

[2] Charles Fried, *Right and Wrong* (Cambridge, Mass.: Harvard University Press, 1978) at 67.
[3] The concept of reactive emotions is discussed above in the text accompanying ch. 10 n 42.

PART III

FINDING THE MORAL CONTENT OF WHITE-COLLAR OFFENSES

In this, the final Part of the book, we examine the moral content of a collection of ten key white-collar offenses or offense-types: perjury, fraud, false statements, obstruction of justice, bribery, extortion, blackmail, insider trading, tax evasion, and a certain class of 'failure-to-comply' regulatory crimes. In most cases, our starting point will be the way in which such offenses are defined under the leading American federal statutes; though I have also endeavored to construct a more universal definition of such offenses, and to note where American and foreign law differ significantly. There is no attempt to be exhaustive in the description of moral content; a comprehensive account of just the harms caused by such crimes could easily fill several volumes. Instead, I want to use the three-part framework developed in Part I, and the discussion of moral norms developed in Part II, as a means to examine those aspects of such offenses that seem to me most interesting and problematic.

12

Perjury

At common law, perjury was considered one of the most odious of offenses.[1] According to William Hawkins, perjury 'is of all Crimes whatsoever the most Infamous and Detestable.'[2] Under the Code of Hammurabi, the Roman law, and the medieval law of France, the punishment for bearing false witness was death; in the colony of New York, punishment included branding the letter 'P' on the offender's forehead.[3] In recent studies of public attitudes toward crime, perjury continues to be viewed as a very serious offense.[4]

My aim in this section is to show exactly what it is that makes perjury morally wrong, and how the contours of such moral wrongfulness shape the contours of the legal doctrine by which the crime is defined. At the end of the section, I want to explain how an understanding of the underlying moral concept of 'lying' illuminates our understanding of the perjury case against Bill Clinton that was first mentioned in the Introduction.

1. The Moral Content of Perjury

Perjury, as defined by the leading US federal perjury statute,[5] and as interpreted by the courts, requires five basic elements: (1) an oath authorized by a law of the United States; (2) taken before a competent tribunal, officer, or person; and (3) a false statement; (4) willfully made; (5) as to facts material to a given proceeding.[6] The closely related crime of false declarations requires that

---

[1] Bennet L Gershman, The 'Perjury Trap' (1981) 129 *University of Pennsylvania Law Review* 624, 636. See also *United States v Carollo*, 30 F Supp 3, 6 (W D Mo 1939) (noting that for centuries perjury has been regarded as an offense involving 'moral turpitude'—an act that offends the moral code of mankind even in the absence of a prohibitive statute); Comment, 'Perjury: the Forgotten Offense' (1974) 65 *Journal of Criminal Law & Criminology* 361, 363 & n 37.

[2] William Hawkins, *A Treatise of the Pleas of the Crown* (London: J. Worrall, 1771; Ayer Company, 1972) vol. 1, at 172.

[3] Law Review Commission, State of New York 'A Study of Perjury,' (1935) Legislative Document 60.

[4] See Marvin Wolfgang, et al., (Bureau of Justice Statistics), *National Survey of Crime Severity* (Washington, DC: US Department of Justice, 1985) ('A person knowingly lies under oath during a trial' ranks as more serious than both 'three high school boys beat a male classmate with their fists. He requires hospitalization' and 'a company pays a bribe to a legislator to vote for a law favoring the company.').

[5] 18 USC 1621. The law in England, Canada, and Australia is discussed in the text accompanying n 16–20 below.   [6] *United States v Debrow*, 346 US 374 (1953).

a 'false material declaration' be made knowingly, under oath, in a proceeding 'before or ancillary to any court or grand jury.'[7]

The harms of perjury are significant: courts and other tribunals are deprived of crucial information material to the decision-making process.[8] Indeed, they may be affirmatively misled into believing that which is untrue. An innocent person might be unjustly convicted and imprisoned. A guilty person might be acquitted and set free to commit other crimes. A witness perjuring himself before a legislative committee or in a civil suit might cause a grave injustice to occur. And even if the jury's verdict turns out to be the correct one, the potential for error has been increased and the integrity of the system seriously undermined.

What is harder to assess is the way in which perjury can be said to be morally wrong. Perjury seems to involve an aggregation of at least two significant norm violations. First, it involves the breaking of an oath or promise to tell the truth (an element that is notably absent from both fraud and the offense of false statements). And what is broken is not just any promise but one typically invoking God. 'Penal sanctions provide temporal punishment; violating an oath suggests ultimate punishment by a supernatural power,' as one commentator has put it.[9] The word 'perjury' itself is derived from the Latin *perjurium*, which refers to the act of invoking a god to bear witness to the truth of a statement although the speaker knew the statement was false.[10] On the other hand, the fact that such promise to tell the truth is frequently made under compulsion seems significant: as suggested earlier, the wrongfulness of breaking of a promise that is compelled is surely less, other things being equal, than the wrongfulness of breaking a promise that is truly voluntary.

My focus here, however, will be on what is probably the more significant form of moral wrongfulness entailed by the crimes of perjury and false declarations—namely, deception. My claim is that perjury, at least under the prevailing rule in Anglo-American jurisdictions, requires not just any kind of deception, but specifically lying. In addition, I want to say something about the way in which perjury incorporates notions of wrongful exculpation and wrongful inculpation.

Perjury and Lies

There are two respects in which the elements of perjury track those of lying. First, like lying, perjury has consistently been interpreted as requiring an

---

[7] 18 USC § 1623. The offense of false declarations differs from perjury in that it: (1) can be proved by means of showing inconsistent sworn statements, see *Ibid* at 1623(c); (2) does not require corroboration through the common law 'two witness' and 'direct evidence' rule; (3) contains a limited recantation defense, see *United States v Norris*, 300 US 564 (1937); (4) has a less demanding oath requirement, see *Christoffel v United States*, 338 US 84 (1949); (5) has a less demanding *mens rea* requirement; and (6) applies in a narrower range of proceedings, see *Dunn v United States*, 442 US 100 (1979).   [8] See Gershman (n 1 above, at 636).
[9] *Ibid* at 636.   [10] 'Perjury,' in *Oxford English Dictionary*.

assertion, the truth or falsity of which can be ascertained with certainty.[11] Thus, statements of belief or opinion cannot constitute perjury.[12] The only exception occurs in those special cases in which the witness states that she holds an opinion or belief that she does not in fact hold.[13] In such cases, the existence or nonexistence of the belief or opinion is itself a matter of material fact that is theoretically capable of verification.

Secondly, under the modern American rule, in order to be perjurious, a statement must be literally false.[14] This requirement of literal falsity reflects a change from the earlier common law rule.[15] It comes not from the literal language of section 1621 (which refers simply to statements that the witness 'does not believe to be true'), but from well-settled case law. The prevailing rule in Australia is to the same effect.[16] In England, the rule is somewhat more ambiguous. While section 13 of the Perjury Act 1911 does seem to follow the literal falsity rule, section 1 does not.[17] Under modern law, this apparent inconsistency has generally been resolved in favor of the more demanding rule.[18] In addition, the Law Commission has recommended that the law be explicitly changed to reflect the requirement of literal falsity.[19] And, according to Smith and Hogan, '[i]n practice, it seems that no one is ever prosecuted for making a

[11] The question of what is an assertion also arises in the context of Federal Rule of Evidence 801(c), which defines 'hearsay' as a 'statement, other than one made by the declarant while testifying at the trial or hearing, offered in evidence to prove the truth of the matters asserted.' This rule is meant to apply to direct statements of fact offered to prove the truth of the matter directly stated. See Paul S Milich, 'Re-Examining Hearsay Under the Federal Rules: Some Method for the Madness' (1991) 39 *University of Kansas Law Review* 893, 900 (discussing various meanings of 'assertion').

[12] Among the kinds of testimony that cannot constitute perjury are statements as to beliefs concerning (1) the cause of an accident, see *Trullinger v Dooley*, 266 P 909 (Ore 1928); (2) the effect of a contract or instrument, see *Goad v State*, 61 SW 79 (Tenn 1900); and (3) one's status as a principal or agent, see *Harp v State*, 26 SW 714 (Ark 1894).

[13] CR McCorkle, Annotation, 'Statement of Belief or Opinion as Perjury' 66 *ALR* 2d 791. English law appears to follow a similar rule. See JC Smith and Brian Hogan, *Criminal Law* (6th edn., London: Butterworths, 1988) ('an expression of opinion, when that opinion is not genuinely held, is perjury') (citing *R v Schlesinger* [1867] 10 QB 670). It appears that the materials on perjury have been omitted from later editions of Smith and Hogan.

[14] See Perovich J D Annotation: Incomplete, Misleading, or Unresponsive but Literally True Statement as Perjury (1976) 69 *ALR* 3d 993.

[15] At common law, a witness could apparently be prosecuted for perjury if he believed that his sworn statement was false, even if it later turned out to be true. *Allen v Westly* [1629] Hetley 97; (1629) 124 ER 372; Smith and Hogan (n 13 above, at 746). Sarah N Welling et al., *Federal Criminal Law and Related Actions: Crimes, Forfeiture, the False Claims Act and RICO* (St. Paul, Minn.: West Group, 1998) vol. 2, 215.

[16] Model Criminal Code Officers Committee, 'Report on Administration of Justice Offences' (July 1998) 13–15 ('In no Australian jurisdiction is it sufficient for the evidence to be misleading as opposed to false.').

[17] Perjury Act 1911 (UK) s.1 ('If any person lawfully sworn as a witness or as an interpreter in a judicial proceedings willfully makes a statement material in that proceeding, which he knows to be false or does not believe to be true, he shall be guilty of perjury');

[18] Smith and Hogan (n 13 above, at 74).

[19] Law Commission, *Report No. 96, Offences Relating to Interference with the Course of Justice* (1979), at ¶ 2.56.

statement which was true.'[20] Only in Canada does the old common law rule prohibiting the literal truth defense rule still apply.[21]

The leading American case concerning literal truth is *Bronston v United States*.[22] Bronston was president of a movie production company that petitioned for bankruptcy. At a bankruptcy hearing, Bronston was asked, 'Do you have any [Swiss bank accounts]?,' to which he responded 'no'; and 'Have you ever?', to which he responded, 'The company had an account there for about six months, in Zurich.'[23] The truth was that Bronston had had Swiss bank accounts for five years, but did not have any at the time of the trial, and so his first answer was correct. As for his second answer, had he said 'no,' he would have been guilty of perjury. Instead, he gave a literally true, though misleading, answer to a question that had not been asked—namely, whether *his company* had ever had a Swiss bank account. In overturning Bronston's conviction, the Court held that the perjury statute is not meant to apply to: (1) statements that are literally true; (2) statements that are untrue only by 'negative implication' (ie, literally true, but evasive, answers); or (3) literally true but misleading or incomplete answers. Under the Court's reasoning, although a witness' testimony might be misleading, it is the responsibility of the questioning lawyer to probe until the truth can be uncovered. If the lawyer fails to do so adequately, the witness is not guilty of perjury.

Like perjury, the closely related crime of false declarations also requires an assertion and literal falsity.[24] Consider, for example, the Fourth Circuit's decision in *United States v Earp*.[25] During the course of his testimony before a grand jury, the defendant, a member of the Ku Klux Klan, was asked whether he had ever burned a cross at the home of an interracial couple. He denied that he had. The truth was that he had *attempted* to burn a cross, but had fled before it was lit. The court, following *Bronston*, reversed his conviction on the grounds that the defendant's testimony, though obviously misleading, was nevertheless literally true, and therefore not perjurious.[26]

[20] Smith and Hogan (n 13 above, at 747).

[21] *R v Farris* [1965] 3 CCC 245 (Ontario Ct App.); *R v Trotchie* [1994] 3 WWR 201 (Saskatchewan Ct App.). Ironically, the relevant Canadian statute uses language that seems more reflective of the literal truth rule than the American or English statutes. Whereas the American and English statutes speak only of the witness' 'not believing his testimony to be true,' the Canadian statute says that the witness must make a 'false statement' 'knowing that the statement is false.' RSC 1985, c. C-46, s131. It is therefore puzzling that the literal truth defense has been embraced by the United States, Australia, and Great Britain, while Canada, under the influence of the common law, seems to have rejected it.   [22] 409 US 352 (1973).

[23] *Ibid* at 354.

[24] See, eg, *United States v Hairston*, 46 F.3d 361, 375 (4th Cir 1995); *United States v Reveron Martinez*, 836 F2d 684, 689 (1st Cir 1988).   [25] 812 F 2d 917 (4th Cir 1987).

[26] *Ibid*. Similar is the Sixth Circuit's decision in *United States v Eddy*, 737 F 2d 564 (6th Cir 1984), in which the court reversed a conviction for false declarations in a case in which the defendant, who had sought to become a Navy doctor, answered 'no' to the question whether he had submitted a 'diploma' and 'official college transcript' from the Ohio State University College of Medicine as proof of his qualifications. Because the diploma and transcript submitted by defendant were, in fact, forgeries, defendant's statement, though misleading, was held to be literally true and therefore not a false declaration.

The reasoning in each of these literal truth cases is strikingly similar to the argument offered above regarding the moral status of lying. Recall that one of the distinctions between lying and evasion and related forms of linguistic and non-linguistic deception is that the latter afford the listener the opportunity for more precise questioning, which bald-faced lies generally do not.[27] Indeed, as Renaissance scholar Debora Shuger has explained, '[i]t was precisely to give witnesses and defendants a way out of the perjury trap that theologians distinguished between a lie and a misleading or equivocal statement.'[28]

This distinction applies *a fortiori* in the courtroom. A lawyer who fails to clarify evasive or nonresponsive statements from a witness bears even more responsibility for improper inferences than does a listener in everyday conversation. As *Bronston* put it, '[i]t is the responsibility of the lawyer to probe; testimonial interrogation, and cross-examination in particular, is a probing, prying, pressing form of inquiry. If a witness evades, it is the lawyer's responsibility to recognize the evasion and to bring the witness back to the mark, to flush out the whole truth with the tools of adversary examination.'[29] What the Court is saying is that perjury requires lying, and that the witness who makes an evasive or unresponsive, but literally true, statement has not lied, and therefore has not committed perjury. (In that sense, perjury can also be seen to involve yet another kind of moral wrongfulness—namely, cheating. The 'rules' of the 'testimony game' say it's okay to mislead the jury, as long as one doesn't use literal falsity to do it.)

A similar rule of *caveat auditor* applies in the equally formal structure of the British Parliament, where there is a convention that MPs 'may not lie when answering questions or making statements, but they can certainly omit, select, give answers that reveal less than the whole relevant truth, and generally give a misleading impression.'[30] And the justification for this rule is closely analogous to that in *Bronston*. As Bernard Williams explained:

It is clear what the point of the convention is. No-one can expect a government to make full disclosure about everything, and often it is unclear anyway what full disclosure would look like. It is equally undesirable that they should be able to get away with anything they like in order to deceive the public. The rule makes it harder to get away with deceit, since answers will be suspiciously inspected and questions pressed, and ministers who are debarred from lying can be forced to a position in which they

---

[27] See, eg Thomas Hill, Jr., 'Autonomy and Benevolent Lies' in *Autonomy and Self-Respect* (Cambridge: CUP, 1991) 41.

[28] Debora Shuger 'Sins of the Tongue' (14 Sept. 1999) *Slate* <http://slate.msn.com/Features/tongue/tongue.asp>. Shuger goes on: 'Henry Mason, an Anglican priest writing in the early 17th century, points out that in traditional Protestant and Catholic ethics "if there be just cause for concealing of a truth", one may use words in a "less known and common signification, and in another meaning than it is likely the hearers will understand them." '

[29] *Bronston*, 409 US at 358–59.

[30] Bernard Williams, *Truth and Truthfulness* (Princeton: Princeton University Press, 2002) 108.

either produce the truth (if they know it) or are left seriously embarrassed and with nothing to say.[31]

Understanding the literal truth rule in this manner also helps to explain the fallacy in the Sixth Circuit's recent opinion in *United States v DeZarn*, which creates a seemingly significant limitation on *Bronston*.[32] The defendant DeZarn was prosecuted for perjury after being questioned, under oath, by Robert Tripp, a staff member in the office of the Army's Inspector General, regarding DeZarn's connection to alleged violations of the Hatch Act, which prohibits the improper solicitation of government employees (in this case, members of the Kentucky National Guard) in political campaigns. DeZarn had been present at two parties organized around a horse racing theme: a 'Preakness Party' in 1990, and a 'Belmont Stakes' party in 1991. Only the 1990 party involved any political fund-raising. Although Tripp *meant* to ask DeZarn about the events surrounding the 1990 party, he mistakenly asked DeZarn whether there had been any political fund-raising activity at the '1991 party.' DeZarn, undoubtedly aware of Tripp's mistake, and seizing on the opening it created, answered '[a]bsolutely not'; he was 'not aware' of any fund-raising at the party.[33] In so doing, DeZarn made a literally true, but arguably misleading, statement.

The Court of Appeals—mistakenly, in my view—upheld DeZarn's conviction for perjury, reading the *Bronston* literal truth rule narrowly to apply only when a defendant responds to a question with a *non-responsive* answer.[34] Since the defendant's answer in this case was responsive, the court viewed it as distinguishable from the non-responsive (and therefore non-perjurious) answer given in the *Bronston* case.

Why did *DeZarn* read *Bronston* in this narrow way? According to *DeZarn*, non-responsive answers (like those in *Bronston*) are 'unique,' because they require 'speculation' by the fact-finder as to what they imply. As a consequence, non-responsive answers allow no 'finding beyond a reasonable doubt that [an] answer is untruthful.'[35] By contrast, *DeZarn* says, 'when the answer given is responsive to the question asked and "it is entirely reasonable to expect a defendant to have understood the terms used in the question," ' the literal truth defense should not apply.[36]

The *DeZarn* opinion has been celebrated as 'nudg[ing] federal criminal law closer to everyday morality.'[37] In reality, however, it seems to have done just

---

[31] *Ibid* at 109.   [32] 157 F3d 1042 (6th Cir 1998).   [33] *Ibid* at 1045.

[34] Recall that Bronston responded to the question, 'Do you have any bank accounts in Swiss banks?' by stating, 'the company had an account there for about six months,' whereas DeZarn responded to the question, did the 1991 party involve 'political fundraising activity?,' by stating, 'absolutely not.' Bronston's answer was non-responsive; DeZarn's was not.

[35] *DeZarn*, 157 F3d at 1047.

[36] *Ibid* (quoting *United States v Slawik*, 548 F 2d 75, 86 (3rd Cir 1977)).

[37] Recent Case, 'Criminal Law—Perjury—Sixth Circuit Sustains Perjury Conviction for Answer to Question with Mistaken Premise' (1999) 112 *Harvard Law Review* 1783.

the opposite. By reading the literal truth rule in this restrictive manner, *DeZarn* tends to blur the distinction in everyday morality between lying and merely misleading. If anything, the questioner in *DeZarn* bore even more responsibility for being misled than the questioner in *Bronston*. In *Bronston*, the questioner asked the right question, but failed to seek a follow-up clarification of the answer. In *DeZarn*, the questioner asked the wrong question. A witness who fails to respond to a question the questioner *meant* to ask, instead of the one he did ask, certainly cannot, in any 'everyday morality' sense of the term, be said to have lied. Nor should he be said to have committed perjury. *DeZarn* is wrongly decided because the distinction it implies between literally true, *responsive* testimony and literally true, *non*-responsive testimony is one without any moral significance.

Responses to Ambiguous Questions

Closely related to—really, a subset of—the literal falsity rule is the principle that ambiguous questions cannot produce perjurious answers. That is, when there is more than one way of understanding the meaning of a question, and the witness has answered truthfully as to his understanding, he cannot be held liable for perjury. The leading case is the DC District Court's opinion in *United States v Lattimore*,[38] in which a witness was questioned before a Senate Subcommittee about his ties to the Communist party. The witness was asked whether he was a 'follower of the Communist line' and whether he had been a 'promoter of Communist interests.' He answered 'no' to both questions, and was subsequently indicted for perjury. In dismissing the charges, the court stated that '"follower of the Communist line" is not a phrase with a meaning about which men of ordinary intellect could agree, nor one which could be used with mutual understanding by a questioner and answerer unless it were defined at the time it were sought and offered as testimony.'[39]

The applicability of the ambiguous question rule is particularly important in cases in which a witness faces a compound question or its functional equivalent. Consider, for example, the Ninth Circuit's decision in *United States v Sainz*.[40] The defendant, a border patrol inspector for the Immigration and Naturalization Service, was charged with making a false declaration before a federal grand jury. During the course of his testimony, the defendant was asked a series of questions regarding his duties at an INS border station. The following colloquy formed the basis for the charge:

Q: Have you ever failed to follow your agency's procedure in running license plates of cars coming into the United States to determine whether or not they were listed as suspicious narcotics vehicles?
A: No, sir.

[38] 127 F Supp. 405 (DDC 1955).   [39] *Ibid* at 410.   [40] 772 F 2d 559 (9th Cir 1985).

The government contended that this response was perjurious because, on two separate occasions, automobiles had traveled through the defendant's lane and he had failed to enter their license plate numbers into the INS computer.

In reversing the conviction, the court explained that the term 'procedure' was ambiguous, and in fact had been used by the questioner to refer to the practice of both routing entering traffic as well as placing a driver's documents in a cone on top of the entering vehicles.[41] Moreover, the prosecutor's question presented 'two distinct alternative questions within one compound question': first, whether the defendant always followed the discrete steps necessary to 'run' plates through the computer[42]; and secondly whether the defendant failed to 'run' license plates for the specific purpose of aiding in the importation of controlled substances while on duty.[43] In light of the ambiguity in the prosecution's questioning, the court held, the defendant's conviction could not stand.

The concerns expressed by cases like *Lattimore* and *Sainz* are exactly congruent with those expressed in *Bronston*. As *Sainz* put it, ' "[p]recise questioning is imperative as a predicate for the offense of perjury." A witness cannot be forced to guess at the meaning of the question to which he must respond upon peril of perjury ... The perjury statute and its goal of truth in our system is served by fostering truthful answers to precise questions, not by penalizing unresponsive answers to unclear questions.'[44] Once again, the principle of *caveat auditor* applies. One who asks an ambiguous question cannot expect an unambiguous answer; one who answers an ambiguous question with a statement that may be misleading cannot be said to have lied.

2. The Case of Bill Clinton

In order to see the significance of these principles in practice, let us now return to the case of Bill Clinton. According to prosecutors, Clinton committed perjury not only during his 17 Jan. 1998 deposition in the *Jones* sexual harassment case (when he denied that he had had 'sexual relations with Monica Lewinsky' as that term was used in the unusually narrow definition that appeared in 'Deposition Exhibit 1, as modified by the Court,'[45]) but also

[41] *Ibid* at 562.
[42] 'For example,' the court pointed out, 'this question might be probing whether the defendant ever negligently or intentionally input incorrect information into the computer.' *Ibid*.
[43] As the court pointed out, 'the prosecutor had preceded this question with three substantially identical questions as to the defendant's direct or indirect involvement in the importation of controlled substances while on duty.' *Ibid*.   [44] *Ibid* (quoting *Bronston*, 409 US at 362).
[45] Referral to the United States House of Representatives Filed in Conformity with the Requirements of Title 28, United States Code §595(c) Submitted by the Office of the Independent Counsel, HR Doc No 105–310 (1998). We will deal with the obstruction of justice aspects of the case in ch. 15 below.

during his 17 Aug. 1998 videotaped appearance before the grand jury.[46] These additional statements concerned: (1) whether he and Lewinsky had ever been alone together in the Oval Office, (2) whether he had any specific recollection of having been alone with Lewinsky in the Oval Office, (3) whether she had ever given him any gifts, and (4) whether he had ever given her any gifts. What I want to suggest is that proper legal disposition of each such allegation makes sense only if one recognizes the way in which the law of perjury mirrors our moral understanding of the concept of lying.

Testimony That Was Non-Responsive, Misleading, and Literally True

According to the allegations contained in the Referral of the Office of Independent Counsel,[47] one of the most significant instances of perjury during the course of President Clinton's deposition in the *Jones* case occurred in the following colloquy:

Q: ... At any time were you and Monica Lewinsky together alone in the Oval Office?
A: ... [A]s I said, when she worked at the legislative affairs office, they always had somebody there on the weekends. Sometimes they'd bring me things on the weekends. She—it seems to me she brought things to me once or twice on the weekends. In that case, whatever time she would be in there, drop it off, exchange a few words and go, she was there. I don't have any specific recollections of what the issues were, what was going on, but when the Congress is there, we're working all the time, and typically I would do some work on one of the days of the weekends in the afternoon.[48]

According to the Referral, Clinton's response constituted perjury because, in fact, Clinton had been alone with Lewinsky in the Oval Office on a number of occasions.[49]

Was this testimony really perjurious? Note that Clinton never actually answers the question asked of him. He never says whether he and Lewinsky were alone together in the Oval Office. Instead, he offers a rather elaborate, and somewhat rambling, explanation of the circumstances in which a legislative aide might have brought him materials in the Oval Office—an explanation

---

[46] Although his alleged perjury during the deposition received at least as much attention in the press and in special prosecutor Kenneth Starr's Referral, as it turns out, only Clinton's alleged perjury before the grand jury was the subject of the impeachment articles themselves. See 'House Resolution 611,' in Merrill McLoughlin (ed.), *The Impeachment and Trial of President Clinton: The Official Transcripts, From the House Judiciary Committee Hearings to the Senate Trial* (New York: Random House, 1999) 445–50.

[47] Referral, above n 45.

[48] *Ibid* at 126. For purposes of analytical clarity, I have omitted the phrase with which Clinton begins his response: 'I don't recall.' Because Clinton was almost certainly lying when he said he could not recall being alone together with Lewinsky in the Oval Office, this statement should be regarded as perjurious. [49] *Ibid*.

that would appear to be accurate on its face. In other words, Clinton offers an evasive, non-responsive, and factually true reply to the question posed.

Was Clinton's testimony misleading? Probably it was. A reasonable inference to be drawn from his statement is that Clinton and Lewinsky were never alone together in the Oval Office, or at least not alone long enough to engage in sexual activity. Bill Clinton—a witness so slippery he makes Bronston look like an amateur—evades the question he does not want to answer by answering a different, relatively innocuous question about White House procedures. Under *Bronston*, however, evasive answers are not perjurious: 'If a witness evades, it is *the lawyer's* responsibility to recognize the evasion and to bring the witness back to the mark, to flush out the whole truth with the tools of adversary examination.'[50] Here, the *Jones* lawyers had the opportunity to obtain a clarification of Clinton's response, but, for whatever reason, they did not pursue it.[51] Any inferences, true or untrue, that can be drawn from such statements would seem to be at least partly the questioner's fault.

Testimony That was Responsive, Misleading, and (Arguably) Literally True

Perhaps the single most infamous example of alleged perjury by President Clinton occurred during his deposition, in the course of the following colloquy with a lawyer for the Office of Independent Counsel. Clinton was asked, 'have you ever had sexual relations with Monica Lewinsky, as that term is defined in Deposition Exhibit 1, as modified by the Court?,' and he responded, 'I have never had sexual relations with Monica Lewinsky.'[52]

Here again, Clinton's testimony was obviously misleading. In normal discourse, one would infer that if *A* and *B* had not had 'sexual relations,' then *A* and *B* had not had sexual intercourse, oral sex, or any other form of sexual contact. But this was not normal discourse. It was a deposition, and the term 'sexual relations' had already been defined in a very specific way. According to Exhibit 1:

[A] person engages in 'sexual relations' when the person knowingly engages or causes
   (1) contact with the genitalia, anus, groin, breast, inner thigh, or buttocks of any person with an intent to arouse or gratify the sexual desire of any person.[53]

Initially, the Jones lawyers had submitted a much broader definition of 'sexual relations,' which included both 'contact between any part of the person's body or an object and the genitals or anus of another person' and 'contact

[50] *Bronston*, 409 US at 358–59 (emphasis added).
[51] For a discussion of other errors apparently made by the *Jones* lawyers, see Robert W Gordon, 'Imprudence and Partisanship: Starr's OIC and the Clinton-Lewinsky Affair' (1999) 68 *Fordham Law Review* 639, 682.   [52] *Referral*, n 45 above, at 133.
[53] *Submission by Counsel for President Clinton to the Committee on the Judiciary of the United States House of Representatives*, HR Prt No 105–16 (1998) [hereinafter, *Clinton Submission*], at 37.

between the genitals or anus of the person and any part of another person's body.'[54] But for reasons that are now difficult to ascertain, Judge Wright narrowed the meaning of the term by striking these last two clauses.

As a result, the remaining definition did not include a number of acts that might ordinarily be thought of as involving sexual activity—including, most significantly, fellatio performed by Lewinsky on Clinton.[55] Thus, assuming that Clinton's sexual activity with Lewinsky was limited to his being fellated by her,[56] it follows that Clinton's response was literally true, that he did not lie, and that, under *Bronston*, he did not commit perjury.

Unlike the testimony discussed above, however, Clinton's testimony here was responsive. In this case, Clinton actually answered the question that was put to him, albeit in a misleading way. Does this mean that *DeZarn's* alternative rule for misleading, literally true, but *responsive* answers should apply?

Clinton's testimony offers another good illustration of why the rule in *DeZarn* is misguided. Recall that, in *Bronston*, the lawyer's only error was failing to follow up on a non-responsive answer. By contrast, the lawyer here, as in *DeZarn*, actually asked the wrong question. By adhering to the idiosyncratic definition of 'sexual relations' contained in Exhibit 1, rather than asking straightforward questions about the precise nature of the sexual relationship between Clinton and Lewinsky,[57] Jones's lawyers drew unwarranted

---

[54] *Ibid.*

[55] The import of the 'oral sex does not constitute sexual relations' defense would not become fully clear until Clinton testified before the grand jury on 17 August 1998. When asked about his understanding of the term 'sexual relations' as defined for use in the deposition, Clinton said it 'covers contact by the person being deposed with the enumerated areas, if the contact is done with an intent to arouse or gratify,' but it does not cover oral sex being performed on the person being deposed. '[I]f the deponent is the person who has oral sex performed on him, then the contact is with—not with anything on that list, but with the lips of another person.' *Referral*, n 45 above, at 16. In other words, assuming again that the only sexual contact Clinton had with Lewinsky consisted of her performing fellatio on him, then what Clinton testified to in his deposition was literally true. Even if Lewinsky had engaged in 'sexual relations' with Clinton, technically speaking, Clinton had not engaged in 'sexual relations' with her, because he had allegedly not had contact with any of her listed body parts with the 'intent to arouse or gratify [her] sexual desire.'

[56] I recognize, of course, that this is a big assumption. According to Lewinsky's testimony, in addition to *her* performing oral sex on him, *he* also touched her in various sexual ways. *Ibid* at 148 ('She described with precision nine incidents of sexual activity in which the President touched and kissed her breasts and four incidents involving contacts with her genitalia.'). If Lewinsky's testimony on this point is to be believed, then Clinton's assertion that he did not have 'sexual relations' as defined in Exhibit 1 would be literally false, and he would thereby have committed perjury. On the other hand, it is also possible that Lewinsky was lying about the precise nature of her sexual contact with Clinton. In any event, under the circumstances, the requirement that the government present the testimony of two witnesses, see *Hammer v United States*, 271 US 620, 626 (1926), or at least one witness and independent evidence corroborating that witness's testimony, see *United States v Ford*, 603 F 2d 1043 (2nd Cir 1979), would have been hard to satisfy.

[57] For example, Jones's lawyers could have asked questions such as: 'Did Lewinsky ever perform fellatio on you?' 'Did Lewinsky ever have "sexual relations" with you?' 'Did Lewinsky ever have contact with any of your following body parts?' 'Did you ever have contact with any of her following body parts?'

inferences about the nature of their relationship. Assuming again that Clinton's contact with Lewinsky was limited to her performing oral sex on him, his statement that he had 'never had sexual relations with Monica Lewinsky' was not perjurious.[58] Under *Bronston*, it would have been unreasonable to expect Clinton to volunteer information that exceeded the scope of the definition given.

Testimony Given in Response to Ambiguous or Imprecise Questioning

At another point in the deposition, the *Jones* lawyers questioned Clinton about the number of times he and Monica Lewinsky had been alone together in the Oval Office, and the following colloquy ensued:

---

[58] It is also worth considering Clinton's denial in the 17 January deposition that he ever had a 'sexual affair' or a 'sexual relationship' with Lewinsky—terms that, unlike 'sexual relations' were never expressly defined. The Clinton defense team argued that the terms 'sexual affair' and 'sexual relationship' both refer to sexual intercourse or coitus, and that since Clinton (even by Lewinsky's own admission) had never had intercourse with her, it follows that they did not have a sexual 'affair' or 'relationship.' See Clinton Submission, above note 51, at 35–36.

This strikes me as a difficult claim to sustain. The problem is the premise that the terms 'sexual affair' and 'sexual relationship' refer exclusively to sexual intercourse or coitus. To be sure, there are a number of sex-like activities that might not necessarily qualify as a 'sexual affair' or 'relationship,' such as kissing and fondling and even phone sex. Similarly, it could be argued that a sexual encounter with an anonymous partner or with a prostitute would not be a sexual 'affair' or 'relationship.' But it strains the limits of language to suggest that a relationship that involves mouth-to-genital contact with intent to arouse is not a sexual relationship. There is little ambiguity about the fact that such conduct *is* sex.

There is, however, a better argument that the Clinton defense team could have made, but apparently did not. We are dealing with three terms that, in ordinary discourse, would be understood as basically synonymous: sexual relations, sexual affair, and sexual relationship. Only the first is defined. In such a situation, one would expect to see the undefined terms used in one of two situations: either because the speaker *intends* to be limited by the defined term, and has simply been careless; or because the speaker intends *not* to be limited by the defined term. If one looks at the deposition transcript, it seems obvious that the *Jones* lawyers did intend to use the undefined terms 'sexual relationship' and 'sexual affair' as synonyms for the defined term 'sexual relations.' For example, consider the following crucial colloquy:

Q: Did you have an extramarital sexual affair with Monica Lewinsky?
A: No.
Q: If she told someone that she had a sexual affair with you beginning in November of 1995, would that be a lie?
A: It's certainly not the truth. It would not be the truth.
Q: *I think I used the term 'sexual affair.' And so the record is completely clear, have you ever had sexual relations with Monica Lewinsky, as that term is defined in Deposition Exhibit 1, as modified by the Court?*
A: *I have never had sexual relations with Monica Lewinsky. I've never had an affair with her.*

Referral, n 45 above, at 117 (emphasis added). As the italicized language indicates, both the *Jones* lawyers and Clinton used the undefined term 'sexual affair' as a synonym for the defined term 'sexual relations.' Therefore, to the extent that the defined term 'sexual relations' does not refer to Clinton's being fellated, it seems reasonable to conclude that the undefined terms 'sexual relationship' and 'sexual affair' are also so limited. Under this construction, and assuming again that Clinton's relationship with Lewinsky was in fact limited in this manner, it appears that Clinton did not make a literally false statement.

Q: So I understand, your testimony is that it was possible, then, that you were alone with her, but you have no specific recollection of that ever happening?
A: Yes, that's correct. It's possible that she, in, while she was working there, brought something to me and that at the time she brought it to me, she was the only person there. That's possible.[59]

Here again, the Office of Independent Counsel maintained that Clinton had committed perjury, on the grounds that he did in fact have a specific recollection of having been alone with Ms Lewinsky.[60]

Under the reasoning of cases like *Lattimore* and *Sainz*, this conclusion is highly doubtful.[61] The question posed to Clinton has two discrete parts: 'is it possible that you were alone with her?'; and 'is it true that you have no specific recollection of being alone with her?' When Clinton answered, 'yes, that's correct,' he could have been responding either to part 1 of the question, or to part 2, or to both parts at once. Under the Independent Counsel's theory, the only truthful answer he could have given would have been something to the effect that, 'yes, it is possible that I was alone with her, but no, it is not true that I have no specific recollection of being alone with her.' The fact that Clinton failed to clarify an ambiguous and poorly framed question in this manner surely cannot mean that he committed perjury.

False Testimony Given in Response to Questioning Regarding Precise Quantities

During the deposition in the *Jones* case, in response to the question, '[h]as Monica Lewinsky ever given you any gifts?,' the President responded, '[o]nce or twice. I think she's given me a book or two.'[62] Here, Clinton misleads his questioner by implying that the *only* gifts he received from Lewinsky were one or two books when in fact, according to Lewinsky, she gave him numerous gifts, perhaps as many as 38.[63] Did this response from Clinton constitute perjury, or is it too protected by *Bronston's* literal truth rule on the grounds that, after all, Lewinsky *did* give Clinton 'a book or two'—in addition to a slew of other gifts?

As a matter of law, the answer to this question lies in footnote 3 of *Bronston*, in which the Court refers to (and distinguishes) an example of perjury given by the District Court below:

'[I]f it is material to ascertain how many times a person has entered a store on a given day and that person responds to such a question by saying five times when in fact he knows that he has entered the store 50 times that day, that person may be guilty of perjury even though it is technically true that he entered the store five times.'[64]

---

[59] *Referral*, n 45 above, 152.   [60] *Ibid.*
[61] See above n 38–44 and accompanying text.   [62] *Referral*, n 45 above, at 156.
[63] *Ibid* at 157.   [64] *Bronston*, 409 US at 355 n 3 (quoting district court opinion).

Indeed, the Court says, 'it is very doubtful that an answer which, in response to a specific quantitative inquiry, baldly understates a numerical fact can be described as even "technically true." '[65] In this case, Clinton seems to have done exactly what footnote 3 says he may not do. He has responded to a quantitative inquiry by 'baldly understat[ing]' the numerical response.[66] Accordingly, this statement should be regarded as perjurious.

Moreover, the approach in footnote 3 is consistent with everyday morality. Imagine that A needs to borrow a car for the evening and asks B how many he owns. B, who in truth owns four cars, replies, 'I have one car, and I'm using it this evening.' Has B lied in saying that he owns 'one car'? Has B made an assertion that is literally false, or has he merely led A to draw an improper inference from a misleading statement? It seems wrong to say that B has merely misled A. After all, B told A that he owns 'one car.' Perhaps A could have asked the follow up question, 'are you saying that you own *only* one car and no more?,' but this seems to take the principle of *caveat auditor* to extremes. In terms of everyday morality, one who responds to a specific quantitative inquiry by baldly understating a numerical fact should be regarded as uttering a lie.

Literally False and Misleading Testimony

At yet another point in the *Jones* deposition, Clinton was asked, 'have you ever given any gifts to Monica Lewinsky?,' to which he replied, 'I don't recall. Do you know what they were?'[67] In light of Lewinsky's testimony, physical evidence (namely, the gifts themselves), and Clinton's own testimony to the contrary,[68] his statement that he could not recall whether he had ever given any gifts to Monica Lewinsky was almost certainly literally false. Assuming that it was also intentional and material, it should be viewed as unproblematically perjurious.[69]

---

[65] *Ibid.*

[66] The fact that Clinton was asked, '[h]as Monica Lewinsky ever given you any gifts?,' rather than 'how many gifts has she given you' should make no difference to the perjury inquiry, given the fact that he responded with a specific quantitative answer.

[67] *Referral*, n 45 above, at 155.

[68] *Ibid* at 155–56 (describing evidence of Clinton gifts to Lewinsky).

[69] Clinton's defense team, presumably at a loss as to how to respond to this particular allegation of perjury, came up with the following, almost comically far-fetched, explanation:

The videotape of the President's January 17 deposition makes clear that the cold transcript can be somewhat misleading. When the President is asked, 'Well, have you ever given any gifts to Monica Lewinsky?', the transcript records his response as, 'I don't recall. Do you know that they were?' Dep. at 75. The videotape reveals the president's response, however, was a run-on sentence, as though the punctuation were omitted, for the real communicative gist of his quoted response (as it appears in the videotape) was, 'Yes I know there were some—please help remind me.'

(*Clinton Submission*, n 53 above, at 39).

Conclusion

The perjury case against Bill Clinton was offered in the Introduction as an example of the kind of moral ambiguity that surrounds white-collar crime. Despite the fact that Clinton undoubtedly did offer, in both his deposition and before the grand jury, misleading testimony concerning his relations with Monica Lewinsky, there are nonetheless serious questions as to whether much of this testimony satisfied the legal requirements of perjury. What I have tried to show here is that the resolution of such questions does, and ought to, closely track our understanding of what it means to lie.

13

Fraud

The concept of fraud is ubiquitous in white-collar criminal law, reflecting a protean and proliferating range of meanings. Not only are the fraud offenses among the most frequently charged, but they are also among the most widely and variously codified.[1] My goals in this section are two: first, to offer a brief survey of the range of moral concepts that have been associated with fraud; and, secondly, to focus in on what I regard as the most central of these concepts—namely, deception—and, in particular, to show how the relatively flexible conception of deceit that helps to define fraud differs from the rigid concept of lying that we saw in our discussion of perjury.

1. THE CONCEPT OF FRAUD

Much of the difficulty in defining the concept of fraud lies in the often inconsistent ways in which the term has been used. My focus here is on two points of contention: the means by which fraud must be carried out, and the object at which it must be aimed.

Means of Fraud

Traditionally, fraud has been thought to require the use of deceit.[2] But while deception seems to be, historically and conceptually, at its core, the means by which fraud must be carried out are, under modern statutes, frequently defined more broadly. As Brenda Nightingale has put it in her comprehensive treatise on the subject:

Given the origin of the concept of fraud, in equity and at common law, as a concept tied, initially to misrepresentations in contractual relations and later to the tort of deceit, deceit was, for a time, the primary concept around which the law relating to the offence

---

[1] For data on the number of fraud prosecutions, see Administrative Office of the US Courts, *Federal Judicial Workload Statistics* (Washington, DC, 1993) 52–57; Bureau of Justice Statistics, *Sourcebook of Criminal Justice Statistics* (Washington, DC: US Department of Justice, 1996). For a count of the number of fraud provisions in Title 18 of the US Code, see Ellen S Podgor, 'Criminal Fraud,' (1999) 48 *American University Law Review* 729, 740.

[2] The *OED*, for example, defines *fraud* as 'criminal deception,' requiring the use of 'false representations.' 'Fraud' in *Oxford English Dictionary*. See also Podgor, n 1 above, at 737 ('In United States federal criminal law the term is often synonymously used with the term "deceit." ').

was developed. While deceit is no longer the defining characteristic of fraudulent conduct, it is still one of the most common means by which the offence is committed.[3]

So what might fraud mean in the absence of deceit? The term that is often used to describe non-deceptive fraudulent means is 'dishonesty.'[4] And what does 'dishonesty' mean? The concept has been defined broadly enough to include, at various times, notions as diverse as breach of trust, conflicts of interest, non-disclosure of material facts, exploitation, taking unfair advantage, non-performance of contractual obligations, and misuse of corporate assets.[5] Indeed, in its broadest sense, the term fraud has been used to refer to a wrongful act of almost any sort—a violation of 'moral uprightness, of fundamental honesty, fair play and right dealing in the general and business life of members of society,'[6] an act that is 'discreditable as being at variance with straightforward or honourable dealings.'[7]

Object of Fraud

There is also considerable variation in the way in which the authorities define fraud's object. The most common use of the term fraud is to refer to criminal acts the purpose of which is to obtain, in the words of the federal mail fraud statute, 'money or property,'[8] or at least something of economic value, such as an accommodation or service of some kind. A classic case of such alleged fraud is that involving Enron Vice President and Chief Financial Officer Andrew Fastow, who, in an effort to find investors for an Enron spin-off investment partnership known as LJM-2, allegedly gave such investors false information about the state of Enron's and LJM-2's finances, and thereby obtained from them nearly $349 million in equity.[9]

---

[3] Brenda L Nightingale, *The Law of Fraud and Related Offences* (Toronto: Carswell Pub., 1996) 2–4.

[4] See, eg *Hammerschmidt v United States*, 265 US 182, 188 (1924) (although fraud has traditionally been committed by means of 'deceit, craft or trickery,' it can also be committed by other 'means that are dishonest'); *R v Olan* [1978] 2 SCR 1175, 1180 ('The words "other fraudulent means" [in what is now s 380(1)] include means which are not in the nature of a falsehood or deceit; they encompass all other means which can properly be stigmatized as dishonest.'). Criminal Code (Canada) 380(1), in turn, provides that '[e]veryone who, by deceit, falsehood, or other fraudulent means, whether or not it is a false pretence within the meaning of this Act, defrauds the public or any person, whether ascertained or not, of any property, money or valuable security or any service' is guilty of fraud.

[5] Nightingale, (n 3 above, at 3–13) (cataloguing meanings of 'dishonest means').

[6] *Gregory v United States*, 253 F 2d 104, 109 (5th Cir 1958).

[7] *R v Doren* [1982] 66 CCC (2d) 448, 450.   [8] 18 USC § 1341.

[9] The solicitations are described in an 15 October 2001 Memorandum from Max Hendrick, III, outside counsel for Enron at Vinson & Elkins law firm, to James V Derrick, Jr., Enron General Counsel, available on *Houston Chronicle* website, <http://www.chron.com/content/ chronicle/special/01/enron/background/index.html>. See also David Ivanovich, 'The Fall of Enron; Bankers Believed Deals Hinged on Investments,' *Houston Chronicle* (20 Feb. 2002), at A9; 'Top Former Enron Executive "to Plead Guilty,"' *The Guardian* (8 Jan. 2004), <http://www.guardian.co.uk/ enron/story/0,11337,1118744,00.html>. Another aspect of the case, concerning threats that Fastow allegedly made to the LJM-2 investors, is discussed in ch. 17 below.

But the term 'fraud' is also used more broadly to refer to schemes not just to obtain money or property, but also to achieve any 'unjust advantage' or to 'injure the rights or interests of another.'[10] As the Supreme Court put it in *Hammerschmidt v United States*, '[t]o conspire to defraud the United States means primarily to cheat the Government out of property or money, but it also means to interfere with or obstruct one of its lawful governmental functions.'[11] Indeed, the term 'fraud' has been used even to refer to objects as broad and nebulous as the 'evasion of statutory prohibitions.'[12]

Under US federal law, one of the most significant contexts in which fraud involves an object other than obtaining property is that contained in the 1988 amendment to 18 USC § 1346, enacted in response to the Supreme Court's decision in *McNally v United States*.[13] Under section 1346, the term 'scheme or artifice to defraud' is expressly defined to include a scheme or artifice to 'deprive another of the intangible right of honest services.'[14] When such fraud occurs in the public sector, the goal is to deny the public its rights to honest governmental services.[15] When it occurs in the private sector, the goal is to deny an employer its right to the honest services of its employee.[16]

The Moral Content of Fraud

The moral content of fraud follows directly from the way in which its statutory elements are defined. For example, according to its core, historically-based definition, fraud involves the use of (1) 'false or fraudulent pretenses, representations, or promises' for the purpose of (2) 'obtaining money or property'[17] Under such a definition, fraud seems to involve two basic, and fairly discrete, forms of moral wrongfulness: deception and stealing.

Under alternative definitions of fraud, however, moral content varies significantly. Here we need to consider both means other than deceit and objects other than obtaining money or property. For example, if the object of a given fraud is some 'unjust advantage' or 'injury to the rights or interests of others' other than the obtaining of money or property, then such fraud would not violate the norm against stealing. And if such fraud is carried out by some

---

[10] 'Fraud' in *Oxford English Dictionary*.   [11] 265 US at 188.

[12] Anthony J Arlidge and Jacques Parry, *Arlidge & Parry on Fraud* (London: Waterlow Publishers, 1985) 30 (criticizing this tendency).   [13] 483 US 350 (1987).

[14] 18 USC § 1346.

[15] For cases involving breach of duty to the public, see *United States v Devegter*, 198 F 3d 1324, 1328 (11th Cir 1999) ('Public officials inherently owe a fiduciary duty to the public to make governmental decisions in the public's best interest. "If the official instead secretly makes his decision based on his own personal interests ... the official has defrauded the public of his honest services." ') (quoting *United States v Lopez-Lukis*, 102 F 3d 1164, 1169 (11th Cir 1997)).

[16] For cases involving breach of duty to private employers, see *United States v Frost*, 125 F 3d 346 (6th Cir 1997), cert denied, 525 US 810 (1998); *United States v Vinyard*, 266 F 3d 320 (4th Cir 2001); *United States v Jain*, 93 F 3d 436 (8th Cir 1996).

[17] 18 USC § 1341; see also, eg the Canadian fraud statute, Criminal Code §380(1), quoted in note 4.

'dishonest' but non-deceptive means of the sort mentioned abov
would involve cheating, exploitation, disloyalty, or promise-breaking, ra..
than deceit. Indeed, if fraud really does refer to any 'evasion of statutory pro-hibitions,' then it would apply, as Arlidge and Parry point out in their treatise on fraud, even to such apparently non-fraud-like crimes as the smuggling of drugs and distribution of pornography.[18]

Such diversity in the definition of fraud obviously poses problems for the analysis that is being developed in this book. My project is to break down specific white-collar offenses into their constitutive moral elements: thus, per-jury is analyzed in terms of lying, bribery in terms of disloyalty, tax evasion in terms of cheating, extortion in terms of coercion, and so forth. But if fraud itself encompassed all of these forms of moral wrongfulness, then it would be virtually impossible to distinguish it from other forms of criminality.

Moreover, such variation in meaning would pose real impediments to the principles of fair labeling and of legality. If fraud really were to encompass not just stealing by deceit, but also deceptive and non-deceptive breaches of trust, conflicts of interest, non-disclosure of material facts, exploitation, taking unfair advantage, non-performance of contractual obligations, and misuse of corporate assets, it would be virtually impossible to distinguish between different offenses in terms of their nature and seriousness, and even to know whether and when one had committed a crime. Under such an approach, and subject to certain contingent jurisdictional limitations, there is no reason why the perjurer, the bribee, the tax cheat, and the extortionist could not all be convicted of fraud.[19]

Unfortunately, I have no immediate solution to this conceptual morass. Certainly, I would recommend that legislatures define, and courts interpret, the concept of fraud narrowly, to avoid such indeterminacy. But to the extent that the goal of the instant project is to describe the moral content of white-collar crime as it currently exists, it will do no good to deny that such problems exist. Instead, I will in the discussion below focus on what seems to me the most characteristic feature of the traditional 'core' notion of fraud—namely, the flexible way in which it defines the notion of deceit.

---

[18] Arlidge & Parry (n 12 above at 30).
[19] Indeed, to cite just one example, acceptance of a bribe constitutes a breach of honest ser-vices under the mail fraud statute, provided that the requisite jurisdictional requirements are met. *United States v Mandel*, 591 F 2d 1347 (4th Cir), *aff'd per curiam by equally divided court*, 602 F 2d 653 (4th Cir 1979), *coram nobis granted*, 862, F 2d 1067 (4th Cir 1988). As the court explained:

[T]he fraud involved in the bribery of a public official lies in the fact that the public official is not exercising his independent judgment in passing on public matters. A fraud is perpetrated on the public to whom the official owes fiduciary duties, e.g., honest, faithful and disinterested service. When a public official has been bribed, he breaches his duty of honest, faithful and disinterested service. While outwardly purporting to be exercising independent judgment in passing on official matters, the official has been paid for his decisions, perhaps without even considering the merits of the matter. Thus, the public is not receiving what it expects and is entitled to, the public official's honest and faithful service.

Fraud As a White-Collar Crime

Before we proceed to our consideration of the nature of deceit in the definition of fraud, there is one more preliminary matter that needs to be addressed. To the extent that I have defined the core concept of fraud as theft by deceit, it is reasonable to ask how such a concept differs from the traditional common law offense of false pretenses, which is defined as using false representations to wrongfully deprive another permanently of his property.[20] More generally, it is worth asking in what sense fraud should be classified as a white-collar crime.

In terms of offense elements, there are three basic differences between fraud and false pretenses. First, whereas the offense of false pretenses always involves an attempt to obtain money or property, the object of fraud, as we have seen, is far more ambiguous. Secondly, whereas false pretenses requires a misrepresentation regarding a past or present fact, fraud can also involve a misrepresentation involving a promise or prediction of a future state of affairs.[21] Thirdly, while false pretenses requires a completed theft, fraud frequently conflates the distinction between complete and inchoate criminality by requiring that the defendant either obtain, or *attempt* to obtain, property (or perhaps some other goal) through deceptive means.[22]

But fraud also differs from false pretenses in more than just its basic formal elements. The term 'fraud' is typically used to describe a statutory offense that is committed by some specialized means or in some specialized context. Under American federal law, for example, there are now dozens of statutory provisions that criminalize offenses such as mail fraud, wire fraud, bank fraud, health care fraud, tax fraud, computer fraud, securities fraud, bankruptcy fraud, accounting fraud, and conspiracy to defraud the government.[23] Fraud is thus distinguishable from false pretenses most significantly in terms of its potential harms, victims, and perpetrators.

Fraudsters use means of mass communication and commerce—television and radio, the Internet, and the mail—to perpetuate frauds that are capable

[20] See Wayne R LaFave, *Criminal Law* (4th edn., St. Paul, Minn.: Thomson/West, 2003) §19.7.
[21] *Durland v United States*, 161 US 306, 313 (1896).
[22] The mail fraud statute, for example, speaks in terms of devising or 'intending to devise' any scheme or artifice to defraud. 18 USC § 1341.
[23] 18 USC § 1341 (mail fraud); 18 USC § 1343 (wire fraud); 15 USC §§ 77x, 78ff (securities fraud); 26 USC § 7201 (tax fraud); 18 USC § 1344 (bank fraud); 18 USC § 1030 (computer fraud); 18 USC § 1347 (health care fraud); 18 USC § 371 (conspiracy to commit fraud against United States); 18 USC § 157 (bankruptcy fraud).
   The scholarly literature on mail fraud alone is enormous. For some leading examples, see Craig M Bradley, 'Foreword: Mail Fraud After *McNally* and *Carpenter*: The Essence of Fraud' (1988) 79 *Journal of Criminal Law & Criminology* 573; John C Coffee, Jr., 'Modern Mail Fraud: The Restoration of the Public/Private Distinction' (1998) 35 *American Criminal Law Review* 427; Peter J Henning, 'Maybe It Should Just Be Called Federal Fraud: The Changing Nature of the Mail Fraud Statute' (1995) 36 *Boston College Law Review* 435; Jed S Rakoff, 'The Federal Mail Fraud Statute (Part I)' (1980) 18 *Duquesne Law Review* 771; Geraldine Szott Moohr, 'Mail Fraud Meets Criminal Theory' (1998) 67 *University of Cincinnati Law Review* 1.

of causing widespread, aggregative harms.[24] Such offenders are often privileged, highly compensated, ostensibly respectable citizens who are perceived as (and may in fact be) providing valuable goods and services, increasing stock value, and creating employment opportunities. They commit such frauds in the context of complex business activities, such as securities offerings, health care financing, and bank transactions. Such activity can be hard to distinguish not only from civil frauds (in terms of their elements, the two offenses are virtually indistinguishable[25]), but also from lawful, if aggressive, business activity—'creative accounting,' 'puffing,' 'sharp dealing,' 'seller's talk,' and the like[26].

The victims of fraud can also be hard to identify. In addition to its immediate targets, fraud also causes (more remote) harms to less easily identifiable victims, including consumers and taxpayers. More generally, it can result in a loss of confidence in the system of free and fair enterprise. And even when a direct victim can be identified, such persons are sometimes themselves held to blame. As in the saying, 'you can't cheat an honest man,' the assumption is often made that only the greedy and dishonest are likely to be defrauded.[27] In light of such characteristics, fraud is appropriately classified as a white-collar offense.

2. The Deceit Element in Fraud

Although deceit is not always a required offense element under modern fraud statutes ('dishonesty,' in all of its ambiguity, is a common alternative), it nevertheless plays a central role in fraud's history and modern understanding. In this section, I want to explore the particular form that deceit takes in the formulation of fraud, and contrast it to the form of deceit required for perjury.

As defined earlier, deception consists of the communication of a message, or attempt to communicate a message, with which the communicator, in communicating, intends to cause a person to believe something that is untrue. Perhaps the clearest way to see the importance of deception in the concept of fraud is in connection with the law of theft. Indeed, it is precisely the element of deception that distinguishes fraud from other stealing offenses such as embezzlement (stealing by breach of trust), extortion (stealing by coercion), and robbery (stealing through force).[28]

---

[24] For a discussion of the social costs of fraud, with particular reference to Canada, see Nightingale (n 3 above, §1.3(a)).

[25] See, eg False Claims Act, 31 USC § 3730 (giving federal government and civil plaintiffs a cause of action against those who submit false claims to the government). Virtually the only differences between criminal and civil fraud concern burden of proof and remedies.

[26] On the subtle difference between fraud and mere puffing, see, eg *United States v Regent Office Supply Co.* Y21 F 2d 174, 1180 (2d Cir 1970) (to be fraudulent, a statement must concern price, quantity, effectiveness, or quality of goods or services); *United States v Brown* 79 F 3d 1550, 1557 (11th Cir 1996); *United States v Gay*, 967 F 2d 322, 328 (9th Cir.1992).

[27] Nightingale (n 3 above, at 1–29).

[28] Moreover, in its decision in *Fasulo v United States*, 272 US 620, 628 (1926), the Supreme Court was explicit that, broad as the conception of fraud is, it does not include obtaining property through threats or coercion.

The fact that property is taken *by deception* significantly affects the way in which fraud is experienced by the victim. One who has been defrauded of 50 dollars by a confidence man is likely to feel very different from a person who has had 50 dollars stolen by a larcener (or extortionist or robber). As Peter Alldridge has noted:

[I]f a victim is going to suffer a particular harm, it is less painful for him or her and less culpable of the person causing it that the harm should be caused without whatever additional unpleasantness comes from the deception of the victim. In the case of frauds there is far more likely to be the loss of self-esteem consequent upon feeling responsible by reason of having been duped.[28]

Indeed, it is the recognition of the distinctive moral character of fraud that explains why, notwithstanding the widespread consolidation of theft law that has occurred in many jurisdictions, the fact that theft is committed by means of deception continues to play a role in various classificatory schemes. Good examples are provided by the Model Penal Code[29] and the English Theft Act of 1968.[30] Both statutes consolidate the traditional acquisitive offenses (larceny, embezzlement, false pretenses, extortion, blackmail, fraudulent conversion, and receiving stolen property) in a manner that obviously reflects the similarity in harms caused.[31] Yet, within the broad rubric of 'theft offenses,' each statute retains categories such as Theft by Deception (in the case of the Model Penal Code[32]) and Obtaining Property by Deception (in the case of the English Theft Act[33]). In both instances, the principal factor that distinguishes such offenses from other theft offenses is the presence of deceit.

Non-Lying Deceit Crimes in Historical Perspective

Although fraud and perjury both involve an element of deceit, the nature of such deceit differs significantly. Perjury, as we saw above, requires a rigidly defined form of deception which we call 'lying.' Fraud, by contrast, allows for a much more flexible, open-ended form of 'merely misleading.' The Supreme Court in *Bronston* noted this explicitly when it said:

[Perjury] is not to be judged by the same standards applicable to criminally fraudulent or extortionate statements. In that context, the law goes 'rather far in punishing intentional creation of false impressions by a selection of literally true representations, because the actor himself generally selects and arranges the representations.' In

---

[28] Peter Alldridge, 'Sex, Lies and the Criminal Law' (1993) 44 *Northern Ireland Legal Quarterly* 250, 251. See also Lloyd L Weinrib, *Criminal Law: Cases, Comment, Questions* (6th edn., New York: Foundation Press, 1998) 395–96 (making a somewhat similar point).
[29] Model Penal Code § 223.1–.2.   [30] Theft Act 1968, c. 60, §§ 1, 7 (Eng.).
[31] See, eg Model Penal Code, Comments to § 223.1, at 131–32 ('[T]heft by a stranger and...theft by a fiduciary represent similar dangers requiring approximately the same treatment and characterization....Prevailing moral standards do not differentiate sharply between the swindler and other 'thieves.' To that extent, at least, consolidation conforms to the common understanding of what is substantially the same kind of undesirable conduct.').
[32] Model Penal Code § 223.3.   [33] Theft Act 1968, c. 60, § 15 (Eng.).

contrast, 'under our system of adversary questioning and cross-examination the scope of disclosure is largely in the hands of counsel and presiding officer.'[34]

In order to understand the role of deception in fraud and related offenses such as false pretenses and theft by deception, it will be helpful to view these offenses in historical context. Although such offenses today reflect a broad concept of deception, this was not always the case. Initially, the role of deception in theft law was limited to a narrowly defined set of circumstances. It was only slowly, over several centuries, that this role broadened.

At early English Common Law, one who obtained title to another's property by force or stealth was guilty of robbery or larceny, respectively, but one who obtained title to another's property by deception was generally held not to have committed a crime.[35] An important exception to this rule was the offense of common law cheat, which consisted of fraud perpetrated by means of some false token, typically false weights or measures.[36] The rationale for the common law exception to the usual rule of *caveat emptor* was clear: unlike other forms of fraud, the use of false weights or false tokens was something against which common prudence could not guard.[37] This explanation thus bears a striking resemblance to the reasoning used above to describe the difference between lying and other forms of deception—ie whereas most forms of deception can be guarded against by common prudence, lying cannot.

Over time, however, this narrow definition of theft by deception could not stand. As commercial relations became increasingly complex, and the principle of *caveat emptor* became harder and harder to sustain, the definition of what constituted actionable deception was bound to become broader. The paradigm of 'lying' thus began to give way to the paradigm of 'merely misleading.'

In 1562, forgery—defined as the fraudulent making or alteration of a writing having apparent legal significance—was first made a crime in England.[38]

[34] 409 US at 358 n.4 (quoting Model Penal Code § 208.20, comt. (Tentative Draft No. 6, 1957)).
[35] The doctrine of *caveat emptor* prevailed: 'A person who deprived another of his property by force or stealth was regarded by all as a very evil person, but he who got the better of another in a bargain by means of falsehood was more likely to be regarded by his neighbors as clever than as criminal.' Rollin M Perkins and Ronald N Boyce, *Criminal Law* (Mineola, NY: Foundation Press, 1969) 363. Much of this history is also considered in Note, 'Whatever Happened to *Durland*?: Mail Fraud, RICO, and Justifiable Reliance' (1992) 68 *Notre Dame Law Review* 333.
[36] On the origins of the law of common law cheat, see Jerome Hall, *Theft, Law and Society* (Indianapolis: Bobbs Merrill, 1952) 40; Joel Prentiss Bishop, *Commentaries on the Criminal Law* (5th edn., Boston: Little, Brown, 1872) vol.2, ch. 10, at 77–94.
[37] See, eg *R v Wheatly* (1761) 97 ER 746 (upholding dismissal of charges for common law cheat where the defendant was alleged to have 'falsely, fraudulently and deceitfully' sold and delivered to victim as 18 gallons of beer what was really only 16 gallons; reasoning that the case involved what was essentially a civil wrong, 'an inconvenience and injury to a private person,' not an offense under the criminal law, which would involve the use of false weights and measures affecting 'all or many of his customers' or which were used in the 'general course of his dealing,' and which 'common care and prudence are not sufficient to guard against').
[38] Perkins and Boyce (n 35 above, at 414). On the origins of the English law of forgery, see JW Cecil Turner, 'Documents in the Law of Forgery' (1946) 32 *Virginia Law Review* 939. On the Roman law history of forgery, see Stuart P Green, 'Deceit and the Classification of Crimes: Federal Rule of Evidence 609(a)(2) and the Origins of *Crimen Falsi*' (2000) 90 *Journal of*

The offense was initially restricted to royal documents, then expanded to sealed documents, and finally to public documents generally.[39] In forgery, the deception is found not in the *content* of the document; rather, it involves deception concerning the genuineness or authenticity of the document itself.[40]

With the advent of the Industrial Revolution, the broadening of fraud offenses began to accelerate. False pretenses was added to the list of deception offenses in England in 1757, under a statute that made it a crime for any person to 'knowingly or designedly' by false pretenses obtain title to 'money, goods, wares or merchandizes' from another person 'with the intent to cheat or defraud.'[41] Although significantly broader in scope than both common law cheat and forgery, false pretenses was still limited in that it required a false representation of an existing fact, rather than merely a false promise,[42] opinion,[43] or prediction.[44] For example, falsely stating that a gem has been appraised at $1,000 constitutes a false representation for purposes of false pretenses, but falsely stating that the gem *will* appreciate in value over the next year does not.[45]

Criminal Law & Criminology 1087, 1096 (at Roman law, forgery limited to falsification of royal seals and official documents). Under the broader Model Penal Code definition, a person commits forgery if, knowingly facilitating fraud or injury of another, the person makes, alters, or authenticates a writing that purports to be another's without authorization to do so. Model Penal Code § 224.1.

[39] See Model Penal Code § 224.1, Comments at 282–83.

[40] Paul H Robinson, *Criminal Law* (New York: Aspen, 1997) 790. Note that, at common law, not every faked document constitutes a forgery. For example, if one wrote out the Gettysburg Address, simulating the handwriting and signature of Abraham Lincoln, and sold it to a collector of antique manuscripts, that would not be forgery, because the Gettysburg Address—unlike, say, a negotiable instrument, deed, mortgage, bill of lading, will, sales receipt, bond, contract, diploma, certificate of marriage, divorce decree, army discharge, or railroad ticket—does not have any immediate legal significance. Perkins and Boyce (n 35 above, at 416–17). Attempting to pass off a copy of the Gettysburg Address as the original would, however, constitute false pretenses.   [41] 30 Geo. II., c. 24 § 1 (1757).

[42] The evolution of the 'existing fact' dogma of false pretenses is described in Arthur R Pearce, 'Theft by False Promise' (1953) 101 *University of Pennsylvania Law Review* 967, 968–78. Pearce advanced a strenuous argument against the then-prevailing common law doctrine which excluded false promises from the scope of false pretenses. He argued that such exclusion was based principally on historical accidents, and that subsequent developments in federal fraud law (which has long included false promises within its scope) point towards an expansion of doctrine in the law of false pretenses as well. The problem with Pearce's argument, however, is that it seems to evade the apparently important moral distinction between situations in which a defendant knows he cannot or will not honor a contract at the time he enters into it, and situations in which the decision not to honor a contract is made later.

[43] The leading case of *R v Bryan* (1857) 7 Cox Crim. Cas. 312, 317, seems to carry this approach to extremes. *D* obtained money from *P* by representing that certain spoons were of the best quality, equal to Elkington's A, and having as much silver as Elkington's A. These statements were known by the defendant to be false. In reversing the conviction, the court held that this was not false pretenses: 'Whether these spoons . . . were equal to Elkington's A or not, cannot be, as far as I know, decidedly affirmed or denied in the same way as a past fact can be affirmed or denied, but it is in the nature of a matter of opinion.' But, as J C Smith points out, this can hardly be true of the statement that the spoons had as much silver on them as Elkington's A. J C Smith, *The Law of Theft* (5th edn., London: Butterworths, 1984) 91.

[44] Perkins and Boyce (n 35 above, at 369–70).

[45] Kathleen F Brickey, *Corporate and White Collar Crime* (2nd edn., Boston: Little Brown, 1995) 119. The idea was that many opinions expressed by sellers of goods are merely

In addition to false pretenses, English law also criminalized a separate offense known as larceny by deceit. At common law, larceny was defined as the trespassory taking of personal property from the *possession* of another. Because false pretenses was limited to cases involving the use of deception to obtain *title* to money or goods, it did not cover cases in which a defendant had used deception to obtain mere possession. The most famous example is *Pear's Case*, in which the defendant fraudulently rented a horse from a stable, intending from the outset to steal it.[46] Because only possession of, and not title to, the horse passed with the rental agreement, the defendant could not be prosecuted for false pretenses. Instead, the defendant was prosecuted for a newly created theft offense—namely, larceny by trick.

This collection of common law deception offenses illustrates two things. The first is the absence of any requirement of assertion. A charge of common law cheat, for example, would lie where a butcher misled a customer into believing that a slab of meat weighs more than it actually does by some action—say, placing an underweight slab on a rigged scale.[47] Likewise, as noted above, the crime of forgery consists not in the falsity of the statements contained in the document, but rather in the misrepresentation of the genuineness or authenticity of the document itself. False pretenses is also frequently committed without an assertion, as when the defendant obtained credit from a shopkeeper by wearing an Oxford college cap and gown to create the false impression that he was an Oxonian.[48] As for larceny by trick, *Pear's Case* itself shows that no statement was necessary for the offense to be committed; it was enough that the defendant *acted* as if he would return the horse.

Secondly, unlike perjury, fraud and the other deception offenses do not require a literal falsehood. This is most obvious in the context of cases such as *R v King*, in which the defendant, a used car salesman, allegedly stated that

---

'puffing,' see, eg *Pizza Hut Inc. v Papa John's International*, 80 F Supp. 2d 600 (ND Tex 2000) (question was whether advertising slogan, 'Better Ingredients, Better Pizza,' was fraud or mere puffing), and cannot be taken as fact. Moreover, there was a reluctance to treat a debtor's breach of contract as the basis for a false pretenses prosecution, the explanation being that 'the act complained of . . . is as consonant with ordinary commercial default as with criminal conduct. . . . Business affairs would be materially encumbered by the ever present threat that a debtor might be subject to criminal penalties.' *Chaplin v United States*, 1587 F 2d 697, 698–99 (DC 1946).

[46] *R v Pear* (1779) 168 Eng. Rep. 208.

[47] One can easily imagine the butcher saying, as he places a 3½ pound slab of beef on the rigged scale, 'there's four pounds for you, Mrs. Soprano.' But such statement would not be a necessary part of the offense.

[48] *R v Barnard* (1837) 173 ER 342; *R v Robinson* (1884) 10 VLR 131 (defendant in Barnard would have been guilty of false pretenses even if he had said nothing); see also *Harris* (1975) 62 Cr App Rep 28 (false pretenses committed when defendant registered as a guest in a hotel, and thereby represented that he intended to pay the bill at the end of his stay); *R v Buckmaster* (1887) 2 QBD 182 (bookmaker, when he takes a bet, represents that he intends to pay if the backed horse wins). Indeed, even a silence can constitute false pretenses when the non-speaker has a duty of disclosure. See, eg *People v Johnson*, 150 NYS 331 (NY 1914).

the mileage shown on the odometer of a second hand car 'may not be correct.' The court held that, though literally true, the statement falsely implied that the defendant did not know the odometer to be incorrect, and therefore constituted false pretenses.[49] Similarly, a 1932 British court 'sent Lord Kylsant to prison because his steamship line had issued a prospectus that had *truthfully* stated its average net income for the past ten years and its dividends for the past seventeen, but had deliberately *concealed* the fact that its earnings during the first three of the ten years had been greatly augmented by World War I as compared with the seven lean years that followed.'[50] In sum, according to LaFave and Scott, a 'statement which though literally true is nonetheless misleading because it omits necessary qualifications—the half-truth which can operate to deceive quite as effectively as the outright lie—constitutes a form of misrepresentation which, when done with intent to deceive, ought to qualify as a false pretense.'[51]

Modern Misleading Offenses: Mail Fraud, Securities Fraud, and Theft by Deception

Like their common law antecedents, the modern fraud-like offenses reflect a significantly more flexible approach to deception than crimes such as perjury and false declarations. Although they obviously can be committed by means of outright lies, literal falsity is seldom, if ever, required. The most prominent example of such flexibility in approaching the requirement of deception is the federal mail fraud statute. Under this statute, the courts have repeatedly recognized that a statement that is literally true may nonetheless constitute fraud, as long as it is both material and made with intent to deceive.[52] Moreover, 'deception need not be premised upon verbalized words alone. The arrangement of the words, or the circumstances in which they are used may convey the false and deceptive appearance.'[53]

The modern fraud offenses are even more flexible than their common law antecedents. They eliminate not only the requirements of assertion and literal

[49] See Smith (n 43 above, at 86).
[50] Louis Loss, *Fundamentals of Securities Regulation* (New York: Aspen, 1988) 714 (citing *R v Kylsant* (1932) 1 KB 442, CA). According to Loss, under false pretenses or common law fraud, '[i]t is now quite clear that a half-truth is as bad as an outright lie.' *Ibid.*
[51] Wayne R LaFave and Austin W Scott, Jr., *Criminal Law* 743–44 (2nd edn., Minneapolis: West Publishing., 1986).
[52] See, eg *Lustiger v United States*, 386 F2d 132, 136 (9th Cir. 1967) ('While the statements in the advertising materials may not have been literally false, taken as a whole they were fraudulently misleading and deceptive.'), cert. denied, 390 US 951 (1968). On the other hand, not all literally false statements made with intent to deceive will necessarily constitute fraud, as demonstrated by the Second Circuit's decision in *United States v Regent Office Supply*, 421 F 2d 1174 (2d Cir 1970) (rejecting application of mail fraud statute premised upon use of false pretenses in the preliminary stages of a sales solicitation). The most important factor is that the statement be material. In the words of the court in *Regent Office Supply*, it must be 'directed to the quality, adequacy or price of the goods' themselves.' *Ibid* at 1182.
[53] *Lustiger*, 386 F 2d at 138.

falsity, but also that of a false representation of an existing fact. Again, mail fraud provides an excellent example. In the Supreme Court's 1896 case of *Durland v United States*,[54] the defendant was charged with making false promises to investors in his investment company. In rejecting the defendant's argument that the mail fraud statute reaches only 'such cases as, at common law, would come within the definition of "false pretenses," ' the Court made clear that the statute reflected a much broader conception of deception, which included 'representations as to the past or present, or suggestions and promises as to the future.'[55]

Securities fraud has followed a similar pattern.[56] In *Lucia v Prospect Street High Income Portfolio, Inc.*, for example, the defendants issued a mutual fund prospectus containing a ten-year profit comparison of junk bonds and United State Treasury notes.[57] Although the junk bonds had in truth outperformed Treasury securities during the preceding 10-year period, the fact was that during the six years immediately preceding each fund's public offerings, Treasury securities had outperformed junk bonds. The court concluded that a triable issue was presented as to whether the defendants had committed fraud:

[T]he fact that a statement is literally true does not preclude liability under federal securities laws. 'Some statements, although literally accurate, can become, through their context and manner of presentation, devices which mislead investors. For that reason, the disclosure required by the securities laws is measured not by literal truth, but by the ability of the material accurately to inform rather than mislead prospective buyers.'[58]

---

[54] 161 US 306 (1896).

[55] *Ibid* at 313–14. It should be pointed out here that the current mail fraud statute has both 'schemes to defraud' and 'false pretenses' provisions. To the extent that a defendant is charged under the false pretenses prong only, he might be able to argue that a common law-like limitation on deception should apply. Cf SN Welling, et al., *Federal Criminal Law and Related Actions: Crimes, Forfeiture, the False Claims Act and RICO* (St. Paul, Minn.: West Group, 1998) vol. 2, at 11, ('Although the federal courts give the concept of affirmative misrepresentation a fairly broad interpretation, the experience under the bank fraud statute demonstrates [that] convictions that would have been upheld under the defraud prong may be reversed if they are brought only under the false pretenses prong.').

[56] See section 17(a) of the Securities Act of 1933, 15 USC § 77q (making it unlawful for any person in the offer or sale of any securities . . . (1) to employ any device, scheme, or artifice to defraud, or (2) to obtain money or property by means of any untrue statement of a material fact or any omission to state a material fact necessary in order to make the statements made, in the light of the circumstances under which they were made, not misleading, or (3) to engage in any transaction, practice, or course of business which operates or would operate as a fraud or deceit upon the purchaser'); Rule 10b-5 of the SEC's regulations, 17 CFR § 240.10b-5, promulgated pursuant to the Securities Exchange Act of 1934, 15 USC § 78j (providing that it is unlawful, in connection with the purchase or sale of any security, to '(a) To employ any device, scheme, or artifice to defraud, (b) To make any untrue statement of a material fact or to omit to state a material fact necessary in order to make the statements made, in the light of the circumstances under which they were made, not misleading, or (c) To engage in any act, practice, or course of business which operates or would operate as a fraud or deceit upon any person.').   [57] 36 F 3d 170 (1st Cir 1994).

[58] *Ibid* at 175 (quoting *McMahan v Wherehouse Entertainment, Inc.*, 900 F 2d 576, 579 (2d Cir 1990). See also Donald C. Langevoort, 'Half-Truths: Protecting Mistaken Inferences by Investors and Others' (1999) 52 *Stanford Law Review* 87 (discussing treatment of half-truths, misrepresentation, and nondisclosure in securities fraud cases). As described in the text accompanying n 34 above, *Bronston* makes a similar point.

Finally, we can look to Model Penal Code section 223.3, theft by deception, which provides that a person is guilty of theft if he 'purposely obtains property of another by deception,' and which, in turn, defines 'deceive' to mean 'creates or reinforces a false impression, including false impressions as to law, value, intention or other state of mind,' as well as certain cases in which the actor knowingly takes advantage of another's misinformation, though he may not have been responsible for disseminating it.[59] As the Comments to section 223.3 make clear, it is the 'falsity of the *impression* purposely created or reinforced that is determinative, rather than the falsity of any particular representations made by the actor. Thus, deception may be accomplished by statements that are literally true or that consist of a clever collection of half-truths.'[60]

In sum, with respect to fraud and other similar offenses, legislatures and courts have defined deception broadly, to allow for a far broader and more flexible conception of deceit than occurs in connection with perjury or false declarations. Not only do these offenses not require a literally false statement, they do not require any statement at all. They can be committed by means of deceptive conduct, gestures, pictures, even silences.

---

[59] Model Penal Code § 223.3.   [60] *Ibid* § 223.3, Comments at 185.

14

False Statements

Having considered both 'lying' offenses such as perjury, and 'misleading' offenses such as fraud, we can now turn our attention to an offense that reflects elements of both lying and misleading—the crime of making false statements.[1] Codified most prominently in 18 USC § 1001, as well as in numerous kindred statutes, the offense of false statements typically requires that the defendant make a materially false statement or representation 'within the jurisdiction of' some government agency.[2] Unlike perjury, there is no requirement that such statements be made under oath. Like perjury, however, most (but not all) American false statements statutes have been held to require literal falsity. What is perhaps most interesting about the offense of false statements, however, is the way in which it distinguishes (or, more accurately, used to distinguish) between wrongful exculpation and wrongful inculpation.

1. The Hybrid Nature of False Statements

In its current form, section 1001 makes it a crime, within the jurisdiction of the United States Government, to (1) make 'materially false, fictitious, or fraudulent statements or representations,' (2) make false writings containing

---

[1] This hybrid nature is also reflected in the different ways the offense is dealt with in the major treatises on white-collar crime. For example, Kathleen Brickey emphasizes the similarities between section 1001 and perjury, see Kathleen F Brickey, *Corporate Criminal Liability* (2nd edn., Deerfield, Ill.: Clark Boardman Callaghan, 1991–94) vol. 3, at 239–326, while Sarah Welling, Sara Beale, and Pamela Bucy emphasize its relation to fraud-type statutes (particularly, fraud against the government), see SN Welling, et al., *Federal Criminal Law and Related Actions: Crimes, Forfeiture, the False Claims Act and RICO* (St. Paul, Minn: West Group, 1998) vol. 1, 505–28.

[2] 18 USC § 1001((a)(2). In addition to section 1001, there are also numerous other 'kindred' federal statutes that make it a crime to make a false statement in one or more specific contexts, frequently involving matters subject to administrative agencies. See, eg 18 USC § 1014 (making it a crime to make a 'false statement or report . . . for the purpose of influencing' various federal bank loan and credit agencies); 18 USC § 287 (making it a crime to make or present a claim to the United States Government knowing such claim to be 'false, fictitious or fraudulent'); 18 USC § 494 (making it a crime, *inter alia*, to 'falsely make, alter, forge, or counterfeit any bond, bid, proposal, contract, guarantee, security, official bond, public record, affidavit, or other writing for the purpose of defrauding the United States'). For a comprehensive listing of federal false statements statutes, see Brickey (n 1 above, vol. 3, at 314–19).

'materially false, fictitious, or fraudulent statements,' or (3) 'falsify, conceal, or cover up by any trick, scheme, or device a material fact.'[3] Although the term 'false claim' was deleted from the statute in 1948,[4] the use of terms such as 'fraudulent,' 'falsify, conceal, or cover up,' and 'trick, scheme, or device,' continues to be understood as signifying a broad, fraud-like conception of deception. At the same time, the use of the term 'false statement' has been interpreted to connote a much narrower, perjury-like conception.

False Statements in Historical Perspective

A brief examination of the history of the false statement statutes will be helpful in explaining the reason for their hybrid nature. The statutory progenitor of section 1001 was enacted in 1863.[5] Entitled 'An Act to Prevent and Punish Frauds Upon the Government of the United States,' it prohibited the filing of 'false, fictitious, or fraudulent' claims against the government.[6] Passed in the midst of the Civil War, the statute was a response to a 'spate of frauds'—particularly, procurement frauds—being committed on the US Government.[7] In 1918, this time at the end of the First World War, the statute was broadened slightly, to cover false statements made 'for the purpose and with the intent of cheating and swindling or defrauding the Government of the United States.'[8] At this point, the concept of deception in the false statements statute was virtually indistinguishable from the concept of deception found in the various fraud-type statutes discussed above.[9] The only difference was the identity of the victim being defrauded.

Starting in the 1930s, however, the crime of false statements began to undergo dramatic changes. With the advent of the New Deal and the creation of numerous new regulatory programs and agencies, self-reporting became an increasingly important element in compliance. The Government's concern was no longer merely with the direct loss of property or money; it now had a strong interest in preventing the loss of information through inaccurate and untruthful reporting—most notoriously in connection with unreported shipments of 'hot oil.'[10]

---

[3] 18 USC § 1001. Non-deceptive violations of the 'concealing' or 'covering up' provisions in the statute are dealt with in Chapter 15.

[4] In 1948, the false claim language was moved into a separate provision, 18 USC § 287. See Act of 25 June 1948, §§ 287, 1001, 62 Stat 698, 749.

[5] Act of 2 March 1863, c. 67, 12 Stat 696–697.

[6] See *Brogan v United States*, 522 US 398, 412 (1998) (Ginsburg, J., concurring) (citing Act of 2 March 1863, c. 67, 12 Stat 696); *Hubbard v United States*, 514 US 695, 705 (1995).

[7] *United States v Bramblett*, 348 US 503, 504 (1955).

[8] Act of 23 Oct. 1918, c. 194, § 35, 40 Stat 1015–16.

[9] See, eg *Brogan*, 522 US at 412 (statute limited to cases in which defendant has allegedly 'cheat[ed] the Government out of property or money') (Ginsburg, J., concurring) (quoting *United States v Cohen*, 270 US 339, 346 (1926)).

[10] *Ibid* at 412 (Ginsburg, J., concurring) (describing New Deal history of section 1001: 'If regulated industries could file false reports with impunity, significant Government interests would

In response to these concerns, Congress took several initiatives. First, it amended the precursor to section 1001 to prohibit not just 'false, fictitious, or fraudulent' *claims* against the government, but also 'any false or fraudulent *statements* or *representations*' made within the jurisdiction of the government.[11] In addition, it began passing or amending various specialized false statements statutes that would apply in specific regulatory contexts. The result was to transform the crime of false statements into one that reflected both the looser 'misleading' and the more restrictive 'lying' models of deception.

False Statements and the Requirement of an Assertion

A good example of how the crime of false statements takes on the rigid contours of the 'lying' offenses can be found in the Supreme Court's opinion in *Williams v United States*,[12] which involved a prosecution under 18 USC § 1014, making it a crime to 'knowingly make[] any false statement' for the purpose of influencing the action of any federally insured bank. The defendant had allegedly engaged in a series of transactions usually characterized as 'check kiting,' a scheme whereby false credit is obtained by the exchange and passing of worthless checks between two or more banks. In rejecting the government's contention that the defendant, by depositing a check that was not supported by sufficient funds, had made a 'false statement,' the Court relied on the fact that:

technically speaking, a check is not a factual assertion at all, and therefore cannot be characterized as "true" or "false." Petitioner's bank checks served only to direct the drawee banks to pay the face amounts to the bearer, while committing petitioner to make good the obligations if the banks dishonored the drafts. Each check did not, in terms, make any representation as to the state of petitioner's bank balance. [13]

Had the defendant been prosecuted for mail or bank fraud, rather than false statements, there is little question that his check kiting scheme would have been viewed as actionable, since one who draws a check on a bank is generally understood to be making a representation that he has sufficient funds in his bank account to cover the check.[14] But since check kiting does not

be subverted even though the Government would not be deprived of any property or money.'). 'Hot oil frauds' were schemes in which petroleum producers falsify shipping documents by stating that their in-state oil wells are producing a certain amount of oil, when in fact they were producing less oil and supplementing it with contraband oil purchased from out of state. *United States v Gilliland*, 312 US 86, 94–95 (1941); *United States v Yermian*, 468 US 63, 80 (1984) (Rehnquist, J., dissenting).

[11] Act of 18 June 1934, c. 587, § 35, 48 Stat 996 (emphasis added). *United States v Gilliland*, 312 US 86, 93 (1941) (1934 amendment removed restriction to matters in which government has financial or proprietary interest) [12] 458 US 279 (1982).

[13] *Ibid* at 284.

[14] See, eg *United States v Giordano*, 489 F 2d 327 (2nd Cir 1973) (affirming conviction for bank fraud in scheme involving check kiting); *United States v Constant*, 501 F 2d 1284 (5th Cir 1974) (upholding mail fraud conviction for scheme involving check kiting), *cert denied*, 420 US 910 (1975).

involve an assertion, it does not constitute a false statement. *Williams* should thus be understood as being consistent with the narrow 'lying' approach to false statements described above.[15]

A different situation arises in false statements cases involving defendants who give no response at all or only an incomplete response to government questioning. Consider the case of then-Governor George W Bush's response (or lack thereof) to a 1996 jury questionnaire, which became something of an issue in the final days of the 2000 presidential campaign. In the questionnaire, Bush was asked to check whether he had ever been an accused, a complainant, or a witness in a criminal case. Despite the fact that he had been arrested on at least two occasions, and despite the instruction that '[t]his form must be completed and returned when reporting for jury duty,' Bush (or his agents) left the question blank.[16] Did Bush's failure to respond constitute a false statement?

What little case law there is seems to indicate that a person who has a duty to answer a question posed by a government official or form, and fails to do so, is guilty of making a false statement. Typical of this view is the Fifth Circuit's opinion in *United States v Mattox*, in which the defendant was prosecuted under 18 USC §§ 1001 and 1920 (making false statements in connection with federal worker's compensation claims).[17] A Labor Department form required applicants to 'report all employment during the past 12 months' and 'account for the entire time, including periods of self-employment or unemployment.' In response to one question, the defendant wrote 'N/A.' Another question he left blank. In rejecting the defendant's apparent

---

[15] Analogous reasoning was followed in *United States v Blankenship*, 382 F 3d 1110, 1135 (11th Cir 2004) ('Like a check, a contract is not a factual assertion, and therefore cannot be characterized as "true" or "false."... Just as a check is not "false" simply because neither the drawer nor the drawee intends that the drawee cash it, a contract is not false simply because neither party intends to enforce it.').

Unfortunately, the courts have not always been clear about what exactly an assertion is. Consider the Second Circuit's decision in *United States v Worthington*, in which the defendant was prosecuted under section 1001 after submitting to the Internal Revenue Service a check printed with the name of a fictitious drawee bank. 822 F 2d 315 (2nd Cir), *cert denied*, 484 US 944 (1987). In upholding his conviction, the Second Circuit wrote:

The rationale of *Williams*—that drawing a check unsupported by sufficient funds is [not] a statement... is simply inapplicable here.... Here, of course, the check contains the name of a drawee 'bank,' which designates where the check may be presented for payment. Naming a bank is a representation that the bank upon which the check is drawn does in fact exist. Thus, unlike *Williams*, the assertion in the instant case constitutes a statement.

Ibid at 318. In this reasoning, the court clearly erred. Submitting a check printed with the name of a fictitious drawee bank, though certainly deceptive, is not an assertion, because it is not a statement with a determinable truth value. If it constitutes any crime, it is probably forgery (See ch. 13, n 4 and accompanying text above), not false statements.

[16] Wayne Slater and Peter Slover, 'Race Heating Up in the Homestretch: Bush Camp Tries to Stem DUI Fallout, Denies Misleading Answers on Arrest,' *Dallas Morning News* (4 Nov. 2000), at A1. Bush was arrested in 1966 for stealing a Christmas wreath from a Connecticut store in a 'fraternity prank,' and again in 1976 for drunk driving. There were also allegations that, on a number of occasions, Bush had lied to, or misled, the media regarding the fact of these arrests. *Ibid*.   [17] 689 F 2d 531 (5th Cir 1982).

argument that his response (or lack of response) did not constitute a statement, the court argued that 'silence may be falsity when it misleads, particularly if there is a duty to speak. The evidence warranted the conclusion that Mattox had a duty to fill in the blank if he had been employed and that his failure to do so was equivalent to an answer, and a false one at that.'[18]

Such reasoning seems to me mistaken. The mere fact that a person is under a legal duty to give a response does not necessarily mean that his failure to do so constitutes a false statement.[19] Indeed, the fact that a person is under a legal obligation to make a statement is no more relevant to the truthfulness of her statement than the fact that she is under *no* such obligation.[20] Here again, morality helps illuminate law. A person who refuses to answer a question that she is morally obligated to answer (say, a child who is asked a question by a parent) may be defiant and obstreperous, but she is not necessarily mendacious.[21] Similarly, while a witness who is subpoenaed to testify and refuses to do so may be guilty of contempt or obstruction, and a party who declines to answer questions required on a government form guilty of failure to file a required form,[22] neither should necessarily be guilty of perjury or false statements.

False Statements and the Requirement of Literal Falsity

Another way in which the crime of false statements reflects the rigid 'lying' approach can be observed in cases involving the literal falsity requirement. A majority of—though not all—courts have held that conviction for false

---

[18] *Ibid* at 532. See also *United States v Irwin*, 654 F 2d 671, 676 (10th Cir 1981) (upholding conviction under section 1001 for submitting a federal grant application to the Economic Development Association and leaving a blank under the column marked 'compensation already paid,' when in fact the defendant had received compensation; 'leaving a blank is equivalent to an answer of "none" or a statement that there are no facts required to be reported.').

[19] I say 'mere' fact because one can easily imagine a scenario in which it would be reasonable to construe a failure to give a response as a negative response. For example: if I say to my class, 'please raise your hand if you did not do the homework for today,' the fact that *A* is one of several people who has not raised her hand can reasonably be understood as an assertion that she did her homework. If in fact she did not do her homework and nevertheless did not raise her hand, we might say that she has lied. (Of course, it is also possible that she did not respond because she did not hear my question or was not paying attention.) Similarly, if a government form said, 'please list all of your assets,' then it might well be reasonable to infer that someone who left the appropriate space on the form blank would be making an assertion that he had no assets. My point, though, is that the mere fact that there is a legal duty to respond to a question does not tell us much about what can reasonably be inferred from a silence. Rather, we need to know more about the precise context in which the question was asked.

[20] False statements prosecutions frequently involve statements that were offered voluntarily. See, eg *United States v Kingston*, 971 F 2d 481, 489 (10th Cir 1992); *United States v Irwin*, 654 F 2d 671, 678 (10th Cir 1981), *cert denied*, 455 US 1016 (1982).

[21] At this point, it is worth distinguishing between refusing to provide a required answer and failing to do so. To the extent that the latter is more likely to be understood as an assertion (see n 19 above) it is also more plausibly characterized as a 'lie.'

[22] For a prosecution for failure to file a required form, see, eg *United States v McCarthy*, 422 F 2d 160 (2nd Cir 1970) (upholding conviction for failure to file report under 29 USC § 432, regarding certain labor practices, where defendant filed a report but failed to list certain payments that were required to be listed).

statements requires a showing of literal falsity. A good example is the Eighth Circuit's opinion in *United States v Vesaas*.[23] In 1972, the defendant had personally guaranteed a Small Business Administration loan made to a corporation formed by a group of his friends. After the corporation failed, the government obtained a default judgment against him. The defendant had held a number of stocks in joint tenancy with his mother, who died in August 1977. In November 1977, the defendant was asked at a deposition if he 'knew of any stocks, bonds, or other property owned by his deceased mother and himself in joint tenancy.' He answered 'no.' Since it is legally impossible to be a joint tenant with a decedent, the defendant's response, though misleading, was literally true. Accordingly, the Eighth Circuit, following *Bronston*, reversed.[24]

In contrast to the rigid lying approach followed in *Vesaas* and elsewhere is the flexible deception formula adopted by the Second Circuit in *United States v Stephenson*.[25] Stephenson was an Export Licensing Officer at the US Department of Commerce. His duties included reviewing applications for federal approval to export high-technology equipment from the United States abroad. In 1987, the Zamax Company sought a Commerce Department license to ship high technology medical equipment to China. Starting in mid-October 1987, Stephenson began pressing Zamax officials, including Wilson Chang, for a bribe to approve the license. During subsequent meetings, Chang, acting as an FBI informant, offered to pay Stephenson at least $35,000 for one of the required licenses. Several months later, Stephenson, fearing that he might be caught, went to Michael Dubensky, a Commerce Department Special Agent, and told him that he, Stephenson, 'had received a bribe offer from a company in New York by the name of Zamax.' As a result of his statement to Dubensky regarding Chang's offer, Stephenson was prosecuted under section 1001.

In his defense, Stephenson argued that his statement to Agent Dubensky—to the effect that he had a received a bribe offer from Zamax—was literally true, and therefore not actionable under section 1001. In upholding Stephenson's conviction, the court said that, even if his statement were literally true,[26] he

[23] 586 F 2d 101, 104 (8th Cir 1978).
[24] See also *United States v Diogo*, 320 F 2d 898, 905 (2d Cir 1963) (reversing conviction for false statements where defendant's statements to immigration officials to the effect that he was the 'spouse of' and 'married to' an American woman were literally true, even if ultimately intended to mislead authorities about the true nature of his immigration status); *United States v Lozano*, 511 F 2d 1, 5 (7th Cir) (similar), *cert denied*, 423 US 850 (1975); *United States v Gahagan*, 881 F 2d 1380, 1383 (6th Cir 1989) (reversing conviction for false statements where defendant, who was required to file financial report listing all of his assets, failed to report his ownership of automobile, after transferring title to vehicle to his girlfriend prior to his completion of financial report; statement of assets held to be 'literally and factually correct').
[25] *United States v Stephenson*, 895 F 2d 867, 873 (2d Cir 1990).
[26] In fact, the court found that Stephenson's statement was literally false: 'Based upon the evidence, the jury easily could have found that by his statement to Dubensky, Stephenson intended to communicate that he was an unwilling victim of a bribery scheme initiated and orchestrated by Chang. So construed, the statement becomes clearly false.' *Ibid* at 874. This argument, however, is clearly specious. When Stephenson told Dubensky that he had received a bribe offer from

would still be subject to prosecution under section 1001. In so doing, the court rejected the literal truth defense, emphasizing the significance of the 'falsifie[d], conceal[ed], or cover[ed] up' language in section 1001, in apparent contrast to the perjury-like term, 'false statement.'

Unfortunately, the legislative history offers little explanation for why Congress made some false statements statutes require lying and others merely misleading. Nor have the courts been helpful in explaining the difference. In large part, the fact that some false statements statutes provisions look like perjury and others like fraud seems to be a result of nothing more than historical accident.

As explained above, however, there are good reasons for maintaining a clear distinction between those contexts in which a defendant has lied and those in which a defendant has merely misled. In light of that analysis, I would propose that legislatures and courts adopt the following approach: when a false statements statute is to be applied to a statement made in a formal or quasi-formal proceeding, in which a government agent has had the opportunity for follow-up questioning, such statute should reflect the requirement of literal falsity. But when a false statement is applied to a statement made in informal proceedings, without the opportunity for 'cross-examination,' it should function like fraud or false pretenses. Such an approach would bring much needed coherence and consistency into the law of false statements.

2. EXCULPATORY NOES

The offense of false statements is violated when a suspect or witness uses deception in dealing with government agents, for the purpose, generally, of either wrongful exculpation or wrongful inculpation. A good example of the former is the recent case of Martha Stewart, who was convicted in March 2004 of making false statements to government agents who were investigating the circumstances surrounding her sale of stock in the biotech company, ImClone.[27] In such cases, false statements charges can be brought instead of, or in addition to, charges relating to the underlying subject of the investigation (in the Stewart case, insider trading).[28] False statements are also committed when an informant or witness gives falsely *incriminating* information to the government about the commission of a crime. For example, in *United States v Rodgers*, the defendant allegedly made false statements when he told the

Chang, the fact is that, no matter how misleading, he was saying something that was literally true. Stephenson's statement was precisely analogous to the misleading, but literally true, statements made in *Bronston, Eddy, Vesaas, Lozano*, and numerous other cases discussed above.

[27] *United States v Stewart*, 323 F Supp. 2d 606, 609–10 (SDNY 2004); 'Stewart Convicted on All Charges,' *CNN/Money* (5 March 2004) <http://money.cnn.com/2004/03/05/news/companies/martha_verdict> (summarizing the case and reporting on the jury's verdict).

[28] Section 1001 can also be violated when a defendant makes a fraudulent statement to the government to obtain money or resist a claim. See, eg *United States v Shah*, 44 F 3d 285 (5th Cir 1995).

FBI that his wife had been kidnapped and the Secret Service that his wife was involved in a plot to kill the President.[29]

The interesting thing about the offense of false statements is that it is (or, more accurately, was) the only crime that acknowledged the moral distinction between inculpation and exculpation, by means of the doctrine of 'exculpatory noes'—a doctrine that was widely recognized in the lower federal courts until its repudiation by the Supreme Court in a 1998 case, *Brogan v United States*.[30]

Under the most common form of the exculpatory no doctrine, a statement that would otherwise violate section 1001 was exempt from prosecution if it satisfied two conditions.[31] First, it had to convey 'false information in a situation in which a truthful reply would have incriminated the interrogee.'[32] Secondly, it had to be limited to simple words of denial (such as 'no, I did not,' 'none,' or 'never') rather than more elaborate fabrications.[33] If, for example, an FBI agent had asked a suspect whether he possessed any drugs, and the suspect had falsely responded, 'no, I do not,' the suspect would have been protected by the exculpatory no doctrine and could not be convicted under section 1001.

Prior to 1998, a majority of the lower federal courts (seven of the nine circuits to consider the issue) had adopted some form of the exculpatory no doctrine.[34] The courts and commentators offered two basic arguments in its favor. First, allowing defendants who utter exculpatory noes to be prosecuted under section 1001 would be inconsistent with the purpose of the statute, which is to criminalize only those acts that 'pervert governmental functions.'[35]

---

[29] 466 US 475 (1984).   [30] 522 US 398 (1998).

[31] Among the variations in the exculpatory no doctrine, as developed in the lower federal courts, were the requirement that defendant be unaware that he is under investigation, that the nature of the government inquiry be investigative and not administrative, that the false statement not impair the basic functions of the government agency, that the statement be unrelated to a privilege or a claim against the government, that the statement be oral and unsworn, and that the statement be a response to an inquiry initiated by the government. See Tim A Thomas, Annotation: 'What Statements Fall Within Exculpatory Denial Exception to Prohibition, Under 18 USC § 1001, Against Knowingly and Willfully Making False Statement Which is Material to Matter Within Jurisdiction of Department or Agency of United States' (1991) 102 *ALR Fed.* 742; Lauren C Hennessey, 'No Exception for No: Rejection of the Exculpatory No Doctrine' (1999) 89 *Journal of Criminal Law & Criminology* 905, 911 n 50.

[32] Scott D Pomfret, 'A Tempered "Yes" to the "Exculpatory No"' (1997) 96 *Michigan Law Review* 754, 755–56. To be incriminating, it would either have to support a conviction under a federal criminal statute or 'furnish a link in the chain of evidence needed to prosecute.' *Ibid* at 755.   [33] *Ibid* at 756–57.

[34] *Moser v United States*, 18 F 3d 469, 473–74 (7th Cir 1994); *United States v Taylor*, 907 F 2d 801, 805 (8th Cir 1990); *United States v Cogdell*, 844 F 2d 179, 183 (4th Cir 1988); *United States v Tabor*, 788 F 2d 714, 717–19 (11th Cir 1986); *United States v Fitzgibbon*, 619 F 2d 874, 880–81 (10th Cir 1980); *United States v Rose*, 570 F 2d 1358, 1364 (9th Cir 1978); *United States v Chevoor*, 526 F 2d 178, 183–84 (1st Cir 1975), cert denied, 425 US 935 (1976). The only circuits to reject the exculpatory no doctrine were the Second, *United States v Wiener*, 96 F 3d 35 (2d Cir 1996), and the Fifth, *United States v Rodriguez-Rios*, 14 F 3d 1040 (5th Cir 1994).

[35] See, eg *United States v Gilliland*, 312 US 86 (1941) (section 1001 is intended to criminalize only those statements that 'pervert governmental functions'). Because exculpatory noes almost always occur in the context of investigatory or adversarial questioning, it is unlikely that any governmental function would be impaired in the matter contemplated by Congress.

Secondly, prosecution of false denials would violate the 'spirit' of the Fifth Amendment by placing a suspect in the 'cruel trilemma' of admitting guilt (and incriminating himself in the underlying crime), remaining silent (and being held in contempt), or falsely denying guilt (and facing a prosecution for perjury or false statements).[36]

In *Brogan*, a majority of the Court rejected both of these arguments. In response to the first argument, Justice Scalia said that even if exculpatory noes do not actually thwart governmental functions, the Court has neither the power nor the desire to apply a construction that would limit 'the unqualified language of a statute to the particular evil that Congress was trying to remedy.'[37] Moreover, reasoned Scalia, 'the investigation of wrongdoing is a proper governmental function; and since the very purpose of an investigation is to uncover the truth, any falsehood relating to the subject of the investigation perverts that legitimate government function.'[38] In response to the second argument, Scalia asserted, the Fifth Amendment gives suspects the right to remain silent, not to lie. Therefore, the Fifth Amendment is inapplicable to exculpatory noes.[39]

As a matter of statutory and constitutional interpretation, Justice Scalia's opinion in *Brogan* is surely correct. Neither the broad wording of section 1001 nor its legislative history evidences any plausible safe harbor for exculpatory noes.[40] Petitioner's suggestion that 'the unqualified language of' section 1001 should be used exclusively to combat 'the particular evil that Congress was trying to remedy' is surely nothing more than wishful thinking. Moreover, Justice Scalia was undoubtedly right that, as a matter of constitutional law, the Fifth Amendment guarantees only the right to silence, not the right to lie.

The interesting question, though, is this: how can we explain the fact that—notwithstanding the lack of textual, legislative, and constitutional support for it—seven of nine federal circuit courts, and numerous other courts and commentators, over the course of some 36 years,[41] were willing to adopt

---

[36] *Brogan*, 522 US at 404. A third argument, emphasized in Justice Ginsburg's concurrence, is that the exculpatory no doctrine is necessary to eliminate the risk that section 1001 will become an instrument of prosecutorial abuse—a means of 'piling on' offenses, sometimes punishing the denial of wrongdoing more severely than the wrongdoing itself. *Ibid* at 410 (Ginsburg, J., concurring).   [37] *Ibid* at 403.

[38] *Ibid* (emphasis omitted).

[39] *Ibid*. Scalia dismissed out of hand the contention that, because a suspect may fear that his silence will be used against him later, or may not even know that it is an available option, silence is an 'illusory' option.

[40] In fact, Congress expressly considered, but never adopted, a provision that would have established a 'defense to prosecution for an oral false statement to a law enforcement officer' if 'the statement was made during the course of an investigation of an offense or a possible offense and the statement consisted of a denial, unaccompanied by any other false statement, that the declarant committed or participated in the commission of such offense.' S Rep No 97–307, at 407 (1981), quoted in *Brogan*, *Ibid* at 410 (Ginsburg, J., concurring).

[41] The earliest appellate court decision endorsing the exculpatory no doctrine was *Paternostro v United States*, 311 F 2d 298, 305 (5th Cir 1962), which ultimately was overruled by *United States v Rodriguez-Rios*, 14 F 3d 1040 (5th Cir 1994) (en banc).

some version of the exculpatory no doctrine? Ironically, I believe, it is precisely the lack of credible legal support for the doctrine that makes its persistence so telling.

The exculpatory no doctrine survived, and flourished, because it is consistent with deeply held moral intuitions. The idea of bringing a prosecution for false statements against one who falsely denies his own wrongdoing seems unfair and demeaning, particularly in cases in which the alternative (viz. remaining silent) would be tantamount to admitting guilt. As I have suggested above, the deception contained in a false denial or exculpatory no is, from a moral perspective, qualitatively different from the deception that occurs in other contexts. It is deception that, though unjustified, often will be viewed as excused. Speaking about the slightly different context of perjury, William Stuntz has made this point well:

Self-protective perjury...looks a good deal like the commission of any victimless crime under great pressure. The defendant's conduct is no doubt wrong, and seriously so, but the harm the conduct causes in any one case is both slight and diffuse while the pressure is both substantial and concentrated. So described, the choice seems to be one for which excuse is classically appropriate. One could hardly imagine punishing a bank robber for leaving the scene of his crime after the robbery in order to avoid immediate arrest; the defendant who lies on the witness stand to avoid confessing is in much the same position.[42]

The fact that the exculpatory no doctrine flourished even in the absence of tenable statutory or constitutional support is a manifestation of the strength of these moral concepts. Given the force of such claims, I would therefore agree with Justice Ginsburg's concurrence in *Brogan* that Congress should amend section 1001 by carving out an exception for exculpatory noes.[43]

---

[42] William J Stuntz, 'Self-Incrimination and Excuse' (1988) 88 *Columbia Law Review* 1227, 1254.   [43] *Brogan*, 522 US at 415–18 (Ginsburg, J., concurring).

15

Obstruction of Justice

The moral ambivalence which the public feels towards white-collar crime is nowhere more apparent than in the case of obstruction of justice. In one high profile obstruction prosecution after another, doubts have been raised as to whether what the defendant did was something that really deserves to be treated as a crime. We have already talked some about the cases of Bill Clinton and Martha Stewart. Not only did Clinton allegedly commit perjury, but he also allegedly committed obstruction of justice by telling Lewinsky to be 'evasive' in her testimony and having Betty Currie go to Lewinsky's apartment to reclaim various gifts that he had given her. As for Stewart, in addition to making allegedly false statements to the FBI, she also allegedly committed obstruction of justice by conspiring with her broker to alter documents that would make it appear that she had sold her stock in ImClone pursuant to a pre-existing standing agreement rather than as a result of any inside information.

What is striking about the reaction to such cases is the suggestion that: (1) in comparison with 'serious' white-collar offenses such as bribery and fraud, mere 'cover-up' crimes like obstruction of justice simply don't merit particularly harsh treatment;[1] (2) such behavior often reflects nothing more than legitimate 'zealous advocacy,' 'witness preparation,' 'routine housekeeping' procedures,[2] or, at worst, 'bad judgment';[3] and (3) there's something somehow unfair or vindictive or petty about prosecutors pursuing charges for obstruction of justice or perjury rather than, or in addition to, charges relating to the conduct being covered up.[4]

---

[1] See, eg James O Goldsborough, 'We Are a Nation Awash in a Sea of Lies,' *San Diego Union-Tribune* (9 June 2004) <http://www.signonsandiego.com/news/op-ed/goldsborough/20030609-9999_mz1e9golds.html>.

[2] See, eg Stephen Gillers, 'The Flaw in the Andersen Verdict,' *New York Times* (18 June 2002), at A23 (arguing that directive given to Arthur Andersen executives, to the effect that a pre-existing document destruction program should not be suspended despite an impending criminal investigation of Andersen's role in the Enron scandal, was not a crime at all, but rather 'the kind of advice lawyers give clients all the time').

[3] Doug Henwood, 'Free Martha!,' *The Nation* (9 Feb. 2004) <http://www.thenation.com/doc.mhtml?i=20040209&s=henwood> (discussing how Martha Stewart's decision to cover up what she believed to be securities fraud by lying to federal investigators reflected 'bad judgment' rather than felonious intent).

[4] Howard Chapman, 'Both Martha and Justice Have Suffered, and Now It Will Get Even Worse,' *Fort Wayne News-Sentinel* (12 March 2004) <http://www.discovery.org/scripts/viewDB/index.php?command=view&program=Misc&id=1926>.

The problem with such judgments, however, is their 'ad hoc-ness.' They seem to be based on little more than subjective and often inconsistent intuitions about particular cases of note. What we need is some more thoroughgoing analysis of the moral content of obstruction-type crimes, a comprehensive framework for thinking about such offenses that could be used across the board in a theoretically consistent manner to evaluate both the statutory treatment of whole categories of criminal behavior and the prosecution and punishment of individual cases. That, in any event, is what I hope to provide here.

1. The Law of Obstruction of Justice

The basic federal obstruction of justice statutes are contained in twenty sections of Chapter 73 of Title 18 of the US Code.[5] Of particular interest to us are sections 1503, 1505, 1510, 1512, 1519, and 1520. These statutes reach a diverse range of obstructive conduct in a wide range of procedural contexts.

Four Formal Distinctions

Before we look at the actual law of obstruction of justice, I want to offer four preliminary distinctions that help define its formal structure. The first is between obstruction by deception and obstruction by non-deceptive means. Imagine a case in which *A* possesses incriminating information about himself or someone else. If *A* seeks to resist the government's attempt to obtain such information, he can do so deceptively (eg by falsely denying guilt during an investigation or on the witness stand) or non-deceptively (eg by admitting that he has such information, but refusing to divulge it).

The second distinction, previously discussed in Chapter 5, is between wrongful exculpation and wrongful inculpation. In the pattern of wrongful exculpation, a person who is under investigation for, or has information about, some alleged course of illegal conduct, gives the government false exculpatory evidence or fails to give it true inculpatory information. In the pattern of wrongful inculpation, a person who purports to have information about another's conduct gives the government false inculpatory evidence (eg by making a false accusation against another) or prevents it from obtaining true exculpatory evidence (eg by destroying or withholding true exculpatory evidence). (Of course, a person who makes a false accusation against another so as to throw the government off the trail of the true suspect would have satisfied both patterns.)

---

[5] 18 USC §§ 1501–20. The elements of the obstruction of justice and other cover-up offenses are discussed in, among other sources, Jamie S Gorelick, et al., *Destruction of Evidence* (New York: Wiley Law Publications, 1989) § 5.6, at 189–94; 200–03; Chris William Sanchirico, 'Evidence Tampering' (2004) 53 *Duke Law Journal* 1215; Lawrence Solum and Stephen Marzen, 'Truth and Uncertainty: Legal Control of the Destruction of Evidence' (1987) 36 *Emory Law Journal* 1085. There is also a wide variety of *state* obstruction of justice statutes, discussed in Gorelick, above at 189–94; 200–03.

The third distinction is between inculpation or exculpation that is done on behalf of oneself and that which is done on behalf of some other party. We can, in turn, identify four variations here: first, a person who is under investigation by government agents and makes a false denial has wrongfully exculpated herself (think of Martha Stewart). Secondly, a person who has inculpatory information about another's wrongdoing and lies to government agents about her knowledge of such wrongdoing has wrongfully exculpated someone else. An example is provided by Arthur Andersen, which sought to cover up not only its own crimes, but also those of its client, Enron.[6] Thirdly, a person who makes a false accusation against another party has wrongfully inculpated another (think of Tawana Brawley). Fourthly, a person who voluntarily confesses to a crime she did not commit has wrongfully inculpated herself and, theoretically at least, should be subject to prosecution for false statements or perjury.[7]

A final distinction is between exculpation or inculpation performed through an act, and that which is done through an omission. A person who offers false inculpatory or exculpatory testimony, intimidates a witness, or destroys or alters evidence has done an act. A person who fails to produce evidence or appear for testimony has performed an omission. Generally speaking, only an affirmative act of exculpation or inculpation can constitute a crime, although there are some interesting exceptions.[8]

---

[6] *Arthur Andersen, LLP v United States*, 125 S Ct 2129 (2005).

[7] While the vast majority of false confessions are the result of coercion, trickery, or mental instability, the kind of cases I have in mind here are those in which a person offers a false confession voluntarily. The interesting question is why someone would do that. Three possible scenarios come to mind: a person might falsely confess in order to protect a child, parent, sibling, spouse, lover, or friend—ie by implicitly providing a false exculpation of such person. Secondly, a person might falsely confess in order to get attention or sympathy of some sort. Thirdly, a person might falsely confess because she hopes to receive some reward for doing so (such as money or professional advancement). Obviously, our moral judgment of such cases would vary: we are more likely to look sympathetically on a person who falsely inculpates herself out of altruistic, rather than selfish, motives. In any event, prosecution for false confession seems to be very rare, though perhaps not unprecedented. In one recent Indiana case, prosecutor Stephen S Pierson was considering bringing charges of false informing against Charles 'Chuckie' Hickman, a man who had falsely confessed to murdering 10-year old Katie Collman. See 'Hickman Released on Bond,' *WAVE3TV.com* (undated), <http://www.wave3.com/Global/story.asp?S=3377448&nav=0RZFa9v2>. In correspondence with the author, Pierson wrote that:

The injury to the Katie Collman murder investigation caused by [Hickman's] false confession was substantial. . . . [T]he person now charged with molesting and murdering Collman had just been interviewed and was slated for follow-up investigation when Hickman confessed. The investigators switched gears and began investigating the persons named by Hickman as having been involved. Those accusations could not be corroborated and a lot of hours were lost. All in all about nine weeks' delay in solving the case can be attributed to Hickman. In terms of dollars wasted, the probable total is in multiple tens of thousands of dollars.

Letter from Stephen S Pierson to the author, 31 May 2005 (on file with the author). At the time of this writing, it was unclear whether such charges would ever be brought.

[8] At common law, misprision of felony was committed by a defendant who, having knowledge of a felony and a reasonable opportunity to disclose it to a responsible official without, failed to report such felony. However, this offense apparently fell into disfavor in Britain and is today virtually obsolete. By contrast, the modern American offense of misprision of felony (see

Each of these distinctions should prove useful as we begin to look at the law of obstruction.

Statutory Framework

The oldest, broadest, and most commonly used obstruction statute is section 1503, which makes it a crime to: endeavor to influence a juror or court officer, retaliate against a juror or court officer, or endeavor to interfere with the judicial system. The first two provisions have resulted in relatively few prosecutions. The third provision, the so-called 'Omnibus Clause,' is by far the most important. Under this clause, the prosecution must prove that the defendant: (1) corruptly, (2) endeavored to interfere, (3) with a pending, (4) judicial, administrative, or congressional proceeding, and (5) that he knew such proceeding was pending. An investigation is not generally regarded as pending until it has reached the grand jury stage.[9] Like other white-collar crimes we have been dealing with here, obstruction of justice typically merges inchoate and completed conduct into a single statute. That is, the defendant need not be successful in obstructing justice; it is enough that he 'endeavored' to do so. Although our main focus here will be on cases in which the alleged obstructer was a party to the proceedings, there are also numerous obstruction cases involving non-party lawyers, informants, witnesses, judges, and legislators.[10]

In contrast to section 1503, which applies to judicial proceedings, section 1505 applies to administrative and legislative proceedings. Otherwise, the two provisions are closely parallel. In addition to its specific prohibition on obstructing justice in connection with proceedings under the Antitrust Civil Process Act, section 1505 also contains a broad, Omnibus-Clause-like provision.[11] Among

---

18 USC §4) does require an affirmative act, such as making a false statement to an investigator, seeking to divert the attention of the police, or harboring a felon. See Stuart P Green, 'Uncovering the Cover-Up Crimes' (2005) 42 *American Criminal Law Review* 9, 22–24. However, there is reason to think that 'false-exculpation-by-omission' statutes are becoming more common. See generally Sandra Guerra Thompson, 'The White-Collar Police Force: "Duty to Report" Statutes in Criminal Law Theory' (2002) 11 *William & Mary Bill of Rights Journal* 3 (discussing recently enacted laws that require individuals to report suspicions of a wide range of criminal conduct, including hazardous waste discharges, money laundering, and child, elder, and domestic abuse). See also the Anti-Terrorism, Crime and Security Act 2001, c. 27 (UK) § 117 (a person who 'has information which he knows or believes might be of material assistance . . . in preventing the commission by another person of an act of terrorism . . . commits an offence if he does not disclose the information as soon as reasonably practicable').

[9] SN Welling, et al., *Federal Criminal Law and Related Actions: Crimes, Forfeiture, the False Claims Act and RICO* (St. Paul, Minn.: West Group, 1998) at 163.

[10] *Ibid* at 162.

[11] Section 1505 makes it a crime to corruptly influence, obstruct, or impede the due and proper administration of law under which any pending proceeding is being had before any department or agency of the United States, or the due and proper exercise of the power of inquiry under which any inquiry or investigation is being had by either House, or any committee of either House or any joint committee of the Congress.

the most common means of endeavoring to obstruct justice under the Omnibus Clauses of §§ 1503 and 1505 are: (1) concealing, altering, or destroying documents that pertain to judicial, administrative, or legislative proceedings, (2) giving or encouraging false testimony in such proceedings, (3) making false statements to government agents (provided that there is a direct connection or 'nexus' between the defendant's act and a pending proceeding),[12] (4) encouraging a witness to assert his Fifth Amendment privilege (at least when there is no valid reason for doing so),[13] and (5) threatening jurors or court officers.[14] Such obstruction can involve both wrongful exculpation and wrongful inculpation.

There are also several other obstruction provisions worth mentioning. The main focus of § 1510 is on the obstruction of criminal investigations, at least in certain limited circumstances, such as by means of bribery.[15] Section 1512 was introduced as part of a major expansion of the obstruction of justice statutory scheme effected by the Victim and Witness Protection Act of 1982.[16] Its focus is on tampering with victims, witnesses, and informants, whether by killing, using force, intimidation, or coercion, engaging in misleading conduct, harassment,[17] or retaliation,[18] and applies to proceedings before federal courts and grand juries, Congress, and federal agencies.[19]

---

[12] *United States v Aguilar*, 515 US 593, 597 (1995).

[13] *United States v Cintolo*, 818 F 2d 980 (1st Cir 1987), *cert denied*, 484 US 913 (1987).

[14] *United States v Bashaw*, 982 F 2d 168, 171 (6th Cir 1992).

[15] 18 USC § 1510. This provision was enacted in order to close a loophole in earlier law which protected witnesses only during judicial proceedings themselves and not during the prior investigation. *United States v San Martin*, 515 F 2d 317, 320 (5th Cir 1975). Subsections (b)(1) and (2) of § 1510 also prohibit officers of financial institutions from notifying anyone about subpoenas for financial records. [16] Pub L 97–291, 12 Oct. 1982, 96 Stat 1248.

[17] 18 USC § 1512.

[18] Retaliation presents a somewhat problematic category, as it will involve covering up only where it is part of a larger process of coercing witnesses and informants through threats of retaliation, and even then the actual retaliation could be seen as part of a cover-up only if it is designed to show others that the threats they face are serious.

[19] The definition of 'official proceeding' as used in §1512 is found in 18 USC § 1515(a). Section 1512 has the effect of increasing protection for victims and witnesses beyond what was previously available only under § 1503, by lowering the threshold of what constitutes obstruction inasmuch as it prohibits tampering by intimidation and harassment as well as force and threats. (Welling, n 9 above, at 185) (citing case law and legislative history). Section 1512 also includes a provision that provides an affirmative defense if the defendant can prove that his conduct consisted solely of lawful conduct and that his sole intention was to 'encourage, induce, or cause the other person to testify truthfully.' Although the Victim and Witness Protection Act eliminated the prior reference in §1503 to witnesses, presumably in deference to §1512's more specialized focus, a majority of courts have held that witness tampering can be prosecuted not only under both §1512 but also under the amended version of the Omnibus Clause of §1503. *Ibid* at 166 (noting circuit split on issue). Also worth mentioning at this point are two recent additions to the prosecutor's obstruction arsenal, enacted as part of the Sarbanes-Oxley Act of 2002. Pub L No 107–204, 116 Stat 745 (codified in scattered provisions of the US Code). Title 18, §1519 makes it a crime to alter, destroy, or conceal any document or tangible object with the intent to impede, obstruct, or influence the investigation or proper administration 'of any matter within the jurisdiction of any department or agency of the United States' or in any bankruptcy case. As such, § 1519 is broader than §1505, which is limited to 'pending proceedings' before federal departments and agencies. The other new provision, 18 USC §1520, makes it a crime to

As a general matter, the closer to formal adjudication that justice is obstructed, the more likely it is to fall within the letter of the obstruction statutes and to be prosecuted as such.[20] Thus, a person who flushes illegal drugs down the toilet as she is about to be arrested for drug possession is less likely to be prosecutable for obstruction of justice than one who destroys the same evidence in the middle of trial. As we shall see below, although the language of the basic obstruction of justice statutes makes little distinction between obstruction that occurs in criminal cases and that which occurs in civil cases, in practice obstruction charges are almost invariably limited to the former. Obstruction charges can be, and often are, accompanied by charges for the underlying crime allegedly covered up; but of course they need not be, as recent cases like that involving Martha Stewart make clear.

Non-Criminal Law Responses to Obstructive Behavior

One of the factors that contributes to the morally ambiguous character of obstruction of justice is the fact that often the same conduct that is treated as criminal obstruction can also be treated not only as one or more related crime (such as perjury, false statements, contempt, or misprision of felony), but also as a violation of rules of court procedure, as a disciplinary breach, or as a civil tort.

For example, there are various kinds of sanctions that can be imposed under the Federal Rules of Civil Procedure and the Federal Rules of Criminal Procedure. Take Federal Rule of Civil Procedure 37: under this provision, a party that fails to obey a court order to 'provide or permit discovery' can be barred from supporting or opposing designated claims or defenses or introducing certain matters in evidence, can have pleadings struck or dismissed, have a judgment rendered by default, or have matters in dispute taken to be established.[21] Under Federal Rule of Civil Procedure 11, an attorney who submits to a court pleadings that are not factually supported or not likely to be factually supported after subsequent discovery can be subject to various monetary and non-monetary sanctions. And, under Federal Rule of Criminal Procedure 16, a defendant who fails to comply with an order to allow the government to inspect and copy various papers, documents, photographs, and the like, or the results of any physical or mental examination or scientific test or

---

violate SEC rules regarding the retention of documents relating to the audit of an issuer of securities. See Dana E Hill, Note, 'Anticipatory Obstruction of Justice: Pre-emptive Document Destruction Under the Sarbanes-Oxley Anti-Shredding Statute, 18 USC §1519' (2004) 89 *Cornell Law Review* 1519.

[20] See Sanchirico (n 5 above, at 1225) (stating that 'the law tends to penalize evidence tampering only when it occurs far downstream in the flow from primary activity through filing, discovery, and trial').

[21] Fed R Civ Proc 37(b)(2). For further discussion of remedies available under the Federal Rules of Civil Procedure, see Gorelick (n 5 above, at 65–137); Sanchirico (n 5 above, at 1262–69).

experiment, can be prohibited from introducing such undisclosed evidence at trial, or subjected to a continuance.[22]

Moreover, in at least half a dozen American jurisdictions, a plaintiff can bring a tort action to recover compensatory, and possibly punitive, damages for the loss of a prospective lawsuit caused by an opponent's spoliation of evidence.[23] In some jurisdictions, the spoliation must be intentional; in others, reckless or negligent conduct will do.[24] A typical spoliation case involves a defendant who, having been sued for engaging in some form of wrongdoing (such as causing a serious personal injury to a plaintiff), covers up such wrongdoing by destroying key evidence, thereby making it more difficult for the plaintiff to pursue his case.[25]

In addition, there are various ethical rules that apply to obstruction-like activity as well.[26] Model Rule of Professional Conduct 8.4(d) and Model Code of Professional Responsibility DR 1-102(A)(5) prohibit conduct that is 'prejudicial to the administration of justice.'[27] Model Rule 3.4 and Model Code DR 7–109(A) prohibit a defendant from obstructing another party's access to evidence or unlawfully altering, destroying, concealing, or suppressing evidence.[28] And Model Rule 3.3 essentially prohibits lawyers from committing or suborning perjury when they make representations to the court or put a witness on the stand.[29] Lawyers who violate such rules are subject to a wide range of disciplinary sanctions, including disqualification from a given case, suspension from law practice, revocation of pro hoc vice status, preclusion of evidence, striking of pleadings, and dismissal of actions.[30]

There is also a host of procedural, constitutional, and disciplinary rules that apply specifically to prosecutors and law enforcement officials who wrongfully inculpate by destroying or failing to turn over exculpatory evidence, suborning perjury, or intimidating a witness. The Jencks Act,[31]

---

[22] Fed R Crim. Proc 16(d)(2). The obligation of the defendant to produce such documents arises only if the defendant first requests similar material from the prosecution and the request is complied with. Fed R Crim P 16(b)(1). Also, the defendant must intend to use such material in its case-in-chief at trial or, in the case of scientific reports, intend to call the witness who prepared the report. *Ibid.*

[23] See Margaret M Koesel, et al., *Spoliation of Evidence: Sanctions and Remedies for Destruction of Evidence in Civil Litigation* (Chicago: Tort and Insurance Practice Section, American Bar Association, 2000) 50–51 (discussing the existence of an independent tort claim for spoliation in certain jurisdictions). [24] *Ibid.*

[25] On the other hand, it should be noted that plaintiffs who seek to recover damages for false inculpatory statements made to the police, in court pleadings, or on the witness stand generally cannot recover for defamation. See, eg David W Eagle, 'Note: Civil Remedies for Perjury: A Proposal for a Tort Action' (1977) 19 *Arizona Law Review* 349, 349 (stating that no tort claim exists for perjury committed at any step in the judicial process).

[26] See generally Gorelick (n 5 above, at 249–74); Sanchirico (n 5 above, at 1283–85).

[27] Model Rule of Professional Conduct 8.4(d) (2003). [28] *Ibid* rule 3.4(a).

[29] *Ibid* rule 3.3.

[30] Gorelick (n 5 above, at 266–70) (discussing sanctions for attorney violation of ethical rules regarding destruction of evidence).

[31] 18 USC § 3500 (2000) (stating government obligations following demands for production of statements and reports of witnesses).

Federal Rule of Criminal Procedure 16,[32] the rule in *Brady v Maryland*,[33] and special prosecutorial ethics guidelines[34] all require federal prosecutors to disclose exculpatory evidence of various sorts.

Finally, there is, as we shall see below, a great deal of ostensibly 'obstructive' conduct, particularly that engaged in by lawyers, that not only is not subject to criminal sanctions, but is not subject even to civil or disciplinary sanctions. Indeed, as Bruce Green has pointed out, such conduct is often regarded as commendable 'zealous advocacy.'[35]

2. THE MORAL CONTENT OF OBSTRUCTION OF JUSTICE: BACKGROUND NORMS

Why do different acts of obstruction (as well as perjury and false statements) result in such a broad range of legal and non-legal responses? One answer is that we need a finely calibrated system of sanctions to provide a level of deterrence that is optimal in terms of social costs and benefits.[36] While deterrence is important, however, my interest here will be in the question of retribution: namely, why are certain acts of obstruction more blameworthy than others, and when does such blameworthiness justify the imposition of criminal sanctions?

Harms Caused, and Victims Affected

Who, or what, is harmed by offenses such as obstruction of justice? In some cases, the harm is done to a witness or informant. For example, section 1512(a)(1) prohibits killing or attempting to kill another person with the intent to prevent his attendance or testimony at an official proceeding, production of a document, or communication with law enforcement officials. Section 1512(b) similarly prohibits the use of intimidation, physical force, or threats. Such crimes cause harms to victims similar to those entailed by murder, attempted murder, assault, and battery.

Also significant are the harms caused to opposing litigants: in a manner similar to perjury, a witness who gives the police false exculpatory evidence

---

[32] Federal Rule of Criminal Procedure 16(a) (stating disclosure obligations of the government).

[33] 373 US 83, 87 (1963) ('[S]uppression by the prosecution of evidence favorable to the accused upon request violates due process where the evidence is material. . . .').

[34] American Bar Association, *Standards for Criminal Justice: Prosecution Function and Defense Function* (3rd edn., Washington, DC: American Bar Association, 1993) 61 (stating the standard for disclosure of evidence by a prosecutor).

[35] Bruce Green, 'The Criminal Regulation of Lawyers' (1998) 67 *Fordham Law Review* 327; Bruce A Green, 'Zealous Representation Bound: The Intersection of the Ethical Codes and the Criminal Law' (1991) 69 *North Carolina Law Review* 687.

[36] For an interesting discussion of the deterrence question in the context of evidence tampering, see Sanchirico (n 5 above).

or fails to divulge true inculpatory evidence impairs their ability to apprehend the correct suspect. An informant who files a police report containing false inculpatory evidence causes harm to a defendant's liberty interests.[37] And a defendant in a tort suit who withholds evidence that would have benefited the plaintiff's case causes harm to the plaintiff's right to receive compensation for his injuries.[38]

Perhaps the most significant harms associated with obstruction of justice are those caused to our system of justice and to society generally. A criminal defendant who destroys evidence that prevents a jury from having sufficient cause to convict has caused a serious harm to the integrity of the criminal justice system. So too has an informant or prosecution witness whose false testimony leads to a wrongful arrest, prosecution, or conviction, or to a wrongful decision to forgo arrest or prosecution. And, as in the case of perjury, such harms to the system occur even if the jury's verdict or prosecutor's decision turns out to be correct.

Wrongs Entailed

Having considered the kinds of harms associated with obstruction-type offenses, we can now turn to the kinds of moral wrongfulness they entail. The first is unique to those cases in which the defendant covers up his own wrongdoing: namely, breach of the supposed duty to take responsibility for one's actions (though exactly whom such a duty would be owed to is a difficult question). But whatever the force of such a norm in our moral lives,[39] it should be obvious that merely failing to take responsibility for one's actions is not ordinarily the sort of thing that is made a crime. In some unusual contexts, it can be a crime to fail to submit to the government certain information that one is specifically required to submit, such as a tax return[40] or a Clean Water Act monthly discharge monitoring report.[41] But, with the possible exception of the now defunct common law offense of misprision of felony,[42] the obstruction-type statutes we are considering here require that the defendant take some affirmative step to cover up his own wrongdoing.

The second form of moral wrongfulness associated with such crimes finds its most familiar expression in the biblical Ninth Commandment, that one shall not bear false witness against one's neighbor. This provision is often interpreted as a general prohibition on lying, or more specifically as a prohibition on lying

---

[37] See, eg *United States v Rodgers*, 466 US 475, 481 (1984) ('The knowing filing of a false crime report, leading to an investigation and possible prosecution, can also have grave consequences for the individuals accused of crime.').

[38] See generally Dale A Oesterle, 'A Private Litigant's Remedies for an Opponent's Inappropriate Destruction of Relevant Documents' (1983) 61 *Texas Law Review* 1185.

[39] See discussion in the text accompanying n 21 in ch. 5.

[40] See 26 USC §7203 (2000) (statute making it a crime to fail to file an income tax return).

[41] See 33 USC §1319(c) (2000) (describing criminal penalties for violations of the Clean Water Act).

[42] See discussion in n 8 above.

under oath.[43] But, given the possibility that, as suggested above, wrongful inculpation poses a greater moral risk than wrongful exculpation, perhaps a better interpretation would focus specifically on what it means to bear false witness 'against' another.[44]

Thirdly, some unusual cases of obstruction involve a form of coercion. For example, section 1512 expressly makes it a crime to 'knowingly use[] intimidation or physical force, threaten[] or corruptly persuade[] another person . . . with intent to . . . influence, delay or prevent' testimony.

Fourthly, under section 1510(a), it is a crime to use bribery to obstruct, delay, or prevent the communication of information relating to a violation of any criminal statute.[45] Obstruction of this sort reflects much the same moral content as the various bribery statutes, discussed below in Chapter 16.

Fifthly, we need to consider the possibility that obstruction-type conduct is wrong because it involves a defiance of governmental authority. Destroying evidence or perjuring oneself in response to a governmental investigation involves more than just the usual breach of the supposed duty to obey the law. People who obstruct the operations of justice wrong the government (and perhaps, by extension, the general polity) at two levels: first by violating the law itself, and then by preventing the government from enforcing that law in a proper manner. Such offenses thus reflect a kind of super-*malum prohibitum* quality. Indeed, it is striking that we speak in this context of parties who show 'contempt' for a court or legislative body or who, in British usage, 'pervert' the course of justice.[46]

A final form of moral wrongfulness worth considering in this context is cheating. As explained in Chapter 4, cheating involves an intentional violation of a rule for the purpose of gaining an unfair advantage over one's rivals—a phenomenon that would seem bound to occur when a litigant destroys evidence, intimidates a witness, or lies on the witness stand.

Focus on the cheating aspect of covering up is also helpful in delineating the often fuzzy distinction between obstruction of justice and mere zealous advocacy. Imagine two cases in which a criminal defense lawyer intentionally engaged in conduct that was calculated to mislead the jury. In the first case,

---

[43] See, eg Nachum Amsel, 'Truth and Lying,' in *The Jewish Encyclopedia of Moral and Ethical Issues* (Northvale, NJ: Jason Aronson, Inc., 1994) 292–93 (explaining how Jewish law has traditionally looked at the obligation to tell the truth under oath).

[44] In fact, the Bible does distinguish between false exculpation and false inculpation. A witness who falsely inculpates is to receive the same punishment as that which would have been given to the falsely accused. *Deuteronomy* 19:18–19. The punishment for false exculpation, on the other hand, does not appear to be stated.   [45] See 18 USC §1510(a) (2000).

[46] In Britain, it is a crime to: (1) intimidate an informant, witness, or juror in an investigation or proceedings for an offense, with the intent to obstruct, pervert, or interfere with such investigation or proceedings; or (2) threaten harm to a person who has been an informant, witness, or juror in such proceedings. Criminal Justice and Public Order Act 1994, c. 33 § 51 (UK). For a discussion of obstruction of justice law in Canada, see Sally Gunz and Steven Salterio, 'What If Anderson Had Shredded in Toronto or Calgary? The Potential for Criminal Liability for Canadian Public Accounting Firms' (29 Aug. 2003), <http://ssrn.com/abstract=465902>.

the lawyer destroys key evidence that would have incriminated his client. Here, there seems to be a clear case of obstruction of justice. In the second case, the lawyer so forcefully and effectively cross-examines a truthful adverse witness that the witness becomes flustered, offers confused and erroneous descriptions of relevant events, and is made to appear mistaken or deceptive in the eyes of the jury. In such a case, virtually every commentator on legal ethics would agree that it would be absurd to bring disciplinary proceedings against the lawyer, let alone a prosecution for obstruction of justice or subornation of perjury, and that in fact she was performing her job admirably.[47]

Given that both cases involve intentional conduct that is in some sense calculated to mislead the jury, the question is why only the first should constitute a crime. One possible answer is simply that the first lawyer has broken the rules, while the second has not. The adversarial system of justice permits, and even encourages, defense lawyers to use clever cross-examination to make truthful prosecution witnesses look like liars, bring motions to suppress otherwise reliable evidence, and advise clients to assert privileges that have the effect of depriving the fact-finder of relevant, inculpatory evidence.[48] But it does not permit lawyers to destroy evidence or put witnesses on the stand whom they know will make literally false statements. In short, it says that certain ways of misleading the jury are permissible, while others are not. Those who comply with the rules play fair; those who do not, cheat.

Unfortunately, this leaves the deeper question of why the line between acceptable and unacceptable conduct has been drawn where it has. Without attempting to develop anything like a comprehensive account, I will simply suggest that the ultimate goal of the prohibitions on obstruction of justice and perjury is to further the interest of truth-finding and allow the prosecution's case to be put to the test; and it seems likely that the destruction and fabrication of evidence foreclose the truth-finding function in a way that clever cross-examination does not.

Two Countervailing Norms: Self-Preservation and Breach of Trust

In the previous section, I enumerated six moral norms that are potentially violated by one who engages in obstruction of justice and related crimes. In

---

[47] See, eg Monroe H Freedman and Abbe Smith, *Understanding Lawyers' Ethics* (3rd edn., Newark, NJ: LexisNexis, 2004) 217 ('Is it ever proper for a lawyer to cross-examine an adverse witness who has testified accurately and truthfully in order to make the witness appear to be mistaken or lying? Our answer is yes—but the same answer is also given by almost every other commentator on lawyers' ethics.'); Geoffrey C Hazard and W William Hodes, *The Law of Lawyering* (3rd edn., New York: Aspen, 2001) § 40.3 ('it is often the *duty* of an advocate to "burden" or "embarrass" an adverse witness, if doing so will make the witness less likely to be believed,' and this is true even for truthful witnesses) (emphasis added).

[48] See Green, 'Criminal Regulation of Lawyers,' (n 37 above, at 362). For a similar analysis, see John A Humbach, 'Just Being a Lawyer' (2001) 4 *Legal Ethics* 155 (book review).

the midst of this discussion, I also described a countervailing norm—namely, that a lawyer who impedes or obstructs the due administration of justice can simultaneously be performing in accordance with the positive norm of 'zealous advocacy' upon which our criminal justice system depends. In the present section, I want to mention two additional countervailing norms that may play a role in fostering the ambivalence we feel towards at least some obstructive acts: first, the view that people have a right of self-preservation; and secondly the view that people ought not to 'rat' or 'snitch' on others with whom they have a relationship of trust.

The first countervailing norm arises in cases of self-exculpation. As discussed in Chapter 5, while most of us would agree that people ought to take responsibility for their wrongful actions, we also recognize a basic human right not to assist the government in causing one's own destruction. Acknowledging the significance of the right of self-preservation also helps to explain the often conflicting range of reactions elicited by the obstruction-type crimes more generally. We recognize that there is something potentially unfair about making it a crime for one suspected of criminal activity to shield himself from government scrutiny. Indeed, it is ironic that the more serious the crime being covered up, and the more severe the penal consequences, the stronger is the defendant's claim of self-preservation and, arguably, the less wrongful is his act of covering up.

The second countervailing norm arises in cases of false exculpation of others. As discussed in Chapter 8, people often feel a moral duty not to reveal secrets about others, particularly when they are in a relationship of trust with the other. The antipathy we feel towards people who take criminal steps to avoid inculpating others may in some cases be mitigated by our sense that such avoidance is, at least in some cases, based on a legitimate sense of loyalty.

3. Assessing The Moral Content of Particular Acts of Obstruction

Having considered some of the background concepts that inform our moral understanding of the obstruction-type offenses, we are now in a position to take a more detailed look at the complex interplay of factors upon which our judgment of specific cases is based. I group them, loosely, into three broad categories, concerning the nature of: (1) the underlying wrongdoing being covered up, (2) the government investigation into, or adjudication of, such wrongdoing, and (3) the cover-up itself.

Underlying Conduct

In assessing the moral content of the obstruction-type offenses, we will want to consider the moral content of the underlying conduct that is being wrongfully exculpated or inculpated, as the case may be. For example, other things being equal, covering up a murder should surely be regarded as a more serious crime than covering up a parking violation, just as falsely alleging that X committed a murder should be regarded as a more serious crime than falsely alleging that she committed a parking violation. Similarly, I would argue that, other things being equal, covering up violations of the Arms Export Control Act and the Boland Amendment (as was done in the Iran-Contra case) should be regarded as a more serious crime than covering up an extramarital affair (as in the Clinton case).[49] But the question is why. One possibility might be that the acts of false exculpation and inculpation somehow derive whatever wrongfulness they entail from the crime that is being covered up or being falsely alleged, just as attempting or conspiring to commit a crime derive their moral content from the crime that is the target of the attempt or conspiracy. Alternatively, it may be simply that the more serious the underlying crime committed, the stronger society's interest is in knowing about it, and the more harmful the cover-up. (Similarly, the more serious the underlying crime, the more serious the penal consequences for the one wrongly accused, and the more harmful the wrongful inculpation.) Under either approach, we face the interesting possibility that, as in the case of jurisdictions that punish attempts or conspiracies in proportion to the seriousness of the target offense,[50] we should want to punish the cover up (or wrongful accusation) of serious crimes more severely than that of minor ones.

The idea that the moral weight of covering up is related to the moral weight of the underlying crime does in fact spell itself out in a crucially important practical context. Although criminal penalties for obstruction of justice are theoretically applicable to obstruction of both civil and criminal proceedings[51] (that is, most of the obstruction statutes make no distinction between the two), the cover-up is far more likely to be prosecuted when the conduct being covered up is the subject of a criminal case than when it is the subject of a civil case. Indeed, cases involving allegations of obstruction of justice and perjury in federal civil proceedings are exceedingly rare; and convictions in such a context are virtually nonexistent.[52]

---

[49] Cf Tom Hays, 'Rapper Lil' Kim Gets 366 Days for Perjury,' *Yahoo.com* (7 July 2005), <http://news.yahoo.com/news?tmpl=story&u=/ap/20050707/ap_en_mu/lil__kim_shootout > (at sentencing proceeding, US District Judge Gerard Lynch opined that rap singer Lil' Kim deserved more prison time for her perjury conviction than Martha Stewart because Kim, unlike Stewart, had lied about a violent crime, not a white-collar scheme).

[50] See Model Penal Code, Commentary to s 5.05, at 484–89 (describing departure of Model Penal Code from traditional approach of grading criminal attempts, solicitations, and conspiracies as less serious than target crimes).

[51] For cases recognizing the theoretical possibility of such prosecutions, see *United States v Meeks*, 642 F 2d 733, 742 n 20 (5th Cir 1981) (Reavley, J., dissenting), vacated, 461 US 912 (1983); *United States v Blohm*, 585 F Supp 1112, 1114 (SDNY 1984).

[52] Several commentators have noted that there are 'no reported criminal convictions for evidence destruction in civil litigation.' Koesel, above n 23 at 69.

The problem is that the cover-up of criminal proceedings is not necessarily more harmful than the cover-up of civil proceedings. For example, the destruction of key incriminating documents in a large scale, multi-million dollar class action products liability or securities fraud case would surely cause more harm than the destruction of cumulative incriminating evidence in a routine drug possession case. So the question is whether a bright-line rule between criminal and civil proceedings is justified.

One argument, offered by Lawrence Solum and Stephen Marzen, is that the prosecution of obstruction of justice in civil litigation would serve little purpose. As they put it:

Even if criminal sanctions are invoked to combat inappropriate destruction of evidence in private lawsuits, they are of inherently limited value. Criminal sanctions cannot restore the accuracy of the original factfinding proceeding, nor do they compensate the victim of evidence destruction for its loss in the civil suit. At most, criminal sanctions could deter evidence destruction in civil litigation. The apparent disinterest [sic] of government prosecutors in evidence destruction in civil suits, however, as reflected in the lack of reported prosecutions, renders the obstruction-of-justice statutes rather toothless against such misconduct. Scarce prosecutorial resources simply do not permit prosecution of spoliation in private lawsuits.[53]

But this argument seems flawed. First, it assumes that the purpose of obstruction of justice sanctions is to compensate or deter or restore accuracy, when in fact most commentators would agree that retribution is at least as important a goal. Secondly, even if the current lack of interest in prosecuting obstruction of civil cases means that the statutes have been rendered toothless, this hardly means that the statutes could not be enforced more aggressively. Thirdly, it begs the question to assume that scarce prosecutorial resources should be used for prosecuting only that sort of obstruction that arises out of criminal proceedings when this is precisely the question that is being considered.

An alternative argument is that there *is* no moral difference between obstruction of justice in civil and criminal cases, and that both should be prosecuted equally. As the Fourth Circuit explained in 1906:

The contention that a violation of section 5399 [the predecessor to 1503], consisting of obstructing the administration of justice in a civil litigation, between private citizens in a federal court, is not an offense against the United States, need not be discussed at any length. One of the sovereign powers of the United States is to administer justice in its courts between private citizens. Obstructing such administration is an offense against the United States, in that it prevents or tends to prevent the execution of one of the powers of the government.[54]

But this argument seems problematic as well, as it rests on the assumption that the only relevant consideration is that a court proceeding was obstructed, without reference to the proceeding's nature or purpose.

[53] Gorelick et al (n 5 above, at 198).
[54] *Wilder v United States*, 143 F 433 (4th Cir 1906), *cert denied*, 204 US 674 (1907).

A better argument is that criminal proceedings—by definition—implicate the public interest in a way that civil proceedings do not, as is evidenced by their being brought on behalf of 'the People' or 'the State.'[55] Thus, even if the obstruction of civil cases sometimes causes *more* harm than the obstruction of criminal cases, the *kind* of interest vindicated by criminal proceedings is qualitatively different from the kind of interest at stake in civil litigation, and the state's interest in preventing and punishing obstruction of justice proceedings is also qualitatively different.

In addition to considering the moral content of the underlying conduct that is being wrongfully exculpated or inculpated, we also need to consider those cases in which the alleged wrongdoing being investigated or adjudicated has not in fact occurred. Consider the following three scenarios: first, suppose a married man is falsely accused of raping a woman he met in a hotel during a business trip and with whom he had a consensual sexual encounter. And imagine that, in order to save his marriage and protect his children, the man falsely denies to investigators that he ever had such an encounter. In that case, the wrongfulness of his covering up obviously could not derive from the wrongfulness of a rape he did not commit; at most, it might derive from the wrongfulness of his marital infidelity. Secondly, imagine a case in which a man is falsely accused of raping a woman he has in fact never met. Out of fear that he is being framed or railroaded by the authorities, he lies about his whereabouts on the night in question. In such a case, there would be no underlying misconduct at all from which this act of 'covering up' could derive moral content. Thirdly, suppose a man who killed in self-defense is accused of murder and, out of fear that the authorities will not believe his story, destroys the weapon. Because the defendant's act was justified, there would once again be no underlying act from which the wrongfulness of the cover-up could be drawn. The wrongfulness of his act would seem to relate solely to the reasonableness of his belief that he was being framed or that the authorities would not believe his story.

There are also cases in which the prosecution believes that the underlying conduct did in fact occur, but nevertheless elects to pursue only the lesser charge of covering up. Often, the prosecutor will determine that it is 'easier' to prove the lesser charge of obstruction of justice or perjury than the underlying case of insider trading or accounting fraud. Such cover-up cases are typically cheaper to prosecute, more comprehensible to the jury, and less subject to subtle nuances in proof. In some cases, of course, the decision to forgo prosecution for the more serious offense will be necessitated by the very destruction of evidence that forms the basis for the obstruction charge. But in those cases

---

[55] See Stuart P Green, 'Victims' Rights and the Limits of the Criminal Law' (2004) 14 *Criminal Law Forum* 335, 343; see also R A Duff, *Punishment, Communication and Community* (Oxford: OUP 2000) 60–64; Jeffrie G Murphy and Jules L Coleman, *The Philosophy of Law* (Boulder, CO: Westview Press, 1990) 113–23; S E Marshall and R A Duff, 'Criminalization and Sharing Wrongs' (1998) *Canadian Journal of Law & Jurisprudence* 7.

in which there does exist adequate evidence to justify pursuing both the less serious cover-up charge and the more serious underlying charge, the question is whether it is improper for the prosecutor to exercise his discretion to prosecute only the latter. One possible answer is that, given limited prosecutorial resources, prosecutors have something like an ethical duty to pursue more, rather than less, serious charges.[56] But it is unclear how far this principle should extend. Assuming that a prosecutor really does have limited resources at her disposal, perhaps the right thing for her to do is to maximize her utility by pursuing those charges which she stands a better chance of proving, or which would have a greater impact on general deterrence.[57]

We will talk more below about cases in which a defendant seeks to 'obstruct injustice.' For the moment, it is enough to note that even a person who covers up a crime he did not commit could be said to have done a morally wrongful act. This suggests that while the wrongfulness of the conduct being covered up is a relevant consideration in determining the seriousness of covering up, it is not a necessary one.

Nature of Investigation into Underlying Conduct

In addition to the nature of the underlying wrongdoing, if any, that is being covered up, we need to consider the circumstances that give rise to such covering up, and particularly the nature of the government's investigation. Here, at least seven possible factors can be identified.

First, there might be cases in which the government is conducting an investigation for the purpose of enforcing an unjust law. For example, imagine that the police in Birmingham, Alabama, in 1963 were investigating a civil rights protester who had violated a local segregated lunch counter ordinance, and that the protester destroyed evidence in order to thwart their investigation. In such cases, we might be tempted to say that what the protester was obstructing was *injustice* rather than justice, and that he was therefore doing nothing wrong.

But this analysis seems to me overly simplistic. The fact that one has a moral right to defy an unjust law does not necessarily give one the right to cover up one's defiance of such law. For a start, it seems unlikely that even

---

[56] Cf Daniel Richman and William J Stuntz, 'Al Capone's Revenge: An Essay on the Political Economy of Pretextual Prosecution' (2005) 105 *Columbia Law Review* 583; Harry Litman, 'Pretextual Prosecutions' (2004) 92 *Georgetown Law Journal* 1135.

[57] On the other hand, there is something to be said for the argument of Dale Oesterle to the effect that, by forgoing the more serious prosecution, 'we lose the public trial, and with it the revelation and condemnation of the core corrupt business practices that attracted the public ire and the prosecutor's attention.' Dale A Oesterle, 'Early Observations on the Prosecutions of the Business Scandals of 2002–03: On Sideshow Prosecutions, Spitzer's Clash With Donaldson Over Turf, the Choice of Civil or Criminal Actions, and the Tough Tactic of Coerced Cooperation' (2004) 1 *Ohio State Journal of Criminal Law* 443, 456. Of course, the obvious rejoinder here is that, in the American criminal justice system, only a very small percentage of cases ever actually go to trial.

a Freedom Rider would be justified in violating section 1512, which makes it a crime to intimidate or harass a witness. More generally, an argument could be made that civil disobedience, by its very nature, requires the defendant to openly accept responsibility for his conduct, and that covering it up would be fundamentally inconsistent with such a device. Moreover, the fact that a particular law or set of laws is unjust does not necessarily mean that all of the other laws in a given legal regime are also unjust. That is, the injustice of the ordinance prohibiting blacks from sitting at the same lunch counters as whites in the Jim Crow South does not necessarily entail that the laws prohibiting the obstruction of justice or perjury in the Jim Crow South were also unjust or immoral. We would have to ask whether such cover-up laws were the product of a thoroughly unjust legal system, whether they were being applied in so discriminatory a manner that they could not be regarded as politically legitimate, and what sorts of punishment, under what conditions, one would suffer if one did not cover up.

Secondly, there are cases in which a defendant is prosecuted for a crime that is not unjust on its face but is being enforced in an unjust manner. For example, imagine that X is prosecuted for engaging in some criminal act for which she has a perfectly adequate defense, such as that she acted out of necessity, or under duress, and that this fact is known to the authorities. Despite the fact that X's conviction for such an offense would once again be unjust, it again does not follow that she would be justified in destroying or fabricating evidence, tampering with the jury, or lying under oath. Even if she is certain that the ultimate just outcome would be her acquittal, X arguably has an obligation to allow the legal system to run its course. The same could be said about otherwise well-founded cases in which a prosecution should properly be barred by a statute of limitations, immunity, or other jurisdictional defect; or in which the investigation was based on speculative information obtained from unreliable informants with no first-hand knowledge of the facts, or on illegitimate political considerations, or solely to embarrass a potential target. On the other hand, we might at least say that such cover-ups were less wrongful than in cases in which the underlying investigation was legitimate.

Thirdly, even when the underlying investigation is itself legitimate, we would need to consider the relevance of the information sought. For example, even if one believed that Kenneth Starr's investigation into the Whitewater land deal was proper, there would still be a question as to whether it was proper to use that investigation as an occasion to subpoena personal items, or ask personal questions, concerning Clinton's relationship with Monica Lewinsky. Assuming that the information sought was not reasonably related to the ostensible subject of the investigation, it seems fair to say that Clinton's covering up should be viewed as less wrongful than it otherwise would be.

A fourth consideration is the probability that the investigation will lead to significant probative evidence. In some cases it appears that law enforcement officials and prosecutors have no reasonable expectation that a given witness interview or document request or line of cross-examination will turn up any probative evidence. The sole or principal purpose of such interviews or document requests is to induce the defendant to make a false statement, perjure himself, obstruct justice, or commit contempt. In the context of section 1001, Justice Ginsburg referred in her concurrence in *Brogan* to the troubling tendency of federal prosecutors to 'manufacture' crimes.[58] In the context of perjury, the phenomenon is known as the 'perjury trap.'[59] There is also at least one case that has spoken of a 'contempt trap.'[60] And we might add to this list the equally plausible notion of an 'obstruction trap.' Thus, if it were the case that the FBI and SEC conducted their interview of Martha Stewart solely or primarily for the purpose of inducing her to make a false statement or, rather than in the belief that such interview was likely to lead to the discovery of any probative evidence, then we should perhaps consider her false statement as less culpable than we otherwise would.

Fifthly, we would want to know the stage of the proceedings at which the information was being sought. Arguably, the farther 'downstream' the obstruction occurs—that is, the closer to formal adjudication—the more blameworthy it is. Certainly, the law of obstruction of justice is structured to reflect such a view.[61] On the other hand, destroying an incriminating document early on in the process, before litigation is pending, and before there has been any opportunity for it to be read or copied, would in some sense be more damaging to the process than destroying it farther downstream, after multiple copies have been made and its contents disseminated.

Sixthly, regardless of the stage of the proceedings, we might think that the degree to which the cover-up should be regarded as wrongful would vary depending on who was doing the investigating. For example, an argument could be made that it is worse to obstruct a legislative body or jury of one's peers than a police department or regulatory agency (or private plaintiff), perhaps in virtue of the fact that legislatures and juries are the more representative institutions. Indeed, the federal scheme of obstruction of justice statutes seem to reflect such a distinction: in terms of sentencing, the obstruction of proceedings before departments, agencies, and committees under section 1505 is almost invariably considered a less serious offense than obstruction of court proceedings under section 1503.[62]

---

[58] *Brogan*, 522 US 398, 411–12 (1998) (Ginsburg, J., concurring).

[59] See, eg *People v Tyler*, 385 NE 2d 1224, 1228–29 (NY 1978); see generally Bennet L Gershman, 'The Perjury Trap' (1981) 129 *University of Pennsylvania Law Review* 624, 645 ('If, under the guise of an otherwise legitimate investigation, a prosecutor solicits testimony for the premeditated design of indicting the witness for perjury, the grand jury is put to an unintended and inappropriate use.').   [60] *People v Fischer*, 423 NE 2d 349, 351 n 1 (NY 1981).

[61] Sanchirico (n 5 above).

[62] Under the Omnibus Clause of section 1503, the penalty is imprisonment for not more than 10 years, a fine, or both. Under the Omnibus Clause of section 1505, the penalty is a fine of not more than $5,000 or imprisonment for not more than five years, or both.

Finally, there are cases in which the person covering up is doing so not in response to an investigation initiated by someone else, but rather on his own initiative. For example, imagine a case in which a plaintiff brought a lawsuit alleging that a defendant manufactured a defective product, and then destroyed evidence of his own contributory negligence. From a moral perspective, such obstruction would seem to be particularly egregious, since the plaintiff could not even claim that he was exercising a right of self-preservation. Consider the case of British thriller writer and life peer, Jeffrey Archer, who in July 2001 was convicted of perjury and perverting the course of justice in connection with a libel case he had initiated 14 years earlier against the tabloid newspaper the *Daily Star*, which had reported that Archer, then deputy chairman of the Conservative Party, had been seeing a prostitute. Archer was alleged to have perverted justice by asking a friend to give him a false alibi, and to have perjured himself by lying in an affidavit to the High Court and during testimony in the libel trial.[63] But even Lord Archer might have an argument that his covering up was in some sense defensive: although it was he who initiated a libel suit against the *Daily Star*, it was the *Daily Star* that arguably first invaded his privacy.

Nature of Covering-Up

Having looked at the significance of the underlying conduct being covered up (or alleged), and the nature of the investigation into such conduct, we can now consider what is probably the most important factor in assessing the moral wrongfulness of obstruction and related offenses—namely, the nature of the cover-up (or the false accusation) itself. Here, we can identify four relevant factors.

For a start, we need to consider the means by which the cover-up was effected. The federal statutes and case law provide a lengthy catalogue: court officials, jurors, and witnesses can be intimidated, bribed, threatened, harassed, and even killed; documents can be destroyed, fabricated, and altered; and witnesses and informants can lie to juries and judges, mislead investigators, and refuse to testify. I assume that, other things being equal, it is worse to cover up a crime by killing a witness than by harassing him, but beyond that, I am reluctant to try to rank the seriousness of various methods of obstruction. Thus, for present purposes, questions such as 'Which is worse—destroying a (true) inculpatory document or fabricating a (false) exculpatory one?,' or 'Is there is any moral difference between ordering the destruction of documents and failing to order the suspension of an already-established document destruction program?' will have to remain unanswered.

---

[63] 'Timeline: Stranger than Fiction' *BBC News Online* (8 Oct. 2002) <http://news.bbc.co.uk/1/hi/uk/1420132.stm>.

A second issue to be considered is the scope of the cover-up. Here we would want to know whether the defendant shredded tens of thousands of documents, like Oliver North,[64] or whether instead she conspired to alter a single document, like Martha Stewart. Was a vast corporate enterprise enlisted to assist in the cover-up, as in the Arthur Andersen case, or was it mostly limited to one or two people, as in the case of Jeffrey Archer? Other things being equal, it would seem that the more extensive the cover-up, the more morally wrongful the act.

Thirdly, we will want to ask what effect, if any, the cover-up or false accusation is likely to have on the resolution of the underlying case. For example, how much other evidence did the government have against the defendant, and how probative was it? To what extent, if any, was the government's investigation hindered by the suspect's false exculpation? Did the informant's false accusation cause investigators to waste limited resources in pursuing a case they otherwise would not have pursued? Did it mean the possibility that a falsely accused might face serious punishment?[65] Did the defendant's covering up cause the prosecution to lose a conviction it otherwise would have obtained? Did it cause the plaintiff to lose a civil suit he otherwise would have won? Did it cause Congress or Parliament to be misled into adopting misguided legislation?

Determining the effect on the government's case of evidence improperly covered up by the defendant is in some sense the converse of the kind of determination that courts make in determining whether perjury by a prosecution witness so affected the jury's deliberations as to justify a new trial. Indeed, this is exactly the inquiry the court was required to make in the Martha Stewart case, after it was alleged that Secret Service Agent and prosecution witness Larry Stewart had lied about his examination of ink samples.[66] Similar is the determination that courts must make in the context of *Brady v Maryland* as to whether the introduction of exculpatory evidence improperly withheld from the defendant by the prosecution would have affected the outcome of the case.[67] Just as there are cases in which the improper introduction of incriminating evidence or the improper withholding of exculpatory evidence is held to be

---

[64] Oliver North was a Reagan Administration aide who in 1989 was convicted of obstructing justice and altering and destroying evidence pertaining to the Iran-Contra Affair, the illegal scheme in which Reagan administration officials sold arms to Iran and diverted the proceeds to right-wing Contra rebels in Nicaragua. North's conviction was subsequently overturned on the grounds that he had previously been granted immunity from prosecution. See *United States v North*, 920 F 2d 940, 948 (DC Cir 1990), *cert denied*, 500 US 941 (1991).

[65] Recall that the biblical approach explicitly links the punishment of the false accuser with the punishment that the falsely accused would have suffered. See n 44 above.

[66] *United States v Stewart*, 323 F Supp 2d 606, 614–23 (SDNY 2004) (holding that a new trial was not justified). In October 2004, Larry Stewart was acquitted of the charges against him. 'Martha Ink Expert Didn't Lie,' *CBSNews.com* (5 Oct. 2004) <http://www. cbsnews.com/stories/2004/06116/national/man 6233516.shtml>.

[67] 373 US 83, 87–88 (1963); see also *United States v Agurs*, 427 US 97, 112–13 (1976) (in order to obtain reversal, defendant must typically show that prosecutor's failure to overturn exculpatory evidence had a material effect on trial's outcome).

harmless error, so perhaps should there be cases in which a defendant's improperly covering up *inculpatory* evidence should be viewed as so inconsequential as to obviate the appropriateness of prosecution for cover-up crimes.[68]

A final factor is the social role played by the person doing the wrongful exculpation or inculpation. As noted at the outset, a surprisingly large number of obstruction and perjury cases involve prominent defendants. Assuming limited prosecutorial resources and two otherwise identical instances of suspected obstruction or perjury, would prosecutors be justified in deciding to prosecute the defendant who is famous, rich, or powerful, rather than the one who is not? From the perspective of general deterrence, prosecutors may well get a bigger 'bang for the buck' by prosecuting the celebrity defendant.[69] But, from the perspective of retributive theory, would such selective prosecution be fair? Most commentators agree that perjury and obstruction of justice occur quite commonly in our criminal justice system,[70] though prosecutions for such offenses are comparatively rare.[71] Given equal protection norms, there is undoubtedly something troubling about the fact that a disproportionate number of defendants in such cases seem to be chosen because of their public prominence.

On the other hand, it may be that prominent people who engage in such conduct should be viewed as somehow more blameworthy than people of modest means who do so. At a minimum, an argument could be made that important public officials such as President Clinton and Deputy Party Chairman Archer should be held to a higher standard of law-abidingness and trust than private persons.[72] The same might also be said generally of lawyers,

[68] For example, the probability that Martha Stewart's alleged lying to the FBI significantly hindered its investigation seems fairly low. On the other hand, it may well be that Arthur Andersen's massive shredding of Enron-related documents did make it significantly more difficult for the government to develop its case against Enron and its top executives, and that it knew that such difficulties would result. Cf Kathleen F Brickey, 'Andersen's Fall from Grace' (2003) 81 *Washington University Law Quarterly* 917, 928 ('Destruction of a paper trail crucial to understanding Enron's complex and sometimes byzantine financial transactions could have jeopardized the government's probe of a potentially massive fraud.').

[69] See Anthony M Dillof, 'Unraveling Unlawful Entrapment' (2004) 94 *Journal of Criminal Law & Criminology* 827, 888; Michael A Simons, 'Prosecutorial Discretion and Prosecutorial Guidelines: A Case Study in Controlling Federalization,' (2000) 75 *NYU Law Review* 893, 964 n 281 (citing cases against prominent sports figures brought because of deterrence value). But cf Stuart P Green, Note 'Private Challenges to Prosecutorial Inaction: A Model Declaratory Judgment Statute' (1988) 97 *Yale Law Journal* 488, 500 n 70 (discussing case in which prosecutors decided not to prosecute rape suspects apparently because of their fame and popularity as professional athletes).

[70] For a critical review of the data regarding the incidence of evidence tampering, see Sanchirico (n 5 above, at 1231–39). On the incidence of perjury, see Myron W Orfield, Jr., 'Deterrence, Perjury, and the Heater Factor: An Exclusionary Rule in the Chicago Criminal Courts' (1992) 63 *Colorado Law Review* 75, 95–114 (discussing police perjury); Keith Soothill, et al., 'Perjury and False Statements: A Criminal Profile of Persons Convicted 1979–2001' (2004) *Criminal Law Review* 926 (analysis of perjury convictions in UK).

[71] Kathleen Maguire and Ann L Pastore (eds.) *Sourcebook of Criminal Justice Statistics 2002* (Bureau of Justice Statistics, US Department of Justice, 2003) at 405, 416 (noting that there were only 114 perjury cases filed in federal district courts in 2002).

[72] See US Sentencing Commission, *Federal Sentencing Guidelines Manual* § 3B1.3 (2004) (sentencing enhancement for 'abuse of position of trust'); cf David A Sklansky, 'Starr, *Singleton*, and the Prosecutor's Role' (1999) 26 *Fordham Urban Law Journal* 509, 531–32 (considering similar issue).

whose obstruction of justice and perjury seem, notwithstanding zealous advocacy norms, particularly noxious crimes.

Postscript: The Case of Scooter Libby

As this book was going to press, another high profile case of obstruction and covering-up reached a significant milestone. In late October 2005, Special Counsel Patrick Fitzgerald announced the indictment of I Lewis "Scooter" Libby, Vice President Dick Cheney's chief of staff, for obstruction of justice, perjury, and false statements, in connection with a federal grand jury's investigation into allegations that Libby and other high-ranking Bush Administration officials had illegally leaked the name of CIA covert operative Valerie Plame Wilson.

The Libby case closely resembles the pattern of prosecution that we have observed in cases like those involving Martha Stewart, Arthur Andersen, Bill Clinton, and the like. Suspected (along with Bush chief political strategist, Karl Rove) of leaking classified information regarding Plame's identity, Libby is ultimately being prosecuted not for the underlying offense of violating the Intelligence Identities Protection Act, but rather for obstructing the government's investigation into such violations.

Fitzgerald was asked at a press conference why his office had chosen to pursue only the cover-up charges, and not the underlying offenses themselves. In response, he offered an insight that is very much consistent with the approach recommended in this chapter. He began by analogizing the underlying act of leaking classified information to a baseball pitcher's hitting a batter in the head. In such circumstances, he said, the umpire could not properly decide whether and how to penalize the pitcher unless he knew the pitcher's intent when he threw the ball. Analogously, Fitzgerald said, in order to determine whether Libby's acts constituted a crime, one would need to know what his intent was in talking to reporters about Valerie Plame. 'And what we have when someone [commits] obstruction of justice,' Fitzgerald said, is that 'the umpire gets sand thrown in his eyes. He's trying to figure [out] what happened and somebody blocked [his] view.'[73]

The significance of Fitzgerald's analogy should be clear: Libby's alleged act of covering up was harmful because it made it more difficult, perhaps impossible, to know the facts of the underlying leak case. And herein lies a kind of paradox: It is precisely in those cases in which the defendant's act of covering up is most effective that prosecution for cover-up crimes will be most clearly justified. And yet it is in those very same cases—where proof of the underlying offense is wanting—that prosecution for the cover-up alone is most likely to seem unfair or petty or vindictive.

---

[73] Transcript of Fitzgerald News Conference (28 Oct. 2005), *Washington Post* (28 Oct. 2005), <http://www.washingtonpost.com/wp-dyn/content/article/2005/10/28/AR2005102801340.html>.

16

Bribery

If any of the offenses considered in this book has a claim to being *the* quintessential white-collar crime, it is probably bribery: its perpetrators are typically upper-income professionals (whether they are the bribees who accept the bribes, or the bribers who have enough capital to pay them); it is invariably committed in the context of governmental or commercial activities; its harms are subtle and often attenuated; its victims are difficult to detect; and, often, the only thing that separates bribery from legitimate 'gifts' is a hard-to-prove mental element of willfulness or, even more obscurely, 'corruption.'

The potential for moral ambiguity in the crime of bribery is illustrated by the case of House Majority Leader Tom DeLay, which was mentioned in the Introduction. Recall that DeLay and several of his Republican House colleagues allegedly told Congressman Nick Smith that, in return for his vote for President George W Bush's Medicare bill, they would give his son, Brad, substantial financial and political support in his congressional campaign.[1] The question is: was this bribery or just political log-rolling? My aim here is to use this and other problematic cases as a vehicle to analyze two more foundational issues: (1) why is bribery morally wrong?; and (2) where should the outer limits of the offense lie?

1. DEFINING BRIBERY

Before we can say why bribery is wrong, we need to have a preliminary idea of what it is. However, there is an inevitable potential for circularity here: ultimately, a determination of its precise contours will turn on an understanding of why bribery is wrong.

One problem is that there are hundreds of bribery and corruption provisions in force throughout the United States,[2] the United Kingdom,[3] and in virtually

---

[1] See sources cited in the Introduction, n 4. The Congressmen also allegedly told Smith that if he didn't accept their offer, they would ensure that his son would never win his election. The 'extortion' aspect of the DeLay case is dealt with in ch. 17.

[2] For a helpful overview of the American law of bribery, see Sarah N Welling, et al., *Federal Criminal Law and Related Actions: Crimes, Forfeiture, the False Claims Act and RICO* (St. Paul, Minn: West Group, 1998), vol. 1, ch. 7.

[3] In England and Wales, the leading bribery statutes are the Public Bodies Corrupt Practices Act and the Prevention of Corruption Act. There are also a number of special offenses covering

every other legal system around the world[4]—and there is a good deal of variation among them. Although I will be giving special consideration to several of the most interesting and problematic aspects of the leading American bribery statute, 18 USC § 201,[5] my overarching interest here will be in articulating a deeper, more universal conception of bribery, one which is correlated only imperfectly with the concept of bribery that can be found in any specific statute.

As a framework for analysis, then, I propose the following working definition of bribery: X (a bribee) is bribed by Y (a briber) if and only if: (1) X accepts, or agrees to accept, something of value from Y; (2) in exchange for X's acting, or agreeing to act, in furtherance of some interest of Y's; (3) by violating some duty of loyalty owed by X arising out of X's office, position, or involvement in some practice.[6] This section focuses on the questions of who can be a bribee and a briber. The next section focuses on bribery as an agreement.

Like offenses such as conspiracy and dueling, a completed act of bribery requires the voluntary concerted criminal participation of two parties. In order for there to be a bribe, there must be both a briber and a bribee (or at least an intended briber and bribee).

Who Can Be a Bribee?

For most of the history of bribery, the only kind of person who could be a bribee was a public official.[7] And, indeed, the only kind of public official

matters such as bribery in elections. The English law of corruption is described in David Lanham, 'Bribery and Corruption,' in Peter Smith (ed.), *Criminal Law: Essays in Honor of J C Smith* (London: Butterworths 1987), at 92; Peter Alldridge, 'Reforming the Criminal Law of Corruption' (2000) 11 *Criminal Law Forum* 287; G R Sullivan, 'Reformulating the Corruption Laws: The Law Commission Proposals' (1997) *Criminal Law Review* 730. In Scotland, bribery is both a common law and statutory offense, the former apparently being limited to the bribery of judicial officials. Gerald H Gordon, *The Criminal Law of Scotland* (3rd edn., by Michael Christie; Edinburgh: W. Green, 2001), vol. 2, 692–3.

[4] See Hearings Before the Committee on Banking, Housing and Urban Affairs, US Senate, 94th Congress, Second Session, 5 April 1976 (research by the Securities and Exchange Commission failed to identify a single country in which it was not a crime to pay a government official money to induce him to enter into a contract with a private firm).

[5] Section 201 contains two distinct, but closely related, offenses. The first offense, bribery, makes it a crime to 'corruptly' give or receive 'anything of value' in return for influence of an official act. The second offense, giving or receiving gratuities, makes it a crime to give or receive anything of value 'for or because of' an official act.

[6] My formulation of this definition and the analysis that follows were influenced by a reading of the following: Kendall D'Andrade, 'Bribery' (1985) 4 *Journal of Business Ethics* 239; Thomas L Carson, 'Bribery, Extortion, and "The Foreign Corrupt Practices Act"' (1985) 14 *Philosophy & Public Affairs* 66; John R Danley, 'Toward a Theory of Bribery' (Spring 1983) *Business & Professional Ethics* 19; Michael Philips, 'Bribery' (1984) 94 *Ethics* 621; Michael S Pritchard, 'Bribery: The Concept' (1998) 4 *Science & Engineering Ethics* 281.

[7] See generally John T Noonan, Jr., *Bribes* (Berkeley: University of California Press, 1984).

that could be bribed for much of that history has been a judge—a fact that is illustrated by references to bribery in both the Hebrew Bible[8] and early English common law.[9] Over time, however, the universe of people considered capable of being bribees has grown considerably, in two ways: first, the class of people who are considered 'public officials' has grown. For example, under section 201(a), the term 'public official' is now broadly defined to include members of Congress, virtually all officers and employees of all three branches of government, jurors, and persons who act 'for or on behalf of' the federal government, such as private employees who receive federally administered funds.[10] Secondly, despite the non-applicability of section 201 itself to private party bribees, the law is increasingly moving in the direction of criminalizing commercial bribery. For example, separate provisions of federal law now make it a crime for investment advisers, contestants in broadcast quiz shows, bank employees, sellers of alcoholic beverages, labor union officials, railroad employees, and radio disc jockeys to receive bribes of various sorts.[11] There are also numerous other provisions, in the United States and elsewhere, that make it a crime to bribe employees of private firms.[12] In short, although, historically, bribery could be committed only by public officials, and many leading statutes continue to be restricted in this way, cases in which payments are received by department store buyers, contest judges, athletes, and other

---

[8] See, eg *Exodus* 23:9 ('Do not take bribes, for bribes blind the clear-sighted and upset the pleas of those who are in the right.'); *Deuteronomy* 16:19 (similar). It is worth noting that, under the original Israeli law of bribery, bribe-taking by judges was considered a more serious offense than bribe-taking by other kinds of government officials. Cf Penal Law Revision (Bribery and Rewards) Law 1950 § 1(a) with § 2.

[9] See, eg Henry de Bracton (Samuel E Thorne (trans.)), *On the Laws and Customs of England*, (Cambridge, Mass.: Harvard U. Press, 1968) vol. 2, 302–03 (citing biblical sources).

[10] 18 USC §201(a); *Dixson v United States*, 465 US 482 (1984) (applying statute to employee of private nonprofit corporation that administered subgrant from municipality's federal block grant). One of the most notable aspects of section 201(b) is that it prohibits bribery of officials who work for the federal government, but not those who work for state and local governments. When the federal government wants to prosecute state and local government officials for bribery and other forms of corruption, it frequently charges them, under the Hobbs Act, 18 USC §1951, with the offense of extortion 'under color of official right.' It can also use 18 USC § 666, which prohibits bribery of state and local officials of entities that receive at least $10,000 in federal funds. See also *Krichman v United States*, 256 US 363, 366–68 (1921) (concluding that earlier federal bribery statute did not reach federal employees such as 'window cleaners, scrubwomen, elevator boys, doorkeepers, pages…or baggage porters'). Although the Court has not had occasion to revisit the question, the prevailing view in the lower courts is that the current bribery statute is not limited in the same way as the earlier statute, and that every federal employee should be regarded as a 'public official' for purposes of section 201. Welling, et al. (n 2 above, vol. 1, at 201 & n 3).

[11] eg 18 USC § 215 (bribery of bank employees); 27 USC § 205(c) (bribery in alcoholic beverage industry); 29 USC § 186 (bribery of labor representatives); 49 USC § 11907 (bribery of railroad employees). Commercial bribery can also serve as a predicate offense under the mail fraud, wire fraud, RICO, and Travel Act statutes.

[12] See *Perrin v United States*, 444 US 37, 44 nn 9 & 10 (1979) (listing statutes); Gunter Heine, et al., (eds.) *Private Commercial Bribery: A Comparison of National and Supranational Legal Structures* (Freiburg: International Chamber of Commerce, 2003) (study of laws in thirteen OECD countries).

private sector actors are now, arguably, as central to the concept of bribery as those involving more traditional bribees such as judges and legislators.[13]

One interesting question that has arisen in recent years concerns the circumstances under which witnesses should qualify as potential bribees. The leading case is *United States v Singleton*, in which the prosecutor offered a witness 'leniency' in return for his agreeing to testify on behalf of the government, and the defendant subsequently argued that such an offer (ie of 'something of value' in return for testimony) constituted an illegal gratuity under 18 USC §201.[14] Under section 201(b)(4), bribery is explicitly defined to include cases in which a person corruptly receives something of value 'in return for being influenced in testimony under oath or affirmation as a witness.' Clearly, then, the statute would apply to a witness who agreed to give perjured testimony in return for payment. But would it apply to a witness who agreed to give testimony that was truthful? Such a witness might have an argument that, rather than receiving something of value in return for being influenced in his role *as a witness*, he was actually receiving something of value in return for his being influenced to *become* a witness. As such, there would be no positional duty for him to violate. His act would thus be analogous to a private person who accepted payment in return for deciding not to run for some political office[15]—an act that would not on its face appear to constitute receiving a bribe.

Who Can be a Briber?

Having considered who can be a bribee, we can now look at who (or what) can be a briber. Section 201 says simply that bribery is committed by 'whoever' gives or receives something of value in return for influence over an official act. The term 'whoever,' in turn, is defined (along with 'persons') in Title 1, section 1 of the US Code, the 'Dictionary Act,' to include 'corporations, companies,

---

[13] It is for this reason that I am skeptical about the approach to bribery offered by Peter Alldridge, who argues that bribery should be a crime because it involves the 'commodification of government.' Peter Alldridge, *Relocating Criminal Law* (Aldershot: Dartmouth, 2000) 186. The idea is that, just as it a crime to traffic in human beings (as in slavery), or in jury verdicts or votes (as in obstruction of justice and various elections offenses), or (more controversially) in sex or bodily organs, so people should not be permitted to commodify government by buying and selling official acts. Such commodification, he says, undermines the rule of law and the legitimacy of our governmental systems. There are, however, several problems with Alldridge's account. First, it fails to explain why commercial bribery should be a crime. Secondly, it fails to explain why bribery is viewed as a far more serious offense than prostitution or selling bodily organs. Thirdly, it fails to account adequately for the difference between gifts and bribes. At a minimum, we need some explanation of what it means to commodify. For further discussion of these points, see Stuart P Green, 'Review Essay: Broadening the Scope of Criminal Law Scholarship' (Summer/Fall 2001) *Criminal Justice Ethics* 58–59.

[14] *United States v Singleton*, 144 F 3d 1343 (10th Cir 1998), rev'd by 165 F 3d 1297 (10th Cir 1999) (*en banc*), *cert denied*, 527 US 1024 (1999).

[15] See generally Daniel H Lowenstein, 'Political Bribery and the Intermediate Theory of Politics' (1985) 32 *UCLA Law Review* 784, 791–95.

associations, firms, partnerships, societies, and joint stock companies, as well as individuals.'

Given the breadth of this definition and the all-encompassing manner in which the term 'whoever' has been interpreted in other federal criminal statutes,[16] it is hard to see how any person or legal entity could be held incapable of being a briber. Nevertheless, this is exactly what the Tenth Circuit *en banc* opinion held in the *Singleton* case. Indeed, the court was so anxious to avoid the conclusion that a promise of leniency in return for testimony might constitute a crime that it gave a wholly implausible answer to the 'who can be a briber' question (or, more precisely, the 'who can be a gratuity-giver' question).

The court's argument, as best it can be summarized, was as follows: (1) The prosecutor in federal criminal cases works not on behalf of herself, but rather on behalf of the U.S. Government. (2) The Government cannot prosecute 'itself.' (3) Therefore, a federal prosecutor, acting in her capacity as a representative of the 'sovereign,' cannot be prosecuted for a crime that is committed in the course of her regular duties. And, because a prosecutor who promises leniency in return for true (as opposed to false) testimony is functioning within 'the limits of his or her office,' she cannot be prosecuted under section 201.[17]

This argument reflects at least four major flaws: first, it is simply wrong that a government-initiated prosecution against a federal prosecutor acting in her official capacity would constitute a prosecution by the government of 'itself'[18]; the government and its representatives are, and always have been, viewed as distinct. Secondly, it obviously begs the question to say that a prosecutor who offers leniency in return for testimony is functioning within the limits of her office; whether a prosecutor who offers such a deal is acting illegally is precisely the issue the court was called upon to answer. Thirdly, the court offers no explanation for why a government prosecutor is incapable of bribing a witness to tell the truth, but fully capable of bribing a witness to lie. Fourth, the decision fails entirely to address the deeper question of whether and how such conduct can be distinguished from conduct that should properly be regarded as bribery. This is a question that will be addressed below.

Bribery as an Agreement

In this section, we consider two related issues: (1) how bribes differ from gifts, tips, and campaign contributions; and (2) what it means for the briber to give the bribee 'something of value' in return for the bribee's acting on the briber's behalf.

---

[16] Cf Stuart P Green, 'The Criminal Prosecution of Local Governments' (1994) 72 *North Carolina Law Review* 1197, 1215–17 (concerning application of federal environmental crime statutes to municipalities).   [17] *Singleton*, 165 F 3d at 1302 & n 2.

[18] I have previously dealt with the supposed problem of self-prosecution in Green, above note 16, at 1209–10.

The supposed difficulty of distinguishing bribes from gifts, tips, rewards, and campaign contributions has frequently been noted.[19] Although it may well be difficult to make the distinction in practice, in theory it is clear: bribes involve an agreement to exchange something of value in return for influence, whereas gifts, tips, and campaign contributions involve no such agreement.[20]

A bribe involves a bilateral agreement between two parties in which something of value is given or promised *in exchange for* the bribee's acting on the briber's behalf. There can be no completed bribe without a meeting of minds. Thus, as in the case of conspiracy,[21] if the briber or bribee is intoxicated or is mistaken, or is an undercover agent feigning agreement (as in the notorious Abscam case[22]), the bribe would be incomplete. Therefore, assuming for purposes of discussion that *Singleton* is right, and that government attorneys acting within the scope of their office are incapable of committing bribery, it would seem to follow that, if a witness who accepts consideration from such a person in return for testifying is a bribee at all, he is party to an *incomplete* bribe (though it should be noted that, for all practical purposes, section 201 makes no real distinction between 'choate' and 'inchoate' bribes).

In contrast to bribes, gifts, tips, rewards, and donations are unilateral; they are given without any agreement to reciprocate. This is not to deny, of course, that gifts are often given either in return for some service that has already been rendered (as in the case of tips or rewards), or in expectation of receiving something in return (as in the 'exchange' of family gifts at holiday time). We have all encountered circumstances in which such ambiguity is manifest.[23] Nevertheless, there is, at least as a conceptual matter, a significant difference between 'exchanging' goods or services through an agreement and doing so gratuitously. Similarly, there is a significant conceptual difference between completed bribes and gifts.

What the Briber Offers: 'Something of Value'

Bribery statutes typically say that a briber must offer or give 'something of value' in return for some service rendered by the bribee. Although the idea of bribery typically conjures up images of fat envelopes stuffed with $100 bills,

---

[19] See, eg Noonan (n 7 above, at 687–90); James Lindgren, 'The Theory, History, and Practice of the Bribery-Extortion Distinction' (1993) 141 *University of Pennsylvania Law Review* 1695, 1707.

[20] A similar distinction is made in Susan Rose-Ackerman, *Corruption and Government: Causes, Consequences, and Reform* (Cambridge: CUP, 1999) 93; and Philips (n 6 above, at 632).

[21] At common law, the traditional rule was that there was no conspiracy unless the plurality requirement was satisfied—ie unless at least two persons possessed the requisite intent to conspire. See *Morrison v California*, 291 US 82, 92 (1934) (Cardozo, J.).

[22] Described in Stuart P Green, 'Federal Bribery Statute,' in Brian K Landsberg (ed.), *Encyclopedia of Major Acts of Congress* (New York: Macmillan, 2003).

[23] See, eg *The Simpsons: Lisa's Substitute* (Fox television broadcast, 25 April 1991) (Homer is bemused to learn that while local art museum does not charge 'admission' per se, patrons are expected to give 'donation' upon entering).

the thing of value given by the briber to the bribee need not, of course, be money. Bribes have been premised on a wide range of things of value, such as offers of future employment, unsecured short-term (and subsequently repaid) loans, restaurant meals and tickets for athletic events, ostensibly valuable (but actually worthless) stock certificates, and even sexual favors.[24] Indeed, in the Talmudic tradition, bribes could be effected even by means of 'pleasant words' of flattery.[25]

On the other hand, as I have discussed elsewhere in the context of theft law, the term 'thing of value' cannot always be taken literally.[26] We need to think about the term in relation to the underlying purposes and policy concerns of the relevant statute. In the case of bribery, we would need to inquire into the extent to which an expansive interpretation of the term 'thing of value' might create a chilling effect in the context of, for example, dealings between department store buyers and suppliers, political fundraising activities, and the social lives of government officials.

The question of chilling effect also arises in the legislative context. If legislator *A* offers legislator *B* $100,000 in return for voting for some piece of legislation, then it would not be hard to conclude that the 'something of value' requirement had been satisfied. But what if legislator *A* offered legislator *B* not money, but rather his endorsement in the next election, or perhaps his support for some other piece of legislation in which *B* had a special interest? Would that be bribery, or merely log rolling, legislative 'business as usual'? Given the interest our society presumably has in a legislative process unconstrained by outside control, including by courts and prosecutors, we would do well to approach such situations with caution. Conceptually, one way to do so is simply to decide that endorsements and votes will not constitute things of value for purposes of bribery law.

Another interesting context in which the 'thing of value' question arises is provided, again, by a case in which a prosecutor made a deal with a witness to give something in return for testimony. In *United States v Medina*, the defendant, charged with drug trafficking, sought to exclude testimony given by a cooperating government witness who had, in exchange for his agreement to testify on behalf of the government, received not only a promise of leniency but also cash payments of over $105,000.[27] In ruling on the motion, the court seemed reluctant to follow the approach used by the Tenth Circuit in *Singleton*, and refused to hold that prosecutors acting within the scope of their duties could never violate s 201. Instead, the *Medina* court distinguished between

---

[24] See, respectively, *United States v Biaggi*, 909 F 2d 662, 684–85 (2nd Cir 1990); *United States v Gorman*, 807 F 2d 1299, 1304–05 (6th Cir 1986); *United States v Sun Diamond Growers*, 526 US 398, 401–02 (1999); *United States v Williams*, 705 F 2d 603, 623 (2d Cir 1983); *Scott v State*, 141 NE 19, 23 (Ohio 1923).

[25] Meir Tamari, *Al Chet: Sins in the Marketplace* (Northvale, NJ: Aronson, 1996) at 137.

[26] See Stuart P Green, 'Plagiarism, Norms, and the Limits of Theft Law: Some Observations on the Use of Criminal Sanctions in Protecting Intellectual Property Rights' (2002) 54 *Hastings Law Journal* 167, at 211–21.   [27] 41 F Supp 2d 38 (D Mass 1999).

prosecutorial promises of leniency and payments of cash, arguing that while there was a long 'tradition' of giving witnesses the former, the ethical issues raised by the latter were 'troubling.'[28] In essence, the court said, while cash is a 'thing of value' for purposes of the bribery statute, prosecutorial leniency is not.

What the Bribee Gives Back: Influence

Section 201(b)(2) requires that the bribee agree to accept something of value 'in return for . . . being influenced in the performance of any official act.' As we shall see below, it is this 'being influenced' requirement on which the moral wrongfulness of bribery largely depends, and in which the moral ambiguity inherent in some cases of bribery chiefly resides.

For the moment, we can simply observe that the federal courts have interpreted the 'being influenced' element quite broadly, upholding convictions despite the fact that the act had already been contemplated before the bribe was solicited.[29] The courts have also read broadly the requirement that the bribe relate to acts that are 'official,' rejecting, for example, the claim by a defendant congressman that such acts must occur exclusively within the legislative process itself.[30]

In this context, it is worth asking whether the 'being influenced' requirement of the statute would be satisfied by a witness who receives consideration in return for agreeing to testify truthfully as a fact witness in a criminal trial. Such a witness would presumably want to argue that she was not being influenced in her act, since she would have given the same true testimony regardless of whether she received consideration for doing so. Moreover, it could be argued that the service the witness was providing was not giving *true* testimony per se but, rather, waiving her right not to testify in the first place. In any event, to really understand what it is the bribee must give back to the briber, we need to look more deeply at why bribery constitutes a morally wrongful act.

2. THE MORAL CONTENT OF BRIBERY

Having considered the formal elements of bribery, I now want to turn to its moral content. Here we apply our three-part framework in considering its *mens rea*, harmfulness, and moral wrongfulness.

---

[28] Nevertheless, the court ultimately denied the motion on the grounds that the witness was being paid not for his testimony as a witness but rather for his help as an informant. 41 F Supp 2d at 48–53. See also *United States v Murphy*, 193 F 3d 1, 9 (1st Cir 1999) (recognizing distinction between offering witnesses leniency and 'just pay[ing] witnesses money for their testimony'); *United States v Condon*, 170 F 3d 687, 689 (7th Cir 1999), *cert denied*, 526 US 1126; *United States v Hunte*, 193 F 3d 173, 176 n 4 (3rd Cir 1999).

[29] *United States v Quinn*, 359 F 3d 666, 675 (4th Cir 2004).

[30] *United States v Biaggi*, 853 F 2d 89, 97–99 (2d Cir 1988), *cert denied*, 489 US 1052 (1989).

Mens Rea

Under section 201, a thing of value must be given or received 'corruptly' in order for such act to constitute bribery. Indeed, the requirement of 'corruptness' is often said to be the principal factor that distinguishes bribery from the lesser offense of giving or receiving gratuities.[31] In reality, corruptness is as much a form of moral wrongfulness as it is of *mens rea*. But because the courts tend to regard it as a form of *mens rea*, and it appears as such in the leading statute, I will treat it this way here. The question is, what exactly does 'corrupt' mean in the context of bribery?

Under American law, the term 'corruptly' has been interpreted to mean that the defendant desires that, in exchange for something of value, the public official will perform some act.[32] Thus, the briber must presumably intend that the bribee be influenced, while the bribee must intend that she herself be influenced.

An interesting question arises in cases in which the bribee takes money from a briber with no intention of allowing herself to be influenced. For example, in the Abscam case, the defendant, Congressman Michael Myers, argued that although he had been captured on videotape ostensibly agreeing to introduce a private immigration bill in return for a payment of $50,000, in fact he had merely been 'playacting,' and had never actually intended to follow through on his promise.[33] In rejecting what it characterized as a 'bizarre defense,' the court said simply that it understood the 'agreeing to be influenced' language of the statute to refer not to the bribe taker's 'true intent,' but rather to 'the intention he conveys to the briber in exchange for the bribe.'[34]

The court's reasoning in *Myers* is surely wrong. One who accepts money ostensibly in return for performing an official act he has no intention of performing has no more accepted a bribe than one who accepts money ostensibly in return for committing a killing he has no intention of carrying out has conspired to commit murder. An official who takes money in exchange for a service he does not intend to carry out has presumably committed not bribery, but fraud. On the other hand, an official who accepts money to perform an official act that she does intend to perform, but is unable to do so, either because she lacks authority, or because the act has already been performed, could properly be held to have accepted a bribe.[35]

---

[31] See, eg *United States v Muldoon*, 931 F 2d 282, 287 (4th Cir 1991).

[32] Welling, et al. (n 2 above, at § 7.4, at 210–11).

[33] *United States v Myers*, 692 F 2d 823 (2nd Cir 1982), *cert denied*, 461 US 961 (1983). A similar case, from South Africa, is *S. v Van Der Westhuizen*, 1974 (4) SA 61. See also *R v Dillon* [1982] VR 434.　　　　　　　　　　　　　　　　[34] 692 F 2d at 841–42 & n 19.

[35] See, eg *United States v Carson*, 464 F 2d 424, 433 (2d Cir) (bribe taker had no authority to take the requested action), *cert denied*, 409 US 949 (1972); *United States v Heffler*, 402 F 2d 924 (3rd Cir 1968) (similar), *cert denied*, 394 US 946 (1969).

Harmfulness

Much of the literature on bribery and other forms of corruption focuses on the numerous ways in such acts are believed to be harmful to society.[36] Bribery 'corrupts' political and commercial life by inviting inappropriate grounds for decision-making.[37] It creates political instability, distorts markets, undermines legitimacy, retards development, wastes resources, undercuts confidence in decision-making institutions, and leads to injustice, unfairness, and inefficiency. In the Talmudic view, even a wise person who accepts a gift but otherwise intends to maintain objectivity in the case before him will find that his judgment is distorted.[38]

The precise nature of the harm that a given act of bribery causes will vary depending on the nature of the official act that is compromised, whether by judge, legislator, administrator, juror, witness, executive, or other official. Consider, for example, the difference in harm between cases in which, in return for payment: (1) a military officer agrees to share secrets that could result in loss of life, and (2) a waiter agrees to give a patron a better table in his restaurant (if in fact the latter case involves a bribe at all[39]).

Of course, none of this is to say that every act of bribery will necessarily lead to any actual bad decisions. As we shall see below, a legislator or judge can be bribed into making the same correct decision she would have made absent the bribe. All that is required is that the decision-making process itself be corrupted by the payment of the bribe.

Moral Wrongfulness

So far, we have been talking about 'bribes' as if they were single, uni-directional transactions. In fact, however, bribes involve two distinct parts: a bribe must be given (or at least offered) by a briber; and it must be received (or at least solicited) by a bribee. Although the modern American statutory approach is to impose the same penalty for bribe-taking and bribe-giving, there is some evidence that the general public regards bribe-taking as the more serious offense,[40] and it is in fact treated as such in some foreign statutes.[41]

---

[36] See, eg Rose-Ackerman (n 20 above) and sources cited n 44 below.
[37] See Noonan (n 7 above, at 3).   [38] See source cited in n 25 above.
[39] See discussion in text following n 43 below.
[40] In a recent study, respondents were asked which they regarded as more serious: a public official accepting a bribe, or a private citizen giving a bribe to a public official. Seventy four per cent said they regarded the former as more serious; 12 per cent said the latter was more serious; 14 per cent said they were equal in seriousness. Training and Research Institute, National White Collar Crime Center, *The National Public Survey on White Collar Crime* (2000) <http://www.nw3c.org/research_topics.html> accessed 22 Aug. 2005. Of course, it should be pointed out that such data could also be consistent with the view that what respondents thought was more serious was corrupt action by officials (whether offering or taking bribes) as opposed to corrupt action by private individuals.
[41] eg Israel Penal Law Revision (Bribery and Rewards) Law, 1950 § 3 (person giving bribe is liable for only half the penalty applicable to person accepting bribe).

In terms of understanding why bribery is morally wrongful, the distinction is crucial. In the analysis that follows, I focus first on the moral wrongfulness of *receiving* a bribe, and then on the moral wrongfulness of *giving* a bribe.

Receiving a Bribe as a Form of Disloyalty

My proposal is that we think about the act of receiving or soliciting a bribe as a form of disloyalty. Let us begin with what is presumably a paradigm case: L is a legislator who has been elected to represent a particular constituency. L is offered a substantial sum of money by X in return for L's agreeing to vote for some piece of legislation that X favors, but which is directly contrary to the interests of L's constituents. L accepts the payment and votes in favor of X's favored legislation. In this case, we can clearly see that L has been disloyal to his constituents and to the ideals of his job. Loyal public officials are expected to resist the temptations that may come their way. They are expected to work in the best interests of their constituents or institutions, rather than in the interests of third parties who tempt them. Loyalty faces its most important test when temptation is strongest. To accept a bribe is to give in to such temptation, and therefore be disloyal.

Now let us change the facts a bit and see how far the idea of disloyalty will take us. Suppose that J is a judge presiding over a case involving X and Y, and that J accepts money from X in return for deciding the case in X's favor, rather than on the merits (which would have favored Y). Clearly, J has violated her duty to decide cases impartially. She has *misused* her office. But has she been disloyal, and, if so, to whom or to what? The first thing to note is that, although J surely wrongs or harms Y by denying him the decision he deserves, J has not been disloyal to Y, since J never had a duty of loyalty to Y to begin with. Instead, we should say that J has been disloyal to her judicial office, to the ideal of impartial justice, or to the public. But in order to accept this characterization of the case, we need to believe that one can be loyal not just to other people but also to principles or ideals—an issue that has generated some controversy, as we saw in Chapter 8.

Next, let us imagine that B is a boxer who accepts a payment to throw a fight to his opponent. Unlike L and J, B holds no official position. But, as Michael Philips has put it in analyzing such a case, what B is 'paid to do is act in a manner dictated by some person or organization rather than to act according to the understandings constitutive of' his practice.[42] In this sense, we can say that B has been disloyal to the practice of boxing or to the ideals of athletic competition. But, once again, this move is available only if we believe that it makes sense to talk about loyalty to ideals or principles, and not just to persons or groups of persons.

---

[42] Philips (n 6 above, at 623).

Distinguishing Between Breaches of Loyalty and Other Kinds of Breach

The kind of wrongfulness associated with accepting a bribe needs to be distinguished from two other kinds of moral wrongfulness with which it might be confused. First, it is not disloyal to accept payment to violate a 'non-positional' moral duty. That is, the act that is committed must involve a breach of duty arising out of some office or position or involvement in some practice. Thus, it is not bribery for a hired killer to accept payment in return for violating her duty not to kill, since the duty not to kill does not arise out of a position or practice.[43]

Secondly, not even every breach of positional duty involves disloyalty. Judges, legislators, and other office-holders clearly breach positional duties when they abandon impartiality or make decisions on the basis of frivolous or selfish reasons. Witnesses also breach a positional duty when they lie on the witness stand. All of these acts are wrongful in their own way, but none of them involves disloyalty per se. Disloyalty requires that the agent charged with being loyal 'go over' to the other side: that is, act in a way that is intended to further the interests of someone or something other than the party or cause to which he is charged with being loyal. Where the official or witness is merely being lazy or malicious, and no third party is involved, there is no disloyalty.

Disloyalty Defined in Reference to Scope of Positional Duty

In determining whether someone has committed bribery, it is necessary to determine whether he has in fact violated a positional or practice-related duty. For example, if W, a waiter in a restaurant, accepts money from C, a customer, in return for giving C a better table than he otherwise would have received, we cannot know whether W has accepted a bribe unless we know exactly what W's position entails, including whether he is under any duty to assign tables 'impartially.' It may be that W's duty is merely to provide adequate service to some designated group of customers. On the other hand, if W accepted money from C in return for ignoring all of the other customers and attending exclusively to C, then it seems that W would have breached a positional duty.

Focusing on the scope of the alleged bribee's positional duty is also helpful in understanding what appears at first glance to be a kind of cultural variation in attitudes towards bribery. It is often assumed that bribery is less tolerated in modern Western democracies than in, say, Russia or certain countries in the Third World.[44] And, indeed, one of the goals of legislation such as the

[43] This point is also made by Philips, *ibid*, at 622.

[44] eg Gunnar Myrdal, 'Corruption as a Hindrance to Modernization in South Asia,' in Arnold J Heidenheimer, et al. (eds.), *Political Corruption: A Handbook* (New Brunswick, NJ: Transaction Pub. 1989) 405; John Girling, *Corruption, Capitalism and Democracy*

US Foreign Corrupt Practice Act and the OECD Anti-Bribery Convention is to encourage the proliferation of anti-bribery norms that will apply universally.

So, are people in such societies really more inclined to commit bribery, or more tolerant of the act, than people in the West? At the risk of armchair anthropologizing, let me suggest that the cultural differences here may have less to do with the degree to which bribery and disloyalty are tolerated than with the different ways in which positional duties are defined in various systems.[45] For example, if a customs agent at the border crossing between (let us say) Nigeria and Cameroon is more likely than her counterpart at LAX to 'look the other way' in return for a cash payment, it may be simply because the two agents have different understandings of the duties their respective positions entail, rather than because they have different views about the wrongfulness of bribery (or disloyalty) itself.

Accepting a Bribe to do the 'Right Thing'

In this section, I want to consider several additional cases that may at first seem problematic for my (dis)loyalty-based theory of bribery. First, imagine that *L*, a legislator, accepts a payment to do precisely what is in the best interests of her constituents and, in fact, in the best interests of the polity as a whole. Secondly, imagine that *G*, a prison guard at Auschwitz, accepts payment in return for agreeing to allow a prisoner to escape. Thirdly, consider again the scenario in *Singleton*, in which the witness Napoleon Douglas was given something of value in return for a promise to offer (true) testimony in a criminal trial. In all three cases, it might be argued, the bribee has taken money to do 'the right thing.' Which, if any, of these cases can properly be said to involve taking a bribe?

In the first case, does it make sense to say that *L*, who was doing what was in fact in the interests of his constituents, was disloyal? In arguing that bribery involves a form of disloyalty, I have adopted a view that is similar to that adopted by the English Law Commission's 1997 *Consultation Paper on Corruption*.[46] According to that paper, the paradigm of bribery involves three parties: *A*, the briber; *B*, the recipient of the bribe ('the bribee'); and *C*, *B*'s principal. The purpose of *A*'s bribing *B* is to cause *B* to act in *A*'s interest, which in turn is likely to involve *B*'s acting against the interests of *C*, to whom *B*, as *C*'s agent, owes a duty of loyalty.

So far, so good. But curiously, the *Consultation Paper*'s characterization of the 'essential character of corruption' was rejected by its successor,

(London: Routledge, 1997); Richard T De George, *Competing With Integrity in International Business* (Oxford: OUP, 1993); Sabrina Tavernise, 'A Russian Tilts at Graft,' *New York Times* (10 Feb. 2003), at A3 (in Russia, business owners pay public officials an estimated $33 billion in bribes yearly).

[45] A similar argument is offered in Danley (n 6 above, at 22).

[46] Law Commission for England and Wales, *Consultation Paper No. 145: Legislating the Criminal Code: Corruption* (HMSO, 1997), at paras 1.12–1.15.

the Commission's 1998 *Report on Corruption*.[47] According to the latter, 'an agent can act corruptly by doing something which is not, and which the agent knows is not, contrary to the principal's interest.' One example is where the agent 'demand[s] a bribe for doing what the agent's duty to the principal already requires the agent to do.' Another is when 'of a range of choices open to the agent, two or more appear equally advantageous to the principal, and the agent is bribed to choose one of these acceptable options rather than another.' Indeed, the *Report* views these hypotheticals as so problematic that it 'conclud[es] that a definition [of corruption] couched in terms of breach of duty, or even in terms of the principal's best interest as the agent perceives them, would be too narrow.'[48]

In my view, the *Report* is wrong to suggest that these hypotheticals undermine a loyalty-based theory of bribery. The *Report*'s understanding of what loyalty entails is overly narrow. In cases such as those hypothesized, the wrongfulness of L's conduct comes not from the actual decision that L makes, but rather from the fact that L makes her decision based on the wrong sorts of reasons.[49] The duty of loyalty that L owes to her principals is not to make one particular decision or another, but to make decisions *because* they are in her principals' interests. If L accepts money from a briber to do an act that is in the briber's interest, but which also happens, fortuitously,[50] to be in the interest of her principal, it is hard to see how we can say that she has been true to her principal.[51] Accordingly, I would conclude that L would be guilty of bribery under a loyalty-based theory, notwithstanding the fact that she voted 'correctly.'

In the second case, G, the prison guard, accepts money to allow a prisoner to escape from Auschwitz. Can we say that G has been disloyal and that he has therefore taken a bribe? Recall the two senses in which 'loyalty' and 'disloyalty' are used: to the extent that G has taken money to work against the interests of the Nazis, he is being disloyal in the descriptive or empirical sense of the term, but not in its moral or normative sense, since one cannot be loyal in the moral sense to a thoroughly evil principal. Thus, in determining

---

[47] Law Commission for England and Wales, *Report No. 248, Legislating the Criminal Code: Corruption* (HMSO, 1998), at paras 5.4–5.10.   [48] *Ibid* at 54.

[49] Cf RA Duff, 'The Limits of Virtue Jurisprudence' (2003) 34 *Metaphilosophy* 214 ('A judge's duty is to decide the cases that come before her through a process that accords with the requirements of justice . . . . [A] judge who decides in favour of the party who is legally entitled to win only because she was bribed to do so has failed to observe a basic requirement of natural justice, that she attend only to legally relevant considerations in making her decision.').

[50] I say fortuitously, although one could imagine a legislator or judge who would accept a bribe only in circumstances in which he was able to vote the 'correct' way.

[51] Maimonides, the great 12th century Talmudic commentator, makes a similar point: Bribery involves an intention to pervert justice, and such intention exists even when the judge is bribed to acquit the innocent or convict the guilty. Thus, it is not surprising that modern Israeli bribery law makes explicit 'that the crime of bribery takes place not only when the purpose of the bribe is to induce an unlawful act or to pervert justice, but also when the object is to obtain performance of a lawful act which it is the duty of the recipient to perform in any case.' Israeli Penal Law, Art 5, § 293(7).

whether G has taken a bribe, we need to know which kind of disloyalty bribery entails—descriptive or normative. I suggest that the offense of bribery should be understood as entailing disloyalty in the normative sense, since it would be a perverse use of the criminal sanction to prosecute someone for betraying a loyalty that was so misplaced from the start. To be sure, G, by doing the right thing for the wrong reasons—that is, allowing the prisoner to escape because he was paid to do so, rather than out of any genuine moral commitment—acts in a manner that is formally similar to the way in which L acted in the previous hypothetical. But if I am right that bribery requires disloyalty in the moral sense, then we should say that G has not accepted a bribe.

Finally, let us consider the case in which a witness such as Napoleon Douglas agrees to offer (truthful) testimony against the defendant Singleton in return for a promise of leniency. Like L (the legislator who accepted money from a third party to do an act which, fortuitously, was in the best interest of his constituents), Douglas seems to have done the right act for the wrong reason: witnesses are supposed to offer true testimony in order to aid the truth-finding function of the trial, not because they are paid to do so.[52] But to recognize this is different from saying that Douglas has been disloyal. The problem is that, unlike L, who violated a well-defined duty to act in the interest of his constituents, a witness's duties are much less clear. Douglas, a private citizen with knowledge of a crime, agrees to waive his right to silence and testify in return for something of value. At a stretch, we could perhaps say that Douglas has somehow been disloyal to himself. But if this really is disloyalty, it is of the most elusive kind,[53] and not the sort of disloyalty that is, or should be, the concern of bribery law.

Coerced and Coercive Acceptance of Bribes

There are two final situations I want to consider in which the moral status of receiving a bribe may deviate from the norm. The first occurs when the putative bribee is also the victim of the briber's coercion. The second occurs when the bribee herself uses coercion against the briber. (Cases in which the putative *briber* is the victim or user of coercion are considered below.)

Consider again the case of retiring Congressman Nick Smith. Had he succumbed to alleged pressure from the House Republican leadership, and agreed to vote for the President's Medicare plan in return for substantial financial and political support for his son Brad's congressional campaign, would Smith have accepted a bribe? Would the fact that he was pressured into taking it give him a defense? The case is a complex one. Recall that the real test of loyalty is temptation. Had Nick given in to temptation and agreed to

---

[52] Although, admittedly, this is exactly what *expert* witnesses do all the time.

[53] Cf the brief discussion of the extent to which moral duties to self are comparable to moral duties to others, ch. 4 p. 65 above.

vote in the interests of the House Republicans rather than his constituents, he would surely have been disloyal to those constituents. On the other hand, it seems that Nick's loyalty to his constituents was in competition with the loyalty he presumably had to his son. Moreover, had the threat been more dire—say, if his colleagues had threatened to kill Brad unless Nick voted their way—then we might well conclude that such coercion should relieve him of whatever competing moral or legal duties he might have.

Now let us imagine a case in which a police officer, *P*, offers, in return for a payment, to forgo arresting *D* for a crime that *D* has committed[54] (another way to put it is that *P* threatens to arrest *D* for a crime that *D* has committed unless *D* pays *P*). Here, *P*, the would-be bribee, is using coercion to obtain a bribe. As such, *P* has simultaneously committed bribery and some additional offense, such as extortion, criminal coercion, or blackmail.[55]

3. THE MORAL WRONGFULNESS OF OFFERING OR GIVING A BRIBE

So far, we have been focusing on the moral wrongfulness of *accepting* a bribe. At this point, we need to change gears and inquire into the moral wrongfulness of *offering* a bribe, which under modern law merits an equivalent punishment. Because the briber typically breaches no duty of loyalty,[56] our analysis of moral wrongfulness will have to follow a different course. The question I want to ask is: what exactly is wrong with offering or giving a bribe? In this section, my focus is on the idea that offering a bribe involves inducing another to do a wrongful act.[57]

Inducing Another to be Disloyal

Most of the theoretical literature on the wrongfulness of inducing another to do wrong focuses on the wrongfulness of doing so by means of coercion or exploitation. But while there certainly are bribes that involve coercion and exploitation, neither device is necessary. Thus, for the moment I want to ask two less frequently asked questions: first, why is it wrong to induce, or attempt to induce, another to do wrong, even when one does so without engaging in coercion or exploitation? Secondly, is there something in particular wrong

[54] The hypothetical is James Lindgren's (n 19 above).
[55] On the non-mutual exclusiveness of bribery and extortion, see Lindgren (n 19 above). On the differences between extortion and blackmail, see ch. 17.
[56] I say 'typically' because there could be cases in which a briber's offer of a bribe violated a duty of loyalty to the *briber's* principal—for example, if the briber were subject to ethical guidelines that forbade the offering of bribes.
[57] For another possible theory of why accepting or giving a bribe is morally wrong, see n 13 above (critiquing Peter Alldridge's 'commodification of government' theory).

about inducing another to do wrong by offering such person something of value?

As a start, it seems obvious that the wrongfulness of inducing another to do wrong is in some way derivative of the wrongfulness of the act being induced. Thus, it is clearly worse to induce X to commit murder than to induce her to park in a no-parking zone. On the other hand, we should not assume that inducing another to do a wrongful act and doing the act are necessarily morally equivalent. As bad as it is to induce another to kill, it is likely that we would reserve our most serious condemnation for the actual killer, since it was she who made the ultimate decision to pull the trigger.[58] In comparing the wrongfulness of inducing a wrongful act and doing the act, we will certainly want to assess the circumstances of the relationship between inducer and doer, particularly the balance of power between the parties, and the extent to which one party can be viewed as the moving force behind the wrongdoing. (In the case of bribery itself, such nuances are captured in part by the particular choice of words we make in describing a bribe as having been 'solicited' 'taken,' 'sought,' 'demanded,' 'accepted,' or 'received.')

The criminal law often must confront questions about how to treat parties who influence, solicit, provoke, incite, advise, counsel, command, encourage, procure, instigate, or persuade others to commit a crime.[59] It is not possible here to sort out all of the complex differences among solicitation, attempt, conspiracy, and accomplice liability, except to say that inducers are sometimes treated as seriously as those they induce to engage in wrongdoing, and sometimes not.[60]

In the case of bribery, assessment of the briber's wrongfulness is, in theory at least, fairly straightforward. If X offers Y money in the belief that doing so will induce Y to breach a duty of loyalty, then X has done a morally wrongful act. But if X does not believe that his offering Y money will induce Y to breach a duty of loyalty, then it would seem to follow that X has not done anything wrongful. Of course, in practice, determining whether X has such an intention in a case in which, for example, he made a large contribution to the re-election campaign of a judge before whom he often appears, is likely to be difficult.[61]

---

[58] Presumably, this intuition is reflected in laws that prohibit the application of the death penalty to non-trigger persons. See generally *Tison v Arizona*, 481 US 137 (1987).

[59] This list of terms is derived from Sanford H Kadish, 'Complicity, Cause and Blame: A Study in the Interpretation of Doctrine' (1985) 73 *California Law Review* 323, 343.

[60] See generally Herbert Wechsler, et al., 'The Treatment of Inchoate Crimes in the Model Penal Code of the American Law Institute: Attempt, Solicitation, and Conspiracy' (1961) 61 *Columbia Law Review* 571.

[61] See generally Daniel H Lowenstein, 'When is a Campaign Contribution a Bribe?,' in William C Heffernan and John Kleinig (eds.) *Private and Public Corruption* (Lanham, MD: Rowman & Littlefield, 2004). For a discussion of a recent case that presents this ambiguity in dramatic fashion, see Andrew Longstreth, 'Mississippi Maelstrom,' American Lawyer (August 2004) (concerning controversial bribery prosecution of Paul Minor, a prominent Mississippi lawyer who gave campaign contributions to local judges). See also *United States v Brewster*, 506

Thus, returning to an earlier hypothetical in which the duties of a customs official in Cameroon were assumed to be different from the duties of her counterpart in Los Angeles, I would argue that a Western business person who gives a 'grease payment' to the Cameroonian believing that the action requested is proper has not induced a breach of loyalty, and therefore should not be viewed as having committed bribery either.

Coerced and Coercive Giving of Bribes

In the discussion of why it is wrong to accept a bribe, I considered one case in which a putative bribee was coerced and another case in which a bribee did the coercing. Now, in the interest of completeness, I want to consider those circumstances in which being coerced and coercing are relevant to the moral status of the *briber*.

First, let us return to the case in which a police officer, P, offers not to arrest (or threatens to arrest) D for a crime that D has committed if (or unless) D pays P some amount of money. In the event that D agrees to pay P the money demanded, it would appear that D has satisfied the formal requirements of being a briber. But, from a moral perspective, it may seem harsh to hold D to account, given that he has been the victim of coercion.

Secondly, there are also cases in which bribers themselves use coercion. In the Nick Smith case described above, it is arguable that his fellow congressmen committed not only the morally wrongful act of attempting to induce him to breach his duty of loyalty to his constituents, but also the morally wrongful act of using coercion to do so. Once again, in such cases there should be no theoretical bar to charging the briber with bribery as well as extortion, blackmail, or criminal coercion.

Conclusion

In the foregoing discussion, I have sought to describe some of the moral complexity that surrounds our conception of bribery. One of the keys to understanding, I have argued, is to recognize the distinction between bribe-taking (which involves a breach of loyalty) and bribe-giving (which involves inducing another to breach such a duty). Such distinctions, I believe, are of more than merely academic interest. As the analysis of cases like *Singleton*

F 2d 61 (DC Cir 1974) (discussing application of bribery statute in context of putative campaign contributions); *United States v Biaggi*, 909 F 2d 662, 695 (2d Cir 1990), *cert denied*, 499 US 904 (1991) (distinguishing between campaign contributions and illegal transactions by considering evidentiary factors such as 'whether the contribution was reported, whether it was unusually large compared to the contributor's normal donations, whether the official threatened adverse action if the contribution was not made, and how directly the official or those soliciting for him linked the contribution to specific official action').

illustrates, there are very real issues of doctrine that turn on fairly fine features of moral analysis, such as whether a witness should be viewed as having taken a bribe if he accepts something of value in return for doing what is arguably 'the right thing.' As I hope to have shown, only if we are clear about exactly why it's wrong to commit bribery can we be clear about exactly where the outer limits of the offense should lie.

17

Extortion and Blackmail

From the perspective of criminal practice, blackmail and extortion seem like fairly exotic offenses; prosecution for either is a relatively rare event. Yet no white-collar offense has received more serious and sustained philosophical attention than blackmail (and, indirectly, extortion). What explains this anomaly? The answer is that the very factors that make the so-called 'blackmail paradox' such a compelling subject of theoretical analysis—in particular, the uncertain moral basis on which the offense rests—also make blackmail and extortion disfavored in the real world of criminal prosecutions. My aim in this chapter is not to attempt to resolve the blackmail paradox, but rather to show how it fits into the broader theory of white-collar criminal law that I have been developing.

1. COERCION CRIMES

Let us begin our discussion of extortion and blackmail by recalling the facts of two cases mentioned previously. In the first, Enron CFO Andrew Fastow allegedly told investors that, unless they agreed to invest in LJM-2, Enron would no longer do business with them.[1] In the second, House Majority Leader Tom Delay and fellow Republican members of Congress allegedly told retiring Congressman Nick Smith that unless he voted for controversial proposed Medicare legislation, they would take steps to ensure that his son Brad, who was running to take over Nick's seat in the House, would never win.[2] In order to assess the criminality, if any, of such acts, I want first to consider the difference among three 'coercion offenses': extortion, blackmail, and criminal coercion.

Extortion

The definition of extortion varies from jurisdiction to jurisdiction. Under the leading American federal statute, the Hobbs Act, extortion is defined as the 'obtaining of property from another, with his consent, induced by wrongful

---

[1] The Fastow case was mentioned in the discussion of fraud in ch. 13 above.
[2] The DeLay case was referred to in the Introduction and in ch. 16.

use of actual or threatened force, violence, or fear, or under color of official right.'[3] In France, extortion requires that a defendant use 'violence[,] ... a threat of violence or constraint' to obtain 'the handing over of funds, securities or of any asset.'[4] In Great Britain, there is no crime known as extortion; rather, there is a broadly defined offense known as blackmail, discussed below. In this discussion, I shall focus primarily on the way in which extortion is defined in the American federal system.

The first thing to note about the Hobbs Act is that it identifies two principal kinds of extortion: (1) obtaining property through wrongful threats; and (2) obtaining property under color of official right. The moral content of the second kind of extortion—under color of official right—is, as mentioned above,[5] similar to that of soliciting a bribe, and will not be dealt with here. It is the first kind of extortion that will be the focus of our analysis.

We can begin by observing five preliminary points about the Hobbs Act definition of extortion by threat, each of which will be considered in greater detail below: first, extortion requires that the defendant use a threat to obtain 'property.' As such, extortion is a species of theft. Making a threat to obtain something other than property, such as sexual favors or political endorsements, is not extortion, although it might constitute the separate offense of criminal coercion. Secondly, such property must be obtained with what is referred to as the victim's (admittedly invalid) 'consent.' This requirement distinguishes extortion (and fraud) from other forms of theft, such as larceny and embezzlement, in which the victim's property is taken without the victim's acquiescing in the act, or even necessarily being aware that the property is being taken. Thirdly, the victim's so-called consent must be obtained by means of a 'threat.' Fourthly, what the extortionist threatens the victim with— at least in the kinds of cases dealt with here—is future economic harm. Extortion of this sort is thus distinguishable from robbery, in which property is obtained through threats of immediate physical harm. Finally, the extortionist's threat must be a 'wrongful' one. Notice that the Hobbs Act does not explicitly require that the defendant threaten to do an 'unlawful' act. Thus, a threat to do a lawful act could theoretically constitute extortion. Nevertheless, as I shall argue below, a better construction of the statute is that the term 'wrongfulness' should be understood as meaning 'unlawfulness,' and that a threat should be viewed as extortionate only if the act threatened would violate some underlying provision of positive law.

Blackmail

The term 'blackmail' is used in four distinct senses: a narrow sense, a broad sense, and two different in-between senses. In the narrow, mostly American, sense, the term refers to cases in which an offender threatens to do one

---

[3] 18 USC § 1951.   [4] Code Pénal Art 312-1.   [5] See ch. 16, n 10 above.

particular kind of unwanted but putatively lawful act unless paid money—
namely, revealing true embarrassing information about another.[6] We can also
refer to this as 'informational blackmail.' A somewhat specialized example of
this kind of blackmail can be found in the federal blackmail statute, which
makes it a crime to demand money or other valuable things from a person in
return for not informing on the person's violation of federal law.[7]

Informational blackmail has several elements in common with extortion
under the Hobbs Act: (1) like the extortionist, the blackmailer must use
a threat to obtain 'property,' (2) the property must be obtained with the victim's
'consent,' and (3) the victim's consent must be obtained by means of a 'threat.'
The difference between extortion and informational blackmail is that, whereas
extortion can potentially involve a threat to do anything that is deemed to be
wrongful, blackmail involves one particular kind of threat—namely, to expose
information that would be embarrassing to the one threatened.

A much broader use of the term 'blackmail' occurs under British law, which
has no separate offense of extortion. Under section 21 of the UK Theft Act of
1968, a person is guilty of blackmail if, 'with a view to gain for himself or
another or with intent to cause loss to another, he makes any unwarranted
demand with menaces.'[8] This kind of blackmail is broader than informational
blackmail in two significant ways: first, the 'view to gain . . . or intent to cause
loss' language encompasses both demands for money and demands for something other than money, such as that the victim give the blackmailer a job, that
the victim permit the blackmailer to take indecent photographs of her, or that
the victim destroy letters written by the blackmailer to her.[9] Secondly the 'any
unwarranted demand with menaces' language is—at least on its face—broad
enough to encompass threats of a very wide range of conduct, both lawful and
unlawful.[10]

---

[6]   eg Michael Gorr, 'Liberalism and the Paradox of Blackmail' (1992) 21 *Philosophy & Public
Affairs* 43, 46.
[7]   18 USC § 1873. See also Stuart P Green, 'Federal Blackmail Statute' in Brian K Landsberg
(ed.), *Encyclopedia of Major Acts of Congress* (New York: Macmillan, 2003).
[8]   Theft Act 1968, c. 60, § 21 (UK).
[9]   See cases cited in Edward Griew, *The Theft Acts 1968 & 1978*, (London: Sweet & Maxwell,
1990) at 220; see also Grant Lamond, 'Coercion, Threats, and the Puzzle of Blackmail,' in
AP Simester and ATH Smith (eds.) *Harm and Culpability* (Oxford: OUP, 1996), at 216 (using the
term in the broad sense).
[10]   A threatened course of conduct will be viewed as violative of the Theft Act's blackmail
provision only if it is deemed an 'improper' means of reinforcing a demand. *Ibid* at 216–19. In
Harvey, (1980) 72 Cr App R 139, the court held that no act known by the defendant to be unlawful can be deemed to be proper. What is much less clear under British law is when, if ever, threats
to do what is *lawful* will be regarded as improper, and therefore extortionate. See Griew (n 9
above, at 214–19); see also Gerald H Gordon, *The Criminal Law of Scotland* (Michael Christie
ed.) (3rd edn., Edinburgh: W. Green, 2001), vol. 2, at 247–54. Thus, British blackmail law
reflects an ambiguity similar to that seen under American extortion law. Suffice it to say that
British courts might wish to consider the possibility of interpreting the terms 'unwarranted' and
'improper' under the Theft Act in a manner similar to that recommended for interpreting the
term 'wrongful' under the Hobbs Act.

There also two distinct 'in-between' senses of the term blackmail. One such sense is illustrated by the blackmail statute in effect in France.[11] Under this statute blackmail is defined as threatening to 'reveal... facts liable to undermine a person's honor or reputation' unless the person hands over 'funds valuables or any asset' *or* agrees to do or not to do some other act demanded by the blackmailer. Thus, like blackmail in the narrow American sense, such blackmail is limited to threats to expose embarrassing information; but, unlike American blackmail, it is not limited to demands for money. There is also a second in-between sense of blackmail. Under this approach, which tends to be found in the work of various academic commentators, including Leo Katz,[12] blackmail is limited to demands for money, as opposed to other kinds of compelled conduct. But, unlike blackmail in the usual American sense, such blackmail is not limited to threats to expose embarrassing information; it also includes threats to do other putatively lawful acts, such as filing a lawsuit, staging a work stoppage, or even going on a hunger strike.[13] As we shall see below, however, the problem is that blackmail in both this second in-between sense as well as under the broad 'unwarranted demand with menaces' language of the English Theft Act offers no clear basis for distinguishing between those threats to do what is lawful that should be treated as a crime and those that should not.

The Offense of Criminal Coercion

As defined in the Model Penal Code, the state law offense of criminal coercion consists of 'unlawfully... restrict[ing] another's freedom of action to his detriment' by threatening to: (1) commit a criminal offense, (2) accuse anyone of a criminal offense, (3) 'expose any secret tending to subject any person to hatred, contempt, or ridicule, or to impair his credit or business repute,' or (4) 'take or withhold action as an official, or causing an official to take or withhold action.'[14] Criminal coercion is thus distinguishable from extortion and from blackmail (at least in the narrow, informational sense of the term) in two important ways. First, as noted, it does not involve obtaining any property from the victim. Secondly it can involve threats to engage in either lawful or unlawful conduct, so long as it is intended to be detrimental to the victim. For example, a teacher who demands sexual favors in return for not flunking a student presumably would have committed the offense of criminal coercion.

---

[11] Code Pénal § 312-10 ('Blackmail is the act of obtaining either a signature, a commitment or a renunciation, the revelation of a secret, or the handing over of funds, valuables or any asset, by threatening to reveal or to impute facts liable to undermine a person's honor or reputation.').

[12] See, eg Leo Katz, 'Blackmail and Other Forms of Arm-Twisting' (1993) 141 *University of Pennsylvania Law Review* 1567, 1568.   [13] *Ibid.*

[14] Model Penal Code § 212.5(1).

2. The Blackmail Paradox and Mere 'Hard Bargaining'

Had DeLay or Fastow threatened their alleged victims with some unambiguously unlawful act, such as having their 'knees broken,' unless they did what was demanded, it seems obvious that they would have done something criminal. But what both DeLay and Fastow allegedly did threaten their victims with—namely, working to defeat Brad Smith and no longer doing business with their banks, respectively—was something that seems, on first sight, to be perfectly lawful. So, unless we are prepared to treat as a crime every threat of X's to do some unwanted but putatively lawful action unless Y pays him to forgo it, we have a problem. And it is a problem that is likely to arise in any context in which people attempt to obtain money by threatening to engage in unwanted but putatively lawful actions, such as litigation (threatened lawsuits), labor negotiations (threatened strikes), and tender offers (threatened corporate takeovers).

The broader issue I want to consider is whether it is possible to draw any conceptually clear distinction between those threats to do what is putatively lawful that should be treated as a crime (whatever specific offense that may turn out to be) and those threats to do what is putatively lawful that should be treated as mere hard bargaining. The most obvious place to look for an answer to this question is the voluminous literature on the so-called paradox of blackmail, which is to criminal law theory what Fermat's Last Theorem is to mathematics. As legions of legal theorists have pointed out, the act of exposing another's lawfully obtained private information is generally not a crime; nor is it generally illegal to ask another for money. But combine the two acts and you get a crime. The challenge of the blackmail paradox is thus to offer a justification for making it a crime to demand money to refrain from doing acts that would otherwise be lawful, or at least from doing the particular act of exposing embarrassing information. My goal here is not to assess the overall validity of the arguments offered in favor of, or in opposition to, the criminalization of such threats. Rather, I want to see if such literature can shed any light on the more practical problem of distinguishing criminalizable threats to do what is lawful from non-criminalizable ones.

For present purposes, the arguments offered in favor of the criminalization of blackmail can be grouped into two basic categories: the first category, which is discussed in the next section, consists of theories that focus on justifying the criminalization of informational blackmail specifically. As such, they are too narrow to be of much help in identifying threats to do other kinds of putatively lawful conduct, if any, that should be criminalized. The second category, which is discussed in the succeeding section, consists of theories that seem intended to justify the criminalization of threats to do a much broader range of putatively lawful acts than in the first group, but which ultimately offer no satisfactory criteria for making a practical distinction between those threats that should be criminalized and those that should not.

Theories that are Underinclusive

Consider the argument for criminalizing blackmail offered by Richard Epstein.[15] Epstein argues that the reason we need to criminalize informational blackmail is that legalizing it would produce at least two undesirable consequences: first, it would lead to more blackmail victims and, consequently, more thefts and frauds committed by those desperate to raise the funds necessary to pay off their blackmailers.[16] Secondly, it would encourage victims to commit various frauds against the third parties to whom the disclosure would otherwise be made.[17] In other words, Epstein argues, the best reason for criminalizing informational blackmail is that legalizing it would lead to additional forms of corruption and deceit. Unfortunately, Epstein's theory, even if it were adequate to justify the criminalization of informational blackmail itself, offers little practical help where we need it. The theory is so narrowly focused on offering a justification for informational blackmail that it fails to explain whether any other kinds of threats to do lawful acts should be treated as a crime. In answering such a question, Epstein would presumably have us consider whether legalization of such threats would lead to the kind of chain of criminal activity that he foresees in the case of informational blackmail. But his work leaves unclear how we should evaluate such threats, and what he thinks the outcome would be.

Like Epstein, Jeffrie Murphy offers a theory of blackmail that focuses primarily on the criminalization of threats to expose embarrassing information, and on the negative social consequences that would result from the legalization of such acts.[18] According to Murphy, legalizing blackmail would, at least in the case of non-public figures, create economic incentives for invasions of privacy with no identifiable social value.[19] Unfortunately, like Epstein, Murphy is so focused on threats to expose embarrassing information that he is unable to explain whether, and if so which, other kinds of 'hard economic transactions'[20] should be subject to criminal sanctions.

A third influential theory of blackmail, that offered by James Lindgren,[21] is similarly inadequate for our purposes. Once again, the focus is almost exclusively on informational blackmail. According to Lindgren, what characterizes such conduct is that the informational blackmailer attempts to gain an advantage for himself (typically, money from his victim) by using leverage that properly belongs to another.[22] For example, when a blackmailer threatens

---

[15] Richard Epstein, 'Blackmail, Inc.' (1983) 50 *University of Chicago Law Review* 553.
[16] *Ibid* at 562.   [17] *Ibid* at 564.
[18] Jeffrie G Murphy, 'Blackmail: A Preliminary Inquiry' (1980) 63 *The Monist* 156.
[19] *Ibid* at 163–64.   [20] The term is Murphy's. *Ibid* at 163.
[21] James Lindgren, 'Unraveling the Paradox of Blackmail' (1984) 84 *Columbia Law Review* 670.   [22] *Ibid* at 701.

to expose *V*'s marital infidelities unless *V* pays him money, the blackmailer is using, for his own advantage, 'bargaining chips' that properly belong to someone else—in this case, *V*'s spouse.[23] While Lindgren's account does offer a useful description of the dynamic involved in many cases of informational blackmail, it tells us little about what other kinds of threats, if any, he believes should be subject to criminal sanctions. Indeed, it fails to explain not only whether other kinds of threats to engage in putatively lawful conduct, such as filing a lawsuit or withholding found property, should be criminalized,[24] but, more fundamentally, why it should be a crime to threaten *unlawful* conduct that does not involve the 'triangular' kind of relationship involved in informational blackmail.[25]

Theories that are Overinclusive

The second group of theories intended to justify the criminalization of blackmail also fail to offer a basis for deciding which kinds of threats to do what is lawful, if any, should be treated as a crime, though they fail for a converse reason—namely, *overinclusiveness*. Consider the argument offered by George Fletcher, which can be summarized in the following three steps: (1) the central concern of the criminal law is to deter conditions of 'dominance and subordination'; (2) blackmail, through the prospect of repeated demands, creates a serious potential for a continuing relation of this sort; (3) therefore, blackmail should be criminalized.[26] Even if Fletcher's rationale could justify the criminalization of threats to expose embarrassing information,[27] however, it is unclear where Fletcher would have us draw the line: to the extent that most, or even all, hard bargaining involves relationships of domination and submission, Fletcher's theory offers no identifiable rationale for distinguishing those threats that should be criminalized from those that should not.

Leo Katz's theory of blackmail is similarly flawed.[28] Katz conceptualizes blackmail in the following way: he begins by imagining a case in which *B1*, a burglar, breaks into *V*'s house to commit larceny.[29] Inside, *B1* threatens *V* that unless he divulges the combination to his safe, *V* will be beaten severely.

---

[23] *Ibid* at 702.

[24] Leo Katz offers a similar critique of Lindgren in Katz (n 12 above, at 1581).

[25] Interestingly, though, as I suggest below in the text accompanying n 68, something like Lindgren's 'triangular' analysis may help provide an argument for criminalizing cases in which a union leader threatens that his union will go out on strike unless management pays a kickback to him personally.

[26] George P Fletcher, 'Blackmail: The Paradigmatic Crime' (1993) 141 *University of Pennsylvania Law Review* 1617, 1629–35.

[27] And even this is doubtful, since many acts of informational blackmail present no reasonable apprehension of repeated demands, as in the case of the nominee who on the eve of his confirmation hearings is threatened with the exposure of embarrassing secrets. See Mitchell N Berman, 'The Evidentiary Theory of Blackmail: Taking Motives Seriously' (1998) 65 *University of Chicago Law Review* 795, 825. Therefore, Fletcher's theory is also under-inclusive.

[28] See Katz (n 12 above).   [29] *Ibid* at 1582.

V declares that he would prefer to submit to the beating rather than lose the contents of the safe. *B1* then beats *V* savagely. In a separate case, a different burglar, *B2*, breaks into *V*'s house and the same scenario ensues. But, this time, just as the burglar is about to strike *V*, he notices a scrap of paper containing the combination to the safe. Despite *V*'s plea that he would prefer to be beaten than lose the safe's contents, *B2* opens the safe and takes off with the contents. Katz then asks, why should the law punish the defendant in scenario 1 more severely than the defendant in scenario 2 (as it surely would), notwithstanding the fact that the victim in scenario 2 obtained his preference while the victim in scenario 1 did not?[30] The answer, says Katz, is that when the defendant 'has the victim choose between either of two immoralities which he must endure, the gravity of the defendant's wrongdoing is to be judged by what he actually did (or sought to achieve), not by what he threatened to do.'[31] Thus, *B2* should be punished more severely than *B1* because battery is morally worse than theft. And what does all of this have to do with blackmail? Well, says Katz, we need to think about the wrongfulness of blackmail not in terms of what the blackmailer threatens to do (ie expose *V*'s embarrassing information), but rather in terms of what the blackmailer actually does (ie steal money from *V*).[32]

Unfortunately, Katz's approach provides little help in resolving the doctrinal issue being considered here. Although I am sympathetic to the idea of asking whether *X* has 'stolen' from *V*, it seems that Katz takes this idea too far. For the question remains, should we really say that *X* 'steals' from *V* every time *X* threatens *V* with bad consequences unless *V* pays up? If so, such an approach would invalidate, and indeed criminalize, a vast range of conduct that currently passes for hard bargaining in our commercial world. In short, Katz's approach seems—at least for present purposes—overly inclusive.[33]

Finally, there is Mitchell Berman's theory.[34] Berman begins by identifying two conditions that are presumptively sufficient to justify criminalization: an act must be harmful and it must be undertaken by a morally blameworthy actor. Berman believes that blackmail meets this test. The harm condition requires that the conduct at issue cause or threaten identifiable harm—a condition, he suggests, that is met in the case of informational blackmail (where what is threatened is harm to *V*'s reputation). As for impermissible motive, Berman argues that 'conditional threats can offer powerful (albeit not conclusive) circumstantial evidence of impermissible motive.'[35] In other words, evidence that *X* has offered to withhold disclosure in exchange for a

---

[30] *Ibid* at 1582–83.   [31] *Ibid* at 1598 (emphasis omitted).   [32] *Ibid* at 1597.

[33] Katz does concede that 'the mere threat to be nasty or unpleasant won't suffice' to justify criminalization. *Ibid* at 1597. But this concession seems too little too late, particularly as he fails to explain why it wouldn't be 'stealing' to obtain money by threatening to be nasty or unpleasant.

[34] Berman (n 27 above). For an alternative critique of Berman, see Ronald Joseph Scalise, Jr., Note, 'Blackmail, Legality, and Liberalism' (2000) 74 *Tulane Law Review* 1483, 1491–1501.

[35] *Ibid* at 877–78.

fee is 'probative' of the impermissible motive needed to justify criminalization. But since such an offer is only probative of bad motives, not conclusive, more justification is needed. Where the threat is to engage in criminal activity, we have no problem in concluding that there is an impermissible motive, and that the act is extortionate: people usually threaten to commit crimes out of bad motives. But where the threat is to engage in lawful activity, the task is more difficult: people threaten to disclose embarrassing information (and engage in other kinds of lawful acts) out of all kinds of motives, both good and bad (think, for example, of investigative reporters). But people who threaten to disclose embarrassing information *only if they are paid money not to do so* are significantly more likely to be driven by bad motives than those who impose no such conditions. Therefore, according to Berman, criminalization of informational blackmail is justified.

Once again, Berman's theory, even if it did provide an adequate justification for criminalizing the core case of informational blackmail, would be incapable of providing a clear test for distinguishing between other kinds of threats that should be criminalized and mere hard bargaining. First, it is hard to see why the notoriously slippery requirement of 'harm' could not be met every time X threatens Y with a lawsuit, a strike, a tender offer, or the like. Berman offers the hypothetical of an antiques dealer who seeks to charge an eccentric millionaire an exorbitant price for a cheap and ugly vase that the millionaire needs to complete his collection.[36] He reaches the quite sensible conclusion that dealer's conduct should not be subject to criminal sanctions, but his rationale for doing so is problematic. Berman argues that the millionaire has no 'legally protected interest in the vase' and hence cannot be 'harmed.'[37] But if the millionaire has no legally protected interest in the vase, why exactly should the victim of informational blackmail have a legally protected interest in not having embarrassing information exposed? Such legal interest exists only if there is some law independent of blackmail and extortion law that creates it. And it is precisely the lack of any such independent legal protection in the case of embarrassing information that gives rise to the blackmail paradox.

Equally problematic is Berman's requirement of bad motives. According to Berman, an actor has 'morally bad motives' when he acts with the knowledge that his conduct will cause, threaten, or risk harm to others, unless: (1) he actually believes that his action will produce more good than evil; (2) such belief is a but-for cause of his action; and (3) the standards the actor employs for measuring and evaluating evil and good in the case are defensible under common moral standards.[38] While such definition seems on its face unobjectionable, in application it is likely to be, at best, subjective, and, at worst, to apply to so broad a range of hard-bargaining-type conduct that it would have the effect of putting undue additional weight on the already problematic requirement of harm.

---

[36] *Ibid* at 856 at 795.   [37] *Ibid.*   [38] *Ibid* at 839–40.

3. Conceptually Isolating Extortion

The conclusion of the previous section was that the literature on the blackmail paradox contains no clearly defined basis for distinguishing between those threats to do what is putatively lawful that should be treated as a crime and those that should not. Having in some sense given up on this more ambitious goal, I now want to lower expectations and see if it is possible at least to distinguish between those threats that should be treated specifically as extortion and those that should be treated either as some other crime or as no crime at all.

Obtaining Property: Extortion as a Form of Theft

The first order of business will be to reexamine the four basic elements of extortion mentioned above: obtaining property, threats, consent, and wrongful use. One of the keys to understanding the moral content of extortion is to think about the offense as a form of theft. (For the moment, we can set aside the question whether informational blackmail should also be thought of as a form of theft.) Theft is typically defined as the unlawful taking of, or exercising unlawful control over, movable property of another with the intent to deprive the owner of such property thereof.[39] Theft, as we have seen, can be committed in a variety of ways: larceny is theft by stealth; embezzlement is theft by breach of trust; robbery is theft by force; false pretenses or fraud (at least in its narrow sense) is theft by deception; extortion (and possibly blackmail), as I shall argue here, should be understood as theft by threat or coercion.[40] Despite the feature of property-misappropriation common to each of these offenses, however, there are nevertheless some important differences among them. For example, while the Model Penal Code-inspired trend in the US has been towards the consolidation of larceny, embezzlement, and false pretenses into a single offense of 'Theft by Unlawful Taking,' neither extortion nor robbery has been part of that consolidation.[41] Moreover, while the core theft offenses are typically graded on the basis of how much property is stolen, extortion and robbery are not.[42] On the other hand, while robbery

---

[39] Model Penal Code § 223.2(1) (Theft by Unlawful Taking or Disposition of Movable Property). For a useful discussion of the underlying moral structure of theft, see A P Simester & GR Sullivan, 'On the Nature and Rationale of Property Offences,' in RA Duff and Stuart P Green (eds), *Defining Crimes: Essays on the Criminal Law's Special Part* (Oxford: OUP, 2005).

[40] There is an interesting question—which, for present purposes, need not be resolved—whether robbery (involving the threat of immediate physical harm) should properly be viewed as a subset of extortion.

[41] Cf Model Penal Code § 223.2 (Theft by Unlawful Taking, expressly consolidating the common law offenses of larceny, embezzlement, and fraud) with Model Penal Code § 223.4 (Theft by Extortion, consolidating the traditional offenses of extortion and blackmail).

[42] *Ibid.*

is classified as an offense involving danger to the person, extortion resembles the other theft offenses in that it is classified as an offense against property.[43]

Because extortion, like theft generally, requires that the defendant seek to obtain property, using a threat to obtain something other than property is not generally recognized as extortion.[44] Thus, given that the House Republican leaders allegedly sought Nick Smith's vote for the Medicare bill, rather than his money, it seems clear that they did not commit extortion. Similarly, if *X* threatens to terminate *V* from *V*'s job unless she consents to having sex with him, *X* has not committed extortion, since sexual favors are not considered property.[45] Moreover, as the Supreme Court recently recognized in the case of *Scheidler v National Organization for Women*, the extortionist must use a threat to 'obtain' or 'acquire' such property, rather than merely to divest the victim of it.[46] In the case of Andrew Fastow, on the other hand, the 'obtaining property' requirement would easily be satisfied: the allegations are clear that he used threats to obtain from the LJM-2 investors nearly $350 million in equity.

Coercion and Consent

Did Fastow also threaten, or coerce, the bankers into investing in LJM-2? Not surprisingly, the answer to that question turns, first, on whether Fastow was promising to make the bankers worse off in relation to some relevant baseline than if they did not accept his proposal; and, second, whether that baseline is defined empirically or morally. According to the *Houston Chronicle*, Fastow approached two kinds of potential investors in LJM: those who had not

---

[43] *Ibid.*

[44] It should be noted, however, that a handful of states define extortion to consist of threats to obtain property *or* compel action. See Craig M Bradley, '*Now v. Scheidler*: RICO Meets the First Amendment' (1994) *Supreme Court Law Review* 129, 144 (citing Wayne LaFave & Austin Scott, *Substantive Criminal Law*, (1986) vol. 2, § 8.12, at 460).

[45] As I have noted elsewhere, what constitutes 'property' for purposes of theft law is not necessarily the same as what constitutes 'property' for purposes of bribery or intellectual property law. Stuart P Green, 'Plagiarism, Norms, and the Limits of Theft Law: Some Observations on the Use of Criminal Sanctions in Enforcing Intellectual Property Rights' (2002) 54 *Hastings Law Journal* 167, 211–21. Even if property is not what the defendant has obtained, however, he might still be charged with (1) criminal coercion, see eg Alaska Stat § 11.41.530; Tenn Code § 39-4301; *Furlotte v State of Tennessee*, 350 SW 2d 72 (1961); Bradley, (note 42 above, at 144 n 82); Model Penal Code § 212.5(1); (2) the civil wrong of sexual harassment, see Title VII of the Civil Rights Act of 1964 (Pub L 88-352), codified at 42 USC §§ 2000e et seq; or (3) even rape, see Patricia J Falk, 'Rape by Fraud and Rape by Coercion' (1998) 64 *Brooklyn Law Review* 39 (1998). See also Carrie N Baker, 'Sexual Extortion: Criminalizing Quid Pro Quo Sexual Harassment' (1994) 13 *Law and Inequality* 213 (acknowledging that traditional extortion statutes do not apply to such cases, but arguing for creation of new offense of 'quid pro quo sexual harassment').

[46] 537 US 393 (2003). In *Scheidler*, the Court was called upon to determine whether it was extortion for a collection of anti-abortion groups to use fear and intimidation to shut down various abortion clinics throughout the nation. Because the plaintiffs had failed to show that the defendants had 'obtained' or 'acquired' any of the plaintiffs' property, the Court held that no extortion had been committed (though it noted that the protesters may have committed the misdemeanor crime of coercion). *Ibid* at 405.

previously done business with Enron, but hoped to do so; and those who were already doing business with the firm.[47] Fastow allegedly told those in the first group that they would have an opportunity to do business with Enron, but only if they first invested in LJM-2. This was an offer, not a threat, since such investors were given a chance to be made *better off* in relation to their baseline position of not doing business with Enron. Thus, with respect to this first group of investors, Fastow's behavior was not coercive, and their consent was not thereby invalidated (whether such consent was obtained fraudulently, of course, is another question). The investors in the second group, by contrast, were allegedly told that if they wanted to *continue* doing business with Enron, they would have to invest in LJM-2. By threatening to make such investors *worse off* in relation to their relevant baseline position, it would seem that Fastow was acting coercively, at least in the empirical sense of the term.

The requirement that a transfer of property be uncoerced, informed, and competent in order for it to be valid raises two interesting issues. First, given that the kind of consent obtained by the extortionist will, by definition, be invalid, why should 'consent' be included as an element of extortion in the first place? Why not say simply that the defendant must wrongfully appropriate the victim's property? The answer seems to be that the law implicitly views the obtaining of property through *invalid* consent (as in the case of extortion and fraud) as distinguishable—at least formally, and perhaps morally as well—from the obtaining of property *without* consent (as in the case of larceny and embezzlement). And, indeed, intuitively, the fact that Fastow obtained money from the *LJM-2* investors by getting each of them to write a check does give his act a quality quite different from what it would have had if he had obtained such money by, say, sneaking into their homes and taking it without their knowledge.[48]

Secondly, although extortion and fraud both involve the obtaining of property through invalid consent, the two offenses differ in a striking way. When property is obtained by means of consent gained through *deception*,

[47] See David Ivanovich, 'The Fall of Enron; Bankers Believed Deals Hinged on Investments,' *Houston Chronicle* (20 Feb. 2002), at A9.

[48] So as to avoid the confusion caused by use of the term 'consent,' Stephen Shute and Jeremy Horder cast the distinction in terms of 'voluntary' and 'involuntary' transfers of property. Voluntary transfers (such as those which occur in fraud and extortion) are those in which property is given. Involuntary transfers (such as those that occur in larceny and robbery) are those in which property is taken. Stephen Shute and Jeremy Horder, 'Thieving and Deceiving: What is the Difference?' (1993) 56 *Modern Law Review* 548, 551. And, according to the authors, there is a moral difference between voluntary and involuntary transfers. As they put it, '[t]here is in our society a general social practice of uncoerced voluntary transfers ("givings"), even when they are the product of another's advice, influence or persuasion.... By way of contrast, there is generally little of value in involuntary transfers of property ("takings"), which—as in the case of theft—serve mostly to reduce rather than enhance the "transferor's" autonomy.' They go on: 'This moral difference underpinning the distinction between voluntary and involuntary transfers...means that, on the voluntariness view, the nature of the wrongdoing in theft has a separate moral foundation from that of obtaining by deception.' *Ibid* at 553.

such consent will almost invariably be held to be invalid, and the obtaining fraudulent. But when property is obtained by means of consent gained through *coercion*, such consent will only sometimes be viewed as invalid, and the obtaining extortionate. Before we turn to the question of which kinds of coercion should constitute extortion, it is worth asking why the effects of deception and coercion diverge in this manner. The most straightforward answer is simply that we as a society are more tolerant of coercion than we are of deception, at least in the sphere of commercial life. We recognize that people use threats to achieve commercial aims all the time, and we are unwilling to make such conduct criminal except in the most egregious of circumstances. By contrast, for reasons that obviously call for further investigation, we are considerably less willing to validate commercial transactions conducted by means of deception.

When are Threats 'Wrongful' for Purposes of Extortion Law?

Having determined that Fastow allegedly 'obtained property' from others, with their 'consent,' induced by 'threats' of economic harm, we are finally in a position to ask whether such threats should be viewed as 'wrongful' (and therefore extortionate) within the meaning of the Hobbs Act. Unfortunately, the Act does not say what it means for a threat to be 'wrongful.' In particular, it makes no distinction between threats to do what is lawful and threats to do what is unlawful.

When X threatens V with an act that is itself criminal (eg breaking V's knees) unless V pays X's demand, it seems uncontroversial that X's threat is wrongful and therefore extortionate. In such cases, X 'steals' from V by charging him money for something he has no right to charge him for—namely, being free from unjustified physical harm.[49] The more interesting question, though, is under what circumstances, if any, it is wrongful within the meaning of the Hobbs Act for X to threaten to do a putatively *lawful* act. It is to this question that we now turn.

4. Finding Extortion

This final section takes the following form: first, I identify eight contexts, other than those already discussed, in which persons regularly make threats to engage in unwanted but putatively lawful conduct unless they receive money to forgo it. Secondly, I offer a test for determining when such threats should be regarded as 'wrongful' within the meaning of the Hobbs Act. Thirdly, I apply the test to the eight contexts in determining which cases, if any, should be treated as extortion.

---

[49] A similar point is made in Katz (n 12 above, at 1576).

Eight Kinds of Threats to Do What Is Putatively Lawful

Threats to file, or fail to settle, a lawsuit

Two closely analogous stories recently in the news are illustrative. In the first, Andrea Mackris, a former producer at Fox News, allegedly threatened to sue Fox News television host Bill O'Reilly for sexual harassment unless O'Reilly paid her $60 million.[50] In the second, Golan Cipel, a former New Jersey state official, allegedly threatened to sue then-New Jersey Governor James McGreevey, also for sexual harassment, unless McGreevey paid him as much as $50 million.[51]

Threats to inflict political damage or withhold political support

We have already seen how the Tom DeLay/Nick Smith case involved a threat to actively work against a candidate unless some condition was met. Another case, also recently in the news, reflects a similar pattern: Clarence Norman, chairman of the Brooklyn Democratic Party, and Jeffrey Feldman, the party's Executive Director, allegedly told candidates running for civil court judge that they would not receive the party's wholehearted support unless they used certain selected vendors and consultants.[52]

Threats to withhold found property from its rightful owner

In *United States v Taglione*, the defendant, who had found a box containing $100,000 worth of credit card invoices belonging to the Shell Oil Company, allegedly told Shell that he would not return the invoices unless he received a 'finder's fee' of $25,000.[53]

Threats to engage in union work stoppages

In *United States v Clemente*, the defendants, part of an enterprise that controlled various waterfront businesses in New York and New Jersey, allegedly demanded money from various shipping companies in return for agreeing not to stage labor stoppages and interruptions.[54]

Threats to take over another company unless stock is bought at a premium price (Greenmail)

In the case of *Viacom International, Inc. v Icahn*, corporate raider Carl Icahn and his associates acquired approximately 17 per cent of Viacom

---

[50] Howard Kurtz, 'Bill O'Reilly, Producer Settle Harassment Suit: Fox Host Agrees to Drop Extortion Claim,' *Washington Post* (29 Oct. 2004), at C1; Bill Carter, 'Star of *Fox News* Program Named in Harassment Suit,' *New York Times* (14 Oct. 2004).

[51] 'Former McGreevey Official Sought $50 Million, Aides Say,' *CNN.com* (14 Aug. 2004) <http://www.cnn.com/2004/ALLPOLITICS/08/14/governor.resigns.ap/>.

[52] Andy Newman, 'Case Turns on Whether Usual Politics is a Felony,' *New York Times* (19 Nov. 2003).   [53] 546 F 2d 194 (5th Cir 1977).

[54] 640 F 2d 1069 (2d Cir 1981).

International and then threatened to issue a tender offer unless the company agreed to repurchase their shares at a price well above the market price—a practice popularly known as 'greenmail.'[55]

Threats to fire, or fail to hire, an employee

In *United States v Capo*, an employment counselor at Eastman Kodak allegedly told a job-seeker at one of the company's manufacturing plants that unless he paid the counselor a 'kickback' of $500, he would not get the job for which he had applied.[56]

Threats to disclose embarrassing information

In *Flatley v Mauro*, Mauro and Robertson threatened to 'go public' with allegedly false and defamatory statements (to the effect that Flatley, a well-known entertainment entrepreneur, had sexually assaulted Robertson) unless Flatley made a 'sufficient' payment to them.[57] Contrast this to a case in which *D* threatens to publish true, innocently obtained, but nevertheless embarrassing, information about *V* unless *V* pays up.

Leo Katz's hypotheticals

Consider three hypotheticals offered by Leo Katz: (a) 'Pay me $10,000, or I will persuade your son that it is his patriotic duty to volunteer for combat in Vietnam'; (b) 'Pay me $10,000, or I will give your high-spirited, risk-addicted 19-year-old daughter a motorcycle for Christmas'; (c) 'Pay me $10,000 or I will hasten our ailing father's death by leaving the Catholic Church.'[58]

'Wrongfulness' as Unlawfulness: A Test for Distinguishing Extortion from Blackmail

As noted previously, while the Hobbs Act says that property must be obtained through threats that are 'wrongful,' it does not say what wrongfulness means. The suggestion offered here is that we should understand extortion to be limited to those threats to engage in conduct that is in fact unlawful. More precisely, we should say that a threat to do a putatively lawful act should be regarded as wrongful for purposes of the Hobbs Act if and only if the threatened conduct turns out, upon further analysis, to be unlawful. And in order to determine if such conduct is in fact unlawful, we should look to the relevant law governing the conduct threatened. Note that this has the effect of incorporating into extortion law a kind of *malum prohibitum* quality. Just as we need to look to the legal definition of 'human being' to determine what

---

[55] 747 F Supp. 205 (SDNY 1990).   [56] 817 F 2d 947, 951 (1987).
[57] 18 Cal Rptr 3d 472 (Cal Ct App 2004), review granted, 102 P 3d 904 (Cal 2004).
[58] Katz (n 12 above, at 1567–68).

constitutes murder, so we need to look to the relevant law to determine what should be regarded as 'wrongful' for purposes of extortion.

For example, if X threatens to go out on strike unless V pays him money, we need to look to labor law to determine if it is lawful for X to go out on strike. Similarly, if X threatens to file a law suit unless V pays him to forgo it, we should look to the law governing what constitutes a frivolous law suit to determine if X has the right to file such a suit. If, upon examining such independent sources of law, we determine that X has no such right, then we should say that X's putatively lawful threat was not in fact lawful, and should, for purposes of extortion law, be regarded as 'wrongful.' If, on the other hand, it turns out that the putatively lawful conduct threatened by X was *actually* lawful, then the threat should not be regarded as wrongful for purposes of the Hobbs Act, and should not be understood as constituting extortion (although, as I explain below, such a threat might constitute a different crime altogether).

Such an approach would reflect three significant advantages over the uncertainty that now prevails in this area: first, by referring to the relevant underlying law governing the conduct threatened, it would provide an objective, independent, relatively easy-to-understand set of criteria for distinguishing between threats that should be regarded as extortionate and those that should not, thereby promoting the principle of legality. Prosecutors, judges, and juries—not to mention business people and others who wish to engage in various forms of hard bargaining—would no longer have to guess as to which conduct is permissible and which is not. Secondly, the results obtained under the test recommended here would more or less track the results already reached by courts in a range of specific factual contexts, but would do so under a generalizable test of law. Thus, such an approach would represent no dramatic break with previous practice. Thirdly, the test would do a good job of placing extortion within the context of theft law more generally. For example, in a case in which X threatens to file a frivolous law suit against V unless V pays up, it would make sense to say that X 'steals' from V by charging him money for something for which he has no right to charge him.

Applying the 'Unlawfulness' Test

With the above-described approach in mind, let us now return to each of the various kinds of case in which X threatens to do a putatively lawful act unless paid, and ask whether such threats are appropriately recharacterized as unlawful and therefore extortionate.

Threats to initiate, or fail to settle, a lawsuit

When, if ever, should it be extortion for P to threaten that, unless D pays him a 'settlement,' he will file, or refuse to settle, a lawsuit against her? The case law is divided on this question. Some cases have held that a threat to file a lawsuit, even if made in bad faith, can never constitute extortion.[59] Other courts have allowed an extortion charge to lie if the threatened lawsuit is shown to be frivolous.[60] Which is the better view?

One possible argument against treating threatened frivolous litigation as extortion is that prosecuting plaintiffs who bring such lawsuits might result in overdeterrence, causing even plaintiffs with legitimate, though perhaps novel, kinds of legal claims to forgo filing.[61] In response to this, there are at least four counter-arguments: first, the main thing such prosecutions would chill would be not the *filing* of lawsuits, but rather attempts to reach settlement prior to the filing of lawsuits—an arguably less serious problem. Secondly, lawyers who engage in certain kinds of egregiously frivolous litigation behavior are already subject to the prospect of criminal prosecution for obstruction of justice and related offenses, and such prosecutions do not seem to have had an undue chilling effect. Thirdly, to hold, as some courts have done, that threats to file a lawsuit could never constitute extortion would be to invite potential blackmailers to evade the law by couching their threats to expose private embarrassing information in the form of a threatened lawsuit, as Golan Cipel and Andrea Mackris did in fact allegedly do. Fourthly, and most importantly, it appears that threatening to file a frivolous lawsuit unless the potential defendant pays one's demand involves an 'unlawful taking' and violation of the threatened party's property rights of just the sort that extortion law is meant to prevent and punish. In my judgment, therefore, the better view is that there should be no per se bar against treating as extortion certain egregious cases of threatening to bring a frivolous lawsuit unless 'settlement' is paid; but that, in order to minimize the chilling effect of such a doctrine, where the legitimacy of such a suit is ambiguous, courts should err on the side of finding such threats non-extortionate.[62]

Threats to inflict political damage or withhold political support

We saw two cases above in which powerful political leaders allegedly threatened to withhold political endorsements unless certain conditions were met. One case involved Brooklyn Democratic leaders and a civil court judicial election; the other, Republican House leaders and the Medicare bill.

With respect to the Brooklyn case, there is little dispute that Norman and Feldman met with candidates running for civil court judge and told them that

[59] See *United States v Pendergraft*, 297 F 3d 1198, 1204 (11th Cir 2002); *First Pacific Bancorp, Inc. v Bro*, 847 F 2d 542, 547 (9th Cir 1988).

[60] eg *State v Roth*, 673 A 2d 285 (NJ Super Ct 1996).

[61] For a related discussion involving the claim that class action litigation has the effect of putting 'blackmail'-like pressure on defendants to settle, see Charles Silver, '"We're Scared to Death": Class Certification and Blackmail' (2003) 78 *New York University Law Review* 1357.

[62] For example, the fact that Bill O'Reilly has reportedly agreed to pay Mackris a multi-million dollar amount to settle her lawsuit against him would seem to suggest that her lawsuit did have at least some merit and that she was not in fact committing extortion. See Kurtz (n 50 above). It is less clear whether Cipel's threat would satisfy the proffered test.

they would not receive the party's wholehearted support unless they used certain selected vendors and consultants. But there is serious disagreement about the criminality of such conduct. According to Brooklyn District Attorney Charles Hynes, such conduct constitutes the very 'definition [of] extortion.' According to lawyers for Norman and Feldman, as well various prominent political figures in Brooklyn, however, there was nothing illegal about what the defendants did. As Norman's lawyer, Roger Bennet Adler put it, 'If you take [the allegations] at face value... imposing certain conditions on candidates running on a joint slate, there was nothing unreasonable about those conditions. Suggesting that if you don't basically agree to these expenditures we're not going to be as effective for you on primary day, I think, is a statement of the obvious. It's not extortion.'[63]

For two reasons, I agree that the Brooklyn case did not constitute extortion. First, it appears that what the party bosses made was an offer, rather than a threat. They allegedly promised candidates an opportunity to be in a better position relative to the 'natural or expected course of events' than they otherwise would be. If they committed any crime at all under this scenario, it was most likely soliciting a bribe (but even this seems doubtful, since endorsing a candidate for civil court judge probably does not constitute the sort of 'official act' to which bribery law is meant to apply). Secondly, even if the bosses had threatened the candidates with worse treatment than they had a right to expect if they failed to use the appropriate vendors, it still appears that they were not threatening to do anything unlawful. In the absence of some separate provision of election or anti-corruption law saying that one who receives a political endorsement may not be required to give property in return, I would argue that no extortion has been committed.

The DeLay case also escapes characterization as extortion. First, what the House Republican leaders allegedly demanded of Smith was not money but rather his vote for the Medicare bill. Thus, the case would not satisfy the 'obtaining property' requirement of the Hobbs Act, although it could conceivably constitute solicitation of a bribe and perhaps criminal coercion.[64] Secondly, it is doubtful that working to defeat a candidate for political office could, by itself, properly be characterized as unlawful.

The DeLay case also presents another important issue that we have so far avoided. All of the other cases we have been considering involve threats to do an unlawful act that would harm the victim of extortion directly. But how should we deal with cases in which X threatens that, unless V meets his demand, he will do an unwanted act against some third party? In other words, should it matter that House Republican leaders allegedly threatened harm not to Nick Smith himself but rather to his son Brad?

---

[63] Newman, above note 52, at B1.
[64] The bribery aspects of the DeLay case are dealt with in ch. 16.

To the extent that I have analyzed extortion in terms of theft law, such cases might at first seem problematic. One might think that *X*'s property rights would be violated only if *X* himself was threatened. However, this view would be mistaken. The Hobbs Act requires only that one obtain property through wrongful use of a threat. I have argued that 'wrongful' should be understood as meaning 'unlawful.' But there is nothing in my analysis that requires that *X* threaten *V* with unlawful conduct that would directly harm *V* in order for *X*'s threat to be wrongful. Under my theft-law approach to extortion, the key is not that *V* would suffer the threatened harm, but that *V* suffers loss of property. The fact that the threat is against some third party does not seem to change this analysis.

Threats to withhold found property

Should it be extortion to promise to withhold found property from its rightful owner unless the owner pays the finder a 'reward'? Note that such a promise should be viewed as a threat rather than an offer (at least in the normative sense of the term) because the finder of the property is promising to make the rightful owner worse off in relation to his baseline than he has a right to be. Once again, we need to look to the relevant applicable law—here, the law of found property—to determine if such a threat should be regarded as 'wrongful' for purposes of the Hobbs Act. In most jurisdictions, '[i]t is the duty of a finder of lost goods to return them to the owner if he is known. The finder of goods is entitled to recover from the owner only the necessary and reasonable expenses incurred in the successful recovery and preservation of the goods.'[65] Merely asking for more than that is no crime, of course, so long as the finder does not threaten to withhold the property entirely unless the higher fee is paid.[66] But where such a demand is made, then it would seem that an unlawful taking is threatened, and that the charge of extortion would be proper.

Threats to strike

Should it be extortion for a union leader to threaten to have his union strike or engage in other putatively lawful job actions unless management meets some demand? Here, we can identify two scenarios: in the first, the leader threatens to have the union strike unless management makes a concession to the union, such as higher wages, shorter hours, or better benefits. In the second scenario, the union leader threatens to have the rank-and-file strike unless he, the leader, is given some personal economic benefit.

---

[65] *United States v Taglione*, 546 F 2d 194, 198 (5th Cir 1977). See also *Ganter v Kapiloff*, 516 A 2d 611 (Md 1986) (original owner of stamps prevails against finder); *Armory v Delamire* (1722) 1 Strange 505 (KB). In some jurisdictions, in some circumstances, the finder is entitled to a finder's fee, but such a fee is determined by statute rather than by negotiation.

[66] This is the import of the court's holding in *Taglione, ibid.*

Under the first scenario, the concession demanded would accrue to the benefit of the union itself. There is nothing improper in this. It is well established that workers have the right to strike and to demand concessions in return for not striking, so long as they do not use illegal techniques such as violence against persons or property, taking possession of the employer's property, or illegal work slowdowns.[67] Where workers use legal methods to extract a concession from management, there is no violation of management's property rights, and no extortion.

A different result, however, is reached in the second scenario, in which the labor boss uses the threat of a work stoppage to enrich himself personally. Here, the boss is, to use a phrase that James Lindgren has employed in the context of informational blackmail, using leverage or 'bargaining chips' that properly belong not to him but to the union members he is supposed to represent.[68] Labor law gives him no right to use the threat of a strike in this way. Accordingly, management's property rights would be violated and the union leader would properly be charged with extortion, as the court in the *Clemente* case in fact held.[69]

Greenmail

Do corporate raiders who threaten to take over another's company unless their stock is repurchased from them at a premium price commit extortion? The term 'greenmail,' which has been used to describe such transactions, is presumably intended to suggest that they do.[70] But should such conduct really be viewed as criminal? My approach suggests that it should not, and the case law would seem to agree. For example, in the *Viacom International* case, Carl Icahn and his associates, after acquiring approximately 17 per cent of Viacom International, threatened to take control of the company unless it agreed to buy out their shares for well above the market price.[71] In holding that the defendants had not committed extortion, the court stated that they 'did not obtain property from plaintiff to which they had no lawful claim.'[72] 'At this point in history,' the court said, 'the plaintiff does not have a pre-existing right to be free from the problems and fears of a takeover threat.'[73] In other words, in determining whether a defendant has committed extortion in such circumstances, a court should ask whether the defendant is threatening to violate any of the plaintiff's rights. Assuming he has not, he has not committed extortion.

---

[67] Section 7 of the National Labor Relations Act gives workers the right to engage in concerted activities relating to collective bargaining and the mutual aide and protection of employees. 29 USC § 157. See generally Douglas E Ray, *Labor-Management Relations: Strikes, Lockouts and Boycotts* (Deerfield, Ill.: Clark Boardman Callaghan, 1992).

[68] Lindgren, (n 21 above, at 702).   [69] 640 F 2d 1069 (2nd Cir 1981).

[70] See, eg Tracy Greer, 'The Hobbs Act and RICO: A Remedy for Greenmail?' (1988) 66 *Texas Law Review* 647 (suggesting that greenmail be prosecuted as extortion).

[71] 747 F Supp 205 (SDNY 1990).   [72] *Ibid* at 213–14.

[73] *Ibid* at 213. For similar reasoning, see also *Dan River, Inc v Icahn*, 701 F 2d 278 (4th Cir 1983); *Chock Full O'Nuts Corp. v Finkelstein*, 548 F Supp. 212 (SDNY 1982).

Threats to fire, or fail to hire, an employee

Is it extortion for a company official to threaten to fire, or not to hire, an employee or prospective employee unless such person pays the official a 'kickback'? Once again, we need to ask whether the official is threatening to do anything it is unlawful for him to do.

The general rule in the United States is that employees serve their employers 'at will,' meaning that, absent an employment contract of specified length, such employees may be fired (or may quit their jobs) at any time, for any reason or lack of reason, without legal liability.[74] Thus, it does not seem that an employee's property rights would be violated if he was required to pay a kickback in order to keep his job—as odious as such a practice would undoubtedly be. Nor, *a fortiori*, would such right be violated if he was required to pay a kickback in order to obtain the job in the first place. The company official who engaged in such conduct might well have committed fraud against his employer or, as the court recognized in *Capo*, have taken a commercial bribe[75]—but he would not have committed extortion.

Threats to disclose embarrassing information

Was it extortion for Mauro and Robertson to threaten to go public with allegedly false information about Flatley's sexual liaison with Robertson? The answer is surely yes.[76] Defamation law is meant to protect people in their reputations. By threatening to publish falsely embarrassing information about *V*, *D* would be threatening to commit an unlawful act. The same would be true if *D* threatened to expose *V*'s trade secrets. Such cases are clearly distinguishable from those in which *D* threatens to publish true, innocently obtained, embarrassing information about *V* unless *V* pays up— the paradigm of informational blackmail. Absent violation of some free-standing, statutorily-created privacy right of *V*'s through the publication of such information, it seems clear that such a threat would not constitute extortion.

Leo Katz's threats

There is a seemingly endless list of other kinds of putatively lawful conduct *X* might threaten to engage in unless *V* pays him money to desist. In addition to those imagined by Leo Katz (unless *V* gives *X* $10,000, *X* will: persuade *V*'s

---

[74] See, eg *Toussaint v Blue Cross & Blue Shield of Michigan*, 292 NW 2d 880, 885 (Mich 1980). There are of course exceptions to this general rule. For example, an employee may not be fired because of his race, gender, religion, or ethnic origin; and he may not be fired for refusing to do some illegal act or, generally, in retaliation for asserting some legally protected right. See, eg *Peterman v International Brotherhood of Teamsters*, 344 P 2d 44 (Cal Ct App 1959). Nor may an otherwise qualified prospective employee be refused employment on account of such illegitimate considerations.   [75] *Capo*, 817 F 2d at 951.
[76] This was in fact what the court in *Flatley* assumed, see 18 *Cal Rptr* 3d at 485–86.

son that he should sign up for the army, give *V*'s daughter a motorcycle, or tell *V*'s and *X*'s dying father that *V* is leaving the church), we can think of examples such as a teacher's threatening to flunk a student unless the student pays him money, or an employee's threatening to quit unless his wage demands are met. Would any of these cases constitute extortion? On first glance, it seems unlikely, but in each case, we would have to look to the relevant law concerning the underlying conduct threatened, and ask whether such conduct was itself unlawful.

Threats to withhold business

Finally, we need to consider whether it was extortion for Andrew Fastow to allegedly threaten various banks that Enron would no longer do business with them unless they invested in LJM-2. More generally, is it extortion for *X* to threaten that he will no longer do business with *V* unless *V* pays *X* money or invests in some venture of *X*'s?

Here, we need to distinguish between two kinds of cases: in the first, *X* and *V* have been doing business with each other without any specific contract, and *X* threatens to stop doing business with *V* in the future unless *V* meets his demand. Under my approach, such cases clearly would not constitute extortion. Given that *V*, *ex hypothesi*, has no existing contractual agreement with *X*, he cannot claim that his rights have been violated or that *X* has threatened anything unlawful. As in the *Viacom* greenmail case, it cannot be said that *X* was seeking to obtain property to which he had no lawful claim. And, in fact, as far as I have been able to ascertain, Fastow did not threaten to breach any contracts when soliciting investments in the *LJM-2* partnership. Accordingly, as coercive as his alleged conduct undoubtedly was, it did not constitute extortion.

The more difficult case is that in which *X* and *V* do have a contract, and in which *X* threatens to breach that contract unless *V* pays up. The question is whether a threat to breach a contract should be understood as constituting a threat to engage in 'unlawful,' therefore 'wrongful,' therefore 'extortionate' conduct. This seems to me a close case. On the one hand, the notion of the so-called 'efficient breach' may make us somewhat uncomfortable thinking of contractual breaches as 'unlawful.'[77] On the other hand, there is no obvious reason to say that breaching a contract is any less 'unlawful' than filing a frivolous lawsuit, withholding found property, or making defamatory statements. On balance, I am inclined to say that threatening to breach a contract unless one is paid probably should be treated as extortionate, at least in some particularly egregious cases.

---

[77] The *locus classicus* is Oliver Wendell Holmes, 'The Path of the Law' (1897) 10 *Harvard Law Review* 457, 458 ('The duty to keep a contract at common law means a prediction that you must pay damages if you do not keep it, and nothing else.'); see also Richard Posner, *Economic Analysis of Law* (2nd edn, Boston: Little, Brown, 1977), § 4.9, at 89–90.

Conclusion

Under the approach developed above, a threat should be regarded as 'wrongful,' and therefore extortionate, if and only if the act threatened would violate some provision of underlying positive law. Such an approach would create a sharp conceptual and doctrinal distinction between threats that constitute extortion and threats that do not. As such, it could help clarify a currently muddled area of the law and thereby promote the principle of legality.

But it is important to recognize what this approach would not do. It makes no claim to having solved the admittedly more difficult problem of distinguishing between threats to do what is lawful that should be regarded as blackmail (in the broad sense of the term) and threats to do what is lawful that should be regarded as mere hard bargaining. Instead, it makes the more modest point simply that such threats should not be treated as 'extortion.'

So, under what circumstances, if any, should it be a crime to threaten to do a lawful act unless one is paid to forgo it? Well, threats to expose embarrassing true information are an obvious candidate for criminalization, if only because of the cultural understanding traditionally associated with the offense of informational blackmail. Beyond that, the question becomes more difficult. Let me mention two possible approaches to its solution.

The first approach would focus on the concept of theft. I argued above that, where X threatens that she will perform some unlawful and unwanted act affecting V unless V pays up, X 'steals' from V by charging him money for something for which she has no right to charge him. The question we would need to ask, then, is whether it is also 'stealing' for X to threaten to do an unwanted but *lawful* act to V unless V pays up. To put it another way, assuming that extortion is properly thought of as a form of theft, we would want to ask whether blackmail should also be regarded as such. Framing the question this way obviously would not solve the underlying conceptual problem, but it might at least allow us to see it in a different, and possibly useful, light.

Alternatively, we could decide to depart from the stealing paradigm, and instead pursue what we might think of as a separate 'regulatory' path to criminality. Under such an approach, we would ask whether threatening to do an otherwise lawful act unless one was paid was so anti-social, coercive, and harmful that criminal penalties would be called for. Such an approach would focus not on the property wrongfully obtained by the coercer (as under the theft paradigm), but, rather, on the harms and wrongs of coercion itself. This is just the sort of approach that seems to have been used in connection with the offense of criminal coercion, as well as with 'exploitation'—type offenses such as price gouging and ticket scalping. Whether we should also want to criminalize threats to do lawful acts such as bringing a tender offer, firing an employee, or withholding political support, unless one is paid, does of course lie beyond the scope of the present inquiry.

18
Insider Trading

The law of insider trading demonstrates with particular clarity the doctrinal relevance of the concept of moral wrongfulness. As we shall see, the question of whether and how insider trading wrongs its victims (if at all) bears directly on the scope of the doctrine. In the United States, the dominant, Supreme Court-formulated theory has been that insider trading is wrongful because it involves a breach of fiduciary duty—either to the shareholder from whom the stock was purchased, or to the person from whom confidential information was misappropriated. Doctrinal results differ significantly based on which theory is adopted. In this chapter, I will argue that, rather than thinking of insider trading as involving a breach of fiduciary duty, we would do better to think of it in terms of cheating. The stock market is viewed as a highly formalized, rule-governed game. Confidence in the market depends on investors feeling that the game is being played fairly. The fact that some investors have better *information* than others is not viewed as unfair. What is viewed as unfair is the possibility that some investors might have *access* to information to which other investors do not. Market participants who trade on undisclosed inside information in these circumstances are viewed as cheaters, and punishment is viewed as warranted.

1. ASSESSING THE MORAL CONTENT OF INSIDER TRADING

In the United States, insider trading is a crime under both section 10(b) of the Securities Exchange Act of 1934, which prohibits any 'manipulative or deceptive device or contrivance,'[1] and Securities and Exchange Commission Rule 10b–5, which prohibits any 'act, practice, or course of business which operates or would operate as a fraud or deceit upon any person, in connection with the purchase or sale of any security.'[2] What exactly 'insider trading' consists of, however, is not defined in either provision, so one must look elsewhere—to SEC rulings and federal case law—for enlightenment.

---

[1] 15 USC § 78j(b).
[2] 17 CFR § 240.10b-5. Insider trading is also prohibited, though not necessarily criminalized, in numerous other countries. See Emerging Markets Committee, International Organization of Securities Commissions, 'Insider Trading: How Jurisdictions Regulate It' (Mar. 2003).

In its 1961 decision, *Cady, Roberts & Co.*, the SEC enunciated the basic rule that a trader who possesses material non-public information that would affect his or her judgment about a given securities transaction must either 'disclose' such information or 'abstain' from trading.[3] In subsequent years, the courts and commentators have struggled to explain why violation of the 'disclose or abstain' rule should be prohibited in some circumstances, but not others.[4]

Harmfulness

Much of the scholarly literature on insider trading involves the question of whether and to what extent such conduct is harmful. A number of prominent law and economics scholars have argued that, in fact, insider trading makes the market more efficient, by causing market prices to reflect more complete information about the value of the traded securities than would otherwise be possible, and that insider trading therefore ought not to be criminalized at all.[5] Suffice it to say that the question whether insider trading is harmful, and precisely how, is a controversial issue that cannot be resolved here.[6]

For our purposes, the most interesting thing to note about the law and economics literature on insider trading is the way in which it consistently ignores or trivializes the question of moral wrongfulness. For example, in his influential book on insider trading law, Henry Manne patronizingly reports the outraged reaction of 'an anonymous lady law student who in a classroom discussion of the subject, stamped her foot and angrily declaimed, "I don't care; it's just not right." '[7] In relating this incident, Manne's purpose is to belittle the idea that insider trading might be understood as involving morally wrongful behavior. For Manne, the only relevant question is whether insider trading is harmful.

Moral Wrongfulness

In response to critics such as Manne, a number of scholars argue, on one ground or another, that insider trading is morally wrong. Making exactly the

[3] 40 SEC 907, 912 (1961). Cady, Roberts assumed that the holder of non-public information would be a corporate insider, although subsequent cases have expanded the scope of 'insider trading' to apply to outsiders as well.

[4] Leading commentary includes Stephen Bainbridge, 'The Insider Trading Prohibition: A Legal and Economic Enigma' (1986) 38 *Florida Law Review* 35; Allison Grey Anderson, 'Fraud, Fiduciaries and Insider Trading' (1982) 10 *Hofstra Law Review* 341; Victor Brudney, 'Insiders, Outsiders, and Informational Advantages Under the Federal Securities Laws' (1979) 93 *Harvard Law Review* 322.

[5] The most influential such work is Henry G Manne, *Insider Trading and the Stock Market* (New York: The Free Press, 1996).

[6] For a useful overview of the issues, see Mark Klock, 'Mainstream Economics and the Case for Prohibiting Inside Trading' (1994) 10 *Georgia State University Law Review* 297.

[7] Manne (n 5 above, at 233 n 42).

converse error, however, these scholars suggest that such conduct should be made illegal regardless of whether it is economically harmful. For example, Alan Strudler and Eric Orts have contended that, '[e]ven if economic arguments conclusively favored unfettered insider trading, moral arguments would potentially give an independent reason for prohibiting insider trading....'[8] As I understand them, Strudler and Orts are contending that it would be permissible to criminalize insider trading even if it were shown to be harmless. This position seems to me wrong for the same reason I believe it is wrong to criminalize so-called 'morals offenses' such as adultery, bigamy, and prostitution. In a liberal society of the sort described by Mill, Feinberg, and others, moral wrongfulness by itself is not sufficient to justify criminalization. Under the liberal view, we ought not to make something a crime unless it can also be shown to be harmful.

For our purposes, though, the interesting question is exactly why insider trading *is* morally wrongful. Indeed, there is a direct connection between the way in which the courts have conceptualized this issue and the precise circumstances under which the disclose-or-abstain rule should apply.

Over the years, the courts and commentators have offered three basic theories as to whether, and when, trading on material non-public information is morally wrong and should be made illegal. I shall refer to these as the: (1) 'breach-of-duty-to-shareholder' theory; (2) 'breach-of-duty-to-source-of-information' theory; and (3) 'fraud' or 'deception' theory. In my view, none of these theories adequately captures what is morally wrong with insider trading. After briefly reviewing each of the theories, I offer an alternative characterization of what's wrong with insider trading, based on the idea of cheating.

The breach of duty to shareholder theory (or 'classical' or 'traditional' theory, as it is usually known) is articulated most prominently by the majority opinions in *Chiarella v United States*[9] and *Dirks v SEC*.[10] Under this theory, the rule against insider trading is violated when a corporate insider breaches a fiduciary duty owed to shareholders of his company by using, for his own benefit, non-public information obtained in his role as an insider. A paradigm example is provided by the facts of *SEC v Texas Gulf Sulphur Co.*, in which officers, directors, and employees of TGS learned of their company's rich ore strike in Canada and traded on this information before the news became public.[11] The defendants in *TGS* were liable for insider trading because, under the classical theory, they breached a duty of loyalty owed to the shareholders

---

[8] Alan Strudler and Eric W Orts, 'Moral Principle in the Law of Insider Trading', (1999) 78 *Texas Law Review* 375, 383. Other moralized theories of insider trading can be found in Leo Katz, *Ill-Gotten Gains* (Chicago: University of Chicago Press, 1996); Kim Lane Scheppele, 'It's Just Not Right: The Ethics of Insider Trading' (1993) 56 *Law & Contemporary Problems* 123; Ian B. Lee, 'Fairness and Insider Trading' (2002) *Columbia Business Law Review* 119. I should note, however, that only Strudler and Orts are explicit in minimizing the importance of harm.

[9] 445 US 222 (1980).   [10] 463 US 646 (1983).   [11] 401 F 2d 833 (2nd Cir 1968).

of their company. In contrast, the defendant in *Chiarella*—a financial printer who was able to determine the true identity of five companies that were takeover targets of a client bidder, and to use that information to purchase stock in the target companies—did not, according to the classical theory, commit insider trading. Unlike the defendants in *TGS*, defendant Chiarella owed no fiduciary duty to those with whom he had traded because 'he was not a corporate insider and he received no confidential information from the target company.'[12]

The 'breach-of-duty-to-source-of-information' theory (or 'misappropriation theory' as it is usually known) was adopted by a majority of the Court in *United States v O'Hagan*.[13] Under *O'Hagan*, insider trading is viewed as morally wrongful because it involves a breach of fiduciary duty not to the shareholders of the insider's firm, but rather to the source of the information that is misappropriated.[14] For example, in *O'Hagan* itself, the defendant was a partner in a law firm that represented Grand Metropolitan, which planned to make a tender offer for Pillsbury. After learning of the prospective offer, defendant O'Hagan bought Pillsbury stock and call options. Because O'Hagan was not a corporate insider at Pillsbury, he had no fiduciary duty to Pillsbury shareholders to breach, and his purchase would not have constituted insider trading under the classical or traditional theory of *Dirks* and *Chiarella*. But under the misappropriation theory adopted by the Court in *O'Hagan*, the defendant was liable, since he had breached a duty of loyalty to the *source* of the information—namely, Grand Metropolitan. Likewise, had Chiarella's case been decided under the misappropriation theory, he would have been liable for insider trading, since he had breached his duty to his employer, the printer Pandick Press, by taking and using information to which he was not entitled.

The final approach, based on the concept of 'fraud' or 'deception,' is one that can be found in Chief Justice Burger's theoretically eclectic dissent in *Chiarella*. Although a majority of the Court has never embraced it, the theory continues to find favor with various scholarly commentators.[15] According to this theory, insider trading involves a wrong of omission, rather than of commission. By failing to disclose certain material facts, the offending trader engages in a kind of misrepresentation; hence the term securities 'fraud.' And, like other forms of deceit, such failure to disclose interferes with the other party's deliberative process and thereby infringes on his autonomy.[16] Although its doctrinal implications are not completely spelled out, the theory would surely apply to a broad range of factual circumstances like those involved in *Texas Gulf Sulphur*, *Chiarella*, and *O'Hagan*, since in each case the defendant, whether insider or outsider, allegedly misled the market by failing to disclose material information.

---

[12] 401 F 2d 833 (2nd Cir 1968).		[13] 521 US 642 (1997).		[14] *Ibid* at 652.
[15] See, eg Strudler and Orts n 8 above.		[16] *Ibid* at 380, 408–17.

In my view, none of the three theories adequately captures what's morally wrong with insider trading. The classical theory applies only when non-public information is used by a corporate insider. It does not apply when such information is used by an outsider. From the perspective of the person who buys (or sells) stock without access to such non-public information, however, it makes no difference whether the party on the other side of the transaction is an insider or an outsider. The wrong in both cases is identical. Therefore, the classical theory is too narrow: it fails to capture cases that should be subject to the insider trading laws.

Like the classical theory, the misappropriation theory also does a poor job of reflecting our moral intuitions about what's wrong with insider trading. The misappropriation theory says that the wrong in insider trading comes from a breach of duty to the source of the information. Once again, however, to the victim of insider trading, it makes no difference how the offender has obtained the non-public information on which he relies. What does matter is that the offender enjoys an unfair advantage that is denied to the uninformed trader.

Finally, there is the deceit or fraud theory. Although this approach is preferable to the other two theories (for one thing, it has the virtue of tracking the 'securities fraud' language of the statute under which insider trading is actually prosecuted), the fraud theory nevertheless fails to capture the real moral content of insider trading. As described above, 'fraud' is best understood as theft by deception. Yet it is unclear that insider trading necessarily involves either theft or deception. Unlike the typical fraudster, who makes false representations regarding the quality, price, or quantity of goods or services,[17] the insider trader makes no affirmative representations at all. She simply acts on the basis of information that she knows or believes to be reliable. Indeed, if the insider trader does make any representations, she is signaling, quite accurately, that she regards the stock as either overvalued (which she does by selling) or undervalued (which she does by buying)—precisely the point that the critics of insider trading law make when they argue that insider trading provides an efficient means of telegraphing reliable information to the market.

Perhaps, then, buying stock in a company that one knows will soon be the target of a corporate takeover is like buying a dusty old canvas at a yard sale when one knows that the painting is a previously undiscovered Vermeer. Or perhaps selling stock in a company that one knows, on the basis of non-public information, to be headed for bankruptcy is like selling a used car without disclosing that the transmission is shot. Unfortunately for the fraud theory, the law does not generally regard nondisclosure of material information as deceptive,[18]

---

[17] See *United States v Regent Office Supply*, 421 F 2d 1174, 1179 (2nd Cir 1970).

[18] The leading case is *Laidlaw v Oregon*, 15 US (2 Wheat) 178, 193–94 (1817) (buyers who learned that a peace treaty ending the War of 1812 had been signed, thereby ending the blockade of New Orleans, did not commit fraud when they failed to disclose such information to seller from whom they acquired large quantities of tobacco).

and neither, it seems to me, does morality. As argued in Chapter 5, the concept of deception requires an affirmative act or at least an omission to do an affirmative act that one has an obligation to perform. Thus, if nondisclosure of material information is not regarded as fraudulent in the context of ordinary commercial transactions (eg at a yard sale), it is hard to see why it should be regarded as fraudulent in the context of the securities markets. If we are to explain why nondisclosure should be illegal in the latter context, but not in the former, then we need some moral concept, other than deceit, that allows us to distinguish between the two.

2. Insider Trading as Cheating

A better characterization of what is morally wrongful with insider trading would take into account the notion of cheating. The trader: (1) violates the SEC rule that one must either disclose material non-public information or abstain from trading; and does so (2) with the intent to obtain an advantage over a second party with whom she is in a cooperative, rule-governed relationship. Under this characterization, the stock market is viewed as a highly formalized, rule-governed game, which is distinct from the game that is played at yard sales and on used-car lots.[19] The insider trader violates a rule that is ultimately intended to give investors confidence that the game is being played fairly, and thereby gains an advantage over the uninformed party with whom she is dealing.[20]

I am certainly not the first to characterize insider trading as a form of 'cheating.'[21] But I want to pursue this idea to see where it leads in considering two recurring questions in the law of insider trading: first, why does the law forbid trading securities on information that is not public, but nevertheless allow trading on the basis of vast inequalities in the quality and quantity of information that, theoretically, is publicly available? Secondly, should it be a crime to trade securities on the basis of material non-public information that is obtained by luck rather than through misappropriation?

[19] Cf Boyd Kimball Dyer, 'Economic Analysis, Insider Trading, and Game Markets,' (1992) *Utah Law Review* 1 (characterizing stock market as a 'game market').
[20] The fact that the trader does not ordinarily know the actual identity of his trading partner does not seem to change the analysis.
[21] See, eg William R Lucas et al., 'Common Sense, Flexibility, and Enforcement of the Federal Securities Laws' (1996) 51 *Business Law Review* 1221, 1233, 1237 ('Even though it is not specifically mentioned in the text of the statutes, insider trading, pure and simple, is cheating.' 'Insider trading is about cheating; cheating a shareholder, an employer, a client, or even a friend.'); Strudler & Orts (n 8 above, at 412) (characterizing insider trading as 'cheating' in passing). Although she does not use term 'cheating,' my theory of the morality of insider trading is probably closest to Scheppele, note 8, at 123 (focusing on fairness, level playing fields, equal access to information, and breach of contractarian obligations as key to understanding what is wrong with insider trading).

In order to answer these questions, let us consider the following three hypotheticals:

- *X* is in a bicycle race with *A*. As a result of his exceptional talent, top-notch training, mental toughness, and superior equipment, *A* rides much faster than *X* and wins the race.

- *X* is in a bicycle race with *P*. While *X*'s back is turned, *P* violates the rules of bicycle racing by puncturing *X*'s tire and causing *X* to lose several minutes as a result of having to dismount and change his tire. *P* wins the race.

- *X* is in a bicycle race with *T*. During the course of the race, *X* has the bad luck to run over a nail. It takes *X* several minutes to change his tire. Rather than waiting for him (there is no requirement that he do so), *T* rides on ahead and wins the race.

The first hypothetical helps explain the answer to the first question—namely, why does the law forbid trading on non-public information but allow traders to exploit other kinds of informational advantages, such as those gained by superior research and knowledge of the market? Just as the average competitive bicyclist is unlikely to overcome the extraordinary talents of a Lance Armstrong,[22] the average individual investor is unlikely to outwit the investment savvy of a Warren Buffett.[23] But we would not ordinarily say that it is 'unfair' for such prodigies to exploit their natural talents, hard work, and superior resources. Cheating arises only when an advantage is obtained unfairly, through rule-breaking. The fact that Buffett is smarter, knows more about the stock market, and has access to more and better (at least theoretically) publicly available information than the average investor is not regarded as 'unfair.' What would be regarded as unfair is if he were to rely on information that was not even theoretically accessible to the public (for example, inside information obtained from his friend, Microsoft Chairman Bill Gates).

As for the second question—should it be a crime to trade on the basis of material non-public information that is obtained by luck rather than through misappropriation?—consider the case of the famous American football coach, Barry Switzer.[24] In June 1981, Switzer was in the stands at a high school track meet in Oklahoma when he overheard a man whom he knew to

---

[22] According to a profile of him in *The New Yorker*, Lance Armstrong's heart is almost a third larger than that of the average man. At rest, it beats an astonishingly low 32 times per minute. His VO2 levels—the maximum amount of oxygen the lungs can consume during exercise—have been recorded at levels more than twice as high as the average healthy man. And it is not only his cardiovascular strength that is exceptional; 'his body seems specially constructed for cycling. His thigh bones are unusually long, for example, which permits him to apply just the right amount of torque to the pedals.' Michael Specter, 'The Long Ride: How Did Lance Armstrong Manage the Greatest Comeback in Sports History?,' *The New Yorker* (15 July 2002). I express no opinion, of course, concerning the persistent allegations that Armstrong has also benefited from the use of performance enhancing drugs.

[23] Warren Buffett, chairman of Berkshire Hathaway Co., is known as the world's most successful stock market investor.   [24] *SEC v Switzer*, 590 F Supp 756 (WD Okla 1984).

be a director of a publicly held corporation discussing with his wife the impending merger of one of the corporation's subsidiaries. Trading on the basis of this not-yet public information, Switzer turned a profit of more than $50,000.[25] Although the Supreme Court has not yet had occasion to consider this question straight on, it appears that, following the rule in *O'Hagan*, an outsider who obtains information fortuitously (say, by overhearing it on the train or at the beach), without breaching any fiduciary duty to the source of the information, would not be bound by the disclose-or-abstain rule, and would not have committed insider trading.

Would the result differ under my 'cheating' approach to insider trading? At one level, the question whether Switzer cheated turns on nothing more than whether he violated a rule: if the disclose-or-abstain rule applies to information obtained fortuitously by outsiders, then he has cheated; if the rule does not apply in such cases, then he has not. The problem, of course, is that the precise question we are trying to answer is whether the disclose-or-abstain rule *should* apply in such circumstances.

Here a consideration of hypotheticals 2 and 3 might prove useful. There appears to be, at least at an intuitive level, a significant moral difference between creating a disadvantage for one's rival (eg by puncturing his tire), and exploiting a disadvantage that one's rival has come by naturally (eg by riding on while the rival changes a tire that was punctured as a result of his fortuitously running over a nail). The same distinction should apply in the context of insider trading. The trader who relies on non-public information obtained through his own efforts is analogous to the racer who punctures his rival's tire, while the trader who relies on non-public information that has been obtained fortuitously is analogous to the bicycle racer whose rival runs over a nail. The distinction is between creating an unfair informational disparity and exploiting an informational disparity that already exists. If this analogy is apposite, then the disclose-or-abstain rule should be construed so as not to apply to cases in which an investor comes across non-public information fortuitously (say, by overhearing it in an elevator or on the train), and trading on such information so obtained should not constitute insider trading.

---

[25] The district court held, under then-current law, that Switzer had not committed insider trading. *Ibid* at 760.

19

Tax Evasion

Even compared to other white-collar crimes, the tax crimes seem ambiguous in their moral character: no one likes to pay taxes, and most people take steps to minimize their liability; on the other hand, we recognize that taxes are the fuel on which a liberal society runs, and we resent it when others fail to pay their fair share. Depending on the circumstances, the nonpayment of taxes can be treated as a serious fraud, a minor regulatory violation, or perfectly lawful 'tax avoidance.' Even when it is clear that a violation of law has occurred, there is great variability in whether it will be treated as criminal or civil, and the decision of which kind of remedy the enforcement agency will decide to pursue is made in different ways in different regions, with like cases often being treated in quite divergent ways.[1] Moreover, attitudes concerning the obligation to pay taxes are highly dependent on cultural factors, with wide differences in 'tax morale' observable from country to country.[2]

My goal in this section is not to offer anything like a comprehensive account of the moral content of tax crimes. Rather, I want to identify some basic issues that need to be addressed, and suggest a general and quite tentative characterization of tax evasion based, once again, on the concept of 'cheating.'

1. AVOIDANCE, NON-PAYMENT, AND EVASION

At the outset, we need to distinguish among three related concepts: tax avoidance (or tax mitigation, as it tends to be known in Great Britain), non-payment of taxes, and tax evasion. Tax avoidance is simply the use of lawful 'loopholes' to reduce the amount of tax owed. The tax avoider makes disclosure of all the information he is required to disclose and pays all the tax he is required to pay. At its worst, tax avoidance flouts the spirit of the law while following its letter. Tax avoidance seems to involve an amoral act—neither

[1] See, eg David Cay Johnston, 'Spending It; Where the I.R.S. Aims the Prosecution Ax' *New York Times* (14 April 1996), Section 3, p. 1.

[2] See James Alm and Benno Torgler, 'Culture Differences and Tax Morale in the United States and in Europe,' Center for Research in Economics, Management and the Arts (CREMA) Working Paper No. 2004-14, <http://www.crema-research.ch/papers/2004-14.pdf> accessed 22 Aug. 2005.

supererogatory nor fraudulent; in its most negative light, it is mildly exploitative or selfish.[3]

Non-payment of taxes, by contrast, does involve a violation of the law, but a relatively minor one. Under federal law, failure to file a return is a misdemeanor carrying a maximum penalty of one year in prison or a $25,000 fine.[4] Here, the analogy to the sort of regulatory violations we will discuss in the next section is strongest.

The offense I want to focus on here is tax evasion, under US law a serious felony with a maximum penalty of five years imprisonment.[5] Tax evasion requires not only the non-payment of taxes but also an attempt to evade or defeat the tax, conceal income, or mislead the authorities. In an oft-quoted passage from *Spies v United States*, the Supreme Court explained that evidence of evasion is to be:

inferred from conduct such as keeping a double set of books, making false entries or alterations, or false invoices or documents, destruction of books or records, concealment of assets or covering up sources of income, handling of one's affairs to avoid making the records usual in transactions of this kind, and any conduct, the likely effect of which would be to mislead or to conceal.[6]

2. The *Mens Rea* and Harmfulness of Tax Evasion

One of the distinguishing features of crimes like tax evasion is the use of the *mens rea* term 'willfulness.' The term 'willfulness' is understood to mean a 'voluntary, intentional violation of a known legal duty'[7]—a form of culpability that is highly unusual in criminal law in that it allows mistake or ignorance of the law to be a defense in a much broader array of circumstances than is usually permitted.[8] In *Cheek v United States*, the Court held that a tax evader who sincerely and in good faith believes that he is not violating the tax laws

[3] Cf 'Tax Evasion,' in *Wikipedia*, <http://en.wikipedia.org/wiki/Tax_evasion> accessed 22 Aug. 2005.   [4] 26 USC § 7203.
[5] 26 USC § 7201. There is also a felony provision that makes it a crime to willfully aid or assist in the preparation of a false return. 26 USC § 7206(2).
[6] *Spies v United States*, 317 US 492 (1943). There are also two other possible categories according to which nonpayment of taxes might be classified. First, there are some individuals, particularly in the US, who refuse to pay taxes because they believe, or say they believe, that the tax code itself is unconstitutional or in some other way illegal. Such people are known as tax protesters. There are also individuals who refuse to pay taxes, or part of their taxes, for conscientious reasons, such as that they do not want to see their money used to fight an unjust war. Such people are motivated less by the desire to keep their money (frequently, they donate their unpaid taxes to charity) than by the wish not to see it used for what they regard as immoral purposes. 'Tax Evasion,' in *Wikipedia* (n 3 above).   [7] *United States v Pomponio*, 429 US 10, 11 (1976).
[8] See generally Sharon L Davies, 'The Jurisprudence of Willfulness: An Evolving Theory of Excusable Ignorance' (1998) 48 *Duke Law Journal* 341 (*mens rea* of willfulness is more common than generally thought); Mark C Winings, Comment, 'Ignorance is Bliss, Especially for the Tax Evader' (1993) 84 *Journal of Criminal Law & Criminology* 575.

can avoid liability for willful tax evasion.[9] As the Court explained, the law in criminal tax cases deviates from that in most other criminal cases by rejecting the assumption that citizens know the law: '[I]n our complex tax system, uncertainty often arises even among taxpayers who earnestly wish to follow the law.... [I]t is not the purpose of the law to penalize frank differences of opinion or innocent errors made despite the exercise of reasonable care.'[10] So, for a start, tax evasion is distinguishable from most of the other major white-collar offenses in terms of the level of *mens rea* required and the applicability of the defense of mistake or ignorance of law.

And what about the second prong of our three-pronged approach to the moral content of white-collar offenses—namely, harmfulness? The most obvious harm caused by tax evasion is loss of government revenues. Quite simply, the more taxes are evaded, the less money the government has to administer social programs, fund schools and universities, pave roads, provide police protection, support the military, protect borders, run the court and prison systems, and so forth.[11] And who are the likely victims of such harms? Presumably, the intended recipients of public funds, who suffer a loss of services or benefits; and other taxpayers, who must eventually pay a larger share of taxes to compensate for revenues lost.

But, of course, the same could be said of both tax avoidance and the non-payment of taxes. Like evasion, avoidance and non-payment result in reduced tax revenues and a shifting of the tax burden from those who don't pay to those who do. So, deferring for a moment the issue of moral wrongfulness, it is useful to ask whether tax evasion and tax avoidance can be distinguished in terms of the harms each causes.

A reasonable argument can be made that tax evasion (as opposed to the mere non-payment of taxes) involves greater harms than simply a loss of revenues. As noted above, tax evasion requires more than simple non-payment; the tax evader must also conceal income or mislead the authorities. In order to minimize the appearance of income, the tax evader will engage in various deceptions; establish secret accounts; dispose of money in ways that are unlikely to be socially constructive; and involve family members, colleagues, employees, customers, and suppliers in a web of illegality.[12] Moreover, when tax evasion is widespread, the system itself suffers: confidence in the taxing authority is weakened, citizens are resentful and distrustful of their fellow citizens, potential tax evaders are emboldened in their attempts to evade taxes, and the rule of law suffers.[13]

---

[9] 498 US 192 (1991).   [10] *Ibid* at 205.

[11] On the other hand, in an unjust or repressive regime, where tax revenues are used for socially destructive purposes, such as, say, the funding of terrorists or the stockpiling of weapons of mass destruction, non-payment of taxes might well be regarded as entailing a positive social good.

[12] Cf Linda S Eads, 'From Capone to Boesky: Tax Evasion, Insider Trading, and Problems of Proof' (1991) 79 *California Law Review* 1421.

[13] Admittedly, widespread tax avoidance is also likely to cause resentment from those who are unable or unwilling to take advantage of expensive tax advice and complicated tax loopholes.

3. The Moral Wrongfulness of Tax Evasion

Having looked at the harms tax evasion causes, we can now consider the wrongs it entails. Tax evasion and non-payment of taxes have traditionally been regarded either as a form of 'stealing' or as a violation of the 'moral obligation to obey the law.' In this section, I suggest that a better way of looking at such offenses is in terms of cheating.

To begin with, the characterization of tax evasion as 'stealing'[14] is too narrow. In order to see why this is so, we need to distinguish between two kinds of taxes: on the one hand, income tax, sales tax, estate tax, capital gains tax, and real estate tax (which we can refer to as 'taxes proper'); and, on the other hand, fees, licenses, permits, franchises and special assessments.[15] With the first kind of tax the taxpayer has no automatic right to any of the proceeds. With the second kind, by contrast, the payer pays her fee in order to receive some specific benefit, such as the right to import goods or drive a car, or have a road in front of her business paved.

One who evades taxes of the second kind—say, by obtaining a driver's license or hunting permit without paying for it—can be said to have 'stolen' in the same way as one who receives but fails to pay for, say, cable television transmission. With respect to taxes proper, however, the analogy to theft is strained. Taxes of this type are related to benefits received in only the most attenuated way. A taxpayer in Maine might well have his federal tax dollars used to build a road in New Mexico, even though he derives virtually no benefit from it. Moreover, it is frequently the case that those who pay a great deal in taxes receive relatively little in the way of government benefits, while those who pay little or nothing in taxes receive a lot. And tax revenues are sometime used for purposes that at least some taxpayers are thoroughly opposed to, such as waging unjust wars or subsidizing the construction of professional sports stadiums. In such circumstances, it is doubtful that the evader has 'stolen' anything. Thus, although the metaphor of theft may have some application with respect to the evasion of certain kinds of specialized fees and assessments, it is too narrow to explain why it is wrongful to evade taxes proper.[16]

The overarching problem of an unjust tax code is mentioned below n 18 and accompanying text. For now, it is enough to suggest that the degree of resentment caused by illegal tax evasion is likely to be even greater than that caused by legal tax avoidance.

[14] See Martin T Crowe, *The Moral Obligation of Paying Just Taxes* (Washington DC: Catholic University of America Studies in Sacred Theology No. 84, 1944) 42 (those who 'use fraud and other means to evade just taxes ... sin mortally by committing the sin of theft') (quoted in Leo P Martinez, 'Taxes, Morals, and Legitimacy' (1994) *Brigham Young University Law Review* 521, 522 n 3; Richard H McAdams, 'Group Norms, Gossip, and Blackmail' (1996) 144 University of Pennsylvania Law Review 2237, 2263 n 72 (characterizing tax evasion as a form of theft).

[15] See Robert W McGee, 'Is Tax Evasion Unethical?' (1994) 42 *Kansas Law Review* 411, 412 (citing Martin Crowe, *The Moral Obligation of Paying Just Taxes*, (n 14 above)).

[16] In an earlier version of this argument, I argued that the theft metaphor was also too broad. See Stuart P Green, 'Cheating' (2004) 23 *Law and Philosophy* 137, 173 (2004). The argument

Another common way of talking about the evasion of taxes is in terms of a breach of the moral obligation to obey the law. For example, the Catechism of the Catholic Church identifies '[o]bedience to authority' as the principal ground upon which the obligation to pay taxes is grounded.[17] But the duty-to-obey approach is not without its own problems. First, every violation of a just law involves some form of disobedience. The disobedience theory fails to explain how the moral content of tax evasion differs from (and is more serious than), say, various trivial regulatory violations. Secondly, and more importantly, the disobedience theory fails to capture what there is about tax evasion that is so likely to cause resentment among those who dutifully pay their taxes. By focusing on the vertical relationship between tax evader and state, it loses sight of the crucial breach in the horizontal relationship between tax evader and fellow citizen.

I would propose that a better way of thinking about the moral content of unlawful nonpayment of taxes is in terms of cheating. (In the case of the more serious offense of tax evasion, there is also an element of deception or fraud.) Recall that cheating consists of breaking an equitable and fairly enforced rule with the intent to obtain an advantage over some party with whom the rule-breaker is in a cooperative, rule-governed relationship. Tax evasion surely involves the violation of prescriptive rules. (In this, tax evasion is obviously distinguishable from mere tax avoidance, in which the tax avoider, as ungenerous and crafty as he may be, plays close to, but not does not actually, cross the line.) Whether such rules are sufficiently just, however, to allow us to refer to their violation as a form of cheating is a question that cannot be resolved here.[18] Suffice it to say that, if the tax system were structured so as to impose disproportionate burdens on the poor and middle classes, as compared to the rich; or if tax revenues were used for wasteful, tyrannical, or wicked purposes; or issued or administered by an illegitimate and arbitrary authority, then a

ran as follows: imagine two tax evaders, *X* and *Y*. *X* lives in a country with a liberal, democratically elected government and a just distribution of taxes, and fails to pay moneys that would have been used to provide food and medical care for the poor. *Y* lives in a repressive, totalitarian regime with an unjust distribution of the tax burden, and fails to pay taxes that would have been used to support the country's brutal secret police. I argued that, under the 'theft' rationale, there was no basis for distinguishing between the two cases, since even stealing in a society that is unjust is likely to be viewed as morally wrongful. Therefore, I argued, the problem with the theft metaphor is that it fails to give us the means to distinguish between justified and unjustified tax evasion. I now think that this argument was mistaken. As I suggested above (ch. 6, p. 91), a person who takes property from the government under circumstances like *Y*'s probably should not be said to have stolen, at least in the normative sense of the term.

[17] *Catechism of the Catholic Church* § 2240 (Libreria Editrice Vatican, Provisional Draft, 1992).
[18] See generally Liam Murphy and Thomas Nagel, *The Myth of Ownership: Taxes and Justice* (New York: OUP, 2002); Stephen Holmes and Cass Sunstein, *The Cost of Rights: Why Liberty Depends on Taxes* (New York: W W Norton, 1999); Dennis J Ventry, Jr and Joseph J Thorndike (eds.), *Tax Justice: The Ongoing Debate* (Washington, DC: Urban Institute Press, 2002); Walter J Blum and Harry Kalven, Jr., *The Uneasy Case for Progressive Taxation* (Chicago: University of Chicago Press, 1953).

reasonable argument could be made that tax evasion would not constitute cheating.

And, in fact, this is exactly what empirical studies of people's attitudes regarding tax compliance and evasion seem to suggest. People are less likely to regard tax evasion as morally wrongful if they believe that: their friends and neighbors are evading taxes[19]; the government is using tax revenues unwisely[20]; or the taxing authorities are biased and unfair in their enforcement.[21] In other words, the extent to which tax evasion is likely to be regarded as wrongful is directly related to the extent to which such conduct is viewed as cheating.

A separate question is whether the tax evader: (1) intends to obtain an advantage over (2) some party with whom she is in a cooperative, rule-governed relationship. Taking the second issue first, it seems reasonable to assume that one who earns income or owns property is in a cooperative, rule-governed relationship with her fellow citizens. As for the first issue, it seems that, even if the offender receives little in the way of government benefits, she still obtains an advantage through the non-payment of tax itself. Having avoided taxes that others in her community have paid, she is left with more money in her pocket and thereby obtains a competitive advantage. Indeed, one can easily imagine that what makes tax evasion so particularly worthy of resentment to the average, hard-working, taxpayer in the street is not that it involves theft or a breach of a duty to obey, but that it involves a form of cheating. 'I'm paying my fair share,' the taxpayer might well say, 'while that guy [the tax evader] is not. That's unfair. He's cheating.'

---

[19] John S Carrol, 'How Taxpayers Think About Their Taxes: Frames and Values,' in Joel Slemrod (ed.), *Why People Pay Taxes: Tax Compliance and Enforcement* (Ann Arbor: University of Michigan Press, 1992) 47.

[20] Steven M Shiffrin and Robert K Triest, 'Can Brute Deterrence Backfire? Perceptions and Attitudes in Taxpayer Compliance,' in *Why People Pay Taxes: Tax Compliance and Enforcement* (Ann Arbor: University of Michigan Press, 1992) 203, tbl. 2. See also Eric A Posner, 'Law and Social Norms: The Case of Tax Compliance' (2002) 86 *Virginia Law Review* 1781.

[21] Kent W Smith, 'Reciprocity and Fairness: Positive Incentives for Tax Compliance,' in *Why People Pay Taxes: Tax Compliance and Enforcement* (Ann Arbor: University of Michigan Press, 1992) 233–35.

20
Regulatory Offenses

As the term is generally used, 'regulatory crime' refers to a collection of penal statutes applying to a wide array of matters within the purview of federal, state, and local administrative agencies, including the environment, product and workplace safety, labor, banking, securities, antitrust, transportation, trade, taxation, immigration, customs, agriculture, education, health care, and housing.[1] Given the vast range of conduct covered by the concept of regulatory crime, it is not surprising that such offenses reflect a vast range of harms and wrongs. Some of these harms and wrongs are *sui generis*—eg the death of animals that are members of an endangered species, the exposure of workers to serious workplace hazards, the exposure of consumers to unsafe products, the fixing of prices, and the discharge of toxins into a public water source. Other regulatory violations involve harms and wrongs that are similar to those we saw in connection with other white-collar crimes. Indeed, tax evasion, insider trading, and certain kinds of false statements could all qualify as regulatory crimes. To attempt to catalogue each of these various kinds of harms and wrongs would obviously involve a vast undertaking, one that would take us well beyond the scope of this work.[2]

My goal here is considerably more modest: I want to focus narrowly on those penal statutes that make it a crime to engage in prohibited conduct, subject to regulation, that would not be viewed as entailing significant moral wrongfulness independent of its prohibition. In other words, I want to focus on those

---

[1] See, eg Sanford Kadish, 'Some Observations on the Use of Criminal Sanctions in Enforcing Economic Regulations' (1963) 30 *University of Chicago Law Review* 423, 424; Susan L Pilcher, 'Ignorance, Discretion and the Fairness of Notice: Confronting "Apparent Innocence" in the Criminal Law' (1995) *American Criminal Law Review* 1, 32.

[2] Nevertheless, it is worth asking at this point whether and to what extent regulatory crimes are properly characterized as 'white collar.' Some tentative considerations can be offered: first, the defendant in such cases is frequently a 'white collar' professional or corporate entity. Secondly, the harms caused by such violations are often widely dispersed and aggregative, and the affected victims hard to identify. Thirdly, the same regulatory misconduct is often made subject to both criminal and civil penalties, without any indication of which remedy is preferred or what criteria should be relied on in determining what kind of penalty will be pursued. Fourthly, these statutes are typically codified in titles of the US or state codes that deal principally with matters other than criminal law, and often impose punishments for failure to comply with a separate provision of (civil) law. Finally, compliance with regulatory crime statutes is usually monitored, in the first instance, by specialized administrative agencies, rather than by the Department of Justice or local prosecutors, and matters are referred to prosecutors with general jurisdiction only after there has been an initial determination that probable cause exists.

regulatory offenses that can plausibly be characterized as *mala prohibita*. I have in mind certain generic forms of regulatory crime, such as engaging in one or another activity without a license, failing to file forms required by the government, or failing to comply with some testing requirement.

The question is: when, if ever, is it morally wrong to violate a statute prohibiting some regulated conduct that would not be viewed as morally wrong independent of its prohibition? Note that this question is different from the more general question whether it is morally wrong to violate the law. Even if there is no generally applicable moral obligation to obey the law, there might still be specific cases, or categories of cases, in which conduct that is otherwise morally neutral (or even virtuous) becomes wrongful as a result of its prohibition. In this section, I want to examine the possibility that such offenses are informed by the norms against cheating, promise-breaking, and disobedience.

1. Cheating

One significant way in which such conduct might be viewed as wrongful is if the law violation constitutes cheating. That is, if violating such a regulatory statute constitutes rule-breaking intended to obtain an unfair advantage over another with whom one is in a cooperative, rule-bound relationship, then, under the analysis of cheating developed in Chapter 4, we should say that such violation was prima facie morally wrong.

In fact, many regulatory violations do seem to reflect just such a paradigm. Consider the case of General Motors' alleged violations of the Clean Air Act. Under that Act, automobile manufacturers are required to comply with certain limits regarding carbon monoxide emissions and to supply the Environmental Protection Agency (EPA) with regular, detailed information regarding such emissions.[3] Failure to do so can subject defendant to both criminal and civil sanctions.[4] In 1991, General Motors changed the design of certain Cadillac models, thereby creating better 'performance,' but increasing carbon monoxide emissions to between two and three times the permitted level. Although the cars are typically driven with the climate control on, they were tested with the system off. The result was a misleading set of testing data. While GM allegedly knew about this problem, it failed to tell the agency that it had changed the car's design in a way that resulted in Clean Air Act violations, and for at least four years supplied the agency with inaccurate testing information.[5]

In what way was GM's conduct morally wrong? Well, it presumably deceived EPA by giving the agency misleading data. But did it do anything wrong vis-à-vis its competitors? The answer, I think, is yes. By violating the

---

[3] 42 USC § 7412.   [4] *Ibid* at section 7413(b) & (c).
[5] John H Cushman, Jr., 'G.M. Agrees to Cadillac Recall in Federal Pollution Complaint,' (1 Dec. 1995) *New York Times* A1.

provisions of the Clean Air Act, GM basically cheated; it was, in all likelihood, able to achieve an unfair advantage over competitors that, as a result
of their compliance with the regulations, were forced to manufacture lower
performance, less commercially attractive cars.

To be sure, GM and competitors like Ford do not compete in a formal game
structure like Celtic and Rangers. There is no explicit agreement between
them to comply with 'the rules.' Indeed, most agreements among competitors, such as those concerning prices and boycotts, are themselves violations
of the antitrust laws. Nevertheless, it would be wrong to think of GM and its
competitors as existing in an unrestrained, free market 'state of nature.' GM
and its major competitors all belong to various automobile-manufacturing
trade associations, including the Alliance of Automobile Manufacturers.
They regularly pool their resources to lobby Congress and various regulatory
agencies, formulate industry standards on safety and energy efficiency, gather
information, promote good public relations, encourage innovation, and seek
'consensus' on a wide range of other issues.[6] Moreover, the laws that govern
matters such as carbon monoxide emissions are not ordinarily imposed on
industry participants from 'on high.' Rather, such laws are normally the
product of a protracted administrative rule-making process of lobbying,
notice and comment, and public hearings. One need not believe that there is
an overarching Lockean social contract, or a universally applicable Rawlsian
duty of fair play, in order to believe that GM 'bought into' the system, and
implicitly agreed to 'play by the rules.' By submitting false data in such a situation, GM was presumably able to lower its costs and increase its revenues
in relation to its law-abiding rivals. Such parties act, in Douglas Husak's
words, as 'free riders who exploit a system of mutual forbearance by abro-
gating to themselves a privilege they withhold from others who are similarly
situated.'[7] If that is correct, then it follows that such conduct should be
viewed as 'unfair,' and thereby violative of the norm against cheating.

2. Promise-Breaking

Less significant as a practical matter in assessing the moral content of regulatory crime, though nevertheless of theoretical interest, is the norm against
promise-breaking. Persons engaged in regulated industries—whether it is

---

[6] According to its website, the goals of the Alliance of Automobile Manufacturers are to: 'seek
harmonization of global standards; promote market-based, cost-effective solutions in preference
to mandates on public policy issues; provide credible industry information and data with global
perspective; provide an industry forum for the consideration of issues, through an inclusive and
collaborative process, that facilitates the development of consensus positions; and provide an
essential industry interface with other organizations and coalitions.' <http://www.autoalliance.
org/about/> accessed 22 Aug. 2005.

[7] This language comes from an article by Douglas Husak critiquing an earlier version of my
regulatory-violations-as-cheating argument. Douglas Husak, '*Malum Prohibitum* and

operating a warehouse, mining, or selling real estate—frequently agree to be
bound by the statutes and regulations applicable to such industries, often as
a condition for obtaining a permit or license or other governmental benefit.
In the United States, such 'promise-to-comply' statutory and regulatory
schemes are widely used at both the federal[8] and state[9] level. Even members
of the general public, when they apply for permits to fish or hunt or carry
weapons, may make an explicit promise to abide by certain applicable rules
and regulations.[10] My claim about moral content follows straightforwardly
from the existence of such statutory schemes: where X has (1) made a promise
to comply with some regulatory provision, and (2) fails to keep such a
promise, by violating the provision, it follows that (3) X has engaged in the
prima facie morally wrongful act of promise-breaking.

There are, however, at least three significant qualifications that need to be
made about this claim, each of which is emphasized in a critique by Douglas
Husak of an earlier version of my argument regarding regulatory violations
as promise breaking.[11] First, it is important to note that many, perhaps most,
such promises to comply with some regulatory provision are in some sense
'adhesive.' As Husak puts it, '[t]he terms in a driving or fishing license might
be described as "boiler-plate," offered to applicants on a take-it-or-leave-it
basis.'[12] The fact that such promise-breaking would not give rise to liability
even under contract law, he says, suggests the peculiarity of suggesting that it
might support liability in the criminal context.

It is important, however, not to overstate the significance of such compulsion. There is, it seems to me, a significant difference between being required
to make a promise at the point of a gun and being required to make a promise
in order to obtain a fishing license. Promises need not be spontaneous, unilateral, or unconditional in order to be morally binding. Anyone who wants to
take office as president of the United States, for example, is required by law
to make a promise to 'preserve, protect, and defend the Constitution of the
United States.'[13] The fact that such a promise is a requirement of office in no
way diminishes its moral force. Similarly, the fact that one is required to make
a promise to abide by the laws of the local jurisdiction *in order to* obtain the
privilege of fishing in its waters need not significantly diminish the force of
such promise. If the would-be fisherman is uncomfortable with the prospect of

Retributivism,' in RA Duff and Stuart P Green (eds), *Defining Crimes: Essays on the Special Part
of the Criminal Law* (Oxford: OUP, 2005) 89. The work of mine that Husak was critiquing is
Stuart P Green, 'Why It's a Crime to Tear the Tag Off a Mattress: Overcriminalization and the
Moral Content of Regulatory Offenses' (1997) 46 *Emory Law Journal* 1533. Husak's critique is
discussed further below text accompanying nn 11–14.

[8] See Green (n 7 above, at 1586 n 175) (citing numerous federal statutes and regulations of this
type).   [9] *Ibid* at 1587 n 176 (citing numerous state statutes and regulations of this type).
[10] *Ibid* at 1587–88 n 177 (citing more authority on point).
[11] See Husak (n 7 above).   [12] *Ibid* at 84.
[13] US Const Art II, section I. Cf Kent Greenawalt, 'Promise, Benefit, and Need: Ties that Bind
Us to the Law' (1984) 18 *Georgia Law Review* 727, 737 (making similar argument regarding
political officials who take oath of office).

binding himself to the terms of the required promise, he (unlike the promiser with the gun to his head) is free to withdraw from the application process.

Secondly, Husak argues that a license holder's general promise to abide by applicable rules and regulations is not sufficient to bind the promise-maker to adhere to every single picky rule and regulation contained within a given general regulatory scheme, including even ones that he is not aware of.[14] This seems to me a more substantial criticism than the first. As discussed in Chapter 9 above, when *A* promises *B* that he will do ϕ, *A* states his true intention to do ϕ. If *A* is unaware that he has undertaken to do ϕ, then it is hard to see how he could be said to have promised to do ϕ. Therefore, I should make clear that, in order to do a prima facie morally wrongful act, *A* must fail to do that which he is actually aware he has promised to do—a constraint that admittedly makes the norm against promise-breaking of even less practical significance than I believed previously.

Finally, Husak complains that my argument regarding regulatory-violations-as-promise-breaking applies only to those who actually do go to the trouble of obtaining a license or permit, and not to the 'most egregious violators—those who fish or drive without ever having bothered to apply for a license at all.'[15] I agree with Husak that this situation is 'odd.'[16] But the oddity, I submit, goes not to the suggestion that promise-breaking, when committed within such schemes, should be viewed as morally wrongful, but rather to the whole notion of regulatory schemes that incorporate promise-making in the first place. That is, if prospective fishermen are already bound (legally) to abide by the rules applicable to fishing in a given body of water, having them promise to abide by such laws might seem superfluous. Similarly, if prospective public officials are already bound (legally) to abide by the laws of their respective jurisdictions, then it is natural to ask the point of making them *promise* to abide by such rules. The answer to this conundrum is precisely that promises have significant moral force; most people feel morally bound to honor them. By having regulated parties explicitly take on the moral obligations associated with making promises, regulatory schemes assume additional moral force they otherwise would not possess. The fact that some law violators never make such promises in the first place should not be viewed as diminishing the moral wrongfulness of those law violators who do make, and then break, such promises.

3. DISOBEDIENCE

So far we have considered the possibility that 'failure to comply'-type violations of regulatory law might entail moral wrongfulness insofar as they involve cheating or promise-breaking. But of course many such violations

---

[14] Husak, n 7 above at 83–87.
[15] *Ibid* at 83.   [16] *Ibid* at 83 n 85.

will involve neither. Consider the case of the licensed driver who 'runs a red light on empty streets late at night under perfect conditions of visibility.'[17] Does it make sense to say that such an offender has done anything morally wrong?

As the discussion in Chapter 10 above illustrates, the question is a challenging one. While there is some significant circumstantial evidence to suggest that courts and prosecutors, and perhaps the man in the street, do regard lawbreaking per se as morally wrongful, it is nevertheless difficult to articulate a theory as to exactly why this should be so. Certainly there will be cases in which flagrant and repetitive noncompliance on the part of specific offenders, or which permeates an entire industry, will be harmful. But harmfulness without wrongfulness is not supposed to be enough to satisfy the retributive demands of the criminal law. In the absence of a persuasive argument that lawbreaking per se entails some independent form of moral wrongfulness, I am skeptical that its criminalization can be justified.

[17] Robert P George, 'Moralistic Liberalism and Legal Moralism' (1990) 88 *Michigan Law Review* 1415, 1428.

21

Conclusion

To those readers who have made it thus far (and I trust I am not being overly optimistic in using the plural form here), I owe some concluding thoughts.

I started with the goal of showing that, through sustained analysis of its underlying moral structure, we could clear up some of the confusion and ambiguity that pervade white-collar criminal law. What I hope to have demonstrated is that many of the puzzling fine-grained distinctions we see in the law of white-collar crime are in fact a reflection of equally fine-grained distinctions in our moral thinking. In addition, I hope to have shown that our understanding of various key concepts in *morality* can in turn be sharpened through a careful consideration of the white-collar crimes.

So should we be surprised to discover that the criminal law—that seemingly blunt instrument through which we administer society's most severe sanctions—is so thoroughly dependent on the kind of subtle moral judgments with which we contend in our everyday lives? In the case of the white-collar crimes at least, the answer is no. It is precisely because white-collar criminal law is informed by everyday moral concepts such as cheating, deceiving, coercing, and the like that its moral character can seem so ambiguous. But such ambiguity should not dissuade us from its study. The white-collar offenses constitute an increasingly important part of our criminal law. If we are to really understand that law, we have no choice but to continue exploring the complex relationship between it and morality.

Bibliography

Abelson, R and Glater, J, 'A Style that Connects with Hometown Jurors' (29 June 2005) *New York Times*, C1.

Abrams, N, 'Criminal Liability of Corporate Officers for Strict Liability Offenses— A Comment on *Dotterweich and Park*' (1981) 28 *UCLA Law Review* 463.

Abrams, N and Beale, S, *Federal Criminal Law and Its Enforcement* (St Paul, MN: West Publishing, 2000).

Adler, JE, 'Lying, Deceiving, or Falsely Implicating' (1997) 94 *Journal of Philosophy* 435.

Administrative Office of the US Courts, *Federal Judicial Workload Statistics* (Washington, DC 1993).

Alexander, L, 'Crime and Culpability' (1994) 5 *Journal of Contemporary Legal Issues* 1.

Alexander, L and Kress, K, 'Against Legal Principles', in Andrei Marmor (ed.), *Law and Interpretation* (Oxford: OUP, 1995), 279.

Alexander, L and Sherwin, E, 'Deception in Morality and Law' (2003) 22 *Law and Philosophy* 393.

Alldridge, P, 'Sex, Lies and the Criminal Law' (1993) 44 *Northern Ireland Legal Quarterly* 250.

—— 'Reforming the Criminal Law of Corruption' (2000) 11 *Criminal Law Forum* 287.

—— *Relocating Criminal Law* (Aldershot: Dartmouth, 2000)

Allen, FA, 'The Morality of Means: Three Problems in Criminal Sanctions' (1981) 42 *University of Pittsburgh Law Review* 737.

Alliance of Automobile Manufacturers, <http://www.autoalliance.org/about/> accessed 22 Aug. 2005.

Alm, J and Torgler, B, 'Culture Differences and Tax Morale in the United States and in Europe,' Center for Research in Economics, Management and the Arts (CREMA) Working Paper No. 2004-14, <http://www.crema-research.ch/papers/2004-14.pdf> accessed 22 Aug. 2005.

American Bar Association, *Standards for Criminal Justice: Prosecution Function and Defense Function* 61 (3rd edn., Washington, DC: American Bar Association, 1993).

Amsel, N, *The Jewish Encyclopedia of Moral and Ethical Issues* (Northdvale, NJ: J. Aronson Inc., 1994).

Andenaes, J, 'The General Preventive Effects of Punishment' (1996) 114 *University of Pennsylvania Law Review* 949.

Anderson, AG, 'Fraud, Fiduciaries and Insider Trading' (1982) 10 *Hofstra Law Review* 341.

Angier, N, 'The Urge to Punish Cheats: Not Just Human, But Selfless' (22 Jan. 2002) *New York Times*.

Arenella, P, 'Character, Choice and Moral Agency: The Relevance of Character to Our Moral Culpability Judgments' (1990) 7 *Social Philosophy & Policy* 59.

—— 'Convicting the Morally Blameless: Reassessing the Relationship Between Legal and Moral Accountability' (1992) 39 *UCLA Law Review* 1511.

Arlidge, AJ and Parry, J, *Arlidge & Parry on Fraud* (London: Waterlow Publishers, 1985).

Arnold, DG, 'Coercion and Moral Responsibility' (2001) 38 *American Philosophical Quarterly* 53.

Aron, L, 'Crime and Punishment for Capitalists' (30 Oct. 2003) *New York Times*, A1.

Ash, TG, *The File: A Personal History* (New York: Vintage, 1997).

Ashworth, A, *Principles of Criminal Law* (4th edn., Oxford: OUP, 2003).

—— 'Is the Criminal Law a Lost Cause?' (2000) 116 *LQR* 225.

Atiyah, P, *Promises, Morals, and the Law* (Oxford: Clarendon Press, 1981).

Austin, JL, *How to Do Things With Words* (2nd edn., Oxford: Clarendon Press, 1975) 5–6.

—— 'A Plea for Excuses' in JO Urmson and GJ Warnock (eds.), *Philosophical Papers* (Oxford: OUP, 1961) 123.

Babington, C, 'Ethics Panel Rebukes Delay' (1 Oct. 2004) *Washington Post*, A1.

Babylonian Talmud, 'Ketuvot' (Brooklyn, NY: Soncino Press, 1989) 15b.

Bainbridge, S, 'The Insider Trading Prohibition: A Legal and Economic Enigma' (1986) 38 *Florida Law Review* 35.

Baird, DG, et al., *Game Theory and the Law* (Cambridge: Harvard University Press, 1994).

Baker, Carrie, N, 'Sexual Extortion: Criminalizing Quid Pro Quo Sexual Harassment' (1994) 13 *Law and Inequality* 213.

Balkin, JM, 'Bush v. Gore and the Boundary Between Law and Politics' (2001) 110 *Yale Law Journal* 1407.

Ball, HV and Friedman, LM, 'The Use of Criminal Sanctions in the Enforcement of Economic Legislation: A Sociological Review' (1965) 17 *Stanford Law Review* 197, 206–07.

Barash, DP and Lipton, JE, *Myth of Monogamy: Fidelity and Infidelity in Animals and People* (New York: WH Freeman, 2001).

Barnard, JW, 'Allocution for Victims of Economic Crimes' (2001) 77 *Notre Dame Law Review* 39.

Baron, M, *The Moral Status of Loyalty* (Dubuque, Iowa: Kendall/Hunt Pub., 1984).

—— 'What is Wrong With Self-Deception', in Brian P McLaughlind and Amelie Oksenberg, Rorty (eds.) *Perspectives of Self-Deception* (Berkeley: University at California Press, 1988) at 431.

—— 'Loyalty' in Lawrence C Becker and Charlotte B Becker (eds.), *Encyclopedia of Ethics* (2nd edn., New York: Routledge, 1992) 751.

Barstow, D, 'U.S. Rarely Seeks Charges for Deaths in Workplace' (22 Dec. 2003) *New York Times* A1.

Bayles, MD, 'A Concept of Coercion' in J Roland Pennock and John W Chapman (eds.), *Nomos XIV: Coercion* (Chicago: Aldine/Atherton, 1972) 74.

—— 'Character, Purpose and Criminal Responsibility' (1982) 1 *Law & Philosophy* 5.

BBC News 'Timeline: Stranger than Fiction' (8 Oct. 2002) *BBC News Online* <http://news.bbc.co.uk/1/hi/uk/1420132.stm>.

Becker, LC, 'Property' in Lawrence C Becker and Charlotte B Becker (eds.), *Encyclopedia of Ethics* (New York: Routledge, 2001), vol. 3, 1389, 1390.

Bedau, HA, 'Retribution and the Theory of Punishment' (1978) 75 *Journal of Philosophy* 601.

Benson, BL, 'Enforcement of Private Property Rights in Primitive Societies: Law Without Government' (1989) 9 *Journal of Libertarian Studies* 1.

Bentham, J, *A Fragment on Government and an Introduction to the Principles of Morals and Legislation* (Oxford: Blackwell, 1960).

Berman, MN, 'The Evidentiary Theory of Blackmail: Taking Motives Seriously' (1998) 65 *University of Chicago Law Review* 795.

—— 'The Normative Functions of Coercion Claims' (2002) 8 *Legal Theory* 45.

Bibas, S and Bierschbach, RA, 'Integrating Remorse and Apology into Criminal Procedure' (2004) 114 *Yale Law Journal* 85.

Biographical Sketch of Richard Scrushy <http://www.richardmscrushy.com/bio.aspx?id=1> accessed 22 Aug. 2005.

Bishop, JP, *Commentaries on the Criminal Law* (5th edn., Boston: Little, Brown, 1872).

Black's Law Dictionary (St Paul, MN: West Publishing Co., 2004).

Blackstone, W, *Commentaries* (Philadelphia: University of Pennsylvania Press, 1996) 57.

Blatt, MM and Kohlberg, L, 'The Effects of Classroom Moral Discussion Upon Children's Level of Moral Judgment' (1975) 4 *Journal of Moral Education* 129.

Bloom, C, *Leaving the Doll's House* (New York: Little, Brown, 1996).

Blum, WJ and Kalven, Jr, H, *The Uneasy Case for Progressive Taxation* (Chicago: University of Chicago Press, 1953).

Blumstein, A, et al., *Deterrence and Incapacitation: Estimating the Effects of Criminal Sanctions on Crime Rates* (Washington, DC: National Academy of Sciences, 1978).

Bok, S, *Lying: Moral Choice in Public and Private Life* (New York: Vintage Books, 1979).

—— *Secrets: On the Ethics of Concealment and Revelation* (New York: OUP, 1984).

Bourbeau, H, 'The Redemption of Swine: Can Ken Lay Make a Comeback?' *Slate* (19 Sept. 2002) <http://slate.msn.com/id/2071203>.

Bowman, III, FO, 'Coping With "Loss": A Re-Examination of Sentencing Federal Economic Crimes Under the Guidelines' (1998) 51 *Vanderbilt Law Review* 461.

Bradley, CM, '*Now v. Scheidler*: RICO Meets the First Amendment' (1994) *Supreme Court Law Review* 129.

—— 'Foreword: Mail Fraud After *McNally* and *Carpenter*: The Essence of Fraud' (1988) 79 *Journal of Criminal Law Criminology* 573.

Brembs, B, 'Chaos, Cheating, and Cooperation: Potential Solutions to the Prisoner's Dilemma' (1996) 76 *Oikos* 14.

Brickey, KF, 'Criminal Liability of Corporate Officers for Strict Liability Offenses—Another View' (1982) 35 *Vanderbilt Law Review* 1337.

—— *Corporate Criminal Liability* (2nd edn., Deerfield, Ill.: Clark Boardman Callaghan, 1991–94).

—— *Corporate and White Collar Crime: Cases and Materials* (2nd edn., Boston: Little, Brown, 1995).

—— *Corporate and White Collar Crime: Cases and Materials* (3rd edn., New York: Aspen Publishers, 2002).

—— 'Andersen's Fall from Grace' (2003) 81 *Washington University Law Quarterly* 917, 928.

Bronaugh, R, 'Promises,' in Lawrence C Becker and Charlotte B Becker (eds.), *Encyclopedia of Ethics* (New York: Routledge, 2001), vol. 3, 1386.

Brown, DK, 'Street Crime, Corporate Crime, and the Contingency of Criminal Liability' (2001) 149 *University of Pennsylvania Law Review* 1295.

Brudner, A, 'Agency and Welfare in the Penal Law,' in Stephen Shute, et al. (eds.), *Action and Value in Criminal Law* (Oxford: Clarendon Press, 1993).

Brudney, V, 'Insiders, Outsiders, and Informational Advantages Under the Federal Securities Laws' (1979) 93 *Harvard Law Review* 322.

Bucy, PH, *White Collar Crime: Cases and Materials* (2nd edn., St Paul, Minnesota: West Publishing, 1998).

Bureau of Justice Statistics, US Department of Justice, *Dictionary of Criminal Justice Data Terminology* (2nd edn., Washington, DC, 1981).

Buss, DM, *The Evolution of Desire: Strategies of Human Mating* (New York: Basic Books, 1994).

Butler, J, 'Upon Resentment, and Forgiveness of Injuries,' in *The Works of Joseph Butler (1897 edn.)* (Bristol: Thoemmes Press, 1997).

Caldwell, RG, 'A Re-Examination of the Concept of White-Collar Crime', in Gilbert Geis (ed.), *White-Collar Criminal: The Offender in Business and the Professions* (New York: Atherton Press, 1968).

Callahan, D, *The Cheating Culture: Why More Americans Are Doing Wrong to Get Ahead* (New York: Harcourt, 2004).

Carberry, CM and Gordon, HK, 'To Prosecute or Not to Prosecute: Criminal Enforcement of Non-Fraud Provisions of the Federal Securities Laws' (1997) 4 *Business Crimes Bulletin* 1 (Feb.).

Cardwell L, 'Sure You Shot a 79, Mr. President. Of Course You Did,' (9 May 2003) *New York Times*.

Carrol, JS, *How Taxpayers Think About Their Taxes: Frames and Values*, in Joel Slemrod (ed.), *Why People Pay Taxes: Tax Compliance and Enforcement* (Ann Arbor: University of Michigan Press, 1992) 47.

Carson, TL, 'Bribery, Extortion, and "The Foreign Corrupt Practices Act" ' (1985) 14 *Philosophy & Public Affairs* 66.

Carter, B, 'Star of Fox News Program Named in Harassment Suit' (14 Oct. 2004) *New York Times*.

Catechism of the Catholic Church §2240 (Libreria Editice Vatican, Provisional Draft, 1992).

CBS News 'Martha Ink Expert Didn't Lie' (5 Oct. 2004) <http://www.cbsnews.com/stories/2004/06/16/national/main623516.shtml>.

Chapman, H, 'Both Martha and Justice Have Suffered, and Now It Will Get Even Worse' (12 March 2004) *Fort Wayne News-Sentinel*.

Chevigny, PG, 'From Betrayal to Violence: Dante's *Inferno* and the Social Construction of Crime' (2001) 26 *Law & Social Inquiry* 787.

Chisolm, RM and Feehan, TD, 'The Intent to Deceive' (1977) 74 *Journal of Philosophy* 143.

Chivers, CJ and Arvedlund, EE, 'Russian Tycoon Given 9 Years on Tax Charge' *New York Times* (1 June 2005) A1.

Clark, K, 'Do We Have Enough Ethics in Government Yet?: An Answer from Fiduciary Theory' (1996) *University of Illinois Law Review* 57.

Clarkson, CMV, 'Theft and Fair Labelling' (1993) 56 *Modern Law Review* 554.

Clinard, MB and Quinney, R, *Criminal Behavior Systems: A Typology* (2nd edn., New York: Holt, Rinehart and Winston, 1973).

CNN News, 'Former McGreevey Official Sought $50 Million, Aides Say' CNNCom (14 Aug. 2004) <http://www.cnn.com/2004/ALLPOLITICS/08/14/governor.resigns.ap/>.

CNN News, 'Stewart Convicted on All Charges' CNN-Money (5 March 2004) <http://money.cnn.com/2004/03/05/news/companies/martha_verdict>.

Coady, CAJ, 'The Idea of Violence' (1986) 3 *Journal of Applied Philosophy* 3.

Coffee, Jr, JC, 'From Tort to Crime: Some Reflections on the Criminalization of Fiduciary Breaches and the Problematic Line Between Law and Ethics' (1981) 19 *American Criminal Law Review* 117.

—— 'Does "Unlawful" Mean "Criminal"?: Reflections on the Disappearing Tort/Crime Distinction in American Law' (1991) 71 *Boston University Law Review* 193.

—— 'Modern Mail Fraud: The Restoration of the Public/Private Distinction' (1998) 35 *American Criminal Law Review* 427.

Coke, E, *The First Part of the Institutes of the Lawes of England, or, A Commentarie Upon Littleton* (originally published 1628, Garland Publ. repr. 1979).

Comment, 'Perjury: the Forgotten Offense' (1974) 65 *Journal of Criminal Law & Criminology* 361.

Conklin, JE, *Illegal But Not Criminal: Business Crime in America* (Englewood Cliffs, NJ: Prentice Hall, 1977).

Cooper, N, *The Diversity of Moral Thinking* (Oxford: Clarendon Press, 1981).

Cottingham, J, 'Varieties of Retribution' (1979) 29 *Philosophical Quarterly* 238.

Craswell, R, 'Contract Law, Default Rules, and the Philosophy of Promising' (1989) 88 *Michigan Law Review* 489.

'Criminal Law—Perjury—Sixth Circuit Sustains Perjury Conviction for Answer to Question with Mistaken Premise' (1999) 112 *Harvard Law Review* 1783.

Crosland, TWH, *The English Sonnet* (London: M Secker, 1917).

Crowe, MT, *The Moral Obligation of Paying Just Taxes* (Washington DC: Catholic University of America Studies in Sacred Theology No.84, 1944).

Cushman, Jr, JH, 'G.M. Agrees to Cadillac Recall in Federal Pollution Complaint' (1 Dec. 1995) *New York Times* A1.

D'Andrade, K 'Bribery' (1985) 4 *Journal of Business Ethics* 239.

Damaška, MR, *The Faces of Justice and State Authority: A Comparative Approach to the Legal Process* (New Haven CT: Yale University 1986).

Damon, W, *The Moral Child: Nurturing Children's Natural Moral Growth* (New York: Atlantic Monthly Press, 1988).

Dan-Cohen, M, 'Decision Rules and Conduct Rules: On Acoustic Separation in Criminal Law' (1984) 97 *Harvard Law Review* 625.

Danley, JR, 'Toward a Theory of Bribery' (Spring 1983) *Business & Professional Ethics* 19.

Darnell, SL, 'Self-Deception, Autonomy, and Moral Constitution', in Brian P McLaughlin and Amélie Oksenberg Rorty (eds.), *Perspectives on Self-Deception* (Berkeley: University of California Press, 1988).

Davies, SL, 'The Jurisprudence of Willfulness: An Evolving Theory of Excusable Ignorance' (1998) 48 *Duke Law Journal* 341.

Davis, NA, 'Contemporary Deontology', in Peter Singer (ed.), *A Companion to Ethics* (Oxford: Blackwell, 1991).

de Bracton, H, (Samuel E. Thorne, trans.), *On the Laws and Customs of England*, (Cambridge: Harvard University Press, 1968) vol. 2.

De George, RT, *Competing With Integrity in International Business* (Oxford: OUP, 1993).

DeMott, DA, 'Beyond Metaphor: An Analysis of Fiduciary Obligation' (1988) *Duke Law Journal* 879.

Dershowitz, AM, *Supreme Injustice: How the High Court Hijacked Election 2000* (Oxford: OUP, 2001).

Desphande, P, 'The Role of Women in Two Islamic Fundamentalist Countries: Afghanistan and Saudi Arabia' (2001) 22 *Women's Rights Law Reporter* 193.

Deuteronomy 16:19, 19:18–19.

Devlin, P, *The Enforcement of Morals* (Oxford: OUP, 1965).

Dick, AR, 'When Are Cartels Stable Contracts? (1996) 39 *Journal of Law & Economics* 241.

Dillof, AM, 'Unraveling Unlawful Entrapment' (2004) 94 *Journal of Criminal Law & Criminology* 827.

Dolinko, D, 'Is There a Rationale for the Privilege Against Self-Incrimination?' (1986) 33 *UCLA Law Review* 1063.

—— 'Three Mistakes of Retributivism' (1992) 39 *UCLA Law Review* 1623.

Dubber, M, 'Recidivist Statutes as Arational Punishment' (1995) 43 *Buffalo Law Review* 689.

Dubber, MD, *Victims in the War on Crime: The Use and Abuse of Victims' Rights* (New York: NYU Press, 2002).

Duff, RA, *Intention, Agency and Criminal Liability: Philosophy of Action and the Criminal Law* (Oxford: Blackwell, 1990).

—— *Criminal Attempts* (Oxford: OUP, 1996).

—— *Punishment, Communication and Community* (Oxford: OUP, 2000).

—— 'Harms and Wrongs' (2001) 5 *Buffalo Criminal Law Review* 13.

—— 'The Limits of Virtue Jurisprudence' (2003) 34 *Metaphilosophy* 214.

—— 'Criminalizing Endangerment', in RA Duff and Stuart P Green (eds.), *Defining Crimes: Essays on the Special Part of the Criminal Law* (Oxford: OUP, 2005).

—— 'Theories of Criminal Law, in Edward N Zalta (ed.), *Stanford Encyclopedia of Philosophy*, <http://plato.stanford.edu/entries/criminal-law/> accessed 22 Aug. 2005.

Duff, A and Garland, D, *A Reader on Punishment* (Oxford: OUP, 1994).

Duff, RA and Green, SP, 'Introduction: The Special Part and its Problems', in RA Duff and SP Green (eds.), *Defining Crimes* (Oxford: OUP, 2005).

Duke University, Center for Academic Integrity, <http://academicintegrity.org/samp_honor_codes.asp> accessed 23 Aug. 2005.

Dworkin, R, 'The Model of Rules I' in R Dworkin, *Takings Rights Seriously* (Cambridge, MA: Harvard University Press, 1977).

—— 'Do We Have a Right to Pornography?' in R Dworkin, *A Matter of Principle* (Cambridge, MA: Harvard University Press, 1985).

—— *Law's Empire* (Cambridge, Mass.: Harvard University Press, 1986).

—— *Taking Rights Seriously* (Cambridge, MA: Harvard University Press, 1977).

Dyer, BK, 'Economic Analysis, Insider Trading, and Game Markets' (1992) *Utah Law Review* 1.

Eads, LS, 'From Capone to Boesky: Tax Evasion, Insider Trading, and Problems of Proof' (1991) 79 *California Law Review* 1421.

Eagle, DW, Note, 'Civil Remedies for Perjury: A Proposal for a Tort Action' (1977) 19 *Arizona Law Review* 349.

Edelhertz, H, *The Nature, Impact and Prosecution of White-Collar Crime* (Washington, DC: National Institute of Law Enforcement and Criminal Justice, 1970).

Eichenwald, K, 'Enron Paid Huge Bonuses in '01; Experts See a Motive for Cheating' (1 Mar. 2002) *New York Times* A1.

—— 'Andersen Guilty of Shredding File in Enron Scandal' (16 June 2002) *New York Times* A1.

—— 'White-Collar Defense Stance: The Criminal-less Crime, *New York Times* (3 March 2002) D1.

Eichenwald, K and Walkin, DJ, 'The Double Ups and Downs of a Philanthropist' (30 May 2005) *New York Times* A1.

Eiser, JR, 'Evaluation of Choice-Dilemma Alternatives' (1976) 15 *Journal of Social Clinical Psychology* 51.

Emerging Markets Committee, International Organization of Securities Commissions, 'Insider Trading: How Jurisdictions Regulate It' (March 2003).

Epstein, R, 'Blackmail, Inc.' (1983) 50 *University of Chicago Law Review* 553.

Ewin, RE, 'Loyalty and Virtues' (1992) 42 *Philosophical Quarterly* 403.

Exodus 23:9

Falk, PJ, 'Rape by Fraud and Rape by Coercion' (1998) 64 *Brooklyn Law Review* 39.

Falk, WD, 'Morality, Self and Others' in Judith Jarvis Thomson and Gerald Dworkin (eds.), *Ethics* (New York: Harper & Row, 1968).

Fehr, E and Gachter, S, 'Altruistic Punishment in Humans' (2002) 415 *Nature* 137.

Feinberg, J, 'The Expressive Function of Criminal Punishment', in Joel Feinberg, *Doing & Deserving: Essays in the Theory of Responsibility* (Princeton: Princeton University Press, 1970).

—— 'Justice and Personal Desert', in Joel Feinberg, *Doing and Deserving: Essays in the Theory of Responsibility* (Princeton: Princeton University Press, 1970).

—— 'Noncoercive Exploitation', in Rolf Sartorius (ed.), *Paternalism* (Minneapolis: University of Minnesota Press, 1983) 208.

—— *Offense to Others* (New York: OUP, 1985).

—— *Harm to Self* 189–268 (New York: OUP, 1986).

—— *Harm to Others* (New York: OUP, 1987).

—— 'Some Unswept Debris from the Hart–Devlin Debate' (1987) 72 *Syntheses* 260.

—— *Harmless Wrongdoing* (New York: OUP, 1988).

—— 'The Right to Disobey' (1989) 87 *Michigan Law Review* 1690.

—— 'Coercion', in *Routledge Encyclopedia of Philosophy* (Edward Craig, ed.) (London: Routledge, 1998), vol. 2, at 387.

Finkelstein, C, 'Excuses and Dispositions in Criminal Law' (2002) 6 *Buffalo Criminal Law Review* 317.

—— 'Is Risk a Harm?' (2003) 151 *University of Pennsylvania Law Review* 963.

First, H, *Business Crime: Cases and Materials* (Westbury, NY: Foundation Press, 1990).

Fisse, B and Braithwaite, J, *Corporations, Crime and Accountability* (Cambridge: CUP, 1991).

Flannigan, R, 'The Fiduciary Obligation' (1989) 9 *Oxford Journal of Legal Studies* 285.

Fleming, Jr, J, 'Foreword: Comparative Negligence at Last—By Judicial Fiat' (1978) 64 *California Law Review* 239.

Fletcher, GP, 'Blackmail: The Paradigmatic Crime' (1993) 141 *University of Pennsylvania Law Review* 1617.

—— 'The Recidivist Premium' (Summer/Fall 1982) *Criminal Justice Ethics* 54, 57.

—— *Rethinking Criminal Law* (Boston: Little, Brown), 1978.

—— *Loyalty: An Essay on the Morality of Relationships* (New York: OUP, 1993).

Forster, EM, 'What I Believe' in *Two Cheers for Democracy* (London: Edward Arnold, 1951).

Frankel, T, 'Fiduciary Law' (1983) 71 *California Law Review* 795.

Frankfurt, H, 'Coercion and Moral Responsibility', in Ted Honderich (ed.), *Essays on Freedom of Action* (corrected reprint edn., London: Routledge & Kegan Paul, 1978).

Freedman, L, '3 Expelled for Doping Violations' *Chicago Tribune* (25 Feb. 2002) 5.

Freedman, MH and Smith, A, *Understanding Lawyers' Ethics* (2nd edn., Newark, NJ: LexisNexis, 2002).

Fried, C, 'The Lawyer as Friend: The Moral Foundations of the Lawyer–Client Relation' (1976) 85 *Yale Law Journal* 1060.

—— *Right and Wrong* 54–78 (Cambridge, MA: Harvard University Press, 1978).

—— *Contract as Promise: A Theory of Contractual Obligation* (Cambridge, MA: Harvard University Press, 1981).

Friedrichs, DO, 'White Collar Crime and the Definitional Quagmire: A Provisional Solution' (1992) 3 *Journal of Human Justice* 5.

—— 'Occupational Crime, Occupational Deviance, and workplace Crime: Sorting Out the Difference' (2002) 2 *Criminal Justice* 243.

—— *Trusted Criminals* (2nd edn., Belmont, CA: Wadsworth and Thomson, 2004).

Friendly, HJ, 'The Fifth Amendment Tomorrow: The Case for Constitutional Change' (1968) 37 *University of Cincinnati Law Review* 671.

Gardner, J, 'Rationality and the Rule of Law in Offences Against the Person' (1994) 53 *Cambridge Law Journal* 502.

—— 'Legal Positivism: 5½ Myths' (2001) 46 *American Journal of Jurisprudence* 199.

Gardner, J and Shute, S, 'The Wrongness of Rape,' in Jeremy Horder (ed.), *Oxford Essays in Jurisprudence* (Oxford: OUP, 2000) 193.

Garvey, SP 'Symposium: Punishment as Atonement' (1999) 46 *UCLA Law Review* 1801.

Geis, G, 'Toward a Delineation of White-Collar Offenses' (1962) 32 *Sociological Inquiry* 160.

—— 'White-Collar Crime: What Is It?', in Kip Schlegel and David Weisburd (eds.), *White-Collar Crime Reconsidered* (Boston: Northeastern University Press, 1992) 31.

George, RP, 'Moralistic Liberalism and Legal Moralism' (1990) 88 *Michigan Law Review* 1415.

—— *Making Men Moral: Civil Liberties and Public Morality* (Oxford: Clarendon Press, 1993).

Gershman, BL, 'The Perjury Trap' (1981) 129 *University of Pennsylvania Law Review* 624.

Gert, B, *Morality: A New Justification of the Moral Rules* (New York: OUP 1988).

Gibbs, JP, 'The Sociology of Law and Normative Phenomena' (1966) 31 *American Sociological Review* 315.

—— 'On Crime, Punishment, and Deterrence' (1968) 49 *Social Science Quarterly* 515.

Gillers, S, 'The Flaw in the Andersen Verdict' *New York Times* (18 June 2002) A23.

Girling, J, *Corruption, Capitalism and Democracy* (London: Routledge, 1997).

Goldsborough, JO, 'We Are a Nation Awash in a Sea of Lies' (9 June 2004) *San Diego Union-Tribune*.

Gordon, GH, *The Criminal Law of Scotland* (3rd edn. by Michael Christie ed., Edinburgh: W Green, 2001).

Gordon, RW, 'Imprudence and Partisanship: Starr's OIC and the Clinton–Lewinsky Affair' (1999) 68 *Fordham Law Review* 639.

Gorelick, JS, et al., *Destruction of Evidence* (New York: Wiley Law Publishers, 1989).

Gorr, M, 'Liberalism and the Paradox of Blackmail' (1992) 21 *Philosophy & Public Affairs* 43.

Grasmick, HG and Green, D, 'Legal Punishment, Social Disapproval and Internalization as Inhibitors of Illegal Behavior' (1980) 71 *Journal of Criminal Law & Criminology* 325.

Gray, RL, Note, 'Eliminating the (Absurd) Distinction Between Malum In Se and Malum Prohibitum Crimes' (1955) 73 *Washington University Law Quarterly* 1370.

Green, BA, 'Zealous Representation Bound: The Intersection of the Ethical Codes and the Criminal Law' (1991) *North Carolina Law Review* 687.

—— 'Criminal Regulation of Lawyers' (1998) 67 *Fordham Law Review* 327.

Green, G, *Occupational Crime* (Chicago: Nelson-Hall Publishers, 1997).

Green, MS, 'The Privilege's Last Stand: The Privilege Against Self-Incrimination and the Right to Rebel Against the State' (1999) 65 *Brooklyn Law Review* 627.

Green, SP, Note, 'Private Challenges to Prosecutorial Inaction: A Model Declaratory Statute' (1988) 97 *Yale Law Journal* 488.

—— 'The Criminal Prosecution of Local Governments' (1994) 72 *North Carolina Law Review* 1197.

—— 'Why It's a Crime to Tear the Tag Off a Mattress: Overcriminalization and the Moral Content of Regulatory Offenses' (1997) 46 *Emory Law Journal* 1533.

—— 'Castles and Carjackers: Proportionality and the Use of Deadly Force in Defense of Dwellings and Vehicles' (1999) 1999 *University of Illinois Law Review* 1.

—— 'Deceit and the Classification of Crimes: Federal Rule of Evidence 609(a)(2) and the Origins of *Crimen Falsi*' (2000) 90 *Journal Criminal Law & Criminology* 1087.

—— 'Review Essay: Broadening the Scope of Criminal Law Scholarship' (Summer/Fall 2001) *Criminal Justice Ethics* 58.

—— 'Plagiarism Norms, and the Limits of Theft Law: Some Observations on the Use of Criminal Sanctions in Enforcing Intellectual Property Rights' (2002) 54 *Hastings Law Journal* 167.

—— 'Federal Bribery Statute', in Brian K Landsberg (ed.), *Encyclopedia of Major Acts of Congress* (New York: Macmillan, 2003).

—— 'Victims' Rights and the Limits of the Criminal Law' (2003) 14 *Criminal Law Forum* 335.

—— 'Cheating' (2004) 23 *Law and Philosophy* 137.

—— 'Six Senses of Strict Liability: A Plea for Formalism', in AP Simester (ed.), *Appraising Strict Liability* (Oxford: OUP, 2005) 1.

—— 'Uncovering the Cover-Up Crimes' (2005) 42 *American Criminal Law Review* 9.

Greenawalt, K, 'Silence as Moral and Constitutional Right' (1981) 23 *William & Mary Law Review* 15.

—— 'Criminal Coercion and Freedom of Speech' (1983) 78 *Northwestern University Law Review* 1081.

—— 'Promise, Benefit, and Need: Ties that Bind Us to the Law,' (1984) 18 *Georgia Law Review* 727.

—— *Conflicts of Law and Morality* (New York: OUP, 1987).

Greenspan, P, 'The Problem with Manipulation' (2003) 40 *American Philosophical Quarterly* 155.

Greer, T, 'Note: The Hobbs Act and RICO: A Remedy for Greenmail?' (1988) 66 *Texas Law Review* 647.

Griew, E, *The Theft Acts 1968 and 1978* (London: Sweet & Maxwell, 1990).

Gross, H, *A Theory of Criminal Justice* (New York: OUP, 1979).

Gunz, S and Salterio, S, 'What If Anderson Had Shredded in Toronto or Calgary? The Potential for Criminal Liability for Canadian Public Accounting Firms' (29 Aug. 2003 version), <http://ssrn.com/abstract=465902>.

Hall, J, *Theft, Law and Society* (Indianapolis, IN: Bobbs Merrill, 1952).

—— *Principles of Criminal Law* (Indianapolis, IN: Bobbs-Merrill Co).

Hampton, J, 'Correcting Harms Versus Righting Wrongs: The Goal of Retribution' (1992) 39 *UCLA Law Review* 1659.

—— 'How You Can Be Both a Liberal and a Retributivist: Comments on *Legal Moralism and Liberalism* by Jeffrie Murphy' (1995) 37 *Arizona Law Review* 105.

Harcourt, BE, 'The Collapse of the Harm Principle' (1999) 90 *Journal of Criminal Law & Criminology* 109.

Hardin, G, 'The Tragedy of the Commons' (1968) 162 *Science* 1243.

Hare, RM, *Moral Thinking: Its Level, Method, and Point* (Oxford: OUP, 1981).

Harris, GC, 'Testimony for Sale: The Law and Ethics of Snitches and Experts' (2001) 28 *Pepperdine Law Review* 1.

Hart, Henry, 'The Aims of the Criminal Law' (1958) *Law & Contemporary Problems* 402.

Hart, HLA, 'Are There Any Natural Rights?' (1955) 64 *Philosophical Review* 175.

—— *Law, Liberty and Morality* (Oxford: OUP, 1963).

—— *The Concept of Law* (Oxford: OUP, 1994).

—— *Punishment and Responsibility* (Oxford: OUP, 1968).

Hawkins, K, *Law as a Last Resort: Prosecution Decision-Making in a Regulating Agency* (Oxford: OUP, 2001).

Hawkins, W, *A Treatise of the Pleas of the Crown* (London: J. Worrall, 1771; Ayer Company, 1972 (republished 1974)).

Hays, T, 'Rapper Lil' Kim Gets 366 Days for Perjury' *Yahoo.com* (7 July 2005) <http://news.yahoo.com/news?tmpl=story&u=/ap/20050707/ap_en_mu/lil_kim_shootout>.

Hazard, GC and Hodes, WW, *The Law of Lawyering* (3rd edn., New York: Aspen Publishers, 2001).

Healy, G (ed.), *Go Directly to Jail: the Criminalization of Almost Everything* (Washington, DC: Cato Institute, 2004).

Hearings Before the Committee on Banking, Housing and Urban Affairs, US Senate 94th Congress, Second Session, 5 April, 1976.

Heine, G, et al. (eds.) *Private Commercial Bribery: A Comparison of National and Supranational Legal Structures* (Freiburg: International Chamber of Commerce, 2003).

Hendrick, M, memo to Derick, Jr., J V, Enron General Counsel on 15 Oct. 2001, *Houston Chronicle* website, <http://www.chron.com/content/chronicle/special/01/enron/background/index.html> accessed 23 Aug. 2005.

Hennessey, LC, 'Note: No Exception for No: Rejection of the Exculpatory No Doctrine—*Brogan v United States* 118 S. Ct. 805' (1999) 89 *Journal of Criminal Law & Criminology* 905.

Henning, PJ, 'Maybe It Should Just Be Called Federal Fraud: The Changing Nature of the Mail Fraud Statute' (1995) 36 *Boston College Law Review* 435.

Henwood, D, 'Free Martha!' (9 Feb. 2004) *The Nation* <http://www.thenation.com/doc.mhtml?i=20040209&s=henwood>.

Hill, DE, Note, 'Anticipatory Obstruction of Justice: Pre-emptive Document Destruction Under the Sarbanes-Oxley Anti-Shredding Statute, 18 USC §1519' (2004) 89 *Cornell Law Review* 1519.

Hill, Jr., T, 'Autonomy and Benevolent Lies' in *Autonomy and Self-Respect* (Cambridge: CUP, 1991) 41.

Hobbes, T, (Edwin Curley, ed.), *Leviathan: With Selected Variants from the Latin Edition of 1668* (Indianapolis, IN: Hackett Publishing, 1994).

Holmes, OW, 'The Path of the Law' (1897) 10 *Harvard Law Review* 457.

Holmes, S and Sunstein, C, *The Cost of Rights: Why Liberty Depends on Taxes* (New York: WW Norton and Co., 1999).

Honoré, AM, 'Ownership,' in Anthony G Guest (ed.), *Oxford Essays in Jurisprudence* (Oxford: Clarendon Press, 1961) 107.

Hosseini, K, *The Kite Runner* (New York: Riverhead Books, 2003).

'House Ethics Battle Rages on', National Public Radio, *Morning Edition* (13 April 2005) <http://www.npr.org/templates/story/story.php?storyId=4598160>.

Hudson, WD (ed.), *The Is-Ought Question: A Collection of Papers on the Central Problems of Moral Philosophy* (New York: St Martins Press, 1969).

Huigens, Kyron, 'Virtue and Inculpation' (1995) *Harvard Law Review* 1423.

Hulse, C, 'Compromise in the Senate: Bipartisan Group in Senate Averts Judge Showdown,' (24 May 2005) *New York Times* A1.

Humbach, JA, 'Just Being a Lawyer' (2001) 4 *Legal Ethics* 155.

Hume, D (LA Selby-Bigge ed.), *A Treatise of Human Nature* (Oxford: OUP, 1978).

—— 'Of the Original Contract,' in *Essays: Moral Political and Literary* (Indianapolis, IN: Liberty Classics edn., 1985) 465.

Humphries, J, 'The Logic of Assertion and Pragmatic Inconsistency' (1973) 3 *Canadian Journal of Philosophy* 177.

Husak, D, 'The Criminal Law as Last Resort' (2004) 24 *Oxford Journal of Legal Studies* 207.

—— 'Does Criminal Liability Require an Act?', in RA Duff (ed.), *Philosophy and the Criminal Law: Principle and Critique* (Cambridge: CUP, 1998).

—— 'Malum Prohibitum and Retributivism' in RA Duff and Stuart P Green (eds.) *Defining Crimes: Essays on the Special Part of the Criminal Law* (Oxford: OUP, 2005).

Hyde, A, 'The Concept of Legitimation in the Sociology of Law' (1983) 1983 *Wisconsin Law Review* 379.

Israel, JH, et al., *White Collar Crime: Law and Practice* (2nd edn., St. Paul., Minn.: West Publishing, 2003).

Ivanovich, D, 'The Fall of Enron; Bankers Believed Deals Hinged on Investments', (20 Feb. 2002) *Houston Chronicle* A9.

Jacob, BA and Levitt, SD, 'Catching Cheating Teachers: The Results of an Experiment in Implementing Theory,' in William G. Gale and Janet Rothenberg Pack (eds.), *Brookings–Wharton Papers on Urban Affairs 2003* (New York: Brookings Institution Press, 2003).

James, Jr, F, 'Foreword: Comparative *Negligence* at Last—By Judicial Fiat' (1976) 64 *California Law Review* 239.

Jareborg, N, 'Criminalization as a Last Resort (*Ultima Ratio*)' (2005) 2 *Ohio State Journal of Criminal Law* 521.

Johnson, C, 'Payday Loans: Shrewd Business or Predatory Lending' (2002) 87 *Minnesota Law Review* 1.

Johnston, DC, 'Spending It: Where the I.R.S. Aims the Prosecution Ax' *New York Times* (14 April 1996).

Kadish, SH, 'The Crisis of Overcriminalization' (1957) 374 *Annals of American Academy Political & Social Science* 157.

—— 'Some Observations on the Use of Criminal Sanctions in Enforcing Economic Regulations' (1963) 30 *University of Chicago Law Review* 423.

—— 'Complicity, Cause and Blame: A Study in the Interpretation of Doctrine' (1985) 73 *California Law Review* 323.

Kahan, DM, 'Ignorance of the Law is an Excuse—But Only for the Virtuous' (1997) 96 *Michigan Law Review* 127.

—— 'The Secret Ambition of Deterrence' (1999) 113 *Harvard Law Review* 413.

—— 'Gentle Nudges vs. Hard Shoves: Solving the Sticky Norms Problem' (2000) 67 *University of Chicago Law Review* 607.

Kahan, DM and Posner, EA, 'Shaming White-Collar Criminals: A Proposal for Reform of the Federal Sentencing Guidelines' (1999) 42 *Journal of Law & Economics* 365.

Kant, I (Louis Infield, trans.) *Lectures on Ethics* (Indianapolis: Hackett, 1963) 226.

—— 'On the Supposed Right to Lie from Altruistic Motives' in Peter Singer (ed.), *Ethics* (New York: OUP, 1996).

Katz, L, 'Blackmail and Other Forms of Arm-Twisting' (1993) 141 *University of Pennsylvania Law Review* 1567.

—— *Ill-Gotten Gains: Evasion, Blackmail, Fraud, and Kindred Puzzles of the Law* (Chicago: University of Chicago Press, 1996).

Kelman, M, 'Strict Liability: An Unorthodox View', in Sanford Kadish (ed.), *Encyclopedia of Crime and Justice* (New York: Macmillan, 1983) 1512.

King, Jr, ML, *Why We Can't Wait* (New York: Harper & Row, 1963).

Klock, M, 'Mainstream Economics and the Case for Prohibiting Inside Trading' (1994) 10 *Georgia State University Law Review* 297.

Koesel, MM, et al., *Spoliation of Evidence: Sanctions and Remedies for Destruction of Evidence in Civil Litigation* (Chicago: Tort and Insurance Practice Section, American Bar Association, 2000).

Kohlberg, L (Thomas Likona, ed.), *Moral Development and Behavior; Moral Stages and Moralization* (New York: Holt, Rinehart and Winston, 1976).

Kook, AI (Alter B Metzger, trans.), *Philosophy of Repentance* (New York: Yeshiva University Press, 1968).

Korsgaard, CM, 'The Right to Lie: Kant on Dealing with Evil,' (Fall 1986) 15 *Philosophy & Public Affairs* 325.

Korsgaard, C, *Creating the Kingdom of Ends* (New York: CUP, 1996).

Kupfer, J, 'The Moral Presumption Against Lying' (1982) 36 *Review of Metaphysics* 103.

Kurtz, H, 'O'Reilly, Producer Settle Harassment Suit: Fox Host Agrees to Drop Extortion Claim', *Washington Post* (29 Oct. 2004) C1.

Lacey, N, Normative Reconstruction in Socio-Legal Theory' (1996) 5 *Social & Legal Studies* 131.

Ladd, John, 'Loyalty,' in Paul Edwards (ed.) *Encyclopedia of Philosophy* (London: Routledge & Kegan Paul, 1967, reprint edn. 1972) 9.

LaFave, WR, and Scott, Jr, AW, *Criminal Law* (2nd edn., Minneapolis: West Publishing, 1986).

LaFave, WR, *Criminal Law* (4th edn., St Paul, Minn.: Thomson/West, 2003).

Lakoff, G, *Women, Fire, and Dangerous Things* (Chicago: University of Chicago Press, 1987).

Lamond, G, 'Coercion, Threats, and the Puzzle of Blackmail,' in AP Simester and ATH Smith (eds.), *Harm and Culpability* (Oxford: OUP, 1996) 216.

Landsman, S, 'Death of an Accountant: The Jury Convicts Arthur Andersen of Obstruction of Justice' (2003) 78 *Chicago-Kent Law Review* 1203.

Langevoort, DC, 'Half-Truths: Protecting Mistaken Inferences by Investors and Others' (1999) 52 *Stanford Law Review* 87.

Lanham, D, 'Bribery and Corruption' in Peter Smith (ed.) *Criminal Law: Essays in Honor of J C Smith* (London: Butterworths, 1987).

Law Commission for England and Wales, *Report No. 96, Offences Relating to Interference with the Course of Justice* (HMSO, 1979).

—— *Consultation Paper No. 145: Legislating the Criminal Code: Corruption* (HMSO, 1997).

—— *Report No. 248, Legislating the Criminal Code: Corruption* (HMSO, 1998).

Law Review Commission, State of New York, 'A Study of Perjury' (1935) *Legislative Document* 60.

Lee, IB, 'Fairness and Insider Trading' (2002) *Columbia Business Law Review* 119.

Lehman, GE, '*Force Majeure* Price Gouging: Application of Florida's Deceptive and Unfair Trade Practices in the Aftermath of Hurricane Andrew' (1993) 17 *Nova Law Review* 1029.

Levenson, LL, 'Good Faith Defenses: Reshaping Strict Liability Crimes' (1993) 78 *Cornell Law Review* 401.

Leviticus 19:18

Liebert, RM, 'What Develops in Moral Development?' in William M Kurtines and Jacob L Gewirtz (eds.), *Morality, Moral Behavior, and Moral Development* (New York: Wiley, 1974).

Lindgren, J, 'Unraveling the Paradox of Blackmail' (1984) 84 *Columbia Law Review* 670.

—— 'The Theory, History, and Practice of the Bribery–Extortion Distinction (1993) 146 *University of Pennsylvania Law Review* 1695.

Litman, H, 'Pretextual Prosecutions' (2004) 92 *Georgetown Law Journal* 1135.

Locke, J, (Thomas P Peardon ed.) *The Second Treatise on Government* (Indianapolis, IN: Bobbs Merrill, 1952; orig. publ. 1690).

Logan, WA, 'Criminal Law Sanctuaries' (2003) 38 *Harvard Civil Rights-Civil Liberties Law Review* 321.

Longstreth, A, 'Mississippi Maelstrom,' (Aug. 2004) *American Lawyer*.

Loss, L, *Fundamentals of Securities Regulation* (New York: Aspen Law and Business, 1988).

Lowenstein, DH, 'Political Bribery and the Intermediate Theory of Politics' (1985) 32 *UCLA Law Review* 784.

—— 'When is a Campaign Contribution a Bribe?,' in William C Heffernan and John Kleinig (eds.) *Private and Public Corruption* (Lanham, MD: Rowman and Littlefield, 2004).

Luban, D, *Lawyers and Justice: An Ethical Study* (Princeton: Princeton University Press, 1988).

Lucas, WR, et al., 'Common Sense, Flexibility, and Enforcement of the Federal Securities Laws' (1996) 51 *Business Law Review* 1221.

Luke 15

Lynch, GE, 'The Lawyer as Informer' (1986) 1986 *Duke Law Journal* 491.

MacCormick, N, 'Voluntary Obligations and Normative Powers' (1972) 46 *Proceedings of the Aristotelian Society* 59.

—— 'What is Wrong with Deceit' (1982) *Sydney Law Review* 5.

—— *Legal Reasoning and Legal Theory* (Oxford: OUP, 1995).

MacIntyre, A, 'Truthfulness, Lies, and Moral Philosophers: What We Can Learn from Mill and Kant?' in GB Petersen (ed.), *The Tanner Lectures* (Salt Lake City, UT: University of Utah Press, 1995) vol 16.

Mackie, JL, 'Obligations to Obey the Law' (1981) 67 *Virginia Law Review* 143.

Maguire, K and Pastore AL, (eds.), *Sourcebook of Criminal Justice Statistics 2002* (Bureau of Justice Statistics: US Department of Justice, 2003).

Mann, K, et al., 'Sentencing the White-Collar Offender' (1980) 19 *American Criminal Law Review* 479.

Mann, K, *Defending White-Collar Crime: A Portrait of Attorneys at Work* (New Haven: Yale University Press, 1985).

Manne, HG, *Insider Trading and the Stock Market* (New York: Free Press, 1966).

Mannison, DS, 'Lying and Lies' (1969) 47 *Australasian Journal of Philosophy* 132.

Marmor, A, (ed.), *Law and Interpretation* (Oxford: OUP, 1995).

Marshall, SE and Duff, RA, 'Criminalization and Sharing Wrongs' (1998) *Canadian Journal Law & Jurisprudence* 7.

Martin, MW, *Self-Deception and Morality* (Laurence, Kansas: University Press of Kansas, 1986).

Martinez, LP, 'Taxes, Morals, and Legitimacy' (1994) *Brigham Young University Law Review* 521.

Maynard, J, *At Home in the World* (New York: Picador, 1998).

McAdams, RH, 'Group Norms, Gossip, and Blackmail' (1996) 144 *University of Pennsylvania Law Review* 2237.

McCabe, D, 'Cheating: Why Students Do It and How We Can Help Them Stop' (Winter 2001) *American Educator* 38.

McCorkle, CR, 'Annotation: Statement of Belief or Opinion as Perjury' 66 *American Law Reports* 2d 791.

McFadden, RD, *Outrage: The Story Behind the Tawana Brawley Hoax* (New York: Bantam Books, 1990).

McGee, RW, 'Is Tax Evasion Unethical?' (1994) 42 *University of Kansas Law Review* 411.

McLoughlin, M (ed.), *The Impeachment of Trial of President Clinton: The Official Transcripts, From the House Judiciary Committee Hearings to the Senate Trial* (New York: Random House, 1999).

Meier, RF and Johnson, WT, 'Deterrence as Social Control: The Legal and Extralegal Production of Conformity' (1977) 42 *American Sociological Review* 292.

Merritt, DJ and Cihon, J, 'New Course Offerings in the Upper-Level Curriculum: Report of an AALS Survey' (1997) 47 *Journal of Legal Education* 524.

Milich, PS, 'Re-Examining Hearsay Under the Federal Rules: Some Method for the Madness' (1991) 39 *University of Kansas Law Review* 893.

Mill, JS, *On Liberty* (London, 1859).

Model Criminal Code Officers Committee, 'Report on Administration of Justice Offences' (July 1998).

Moohr, GS, 'Mail Fraud Meets Criminal Theory' (1998) 67 *University of Cincinnati Law Review* 1.

—— 'The Crime of Copyright Infringement: An Inquiry Based on Morality, Harm, and Criminal Theory' (2003) 83 *Boston University Law Review* 731.

—— 'Defining Overcriminalization Through Cost–Benefit Analysis: The Example of Criminal Copyright Laws' (2005) *American University Law Review* 783.

Moore, M, *Act and Crime* (Oxford: OUP, 1993).

—— *Placing Blame: A General Theory of the Criminal Law* (Oxford: Clarendon Press, 1998).

—— 'Causation and the Excuses' (1985) 73 *California Law Review* 1091.

—— 'The Independent Moral Significance of Wrongdoing' (1994) 5 *Journal of Contemporary Legal Issues* 237.

Morris, H, 'Persons and Punishment' (1968) 52 *The Monist* 475.

Murphy, JG, 'Blackmail: A Preliminary Inquiry' (1980) 63 *The Monist* 156.

—— 'Retributivism, Moral Education, and the Liberal Estate' (Winter/Spring 1985) *Criminal Justice Ethics* 3.

Murphy, JG and Coleman, JL, *The Philosophy of Law* (Colorado: Westview Press, 1990).

Murphy, JG and Hampton J, *Forgiveness and Mercy* (New York: CUP, 1988).

Murphy, L and Nagel T, *The Myth of Ownership: Taxes and Justice* (New York: OUP, 2002).

Myrdal, G, 'Corruption as a Hindrance to Modernization in South Asia' in Arnold J Heidenheimer, et al. (eds.), *Political Corruption: A Handbook* (New Brunswick, NJ: Transaction Pub. 1989) 405.

Nagel, I and Hagan, J, 'The Sentencing of White-Collar Criminals in Federal Courts: A Sociological Exploration of Disparity' (1982) 80 *Michigan Law Review* 1427.

Nagel, T, *The Possibility of Altruism* (New Jersey: Princeton University Press, 1979).

Natapoff, A, 'Snitching: The Institutional and Communal Consequences' (2004) 73 *University of Cincinnati Law Review* 645.

National Public Radio, 'House Ethics Battle Rages On,' *Morning Edition* (13 April 2005) <http://www.npr.org/templates/story/story.php?storyId=4598160>.

'National Public Survey on White Collar Crime' (2000) available at <http://www.nw3c.org/research_topics.html>, accessed 22 August 2005.

Newman, A, 'Case Turns on Whether Usual Politics is a Felony' (10 Nov. 2003) *New York Times*.

Nightingale, BL, *The Law of Fraud and Related Offences* (Toronto: Carswell Publishing, 1996).

Nisbett, RE and Wilson, TD, 'Telling More Than We Can Know: Verbal Reports on Mental Processes' (1977) 84 *Psychological Review* 23.

Noah, T, 'Nick Smith Recants: Did the Pressure Get to Him?' *Slate* (Dec 5, 2003) <http://slate.msn.com/id/2092054/>.

Noonan, Jr, JT, *Bribes* (Berkeley: University of California Press, 1984).

Note, 'Selective Incapacitation: Reducing Crime Through Predictions of Recidivism' (1982) 96 *Harvard Law Review* 511.

Note, 'Whatever Happened to Durland?: Mail Fraud, RICO, and Justifiable Reliance' (1992) 68 *Notre Dame Law Review* 333.

Novak, R, 'GOP Pulled No Punches in Struggle for Medicare Bill' (27 Nov. 2003) *Chicago Sun-Times*.

Nozick, R, 'Coercion', in *Socratic Puzzles* (Cambridge, Massachusetts: Harvard University Press, 1997).

Oesterle, DA, 'A Private Litigant's Remedies for an Opponent's Inappropriate Destruction of Relevant Documents' (1983) 61 *Texas Law Review* 1185.

—— 'Early Observations on the Prosecutions of the Business Scandals of 2002–03: On Sideshow Prosecutions, Spitzer's Clash With Donaldson Over Turf, the Choice of Civil or Criminal Actions, and the Tough Tactic of Coerced Cooperation' (2004) 1 *Ohio State Journal of Criminal Law* 443.

Official Baseball Rules, available at <http://mlb.mlb.com/NASApp/mlb/mlb/official_info/official_rules/pitcher_8.jsp> accessed 22 Aug. 2005.

O'Hear, MM, 'Remorse, Cooperation, and Acceptance of Responsibility: The Structure, Implementation, and Reform of Section 3E1.1.of the Federal Sentencing Guidelines' (1997) 91 *Northwestern University Law Review* 1507.

Oldenquist, A, 'Loyalties' (1982) 79 *Journal of Philosophy* 173.

Orfield, Jr, MW, 'Deterrence, Perjury, and the Heater Factor: An Exclusionary Rule in the Chicago Criminal Courts' (1992) 63 *Colorado Law Review* 75.

Orland, L, *Corporate and White Collar Crime: An Anthology* (Cincinnati, Ohio: Anderson Publishing, 1995).

O'Sullivan, JR, *Federal White Collar Crime: Cases and Materials* (2nd edn., St Paul, MN: West Publishing, 2003).

Ozinga, JR, *Altruism* (Westport CT: Prager Publishers, 1999).

Packer, H, *The Limits of the Criminal Sanction* (Stanford, CA: Stanford University Press, 1968)

Pascal, B, (AJ Krailshaimer trans.) *The Provincial Letters* (Baltimore: Penguin Books, 1967).

Patel, P, 'Observers Call Former Dynegy Vice President's Sentence in Loan Case "Overkill"' (26 March 2004) *Houston Chronicle*.

Paternoster, R, et al., 'Perceived Risk and Social Control: Do Sanctions Really Deter?' 17 *Law and Society Review* 457 (1984).

Pearce, AR, 'Theft by False Promise' (1953) 101 *University of Pennsylvania Law Review* 967.

Peisach, E and Hardeman, M, 'Moral Reasoning in Early Childhood: Lying and Stealing' (1983) 142 *Journal of Genetic Psychology* 107.

Pennock, R and Chapman, JW (eds.), *Political and Legal Obligation: Nomos XII* (New York: Atherton Press, 1970).

'Perjury: The Forgotten Offense' (1974) 65 *Journal of Criminal Law & Criminology* 361.

Perkins, RM, 'Criminal Liability without Fault: A Disquieting Trend' (1983) 68 *Iowa Law Review* 1067.

Perkins, RM and Boyce, RN, *Criminal Law* (Mineola, N.Y.: Foundation Press, 1969).

Perovich, JD, 'Annotation: Incomplete, Misleading, or Unresponsive but Literally True Statement as Perjury' (1976) 69 *American Law Report* 3d 993.

Peters, GM, 'The Use of Lies in Negotiation' (1987) 48 *Ohio State Law Journal* 1.

Pettit, P, 'Consequentialism,' in Peter Singer (ed.), *A Companion to Ethics* (Oxford: Blackwell Publishers, 1991).

Philips, M, 'Bribery' (1984) 94 *Ethics* 621.

Piaget, J, *The Moral Judgment of the Child* (New York: Free Press Paperbacks, 1965).

Pilcher, SL, 'Ignorance, Discretion and the Fairness of Notice: Confronting "Apparent Innocence" in the Criminal Law' (1995) 33 *American Criminal Law Review* 1.

Pillsbury, SH, 'Emotional Justice: Moralizing the Passions of Criminal Punishment' (1989) 74 *Cornell Law Review* 655.

Piskora, B, 'The Art of the Steal; Dumped Tyco Chief Kozlowski Indicted,' (5 June 2002) *New York Post* 35.

Plato, 'Crito,' in Edith Hamilton and Huntington Cairns (eds.) and Hugh Tredennick (trans.) *The Collected Dialogues* (Princeton: Princeton University Press, 1961).

Podgor, ES, 'Criminal Fraud' (1999) 48 *American University Law Review* 729.

Podgor, ES and Israel, JH, *White Collar Crime in a Nutshell* (2nd edn., St Paul, MN: West Publishing, 1997).

Pomfret, SD, 'Note: A Tempered "Yes" to the "Exculpatory No" ' (1997) 96 *Michigan Law Review* 754.

Pooley, JHA, et al., 'Understanding the Economic Espionage Act of 1996' (1997) 5 *Texas Intellectual Property Law Journal* 177.

Posner, EA, 'Law and Social Norms: The Case of Tax Compliance' (2002) 86 *Virginia Law Review* 1781.

Posner, RA, *Economic Analysis of Law* (2nd edn., Boston: Little, Brown, 1977).

——— *Economic Analysis of Law* (6th edn, New York: Aspen Publishing, 2002).

Posner, RA, and Silbaugh, K B, *A Guide to America's Sex Laws* (Chicago: University of Chicago Press, 1996).

Postema, GJ, *Bentham and the Common Law Tradition* (New York: OUP, 1986).

Pritchard, MS, 'Bribery: The Concept' (1998) 4 *Science & Engineering Ethics* 281.

Proceedings of the Academic Workshop, *Definitional Dilemma: Can and Should There Be a Universal Definition of White Collar Crime?* (Richmond, Virginia: National White Collar Crime Center, 1996).

Prosser, WL, 'Comparative Negligence' (1953) 51 *Michigan Law Review* 465.

Puka, B, (ed.), *Fundamental Research in Moral Development* (New York: Garland, 1994).

Quinn, MS, 'Practice-Defining Rules' (1975) 86 *Ethics* 76.

Rakoff, JS, 'The Federal Mail Fraud Statute (Part I)' (1980) 18 *Duquesne Law Review* 771.

Ramasastry, A, 'Assessing Anti-Price-Gouging Statutes in the Wake of Hurricane Katrina: Why They're Necessary in Emergencies, But Need to be Rewritten,' *FindLaw. com* <http://writ.news.findlaw.com/ramasastry/20050916.html> (16 Sept. 2005).

Rawls, J, 'Two Concepts of Rules' (1955) 64 *Philosophical Review* 3.

—— 'Obligations and the Duty of Fair Play,' in Sidney Hook (ed.), *Law and Philosophy* (New York: NYU Press, 1964).

—— *A Theory of Justice* (Cambridge, MA: Belknap Press of Harvard University Press, 1971).

Ray, DE, *Labor-Management Relations: Strikes, Lockouts and Boycotts* (Deefield, IL.: Clark Boardman Callagahan, 1992).

Raz, J, 'Promises and Obligations' in PMS Hacker and Joseph Raz (eds.), *Law, Morality, and Society* (Oxford: Clarendon Press, 1977).

—— *The Authority of Law: Essays on Law and Morality* (Oxford: OUP, 1979).

—— 'The Obligation to Obey: Revision and Tradition' (1984) 1 *Journal of Ethics & Public Policy* 139.

—— *The Morality of Freedom* (London: OUP, 1988).

Recent Case, 'Criminal Law—Perjury—Sixth Circuit Sustains Perjury Conviction for Answer to Question with Mistaken Premise' (1999) 112 *Harvard Law Review* 1783.

Referral to the United States House of Representatives Submitted by the Office of Independent Counsel, HR Doc. No. 105–310 (1998).

Regan, Donald, 'Law's Halo' (Autumn 1986) *Social Philosophy & Policy* 15.

Report of the Grand Jury Concerning the Tawana Brawley Investigation, *Court TV.com* <www.courttv.com/legaldocs/newsmakers/tawana/part1.html>.

Richman, DC, 'Obstruction of Justice', in Joshua Dressler (ed.), *Encyclopedia of Crime & Justice* (New York: Macmillan Reference, 2002) vol 3, 1032.

Richman, D and Stuntz, WJ, 'Al Capone's Revenge: An Essay on the Political Economy of Pretextual Prosecution' (2005) 105 *Columbia Law Review* 583.

Robinson, P, 'Rules of Conduct and Principles of Adjudication' (1990) 57 *University of Chicago Law Review* 729.

—— *Criminal Law* (New York: Aspen Publishers, 1997).

Robinson, PH and Darley, JM, *Justice, Liability and Blame* (Boulder, CO: Westview Press, 1995).

—— 'The Utility of Desert' (1997) 91 *Northwestern University Law Review* 453.

Rose-Ackerman, S, *Corruption and Government: Causes, Consequences, and Reform* (Cambridge: CUP, 1999) 93.

Rosenberg, IM and Rosenberg, YL, 'In the Beginning: The Talmudic Rule Against Self-Incrimination' (1988) 63 *New York University Law Review* 955.

Ross, WD, *The Right and the Good* (Oxford: Clarendon Press, 1930).

Rotunda, RD, 'Conflicts Problems When Representing Members of Corporate Families' (1997) 72 *Notre Dame Law Review* 655.

Royce, J, *The Philosophy of Loyalty* (Nashville, TN: Vanderbuilt University Press, 1995).

'Russian Tycoon Jailed for Nine Years,' *The Guardian Online* (May 31 2005) <http://www.guardian.co.uk/print/0,3858,5205164-103610,00.html>.

Sachs, MV, 'Harmonizing Civil and Criminal Enforcement of Federal Regulatory Statutes: The Case of the Securities Exchange Act of 1934' (2001) *University of Illinois Law Review* 1025.

Saletan, W, et al., 'The Worst of Al Sharpton: A Troubling Tale From His Past. Is it True?' *Slate* (8 Sept. 2003) <http://slate.mse.com/id087557/>.

Sanchirico, C, 'Evidence Tampering' (2004) 53 *Duke Law Journal* 1215.

Sandel, MJ, *Liberalism and the Limits of Justice* (2nd edn., Cambridge: CUP, 1999).

Sayre, F, 'Public Welfare Offenses' (1933) 33 *Columbia Law Review* 55.

Scalise, Jr, RJ, Note, 'Blackmail, Legality, and Liberalism' (2000) 74 *Tulane Law Review* 1483.

Scanlon, TM, *What We Owe Each Other* (Cambridge, MA: Harvard University Press, 1998).

Schauer, F, *Playing by the Rules* (Oxford: OUP, 1991).

Scheffer, S, *The Rejection of Consequentialism: A Philosophical Investigation of the Considerations Underlying Rival Moral Conceptions* (Oxford: OUP, 1994).

Schemo, DJ, 'University of Virginia Hit by Scandal Over Cheating' (10 May 2001) *New York Times*.

Scheppele, KL, 'It's Just Not Right: The Ethics of Insider Trading' (1993) 56 *Law & Contemporary Problems* 123.

Schlegel, K, 'Recalling Status, Power and Respectibility [sic] in the Study of White-Collar Crime,' in Proceedings of the Academic Workshop, *Definitional Dilemma: Can and Should There Be a Universal Definition of White Collar Crime?* (Richmond, Virginia: National White Collar Crime Center, 1996) 98.

Schmidt, Jr, BC, 'Principle and Prejudice: The Supreme Court and Race in the Progressive Era. Part The Peonage Cases' (1982) 82 *Columbia Law Review* 646.

Schonsheck, J, *On Criminalization: An Essay in the Philosophy of Criminal Law* (Dordrecht: Kluwer Academic Publishers, 1994).

Schulhofer, SJ, 'Harm and Punishment: A Critique of Emphasis on the Results of Conduct in the Criminal Law' (1974) 122 *University of Pennsylvania Law Review* 1497.

Schur, EM and Bedau, HA, *Victimless Crimes: Two Sides of a Controversy* (Englewood Cliffs, NJ: Prentice Hall, 1974).

Schwartz, GT, 'Contributory and Comparative Negligence: A Reappraisal' (1978) 86 *Yale Law Journal* 697.

Searle, J, *Speech Acts* (Cambridge: CUP, 1969).

'SEC Charges Jeffrey K. Skilling, Enron's Former President, Chief Executive Officer and Chief Operating Officer, With Fraud,' (19 Feb. 2004) <http://www.sec.gov/news/press/2004-18.htm>.

Shachar, Y, 'The Fortuitous Gap in Law and Morality' (Summer/Fall 1987) *Criminal Justice Ethics* 16.

Shapiro, SP, 'The New Moral Entrepreneurs: Corporate Crime Crusaders' (1983) 12 *Contemporary Sociology* 304.

—— 'Collaring the Crime, Not the Criminal: Reconsidering the Concept of White-Collar Crime' (1990) 55 *American Sociological Review* 346.

Shiffrin, SM and Triest, RK, 'Can Brute Deterrence Backfire? Perceptions and Attitudes in Taxpayer Compliance,' in *Why People Pay Taxes: Tax Compliance and Enforcement* (Ann Arbor: University of Michigan Press, 1992).

Shklar, J, *Ordinary Vices* (Cambridge, MA: Harvard/Belknap, 1984).

Shuger, D, 'Sins of the Tongue' *Slate* (14 Sept. 1999) <http://slate.msn.com/Features/tongue/tongue.asp>.

Shute, S and Horder, J, 'Thieving and Deceiving: What is the Difference?' (1993) 56 *Modern Law Review* 548.

Silberman, M, 'Toward a Theory of Criminal Deterrence' (1976) 41 *American Sociological Review* 44.

Silver, C, 'We're Scared to Death': Class Certification and Blackmail' (2003) 78 *NYU Law Review* 1357.

Simester, AP and Smith, ATH, 'Criminalization and the Role of Theory,' AP Simester and ATH Smith (eds.), *Harm and Culpability* (Oxford: OUP, 1996).

Simester, AP and Sullivan, GR, 'On the Nature and Rationale of Property Offences', in RA Duff and Stuart P Green (eds.), *Defining Crimes: Essays on the Special Part of the Criminal Law* (Oxford: OUP, 2005) 168.

Simester, AP and von Hirsch, A, 'Rethinking the Offense Principle' (2002) 8 *Legal Theory* 269.

Simmons, AJ, *Moral Principles and Political Obligations* (Princeton, NJ: Princeton University Press, 1979).

—— 'Consent, Free Choice, and Democratic Government' (1984) 18 *Georgia Law Review* 791.

—— 'Fairness', in Lawrence C Becker and Charlotte B Becker (eds.), *Encyclopedia of Ethics* (New York: Routledge, 1992) vol 1, 355.

Simon, D, *Elite Deviance* (7th edn., Boston, MA: Allyn and Bacon, 2002).

Simon, WH, 'Virtuous Lying: A Critique of Quasi-Categorical Moralism' (1999) 12 *Georgetown Journal of Legal Ethics* 433.

Simons, MA, 'Prosecutorial Discretion and Prosecutorial Guidelines: A Case Study in Controlling Federalization' (2000) 75 *NYU Law Review* 893.

—— 'Retribution for Rats: Cooperation, Punishment, and Atonement' (2003) 56 *Vanderbilt Law Review* 1.

Simpsons, The: Lisa's Substitute (Fox television broadcast, 25 April 1991).

Sklansky, DA, 'Starr, Singleton, and the Prosecutor's Role' (1999) 26 *Fordham Urban Law Journal* 509.

Slater, W and Slover, P, 'Race Heating Up in the Homestretch: Bush Camp Tries to Stem DUI Fallout, Denies Misleading Answers on Arrest' (4 Nov. 2000) *Dallas Morning News* A1.

Slobogin, C, 'Deceit, Pretext, and Trickery: Investigative Lies by the Police' (1997) 76 *Oregon Law Review* 775.

Smith, G, 'The Critical Resource Theory of Fiduciary Duty' (2002) 55 *Vanderbilt Law Review* 1399.

Smith, JC, *The Law of Theft* (5th edn., London: Butterworths, 1984).

Smith, JC and Hogan, B, *Criminal Law* (6th edn., London: Butterworths, 1988).

Smith, KW, *Reciprocity and Fairness: Positive Incentives for Tax Compliance* (Chicago: American Bar Foundation, 1991).

Smith, MBE, 'Is There a Prima Facie Obligation to Obey the Law?' (1973) 82 *Yale Law Journal* 950.

—— 'The Duty to Obey,' in Dennis Patterson (ed.), *A Companion to Philosophy of Law and Legal Theory* (Oxford: Blackwell Publishers, 1999).

—— 'Do Appellate Courts Regularly Cheat?' (Summer/Fall 1997) 16 *Criminal Justice Ethics* 2.

—— 'May Judges Ever Nullify the Law?' (1999) 74 *Notre Dame Law Review* 1657.

Solan, LM, 'Statutory Inflation and Institutional Choice' (2003) 44 *William & Mary Law Review* 2209.

Solum, L and Marzen, S, 'Truth and Uncertainty: Legal Control of the Destruction of Evidence' (1987) 36 *Emory Law Journal* 1085.

Soothill, K, et al., 'Perjury and False Statements: A Criminal Profile of Persons Convicted 1979–2001' (2004, November) *Criminal Law Review* 926.

Soper, P, 'Legal Theory and the Problem of Definition' (1983) 50 *University of Chicago Law Review* 1170.

—— 'The Moral Value of Law' (1985) 84 *Michigan Law Review* 63.

Specter, M, 'The Long Ride: How Did Lance Armstrong Manage the Greatest Comeback in Sports History?' (15 July 2002) *The New Yorker*.

Stephen, JF, *Liberty, Equality, Fraternity* (Chicago: University of Chicago Press, 1991 (orig. publ. 1874)).

Stewart, H, 'Harms, Wrongs, and Set-Backs in Feinberg's *Moral Limits of the Criminal Law* (2001) 5 *Buffalo Criminal Law Review* 47.

Stolberg, SG, 'Inquiry Set on Bribery Claim in Medicare Vote,' (18 March 2004) *New York Times*.

Strader, JK, 'The Judicial Politics of White Collar Crime' (1999) 50 *Hastings Law Journal* 1199.

—— *Understanding White Collar Crime* (Newark, NJ: LexisNexis, 2000).

Strader, JK and Jordan, S, *White Collar Crime: Cases Materials and Problems* (Newark, NJ: LexisNexis, 2005).

Strawson, PF, 'Freedom and Resentment' in *Freedom and Resentment and Other Essays* (New York: Harper & Row 1974) 1.

Strudler, A, 'Incommenurable Goods, Rightful Lies, and the Wrongness of Fraud' (1998)146 *University of Pennsylvania Law Review* 1529.

Strudler, A and Orts, EW, 'Moral Principle in the Law of Insider Trading (1999) 78 *Texas Law Review* 375.

Stuntz, W, 'Self-Incrimination and Excuse' (1988) 88 *Columbia Law Review* 1227.

Sullivan, E, *The Concise Book of Lying* (New York: Farrar, Straus and Giroux, 2001).

Sullivan, GR, 'Reformulating the Corruption Laws: The Law Commission Proposals' (1997) *Criminal Law Review* 730.

Sutherland, EH, 'White-Collar Criminality' (1940) 5 *American Sociological Review* 1, reprinted in Gilbert Geis & Robert F. Meier (eds.), *White-Collar Crime* (New York: Free Press, 1977).

—— 'Is "White Collar Crime" Crime?' (1945) 10 *American Sociological Review* 132.

—— *White Collar Crime: The Uncut Version* (New Haven: Yale University Press, 1983).

Symposium, 'The New Culpability: Motive, Character, and Emotion in Criminal Law' (2002) 6 *Buffalo Criminal Law Review* 1.

Tamari, M, Al Chet: *Sins in the Marketplace* (Northvale, NJ: Aronson, 1996).

Tappan, PW, 'Who is the Criminal?' (1947) 12 *American Sociological Review* 96.

Tavernise, S, 'A Russian Tilts at Graft' (10 Feb. 2003) *New York Times*, A3.

'Tax Evasion,' in *Wikipedia*, <http://en.wikipedia.org/wiki/Tax_evasion> accessed 22 Aug. 2005.

Telushkin, J, *Jewish Wisdom: Ethical, Spiritual, and Historical Lessons from the Great Works and Thinkers* (New York: William Morrow and Co., 1994).

Theroux, P, *Sir Vidia's Shadow* (Boston, MA: Houghton Mifflin, 1998).

Thomas, TA, 'Annotation: What Statements fall Within Exculpatory Denial Exception to Prohibition, Under 18 USC § 1001, Against Knowingly and Willfully Making False Statement Which is Material to Matter Within Jurisdiction of Department or Agency of United States' (1991) 102 *American Law Report Federal* 742.

Thompson, SG, 'The White-Collar Police Force: "Duty to Report" Statutes in Criminal Law Theory' (2002) 11 *William & Mary Bill of Rights Journal* 3.

Tiersma, PM, 'The Language of Perjury: "Literal Truth," Ambiguity, and the False Statement Requirement' (1990) 63 *California Law Review* 373.

Tittle, CR, 'Crime Rates and Legal Sanctions' (1969) 16 *Social Problems* 409.

Tonry, M and Riess, Jr, AJ, (eds.) *Beyond the Law: Crime in Complex Organizations* in M Tonry and AJ Riess Jr (eds.) *Crime and Justice* (Chicago: University of Chicago Press, 1993), vol 18.

'Top Former Enron Executive "to Plead Guilty" ', *The Guardian Online* (8 Jan. 2004) <http://www.guardian.co.uk/enron/story/0,11337,1118744,00.html>.

Travers, ML, 'Note, Mistake of Law in *Mala Prohibita Crimes*' (1995) 62 *University of Chicago Law Review* 1301.

Turner, JWC, 'Documents in the Law of Forgery' (1946) 32 *Virgina Law Review* 939.

Twining, W and Miers, D, *How to Do Things With Rules* (3rd edn., London: Weidenfeld & Nicolson, Ltd, 1991; 4th edn. 1999).

Tyler, TR, *Why People Obey the Law* (New Haven: Yale University Press, 1990).

—— and Darley, JM, 'Building a Law-Abiding Society: Taking Public Views About Morality and the Legitimacy of Legal Authorities into Account When Formulating Substantive Law' (2000) 28 *Hofstra Law Review* 707.

US Department of Justice, Federal Bureau of Investigation, *White Collar Crime: A Report to the Public* (Washington, DC: US Department of Justice, 1989).

US House of Representatives, Committee on Standards of Official Conduct, 'Investigation of Certain Allegations Related to Voting on the Medicare Prescription Drug, Improvement and Modernization Act of 2003', 108th Congress, 2nd Session (30 Sept. 2004).

US Sentencing Commission, *Sourcebook of Federal Sentencing Statistics* (Washington, DC: US Sentencing Commission, 2001).

Van Wyk, RN, 'When is Lying Morally Permissible? Casuistical Reflections on the Game Analogy, Self-Defense, Social Contract Ethics, and Ideals' (1990) 24 *The Journal of Value Inquiry* 155.

Vasagar, J, 'Guilty: Trio Who Cheated Their Way to a Million' (8 Apr. 2003) *The Guardian* 11.

Ventry, Jr, DJ, and Joseph J Thorndike, (eds.), *Tax Justice: The Ongoing Debate* (Washington, DC: Urban Institute Press, 2002).

Vitek, W, *Promising* (Philadelphia: Temple University Press, 1993).

Volokh, A, '*n* Guilty Men' (1997) 146 *University of Pennsylvania Law Review* 173.

von Hirsch, A, *Doing Justice: The Choice of Punishments* (New York: Hill and Wang, 1976).

—— 'Desert and Previous Convictions in Sentencing' (1981) 65 *Minnesota Law Review* 591.

Von Neumann, J and Morgenstern, O, *The Theory of Games and Economic Behavior* (Princeton: Princeton University Press, 1947).

Walker, ADM, 'Political Obligation and the Argument from Gratitude' (1988) 17 *Philosophy & Public Affairs* 191.

Waldo, GP and Chiricos, TG, 'Perceived Penal Sanction and Self-Reported Criminality: A Neglected Approach to Deterrence Research' (1972) 19 *Social Problems* 522.

Wallace, RJ, *Responsibility and the Moral Sentiments* (Cambridge: Harvard University Press, 1994).

Walzer, M, 'The Duty to Disobey,' in *Obligations: Essays on Disobedience, War, and Citizenship* (Cambridge, MA: Harvard University Press, 1970).

Wasserstrom, RA, 'Strict Liability in the Criminal Law' (1960) 12 *Stanford Law Review* 731.

Wechsler, H, '*Mala in se*: Criminal Law' (1930) *Columbia Law Review* 74.

—— 'Note, The Distinction Between *Mala Prohibita* and *Mala In Se* in Criminal Law' (1930) 30 *Columbia Law Review* 74.

Wechsler, H, et al., 'The Treatment of Inchoate Crimes in the Model Penal Code of the American Law Institute: Attempt, Solicitation, and Conspiracy' (1961) *Columbia Law Review* 74.

Weems, ML, *The Life of Washington* (Cambridge, MA: Belknap Press of Harvard University Press 1962).

Weinreb, LL, *Criminal Law: Cases, Comment, Questions* (6th edn., New York: Foundation Press, 1998).

Weinberg, L, 'When Courts Decide Elections: The Constitutionality of *Bush v. Gore*' (2002) 82 *Boston University Law Review* 609.

Weisburd, D, et al., *Crimes of the Middle Classes: White-Collar Offenders in the Federal Courts* (New Haven: Yale University Press, 1991).

Welling, SN, et al, *Federal Criminal Law and Related Actions: Crimes, Forfeiture, the False Claims Act and RICO* (St Paul, MN: West Group, 1998).

Wells, C, *Corporations and Criminal Responsibility* (2nd edn., Oxford: OUP, 2001)

Wertheimer, A, *Coercion* (New Jersey: Princeton University Press, 1988).

—— *Exploitation* (New Jersey: Princeton University Press, 1996).

West, R, *The New Meaning of Treason* (New York: Viking, 1964).

Westen, P, *The Logic of Consent: The Diversity and Deceptiveness of Consent as a Defense to Criminal Conduct* (Burlington, VT.: Ashgate, 2004).

Wetlaufer, GB, 'The Ethics of Lying in Negotiations' (1990) 76 *Iowa Law Review* 1219.

Wheeler, S and Kahan, D, 'White-Collar Crime: History of an Idea', in Joshua Dressler (ed.), *Encyclopedia of Crime & Justice* (2nd edn., New York: Macmillan, 2002) vol. 4, 1672.

White, JJ, 'Machiavelli and the Bar: Ethical Limitations on Lying in Negotiation' (1980) *American Bar Foundation Research Journal* 926.

Williams, B, *Truth and Truthfulness* (New Jersey: Princeton University Press, 2002).

Winings, MC, Comment, 'Ignorance is Bliss, Especially for the Tax Evader' (1993) 84 *Journal of Criminal Law & Criminology* 575.

Wittgenstein, L, (GEM Anscombe, trans.) *Philosophical Investigations* (3rd edn., Oxford: Basil Blackwell, 1968).

Wolfe, NT, '*Mala In Se*: A Disappearing Doctrine ?' (1981) 19 *Criminology* 131.

Wolff, RP, 'On Violence' (1969) 66 *Journal of Philosophy* 601.

Wolfgang, M, et al., *National Survey of Crime Severity* (Washington, DC: US Department of Justice (Bureau of Justice Statistics) 1985)

Zimmerman, D, 'Coercive Wage Offers' (1981) 10 *Philosophy & Public Affairs* 121.

Zimring, F, *Perspectives on Deterrence* (Washington, DC: National Institute of Mental Health, Center for Studies of Crime and Delinquency, 1971).

Zimring, FE and Hawkins, G, *Deterrence: The Legal Threat in Crime Control* (Chicago: University of Chicago Press, 1973).

Index